INSIDE SECRETS
TO FINDING A CAREER IN
TRAVEL

Karen Rubin

Works

Inside Secrets to Finding a Career in Travel

© 2001 by Karen Rubin

Published by JIST Works, an imprint of JIST Publishing, Inc.
8902 Otis Avenue
Indianapolis, IN 46216-1033
Phone: 1-800-648-JIST   Fax: 1-800-JIST-FAX   E-Mail: editorial@jist.com

Visit our Web site at **www.jist.com** for information on JIST, free job search information, book chapters, and ordering information on our many products! Quantity discounts are available for JIST books. Please call our Sales Department at 1-800-648-5478 for a free catalog and more information.

Acquisitions Editor: Michael Cunningham
Development Editor: Lori Cates
Cover Designer: designLab, Seattle
Interior Designer: Aleata Howard
Proofreader: Cheri Clark
Indexer: Tina Trettin

Printed in the United States of America
05 04 03 02 01   9 8 7 6 5 4 3 2 1

Library of Congress Cataloging-in-Publication data is on file with the Library of Congress

We have been careful to provide accurate information in this book, but it is possible that errors and omissions have been introduced. Please consider this in making any career plans or other important decisions. Trust your own judgment above all else and in all things.

Trademarks: All brand names and product names used in this book are trade names, service marks, trademarks, or registered trademarks of their respective owners.

ISBN 1-56370-827-2

DEDICATION

To Eric Friedheim, the "Dean" of Travel

To my parents, who inspired the love of travel

To David and Eric

May every journey be an adventure,
and every voyage lead to discovery.

May each become
all that he or she can be
and humankind realize its humanity.

ACKNOWLEDGMENTS

I would like to express my gratitude to my editor at JIST Publishing, Lori Cates, and, as ever, to Eric Friedheim, who provided the initial rungs to my ladder and the boost up when I needed it.

Karen Rubin, President
Travel Executive Search
Great Neck, NY
2001

CONTENTS AT A GLANCE

CONTENTS

About This Book

We have structured this book quite literally as a guidebook to the $541 billion travel and tourism industry. However, any guidebook must necessarily be a snapshot, freezing a fleeting moment in an ever-changing landscape.

My goal is to speak personally, and arm you with as much information as possible to conduct a realistic and effective job search leading to a career in the travel industry. My approach differs from most careers-in-travel books that take a simplistic view, dwelling on specific (and obvious) job functions such as Travel Agent, Airline Pilot, and Tour Escort.

Each of the chapters on an industry segment describes how the industry is structured, what key issues it faces, and what the future is likely to hold. The information is intended to give you the fundamentals so you can demonstrate to a potential employer some understanding of the business. It will also give you a better handle on whether a field is right for you. No doubt, you will gravitate to a field that you may have heard about or become intrigued about. But I would urge you to look elsewhere, in segments of the industry that may be unfamiliar. You may see that there is more than one way of accomplishing your primary goals. This book will also give you a better idea of what employers are looking for so that you can make a more convincing presentation during an interview. My aim is also to give you enough information about a segment of the industry so that you can visualize yourself in it—or not.

In this guide, I offer you the experience, knowledge, and contacts cultivated over more than 16 years as an editor for the travel trade press and more than a dozen years as an executive recruiter specializing in all aspects of the travel industry. In a word, I am providing you with the "inside secrets" to finding a career in the travel industry.

However, a career is more than any one job—it is a series of steps up a ladder, and a job is only one rung. In travel, especially, you may start off in the hotel business and wind up in airlines, car rentals, travel agencies, or a convention bureau. The travel industry is expanding so rapidly that in most instances the objective is just to get into a field or a company any way you can—reservationist, administrative assistant, accountant. This is particularly true if you are coming from another field to a similar job in travel. You will be able to move up or move over fairly rapidly.

If there is one theme that is common to every facet of this fantastically segmented industry, it is its growing professionalism. The industry is recognizing the need to prepare for middle management by creating more entry-level training and development programs, and even offering better compensation in order to retain employees.

So many people fall into their careers and live with frustration and discontentment until they are able to retire. After more than 25 years of being part of the travel industry, interacting with literally thousands of professionals and watching them rise in their careers, I can honestly say that I have never met so many people who love what they do. Travel is competitive, challenging, frequently beyond control, but it is also fun. There is a certain giddy delight attached to it, a sense of adventure, personal accomplishment, and discovery.

This book is aimed at giving you the inside secrets to help you share in the incomparable experience that working in the travel and tourism industry affords. Let this be your guide to success.

—K.R.

WHY AND HOW TO GET INTO A TRAVEL JOB

these opportunities

Most people dream of working at something that they find interesting, challenging, and fun, something that they enjoy doing even after work hours are over. Travel is such an activity. For many for whom travel is the dream of a lifetime, working at a job that makes it possible to travel can be a dream come true. This book is about fulfilling that dream.

But it is also necessary to dispel the illusions that surround travel careers. A career in travel is considered very glamorous and adventurous. Once inside, however, the reality of hard work, long hours, and low pay dulls the glow.

The Truth About Travel Jobs

INTRO

Most people who haven't simply fallen into a career in travel seek it because they love to travel. If that is your main reason for entering the business, you are better off staying in some other field where you are likely to earn 20 to 40 percent more in salary and have three or four weeks paid vacation a year to travel as you wish. You are not apt to travel as frequently, cheaply, or carefreely as you might expect in the travel industry. Indeed, most of those in the industry who travel do so for business purposes, to the point where it can become too much of a good thing, bringing more stress than satisfaction.

You *should* pursue a career in travel because of the *business* and the *product* itself. Travel and tourism is one of the most dynamic industries anywhere, offering extraordinary opportunities for mobility, creativity,

and personal satisfaction. Indeed, the extraordinary mobility afforded in the travel industry gives you the potential to rise higher, to a position of greater responsibility and compensation than you might in another industry.

Moreover, facilitating travel is a noble enterprise: Having a role that contributes to the betterment of society and world peace is not just an ideal, it is integral to an endeavor that brings together disparate peoples and ideas and redistributes resources more equitably.

In many ways, the travel industry is a business like any other, with many of the same problems and concerns that arise in selling groceries, making women's shoes, or designing office buildings. There are the same concerns for profit and loss, accounts receivable and payable, and the same problems of productivity, market share, and the high cost of investment capital that affect most industries. Like most enterprises, travel entities consist of sales, marketing, finance, operations, human resources, administration, and, increasingly, information technologies and telecommunications. You can be an accountant, a Web programmer, or an account executive anywhere. But people who have had an opportunity to experience other occupations find something special in the travel industry—energy, creativity, fast pace, diversity, challenge, and growth—that they haven't found elsewhere. In fact, so often in this book, people refer to their particular part of the travel business as "fun" and "showtime." And when people are forced to leave the industry for one reason or another, they feel a sense of withdrawal; a surprising number ultimately find a way back into the industry.

A "Life-Changing Experience"

The industry's product—travel—is like no other. Travel becomes addictive—it is for good reason that people say they have been bitten by the "travel bug." Travel is "a life-changing, life-enhancing experience," observed travel agent Richard Dixon. Working in and with "travel" brings an excitement to the job that airline people feel even if they work miles away from the airport, and travel agents feel as they sit for hours on end searching the computer display for schedules and fares. There is a sense of sharing in some marvelous adventure.

Travel is very much a "people" business. No matter how sophisticated airplanes, computer reservations systems, or the Internet get, there is no getting away from the fact that the business is all about serving people. The industry attracts "people-people" who are energetic and open to new experiences, ideas, and...people. Because people tend to stay in the industry even if they move from one area of work to another, a close camaraderie tends to develop, even among those who work for competitors.

In some respects, travel is a service; in others, it is a commodity, just like an item you buy off a shelf. Yet, unlike most other commodities, travel—a seat on an airplane or a room in a hotel—cannot be stored away. The high perishability makes for high risk. It challenges industry professionals to be brilliant forecasters, promoters, and marketers; to excel at information management; and to be efficient operators.

Unlimited Potential and Possibilities

On the other hand, the potential for the industry is unlimited. Unlike a VCR, which you might buy once and have for many years, travel is an experience that has to be renewed each time, and each time it will be different.

Moreover, there are unlimited possibilities in the style of travel: The same customer might take one trip or 12 trips in a year, traveling for business, vacation, a weekend getaway, to visit family and friends, or to take part in an event. And people travel differently during the course of a lifetime: As a college student backpacking through Europe; as a single young professional looking for sun or ski; as honeymooners, a professional couple, a family with young children, a chief executive officer on an expense account, a professional attending a conference, a couple whose children have left the "nest," a retiree; or as a widow or widower.

The customers for travel are no longer confined to any particular stratum of society. A passenger on a $10,000 trek in the Himalayas might be a secretary or a mailman as easily as a stockbroker.

The travel industry is expanding, changing constantly, and new job titles and specialties are being created all the time. Few industries provide as much opportunity for someone with a general education to rise as quickly through the ranks to positions of enormous responsibility and prestige; to be an entrepreneur; to utilize diverse skills, abilities, and creativity; to work for some of the largest or smallest companies; and to see almost instant results from an innovation. Few industries provide as much mobility—moving up in an organization, or to other companies, other fields—the chance to live and work anywhere in the world.

A Vital and Necessary Service

"Tourism" conjures up images of gawking out-of-towners with video cameras and guidebooks in hand, or couples lazing on a tropical beach. In this context, travel and tourism is seen as "frivolous and nonessential." Nothing could be further from the truth. Travel and tourism is a complex network of vital and necessary services that touch virtually every individual and every business in the world. Leisure travel—the vacations for rest and relaxation, cultural pursuits, adventure, or visiting friends and relatives—is only half of what the travel and tourism industry does, but even these seeming luxuries have become necessities to counterbalance the stresses of modern life. Nonetheless, the same airplanes, hotels, car rentals, and trains that are in place to serve tourists also transport and house the businessperson negotiating deals, the diplomat, the politician, and the artist. The travel and tourism industry makes commerce, diplomacy, and exchanges of ideas and cultures possible. Face-to-face contacts between people at any distance whatsoever could not take place without the diverse services provided by travel and tourism.

"The world is becoming a global village," Pope John Paul II told a private audience of 7,000 travel professionals gathered at the Vatican in 1985, "in which people of different continents are made to feel like neighbors. Modern transportation has removed the obstacles of distance, enabling people to appreciate each other, engage in the exchange of ideas and commerce. Tourism can help overcome real prejudices and foster bonds. Tourism can be a real force of world peace."

Travel and tourism plays a critical role in the economies of tiny villages and huge countries. In countries like Mexico, Jamaica, and Spain, tourism is the linchpin for the economy. For countries lacking valuable resources or heavy industry, tourism represents hope in breaking a spiral of poverty and misery. Closer to home, there are countless examples of communities in which tourism is the base for the economy, including Orlando, Atlantic City, and Las Vegas. Others have become commercial centers because of travel and transportation, like New York, Atlanta, Chicago, and Los Angeles. Club Med (which used as its slogan "The Antidote for Civilization") was asked by the Bahamian government to build a resort on San Salvador, where Columbus first landed in the New World, an island now inhabited by only 600 people, in order to create jobs and keep young adults from migrating away.

In a world where so many make their living by selling people what they don't want or shouldn't want or could care less about, most travel industry professionals derive tremendous satisfaction from selling people a "good time," a "meaningful experience," and "a memory to last a lifetime." They sense the importance of what they do and that they are contributing in a real way to the betterment of society through facilitating people-to-people contacts. In short, people feel good about working in the travel industry and promoting tourism, in essence, "fulfilling dreams."

Many are fond of saying that travel dates back to Noah or Moses or the pilgrims. But the travel industry is a phenomenon of the Industrial Revolution, with its social revolution of minimum wages and paid vacations, coupled with the technological revolution that made for buses, airplanes, elevators, and airconditioning. Mass travel and the annual vacation ritual date only from the end of World War II, with the jet plane and the packaged tour.

Travel has not only changed from a luxury to a necessity in the American lifestyle (in polls, travel ranks just after a home and an insurance policy as a necessary expense), but the trend toward greater affluence, more leisure time, and the maturing of the Baby Boom generation into their peak earnings (and travel years) all prompt forecasters to predict fantastic growth for the industry in years to come. In fact, travel and tourism has become the second-largest industry in the world—not just in dollars, but in jobs.

A Strong Job Outlook

All of this bodes extremely well for the job outlook in travel and tourism. Indeed, despite all the technological developments, travel and tourism remains a business of serving people, so it is people-intensive. Nearly eight million Americans already make their living in the industry. The travel and tourism industry has shown an uncanny ability to generate new jobs even when the rest of the economy is in the doldrums, and the industry is expected to show some of the strongest growth rates in new jobs in the future.

It is not just the quantity of jobs that is appealing, but the quality and diversity. Travel and tourism is so diversified, it entails virtually every kind of activity and employs almost every kind of worker. It is common to think of the industry in terms of "Travel Agent," "Flight Attendant," "Airline Pilot," "Tour Escort," and "Front Desk Clerk." People readily recognize airlines, hotels, car rentals, and tours as travel and tourism businesses. But the industry is also real estate, ecology, urban planning, architecture, interior design, engineering, computer science, politics, public relations, marketing, personnel, publishing, telecommunications, e-commerce, finance, law, entertainment, and scores of other fields. Travel/tourism employs Archaeologists, Sociologists, Lawyers, Doctors, Teachers, Computer

Specialists, Artists, Writers, Marine Scientists, Actors, Musicians, and countless other professionals. Indeed, the industry offers an alternative path to fulfill any number of professional dreams.

Industry leaders are even expressing concern about a shortage of workers during this decade. "We will have to be more flexible in establishing split time and flex time for our employees," said a hotel industry executive, "and exert a recruiting effort beyond anything we have seen before, because if we can't service the market, we will lose it."

Snapshot: The Travel Industry

It took Marco Polo 12 years to journey from Italy to China, at great peril all along the way. People take for granted the size, scope, and complexity of the international network of facilities and services that make it possible to retrace Marco Polo's trek today in a matter of weeks.

It is extremely difficult to define precisely what the "travel and tourism" industry is. "[It] has been described, half facetiously, as a collection of diverse products sold by a fragmented industry to segmented markets through a complex distribution chain," noted the U.S. Travel Data Center (USTDC), the Washington D.C.–based travel research affiliate of the Travel Industry Association of America, in its *Economic Review of Travel 1989–90*. "It comprises the airline terminal in the suburbs, the restaurant in town, the highway motel, the travel agency down the block, and a host of other businesses that do not even recognize their dependence on tourism, since visitors are [often] indistinguishable from local customers."

Despite advancements in telecommunications—and sometimes because of them—physically traveling has become more important than ever. Indeed, in 1999, Americans took a total of one billion person-trips (that is, one person on a trip 50 miles or more from home), according to the Travel Industry Association of America (TIA), which measures the economic impact of travel and tourism in the United States.

The Nation's Third-Largest Retail Industry

Travel and tourism is the nation's third-largest retail sales industry and the second-largest private employer, according to data from the TIA Foundation. Spending on travel services in the U.S. totaled about $541 billion in 1999, and generated more than $86.7 billion in tax revenue. Generating a trade surplus of $14.1 billion (that is, international visitors spent more on U.S. travel, tourism, and U.S. carriers than Americans spent abroad), travel and tourism is the nation's largest services export industry.

To put these extraordinary figures into perspective, Americans spent more on travel than on clothing, accessories, jewelry, and personal care combined, or on household utilities, including telephone service. Travel spending in this country averaged $1.42 billion each day, $59.4 million each hour, $989,300 each minute, and $16,400 each second. Most of the money goes to airlines, car rentals, bus companies, cruise lines, the railroad, lodgings, restaurants, tour companies, travel agents, attractions and theme parks, sightseeing companies, and convention centers.

America's Second-Largest Employer

The travel and tourism industry is the country's second-largest employer. The $541 billion spent on travel in the United States generated 7.8 million jobs totaling $157.8 billion in payroll income. Every $60,000 spent by travelers directly supported one job. One out of every 17 U.S. residents was employed due to direct travel spending in the U.S. during 1999.

In 28 states and thousands of localities, tourism has become the first-, second-, or third-largest employer. In many areas, tourism has brought renewed vitality to communities once dependent on smokestack industries.

The travel industry has proved to be an incredibly efficient engine of employment. With all the focus on the New Economy and e-commerce businesses, the travel industry is still the biggest generator of new jobs because it is labor-intensive, unlike the Internet companies, which employ proportionally few people. Over the past decade, travel industry employment has grown 27.7 percent, almost 1½ times as fast as the more modest 19.6 percent increase in total nonagricultural U.S. employment. And travel employment is forecast to grow in excess of 21 percent between 1996 and 2006. Indeed, unemployment levels in the U.S. would have hit 10 percent in 1998 (rather than the very low 4.5 percent) without the influx of travel and tourism dollars supporting new jobs.

There are more than 738,000 executive positions in just four key segments of the travel and tourism industry, according to the TIA Foundation. The number of executive positions is forecast to increase faster by the year 2006 (to 954,000) than employment in the overall economy. TIA forecasts that top executive jobs will grow fastest in the following segments of the industry:

Industry Segment	Executive Job Growth
Food and beverage	32.3 percent
Air transportation	31.3 percent
Lodging	19.1 percent
Amusement and recreation services	28.9 percent

Source: The TIA Foundation.

New Trends: E-Commerce, Globalization, and Professionalism

The 500,000 different businesses involved in travel have their special interests and concerns. But virtually every travel entity and everyone working in travel is affected by three key interrelated developments:

- Technology and the rise of the World Wide Web
- Changing economics due to deregulation, globalization, and consolidation
- Increased professionalism

These are essential to understanding the dynamics of the travel industry.

The past 20 years, the Age of Deregulation, changed the whole economics and structure of the industry— the relationships of travel suppliers (such as airlines) and distributors (such as travel agents) to each other. Even though segments of the industry have been deregulated for some time, the effects are still rippling through, largely reshaped and reformed because of new and emerging technology. Deregulation of the transportation industries replaced what had essentially been a franchise with free market competition, forcing companies to revamp their products, their pricing, and the way they distributed to their customers. The way was open for innovation, new companies, new services, and new ways of doing business. Travel was always an industry with a low profit margin. But deregulation put additional pressure on travel companies' ability to control costs, maximize productivity, boost market share, forge relationships, and maintain brand loyalty against competitors.

The plethora of products and services has made computerized information and reservations systems essential. Consider that there are as many as 2.5 million fare changes a day. Now that same access to inventory and fares is available to consumers through the Internet and a growing category of e-travel entities. As a result, an entirely new dimension has opened up: direct sales and marketing.

Although travel is not generally recognized as high-tech, the industry has been on the leading edge of consumer applications of sophisticated computers, communications, and transportation modes in distribution, marketing, and product services for 25 years. It is no accident that travel is now the biggest consumer category on the World Wide Web.

With the greater premium placed on productivity, resulting in the need for capital-intensive technology and expensive marketing, a third trend has developed: consolidation. Consolidation is most visible among airlines, where mergers, acquisitions, and bankruptcies have whittled down the number to a few major carriers. Consolidation has brought retrenchment; companies have eliminated whole tiers of middle and upper management.

The technology and the need to consolidate and forge marketing alliances even on a global scale have fostered yet another trend: globalization—multinational ownership or alliances of airlines, hotels, travel management companies, and the like—in response to falling barriers and borders and a greater appreciation of the world as a global marketplace. Globalization has changed the orientation of companies and opened new career paths.

Trends Result in Different Opportunities

These trends—deregulation, consolidation, technology, and globalization, are revolutionizing how the travel business is conducted and changing the professional makeup of the industry. New opportunities are opening up all the time. There is enormous demand for Quality Control Coordinators, Computer Specialists, Yield Management Experts, Researchers, Analysts, Trainers, Web Developers, Brand Marketers, and now people with international business and language skills. On the other hand, many entry-level jobs have been eliminated.

Regardless of the kind of travel entity, there are categories of activities that are common to almost every one:

- Product development
- Operations
- Sales and marketing
- Public relations
- Administration
- Information technology/MIS
- Finance

In the past, success was almost universally the bottom-up variety—rising up through the ranks. A second career path has emerged, with a new breed of travel professionals coming out of colleges, universities, and vocational schools. And now a third path is opening up for professionals to come in from other industries, chiefly information technology, marketing, and finance—skills that are becoming vital to an industry

that is reaching a higher level of maturity and sophistication.

A Volatile Industry

Although the outlook for travel and tourism is extremely bright, there is great volatility within it. This year's hot spot may be next year's trouble spot. Changes in airfares, currency values, and political situation all affect interest in and access to destinations; weather, natural disasters, strikes, or even changes in the stock market can also destroy a destination or a company. This is not an industry to go into for security. It is an industry to into for challenge, excitement, responsibility, and personal growth.

An Insider's Guide to Getting into Travel

Ironically, the tremendous demand for workers has not made getting into the travel business easier; if anything, getting in will be tougher. The demand for new employees is concentrated among experienced, or middle-management layers, while the increased reliance on sophisticated computer systems and the extraordinary pace have elevated even entry-level positions. Meanwhile, low profit margins have made it difficult for travel companies to retain their on-the-job training programs.

Helping you get around the Catch-22 of needing experience to get experience is the aim of this book. In the end, it does not matter whether there are thousands of jobs or only a few; all you want is one. Succeeding in getting one requires a strategy. You need to be able to focus in and target your objectives, and convince the potential employer that even if you do not actually have industry experience, you understand the fundamentals and are motivated to learn.

There are no sure-fire methods of landing a job. It often comes down to personalities and the philosophy of the person doing the hiring. Timing can be key to success. But by doing research, preparing, and being proactive, you can create your own opportunities.

AGENTS, OPERATORS, AND PLANNERS

CHAPTER 1

TRAVEL AGENTS AND AGENCIES: FULFILLERS OF DREAMS

In the days when travel was a once-in-a-lifetime event, the Travel Agent was quite literally a "fulfiller of dreams"—the one who made lifelong ambitions of traveling to exotic locales or visiting the family's homeland a reality. Even today, when travel is more of an annual rite than an extraordinary event, most agents continue to see their function as fulfilling dreams—because in essence, the agent sells an experience, the satisfaction of the client's expectations.

Snapshot: The Travel Agency Industry

To most people, the Travel Agent personifies the travel industry. The most visible segment of the industry, the agent is actually the last link in an intricate chain of facilities and services. To travel suppliers such as airlines, hotels, car rental companies, tour operators, and the like, the agent is their retailer—their distribution system—to the public. Travel Agents give the suppliers local contact with the public that they could not afford on their own. They give their customers the benefit of their knowledge of diverse places and services, making appropriate matches to help the customer satisfy their expectations, as well as access to travel product the customer might not have had on their own.

> **INSIDE SECRET:** The travel agency industry affords the greatest opportunity for independence, mobility, and freedom to specialize.

Many people confuse "Travel Agent" with the "travel agency." The agent is essentially a counselor who deals directly with the prospective traveler (the client). But the travel agency is an entire business, performing various sales and marketing functions and administrative tasks. In the smaller agencies, and increasingly with home-based entrepreneurs, a single person can be the counselor as well as the owner/manager, performing all of these tasks; the larger the agency, the more specialization. Some of the largest travel agencies, which handle commercial travel (travel for business purposes), even employ a "Quality-Control Coordinator," who serves as a liaison between the client and the agency.

"The Reports of My Death . . ."

Retail travel agencies are the travel industry's cockroaches—meant in the most complimentary way. Agents possess an uncanny ability to reinvent themselves to a changing environment and survive in a deceptively difficult business.

Originally, travel agencies were the sellers of railroad and steamship tickets. When these forms of transportation were replaced by airplane travel, travel agencies merely shifted over to become the booking agents for airline tickets. At a time when airlines paid very little for agents to book business travel, they were focused predominantly on leisure travelers, booking complex independent itineraries for wealthy travelers. Then, with jet travel, new packaged tour operators arose to provide an easier, off-the-shelf product geared to a rising mass market of traveler. By concentrating sales on a few packagers, agents could earn overrides, increasing the profit on lower-cost products.

When airlines changed their commission structure to make booking business travel lucrative, retail agencies reemerged as corporate travel companies, setting up "in plants" within the companies themselves and devising complicated rebate deals. Airlines came to generate as much as 80 percent of travel agency revenue, while the airline organizations—Airlines Reporting Corporation and International Airlines Travel Agent Network (IATAN)—dictated the rules and procedures for agencies.

But when airlines all but stopped paying commissions, some agencies reinvented themselves again, into corporate travel-management services companies, compensated with management or service fees. Others evolved back into leisure travel agencies, once again booking independent trips as well as packaged products of preferred suppliers and imposing service fees on leisure clients. In effect, the travel agency business seemed to come full circle back to where it began.

As the Internet takes hold and suppliers are going direct to travelers, there are new predictions of the demise of retail travel agencies. But agents have proved resilient again, embracing the Internet and redirecting their business back pretty much to where it began: the discriminating luxury traveler who values service, for whom spending time wisely is more precious than money.

The shifts in the business climate for travel agencies are reflected in the dramatic growth in numbers, sales, and the proportion of airline sales by travel agencies. In 1974 (prior to airline deregulation), there were only 11,400 agency locations, appointed by what was then called the Airline Traffic Conference (now called the Airlines Reporting Corporation). These agencies generated only 40 percent of domestic airline sales.

Rosenbluth International

One of the oldest travel agencies in the U.S., Rosenbluth International was founded in 1892 as a steamship ticket office by Marcus Rosenbluth, a man who spoke nine languages and was entrusted with a few dollars at a time until the client could accumulate the $50 to send to Europe to bring a relative to America.

The agency, now one of the largest in the country, epitomizes the evolution of the travel agency industry: It is a family shop turned mega, and in many ways it still straddles both worlds.

In less than 20 years, Rosenbluth went from a regional travel agency with eight agencies and 250 employees generating $150 million in sales (a substantial amount for the time) to an international behemoth with global links, hundreds of offices, and nearly 5,000 "associates," generating $4.4 billion in sales.

Headed up by a fourth-generation Rosenbluth—Harold F., the President and Chief Executive Officer—the company has grown and prospered because of its focus on technology, innovation, and people. (Harold's brother Lee separated off the leisure part of the travel company, Rosenbluth Vacations.)

The company has the clout to negotiate high override commissions and the resources to invest millions of dollars in state-of-the-art technology to provide value-added services for clients as well as achieve high productivity. An early pioneer of e-commerce, the company launched a new line of business, Customer Interaction Management, providing nontravel-industry customers the same type of telephone and Web-based customer service it provides for travel.

Rosenbluth has applied considerable innovation to its workforce. For example, a "Pay for Quality" incentive program for reservationists produced a 27 percent increase in salaries. The company also places emphasis on quality control and customer service programs, employing specialists in these areas, as well as on training and development. It even opened a special data-processing center in Linton, North Dakota, in order to create jobs for struggling farmers (and is now a leading employer in the town).

The company predominantly handles commercial travel; a separate division handles incentives and meetings ranging in size from 10 to more than 2,000 people.

Apart from travel consultants and reservationists, some of the other job functions include account executives (who interface with major accounts), area managers (who are responsible for overseeing a cluster of agencies, monitoring productivity, and quality control), commercial sales managers (who are responsible for winning new corporate accounts), MIS specialists (there are about 60 programmers), and product development people (who negotiate rates with airlines, hotels, and other suppliers).

Rosenbluth also has a dot-com travel entity, Rosenbluth Interactive, which offers two sites: an online leisure division, travelution.com, and a site for business travelers, biztravel.com. Formed in August 1999 upon its acquisition of biztravel.com, Rosenbluth Interactive is majority-owned by Rosenbluth International; other investors include Sun Microsystems, British Airways, Continental Airways, Marriott International, and Excite@Home. (Check www.rosenbluth.com for job listings.)

The sheer growth in air travel generated by the explosion in new carriers and cheaper fares after airline deregulation caused suppliers to rely more on the travel agency community for their link to customers. Agents were given real-time access to inventory in their own computer systems, giving them an edge that consumers could not get on their own (before the Internet). Deregulation also meant that commission rates were no longer standardized and regulated; once they were opened, the profitability of agencies improved considerably and scores of new entrepreneurs rushed into the field. Deregulation also unleashed chaos on the public in the form of changing schedules, fares, and even airlines. Sheer confusion drove countless new customers into agencies for the first time, while outrageously low fares, pushed down by bloody battles for market share by upstart carriers, also generated new airline travelers.

As a result, dollar volume a decade after deregulation went into effect jumped 231 percent, and agencies were generating 65 percent of airline ticket sales. However, the number of agency locations also doubled, to 29,584. In 1989, agency sales from all sources totaled $79.4 billion, according to the 1990 *Travel Weekly* Louis Harris Survey.

Almost from the beginning, airlines made stabs at cutting agency commissions, but had never been successful in making it "stick." Each time, the travel agency

reaction—shifting bookings to other carriers—was sufficient to force the carrier (usually United Airlines) to reinstate commissions. But in 1995, United was successful in imposing commission "caps," and by 1999 most carriers had capped commissions to $50 for a domestic ticket.

Travel agencies are still a gigantic generator of travel sales. Around $142.8 billion in travel arrangements funneled through some 32,000 appointed agencies in 1999, a 13 percent increase over the $126 billion in 1997—more than one-fourth of the $541 billion in direct travel sales. But travel agencies have changed dramatically from only a few years ago, when airline commissions accounted for 80 percent of agency revenue. According to *Travel Weekly*'s 2000 U.S. Travel Agency Survey, that share dropped to 54 percent, at $76.6 billion. Cruises are the second-biggest segment, with $26.5 billion in bookings amounting to 19 percent of all agency bookings. Agencies also generate $16.4 billion in hotel bookings; $11.4 billion in car rentals; and $11.9 billion in various other travel services.

Just how important are travel agencies to the industry? In 1999 (probably the last year before direct bookings on the Internet become a significant factor), Travel Agents booked 80 percent of all domestic air travel, 85 percent of all international air travel, 95 percent of all cruises, 90 percent of tour packages, 50 percent of car rentals, 25 percent of domestic hotel reservations, and 85 percent of international hotel reservations.

According to the Travel Industry Association, nearly half of all travelers (45 percent) have used a Travel Agent to book a business or pleasure trip, flight, hotel room, rental car, or tour in the past three years. This translates to 64.2 million U.S. adults. Moreover, among the 46.2 million online travelers who did some, but not all, of their travel planning on the Internet, 39 percent also called or visited a Travel Agent in 1999.

The image of the neighborhood mom-and-pop agency hardly holds true anymore. The industry is dominated by global mega-billion businesses with all the mega-merger and acquisition frenzy of other big businesses.

American Express Travel Related Services generates nearly $11 billion in airline volume alone, and has 15,680 full-time employees. Other billion-dollar producers (in airline tickets alone) include the following:*

- **Carlson Wagonlit,** headquartered in Minneapolis, generating $3.9 billion and employing 20,000.
- **World Travel Partners,** Atlanta, generating $3.3 billion and employing 5,900.
- **Navigant International,** based in Englewood, Colorado, generating $2.5 billion and employing 3,600.
- **Rosenbluth International,** Philadelphia, generating $2.4 billion and employing 5,000.
- **Maritz Travel,** St. Louis, generating $1.7 billion and employing 2,500.
- **Sato Travel** (which is owned by airline companies), based in Arlington, Virginia, generating $1.2 billion and employing 2,000.

Sales volumes for these companies more than double when global sales are taken into account.

These are highly sophisticated global businesses and financial enterprises utilizing state-of-the-art technology and e-commerce systems. In 1999, there were 32,200 agency locations, of which 24 percent generated under $1 million in air sales; 26 percent generated between $1 and $1.9 million; 33 percent generated $2 to $4.9 million, and 18 percent generated $5 million or more, according to the 2000 Business Travel Survey. The agencies in the $1 to $4 million range were the ones being gobbled up, while the number of agencies doing under $1 million (24 percent of all agencies) is actually increasing, probably representing single practitioners.

It is a hard business, particularly with agencies still reeling from airlines imposing commission caps on airline bookings. What people fail to realize when they hear the dollar volume of what an agency books is that the agency does not keep that money—they keep on average only about 10 to 15 percent (what used to be the amount of commission and override). That amount is the agency's gross revenue, out of which

they pay salaries, utilities, advertising and marketing costs, computer fees, and rent. After all these expenses, agencies are lucky to clear a margin of 2 to 3 percent. Indeed, the proportion of smallest agencies that made a profit in 1999, according to the *Travel Weekly* 2000 survey, fell from 55 percent in 1997 to 51 percent. Meanwhile, the profitability of larger agencies dropped from 64 percent to 54 percent for agencies in the $1 to $1.9 million category, from 86 percent to 77 percent for agents in the $2 to $4.9 million group, and from 83 percent to 74 percent for those in the $5 million–plus category.

According to a PLOG Research/*Leisure Travel News* "2000 Path to Profitability Survey," the percentage of profitable agencies was about 65 percent in 1999 (with a projection of 76 percent for 2000); 21 percent broke even, and 14 percent lost money. The average agency profit was $250,000, while the average loss was $15,000.

Agencies have proved highly adaptable to the new environment, responding proactively and creatively. The profitable agencies typically charged fees (75 percent do); sold ancillary products such as travel insurance (a few even sell merchandise, luggage, and books); shifted emphasis to leisure products including cruises and vacation packages; established specialties and niche markets; and improved productivity and efficiency through technology by doing more business online.

The smallest agencies generally have one to four people: the owner, the manager, the counselor, and the bookkeeper or clerk. There also may be some commissioned outside sales agents. Medium-sized agencies may have a groups specialist, a commercial department, and counselors who specialize in destinations, such as the Caribbean, Europe, or cruises. The largest agencies are organized much like other big businesses, with personnel, operations, marketing, and sales departments; there may also be a sophisticated mailing department, a resident computer specialist, and training and development experts. The largest agencies may have several different businesses: retail travel, corporate travel, incentive travel, conventions and meetings,

Business Travel News, "2000 Business Travel Survey," May 29, 2000.

groups, wholesale travel, travel school, and even package express, and require many more clerical, secretarial, and other support people.

Deregulation has introduced an entirely new element to the business: negotiations with travel suppliers on rates and commissions and even services. It has also helped create entirely new companies (consortiums, cooperatives, and marketing entities) to give independent agencies more bargaining clout.

> **INSIDE SECRET:** Negotiation skills, forecasting, and preplanning are an increasing part of travel agency operations and will result in new kinds of jobs.

In 1999, agencies averaged 6.2 full-time employees, of which 5.3 were in sales, according to *Travel Weekly*'s 2000 U.S. Travel Agency Survey (August 24, 2000).

The travel agency business offers excellent mobility. Getting in is extremely difficult because experience is at a premium and the pace and economics of the business and its reliance on computers no longer allow for apprenticeships. But once inside, even after only two years of experience, there is enormous opportunity to rise. Mobility is more limited in the smaller agencies; however, the large agency organizations offer all the career paths of any big business.

Frontline Travel Agents

Being a Travel Agent affords the opportunity to become a valued professional, much like a financial planner. The work involves considerable problem-solving ability as well as the ability to fit pieces of a puzzle together. People contact (face-to-face and by telephone) is the essence of the job; in fact, contacts with both clients and suppliers are as important to professional success as product knowledge. Moreover, the contact is not just casual. "You have to involve yourself with the customer," reflected Jaime Patxot, a New York–based agent. "You dig into their personal life in order to come up with appropriate recommendations. We are psychiatrists sometimes."

Having contacts inside travel companies themselves enables the agent to free up space at a hotel that is "booked solid," upgrade an airline ticket, and get that extra or special service for a VIP. Although personal service is still the essence of the business, computers—airline reservations systems, the Internet, and in-house databases—are becoming fundamental to operations. No day is the same; each day presents new challenges and changes at a dizzying pace.

The frontline Travel Agent treads a fine line between the supplier (airlines, car rental companies, hotels, tour operators, and sightseeing companies) and the client. Travel agencies are essentially the "agent" acting on behalf of the travel supplier, paid a commission each time they sell that company's service (although this is changing with airlines eliminating commissions and agents charging service fees). However, travel counselors see their role as providing an objective referral service for their client.

Although there are often monetary incentives (in the form of override commissions) as well as pressure from the agency to book a preferred supplier, the travel counselor's overriding interest is to recommend the supplier that would best satisfy the client's price and service wants. The agent depends heavily on repeat and referral business. Unlike a real estate agency, which sees its client once in 5 years, 10 years, or a lifetime, or the fast-food restaurant that sells a standardized product, the agent services (more than sells) a client once, twice, or perhaps 10 times in a single year. Although travelers are more sophisticated and experienced than in the past, there is still a lot of "hand-holding" by their Travel Agent (even if it is by e-mail), who becomes a trusted professional much like a doctor, a lawyer, or an accountant.

Prior to deregulation, an experienced agent knew the airlines and fares to popular destinations by heart because there were relatively few airlines and rates changed only at specified times after governmental approval. But with deregulation, airlines' services and schedules change daily; there can be literally tens of thousands of new fares daily. Sheer growth of the industry, on one hand, and deregulation on the other, have made it impossible for any agent to keep track of all the fast-changing products, prices, and rules necessary to properly advise clients and book their travel. Increasingly, the Travel Agent functions as an information provider, drawing to some extent on personal familiarity with places, facilities, and companies gleaned with experience, but relying increasingly on powerful computers and online references.

Frontline agents feel a tremendous sense of responsibility about making everything go perfectly, tying together all the myriad details of a trip. "There are times when I am at home at night and I go over and over in my mind all the details of the trip," said Daniela Kelly, a New York agent. "Sometimes I give my home number, like when one of my clients had a trip with 20 different flights."

A mistake such as bringing the client back to the wrong airport or timing a connection badly can have disastrous consequences. Even if the agent performs perfectly, he or she is only a middleman; the tour company or some other supplier can mess up and the client can still hold the agent accountable (and liable).

The pace of work is usually hectic, sometimes frantic. "There are certain days when you have the feeling of 'burnout,' when you get ten people in a row rushing in asking for a 'deal' to Florida. It gets to you," reflected Kelly.

The daily rush is intensified whenever there is an airline strike, a natural disaster, or some other event that would necessitate changing travel arrangements. Travel Agents have to keep abreast of news on a worldwide basis as well as within the industry in order to anticipate problems and provide counsel to clients.

INSIDE SECRET: The emergence of massive travel agency organizations, many with global links, will result in new tiers of management, new specialties, and greater opportunities for graduates of four-year and business administration programs.

The Travel Agent primarily services a client, but the agent also must be a salesperson; the inventory is the brochures on the rack. There has been a deliberate shift away from being mere order-takers to being true counselors. "Most of the people who come in here already know what they want," commented Patxot. "You are just servicing them. But the rest, you do sell." Agents have to learn various techniques of discerning the client's true wants and needs in order to narrow down what part of the world and what type of trip to recommend. "I show the client the world; he buys one piece of it," he said.

There is increasing emphasis on sales techniques, particularly on how to "close" a sale (get the customer to commit to the trip and put down a deposit) because consumers are doing a lot more shopping around in search of the best deal. Agents also actively sell by offering a client more features and services to prepurchase. They also steer clients to purchase "preferred" suppliers, but this is not just because of override commission earnings (and incentives for the agent), but because the agents know the preferred products better and have confidence in the quality and reliability. Agents also act as salespeople by drawing new clients to an agency. Frequently, however, agencies employ outside salespeople who work solely on commission to perform this function.

The average agent in 1999 booked $714,000 worth of travel a year, up from $579,000 just two years before, according to *Travel Weekly*'s 2000 U.S. Travel Agency Survey (August 24, 2000).

Traveling Not Quite So Free

Most people who become Travel Agents do so mainly because they expect they will travel extensively for free. "You don't travel that much, and you don't make any money at all," quipped one 20-year veteran. Still, it is true that most Travel Agents travel considerably more than the average person.

So-called familiarization trips ("fams"), which agents take in order to get to know destinations and facilities and often include organized seminars and hotel inspections, are only occasionally free. Usually they do cost the agent something. Working agents are generally entitled to reduced-rate travel on many airlines and hotels, but airlines are becoming more restrictive on the passes. Also, the employer establishes policy on whether fam trips are to be taken as vacation time or whether extra days are provided for fams; some agencies that consider this an important tool to increase professionalism not only provide the time, but also pay for the trip.

"A Life-Changing Experience"

"Being a Travel Agent is the most difficult job in the world," said Richard Dixon, the owner and manager of Vista American Express, Cranford, New Jersey. "Customers are often irrational. You have to sift through what they think they want and figure what they really want, then choose among 9,000 potential travel products for the right one.

"When I entered the business after leaving Pan Am, this was a regulated business [fares had to be approved by a government agency and were the same for everyone]. We spent the other day cutting coupons from the newspaper in order to give our customers the best deal.

"It's enormously frustrating. But it's the greatest business in the world. Something is always new. Being a Travel Agent gives me the opportunity to live a lifestyle I couldn't otherwise afford," said Dixon. "I've been around the world six times. There's no place I haven't been."

Dixon, a former fine arts major who found his way into travel, epitomizes the new-wave Travel Agent who keeps on top of the best deals and uses innovative marketing programs and good business practices.

For example, seeing a weakening in the economy of Cranford, a town of 30,000 people, Dixon joined forces with other local merchants to create a "Home Town Advantage" promotion to stave off competition from surrounding suburban shopping malls and boost traffic into the local stores. Participating merchants

cross-promoted: A photo store provided a $25 gift certificate to its customers toward the next vacation booked at the travel agency. The local bookstore sponsored a murder mystery weekend at a resort, which the agency booked. A local restaurant donated a dinner that the travel agency used as a prize in conjunction with its promotion with the bookstore. A town-wide treasure hunt was also planned.

The agency has also been successful in turning individual travelers into groups—thus multiplying sales—and at the same time building brand loyalty through its own travel club. Club members pay into an interest-bearing escrow account, with the funds earmarked for some special amenity or activity on the tour. The agency offers six or seven special tours a year for club members.

"We discovered a long time ago that unless people are made to feel special, they will shop price," said Dixon.

Dixon himself helps promote the agency's and his own credibility as a travel expert through a weekly column he writes for the local paper.

He also knows the importance of keeping tight controls on cash flow, and scrutinizes corporate accounts (which represent 30 percent of the agency's volume). "Unless they can convert to a seven-day billing [paying as frequently as the agency has to pay the airlines] or a credit card, we say we can't afford to handle them. I have told clients we think they would be happier in a different environment."

He has had as many as 11 agents working at his agency. "When I hire, I only hire from tour and travel programs because I find these people understand the language and have an interest in travel. As an employer, I will refine the interest." His counselors cultivate specialties, such as cruises or travel for senior citizens.

"The more travel and service-related background you have, the better. Sure, someone who wants to be a Travel Agent should love to travel, love people. But you also need a sense of service and be detail-oriented."

And being a Travel Agent, Dixon notes, does give you the opportunity to travel. "Travel is a life-changing experience. You don't come back the same, or your heart is dead."

Why Choose the Travel Agency Industry?

While we tend to think of "entry level" as people just starting out in their careers, the travel agency industry has traditionally been a popular one for people changing careers, starting over after raising a family, or retiring from something else. This is convenient, too, because many agencies openly admit that starting salaries would be inadequate for someone who depended solely on the one salary.

Increasingly, though, people who are becoming Travel Agents are coming from burnout professions like teaching and nursing, which are higher-paying fields. Although they are content to take lower pay initially, these new agents are still forcing new standards and expectations.

> **INSIDE SECRET:** The ability to travel for free or reduced rates should not be the prime motivation to become a Travel Agent; instead, you should be motivated by a strong desire for people contact, be detail-oriented, and handle stress well.

Sharon Caldwell, for example, was a teacher for seven years and then a nurse before becoming a Travel Agent. "As a nurse, you deal with patients, families, life and death. It takes a lot of energy on a consistent basis. Travel agency work is relaxing in comparison. As an agent, you're dealing with people and dealing with problems, but these are happy problems. I like travel, I like selling it. I love to travel—and I do."

"I had wanted to be an agent for a long time, but stayed away because of the salary," said Caldwell, who had also tried real estate sales, and, though a full-time Travel Agent now, continues to work as a nurse every other weekend.

Joanna Bartolotta, a corporate agent on Long Island, New York, became a Travel Agent just after graduating high school. "My mother wanted me to be a stewardess, but I decided to be a Travel Agent when I was in the 10th grade. I just love hearing about different places; I love sending people away—it makes them happy. But it's nerve-wracking. It takes a lot out of you; people are constantly changing their mind, and businessmen are rough—they actually want you to build them a plane sometimes."

This has always been a field highly dominated by women, and although more men are coming into the travel agency business (typically in management-level positions), women account for 87 percent of frontline Travel Agents and 80 percent of agency managers.

However, the traditional source of new Travel Agents—mature women returning to work after they have reared their children—is drying up because many fewer women are staying home with their children; they are building careers and staying in them through their child-bearing and child-rearing years.

Today, agencies are making a concerted effort to retain women after they have children. Consequently, travel agencies are doing more to make being a Travel Agent more of a career, offering more specialties, more steps on a ladder, and better pay and benefits. Many are offering flexible and reduced work schedules. A few have even opened on-site day-care centers. But a significant new trend is to utilize technology to enable agents to work from home via computer. Thor, a travel agency consortia with more than 13,000 members, in an effort to be competitive in attracting and retaining competent staff, implemented telecommuting so that half of its agents work from home. Similarly, American Express representative agencies also are employing home-based agents who are equipped with technology to sell travel online. Uniglobe Travel, a major franchising company, purchased InHouse Travel Group, a home-based franchise company, seeing home-based business as a leading sector. Navigant International, one of the mega-agencies, also has many of its agents working from home via computer.

McGettigan Corporate Planning Services in Philadelphia has allowed some of its valued employees to work from home via computer. "From an employer's point of view, it is so difficult to find skilled people that this was cost-effective for us," commented Mimi McGettigan, Vice President.

Kathryn Davis, a Texas Travel Agent, gave up a job as an office manager and bookkeeper because she was "tired of staring at the same four walls." Instead, she established a relationship with a local agency and, in effect, works on her own, doing independent itineraries, groups, and corporate travel.

"If I choose to let my family take priority, that's my choice," said Davis, who has been working from her home for several years, linked to a sponsoring agency by computer. "I would never go back to an office setting. I would quit completely first. I like the freedom."

"You get satisfaction in making someone's dreams come true, of doing things for people they can't do as well for themselves," mused Joseph Hallissey, a former chief executive officer of the American Society of Travel Agents. "We are dream makers, still."

 # Jobs in the Travel Agency Industry

The key position in any travel agency is the frontline Travel Agent; however, the larger agencies offer a great number of specialist positions as well as positions associated with the business operations of a travel agency. In addition, there are many different opportunities for entrepreneurs, including buying a franchise or opening a home-based business.

The emergence of mega-agencies—multibillion-dollar companies with hundreds of outlets nationally and internationally, like American Express, Carlson Travel, Navigant, and Rosenbluth—has added the dimension of Big Business to travel agency careers, opened new paths for entry and advancement, and all in all, helped shape travel agency work into a profession.

Best Bets

- Webmaster
- Frontline Agent
- Quality control
- Training
- Information Technology
- Groups Specialist

Small family-run operations—the so-called mom-and-pop shops—may be an excellent training ground for novices, but they offer limited mobility. At a certain point, the only move for an ambitious agent is to go to a larger agency or to open one's own.

Larger agencies (which generally prefer to be known as "travel management services companies" and tend to derive more than 60 percent of their business from corporate travel sales) have more specialization of function and many more management opportunities. For example, they may offer positions for Quality Control and Customer Service people, Account Executives, Area Managers, Commercial Sales Managers, Human Resources, Training and Development professionals, MIS Specialists, Accountants, Product Development Managers, Fare Analysts and Negotiators, Public Relations professionals, and Marketing Managers.

Indeed, one of the "megas" lists 130 different job titles, with most of the new positions in product development, vendor relations, automation, and quality control. Among the job titles are the following: Document Control Specialist, Data Specialist, Disney Sales Administrator, Branch Liaison Coordinator, Cruise Specialist, Promotions Coordinator, Inventory Control Coordinator, Training Coordinator, and Senior Hotel Desk Agent.

Because these companies have hundreds of locations nationwide and even global presence, they also offer more opportunities to relocate (an advantage if you want to live in different places, but a disadvantage when the company says you have to relocate to Minneapolis or Phoenix or leave).

The mega-agencies also generally offer better salaries and benefits and have superior training and development programs.

 # Salaries in the Travel Agency Industry

Travel agencies have traditionally been very low paying. The glamour, the opportunity to travel at reduced cost, the fact that the job was frequently a second income in the household (since most agents tended to be women returning to work after raising their families), and low education and work experience requirements tended to keep wages down. Although it is possible to make a pretty good income (even six figures for the most ambitious commissioned sales agents with an elite following, or for a Vice President of a large, multibranch agency), salary levels are about 20 to 40 percent lower than one could earn doing comparable work elsewhere.

INSIDE SECRET: Base salaries are still on the low side, but this is mitigated by bonuses and incentives and the opportunity to rise up to a higher level of responsibility than other professions might afford.

According to the Institute of Certified Travel Counselors' 1998 Salary and Compensation Survey, the typical frontline agent averages $26,100 annually. Thirty percent of frontline agents receive compensation by salary only, while 14 percent are paid through a commission-only structure. Fifty-six percent receive a combination of salary and commission and/or bonuses.

Compensation levels vary widely with experience, geographical location, size (measured by business volume), and type of agency. *Travel Weekly*'s 2000 U.S. Travel Agency Survey (August 24, 2000) reported the following yearly mean compensation (salary and commission) ranges for frontline Travel Agents (these figures are, however, derived from fairly small bases):

Salary Ranges for Frontline Travel Agents

Experience	Salary Range
Entry-level	$16,646–$22,734
1 to 3 years	$14,533–$26,609
3 to 5 years	$19,068–$29,494
5 to 10 years	$25,527–$34,817
More than 10 years	$34,174–$38,528
Managers	$26,554–$41,593

There are wide variations depending on geographical area, and whether the agency specializes in corporate or leisure travel. In general, agents in big cities like New York, Los Angeles, and Chicago are at the highest end of the scale; corporate agents have higher compensation than leisure agents (however, this too is changing).

About two-thirds of agencies compensate inside sales agents on a salary-only basis; nearly one-fourth use a combination of salary and commission; and 9 percent pay agents on straight commission, according to the 2000 *Travel Weekly* survey.

These average salaries, though, do not take into account specializations and management positions that exist in travel agencies, particularly in larger agencies, which pay considerably more than the typical Travel Agent receives. The following table lists examples of actual salaries:

Examples of Actual Agency Salaries

Position	Salary
Executive Vice President, $150 million regional company	$150,000+
Regional Vice President, $150 million regional company	$85,000 base
President and Chief Executive Officer, large regional agency	$150,000
Executive Vice President dot-com travel company	$200,000

Position	Salary
Regional Manager, corporate agency	$65,000
Account Executive	$35,000
Corporate Sales Manager	$60,000
Branch Manager	$40,000
General Manager, high-volume corporate agency	$60,000
Corporate Agent with five years of experience	$35,000
Regional Sales Director	$55,000
Director of MIS	$60,000
Senior Meeting Planner	$40,000

Salaries for Frontline Agents are improving as well. Because of the complexity and sheer quantity of travel products and offerings and the computerized systems necessary for day-to-day functions, Travel Agents are just beginning to be appreciated as true professionals. Supply/demand balance has also shifted dramatically. There are presently about 235,000 Travel Agents. In all, industry experts estimate there will be a need for 24,000 new Travel Agents per year to cover growth and attrition.

An experienced Agent skilled in using an airline computerized reservation system is in enormous demand. Increasingly, travel agencies are attempting to improve compensation through more use of incentive programs, whereby Agents earn a base salary plus commission.

Benefits

Most agencies view travel as their employees' primary benefit, but policies on travel vary markedly. Generally, agencies offer 4 to 6 days of familiarization trips, depending on experience, plus another 8 to 14 vacation days. According to *Travel Weekly*'s 2000 Agency Survey, most agencies provide at least some type of paid familiarization trip annually, but only 29 percent of the agencies pay the full cost; 38 percent have the

employee and agency share costs. Most agencies provide free or reduced-rate travel as well as career-related educational benefits.

However, agencies tend to be weak in providing most other benefits that have become commonplace in other industries. Only two-thirds of agencies provide health insurance, and 10 percent of the time, the employee pays the entire cost; 50 percent provide medical leave; 35 percent provide a retirement plan; 33 percent provide maternity leave; 31 percent provide life insurance; and 22 percent provide paternity leave.

Your Ticket into the Travel Agent Industry

Getting into the travel agency business is tough even though travel agencies are desperate for agents. In the past, the travel agency industry afforded enormous opportunity at entry level. The industry's version of an apprenticeship was a clerk working for minimum wage but able to look over a more experienced shoulder and ultimately move into a consultant's spot. Many agents started while high school students working part-time and summers.

INSIDE SECRET: Although the industry is desperate for new agents, getting in is still tough without experience; travel schools and professional certification programs are key to landing that first job.

Today, the situation has completely reversed. Computers have virtually eliminated the need for clerks while vastly increasing the complexity and technical knowledge required to do even the most basic functions. The incredibly fast pace of work means there is no time to train, and the very low profit margins mean that training becomes a costly exercise. What is more, many managers fear entrusting their clients to a novice when the tiniest missed detail can cost the agency a client, or worse, a lawsuit.

Jobs for neophytes are scarce, while jobs for agents with only minimal experience (knowing how to operate the airline reservations computer) abound. Agencies today are becoming much more accustomed to going to the placement offices of schools to hire new graduates.

Although you should not confuse a diploma with a ticket into an agency job, some kind of schooling is becoming more and more necessary to break into the field. Even the most skeptical agency managers appreciate the value of the schools for screening out individuals who are interested in travel agency work only for the fun and "fams." Graduates of such programs are regarded as more serious, more committed, and more realistic about what the business is all about. This is important, because agencies make a great investment when they take on a novice.

Today, there is better cooperation between the travel schools and the industry, and more and more are becoming recruitment centers for the entire industry. The American Society of Travel Agents (ASTA) Scholarship Foundation (P.O. Box 23992, Washington, DC 20026; 703-739-2782), as well as the National Tour Foundation, a subsidiary of the National Tour Association (546 E. Main St., Lexington, KY 40508; 800-682-8886) and CHRIE, publish directories of schools.

Also, some of the larger agency groups, plus scores of smaller agencies, have established their own schools largely to meet their own recruitment needs.

Before you enroll in any program, review the curriculum closely. Hiring agencies are looking for knowledge of geography, reservations computer training, courses in agency operations, an understanding of the travel industry in general, and some sales training. Also check that the school is licensed with the state and accredited by appropriate agencies; that instructors have worked or currently work in the industry (it is best if they are CTCs); and that there is placement assistance (check the school's track record). Check with graduates of the program. You may also want to check the school's reputation with local agencies (particularly an agency where you feel you want to work), as well as with the Better Business Bureau. Also be sure it is a member of ASTA.

It is not absolutely necessary to go to a school. Indeed, there are many managers who are firm about taking on new talent and "growing their own." The task is to find these people. The best way to start is to network—ask everyone, starting with the agency you or your company uses, your friends, relatives, and neighbors. Walk into a local agency and ask if there is some entry-level job. If you already have work experience, you may be surprised at how applicable it may be, particularly administrative, sales, or telemarketing. Think about what you can bring to the agency. A desire to travel and even vast experience traveling is nice, but what the agency really wants is contacts for new business. If you are coming from another industry, you may be in a position to bring new commercial business to the agency.

In addition to schools, there are a few correspondence courses that are well respected. These are offered by Solitaire Publishing, Tampa, Florida (800-226-0286; Psolitaire@aol.com); Education Systems/The Center for Travel Education, Sandy, Utah (800-288-3987; www.educationsystems.com); and The Boyd School, Moon Township, Pennsylvania (800-245-6673; www.boydschool.com).

Probably the most well-respected educational institution in the industry is the Institute of Certified Travel Agents, which bestows on working professionals a coveted Certified Travel Counselor (CTC) title upon completion of a rigorous program. ICTA now also offers new certification as Destination Travel Specialist (DTS). Continuing education and certification is becoming a critical element to rising up in the profession.

ICTA, however, has introduced a beginner's program geared to agents who have just entered the industry, but people who want to get in can take it. Those who pass ICTA's national Travel Agent Placement test are allowed to post their resumes on ICTA's employment Web site. For further information about programs, contact the Institute of Certified Travel Agents, 148 Linden St., P.O. Box 56, Wellesley, MA 02181; 617-237-0280.

Commissioned Sales Agents

The easiest (and the most prevalent) way to get in without prior travel agency experience is as an outside salesperson, working on straight commission. This minimizes the risk for the agency, but be aware: You are unlikely to earn more than $9,000 in the first year, perhaps double that the second. On the other hand, commissioned agents who cultivate their own clientele can earn even more than salaried agents over time; some earn six figures.

Outside Sales Agents do not necessarily always work outside the agency, but their function is to bring in business from outside. "You're your own boss," said Bonnie Kogos, a commissioned Sales Agent for more than a decade with Zenith Travel in New York City. "You have your own clientele. When you change agencies, you generally keep your own clients."

"It is not glamorous at all," she said. "You have to slog through each individual booking. You are only as good as your last ticket. You might handle 30 clients at once, do a conference, a vacation, handle commercial clients. I have 40 people going to Bermuda."

The newer agents, she commented, are "computer whizzes but have never been anywhere. The older ones, over 35 years old with 10 years in business, are more Renaissance people. I've been to 82 countries and love to look at hotel rooms. You've got many different breeds of cat in the business," said Kogos, who also publishes her own newsletter for agency clients.

"You have to love the business. If I have a conference, I may work 8 a.m. to 8 p.m. Sometimes I wake in the middle of the night, remembering some detail I had overlooked. There are lots of little details. It pervades life. I don't go on vacation; I go on inspection tours. You are always learning."

A commissioned Sales Agent needs to negotiate with the boss first. There is a lot to negotiate for:

- The amount of the commission split (half of the 10 percent commission for a fairly experienced agent who does his or her own ticketing, but the amount can go higher; 25 percent for an inexperienced agent who does not do the paperwork).

- When it will be paid (at the time of booking, when the client pays, or after the trip).
- What the agent pays for (use of computer, telephone, supplies, or nothing).

You should get promises of a higher pay rate or a future salaried position in writing. Read the contract presented to you carefully, and see what it says about whose clients your clients are (whether you can take them with you if you leave the agency).

Selecting the Right Agency

If you use reasonable care in selecting a travel agency, take any job with it, even at minimum wage, just to get a foot in the door. If you are interested and a bit aggressive, you will learn by being exposed and can create your own position or slip into a vacancy. Once inside, it is easy to move up, or move over to a better position at another agency.

If you are in a position to choose among agencies, there are several matters to consider. Agencies manifest the styles and character of the owner or manager. The clientele and sales volume of the agency (and therefore your own revenue) is further determined by the location, size, facilities (such as computers), advertising and promotion budget, and even number of counselors or outside salespeople.

You can tell a lot about the agency, for example, by whether it is a storefront on Main Street or a mall, or an upper floor in an office building; by how many computer terminals there are; by the brochures that are displayed and how they are displayed; and by the general appearance of the office.

Most agencies have a mixture of leisure and commercial business, although the balance may vary (usually 60/40); but some agencies specialize almost entirely in one or the other, and there are gigantic differences in terms of working environments. The leisure agency is generally warmer; counselors are accustomed to spending a lot of time with clients; they may have to prepare a special itinerary.

In a commercial agency, speed and efficiency are everything; the agent does not deal with the traveler as much as with a secretary or corporate travel department. There is little consultation because the traveler will likely have specific requests. Creativity comes in obtaining the most convenient departures and best rates. Also, agents in commercial departments do not have the same opportunity to travel, because they are not in a position to influence decisions regarding destination and product. Commercial agencies also tend to be larger and more heavily computerized. On the other hand, commercial agents tend to make higher salaries.

There are advantages and disadvantages to starting out in a small operation as opposed to a large organization. The largest organizations probably offer more entry-level positions, better training programs, substantially better mobility, and benefits. But they are also highly specialized; you may be stuck doing reservations for a commercial account (which some compare to a position on an assembly line) for some time. On the other hand, a small agency might also present entry-level opportunities. The training, while not as formatted, can be excellent, with the opportunity of taking on a wide variety of tasks. The rise to a senior position may also be more rapid in a small organization; but because there are very few tiers, there are few places to rise to. A small agency, though, may offer a homier atmosphere and more opportunity to be creative in travel planning, and your own responsibility and fortune can rise as the agency grows.

Clicks and Mortar: Vacation.com

A hybrid between a traditional travel agency consortium and the new world of e-travel, Vacation.com is proving the adaptability and survivability of the retail travel network. Instead of becoming extinct because of the ability of suppliers to use the Internet to sell directly to customers, Vacation.com is harnessing Internet technology to empower its network of traditional travel agencies. In the process, the company has become a powerhouse, generating $20 billion worth of travel sales.

The company has two distinct roots. The first dates back to the 1970s when airline deregulation was taking hold, and the first travel agency consortiums were forming. On the principle that there is strength in numbers, the consortium acted as a marketing company on behalf of its membership—several thousand small, independent travel agencies. The consortium provided combined purchasing power to negotiate higher override commissions and special deals from preferred suppliers, and supplied the agencies with marketing tools and technology they could not have afforded on their own.

The second root, created only in 1995, was "a pure Internet travel play trying to figure out how to build a business selling travel directly to consumers like a Travel Agent, but using a Web site instead of a store," related Andrew McKee, the founder and former chairman and CIO of Vacation.com. In those early days, Vacation.com did not sell airline tickets (which would have required being appointed by ARC), just vacation packages.

Then, two years ago, McKee changed the strategy from a "b2c" (that is, an online agency selling vacation products to consumers) to a "b2b" strategy, using the technology that Vacation.com built for itself and marketing it to agencies.

"It was clear to us, before it was to others, that Travel Agents would need to get on the Web to defend against the pure online travel guys like Travelocity. But no travel agency except the largest, best capitalized, could afford to build a sophisticated Web site. We could help 'webify' the bricks-and-mortar industry by distributing the technology we had built for ourselves to them," McKee said.

"We decided the way we could do that was to use the consortium industry, and the best way to do that was to buy as many as we could and 'webify' the membership of the consortium industry."

With the acquisition of four consortiums, Vacation.com assembled 8,500 agencies in its network—one-fourth of all appointed agencies. The company is now moving to introduce its proprietary technology, Agentnet.com, a members-only b2b exchange. This is a tool for the members to create their own Web sites using the company's content and Web-hosting platform. In essence, the company is hosting thousands of sites—independent businesses—on one system. Vacation.com, acting as a traditional consortium, is also providing the "content"—preferred suppliers, special deals, and marketing programs. The system also provides customer and lead management and provides a "virtual community" so that agency managers can communicate with other agents as well as other agencies.

Because Vacation.com is both a travel agency consortium and an Internet company, it has an unusual cluster of jobs. Like a consortium, there are marketing and salespeople who devise the programs on behalf of the member agencies, as well as the business-development managers who negotiate with preferred suppliers. "Our business is marketing. Technology is one tool," McKee says.

The technology side includes a content group of 50 people who generate the editorial, creative, news and features, and vendor content for publication on the Web site (which goes to agents as well as consumers).

The Producer takes the content and orchestrates the production onto the Web, deciding where it appears, what it links to, and when it is scheduled to appear.

The Community Manager/Leader, part of the content group, is responsible for building an online community of users: scheduling chat sessions, planning events, creating a newsletter, surveying membership, creating content that relates to the community, and monitoring bulletin boards and other interactive forums for exchanging information.

The Product Marketing person (a technology version of a product manager) decides what functionality and what features should be present in the Web site, today and in the future. This person needs to have an understanding of the retail travel industry. They survey the users to determine what they need or want to see on the Web site (content, booking capability, or some other Web-based feature or function). Once this is determined, he writes a Product Requirement Document (PRD), an overview based on conceptual relationships between features of the Web site and what needs to happen.

The Engineering Group then writes the specifications (more technical), which then are handed over to another group, Program Management, which is responsible for scheduling and managing the development team.

The Development Team consists of software programmers who write code. This position is the least travel-oriented, but is geared to people who want to apply their professional skills in the travel industry.

Surprisingly, even the Vacation.com techies get perks. "We get discounted or free vacations from our preferred suppliers and we pass them on to all the employees," McKee related.

The techies for Vacation.com are all based in Boston; the management for the travel consortium is based in Long Island (where the original consortium, GEM, was located), and the executive officers (CFO, CEO, and Senior Vice President of Sales and Marketing) are in Washington, D.C. (See www.vacation.com for more details.) At this writing, Vacation.com had just been acquired by the global distribution system, Amadeus.

Working at Home and Independent Contracting

The travel agency industry is still very entrepreneurial. Ambitious agents who reach their heights at a smaller agency frequently go out on their own, or move into senior management at other agencies. These days, going out alone can be as an independent contractor or creating an Internet-based business that can be operated from home.

INSIDE SECRET: The agency industry affords exceptional opportunities to work at home, either as an employee or as an independent entrepreneur.

Although many Travel Agents are desk-bound, there is a growing number of professional Travel Agents who work outside the usual office environment. Some agents are hired by an agency but work from their homes as outside sales employees, working on commission (that is, they receive a percentage of what they sell).

A second group of home-based agents are independent contractors who may or may not associate themselves with a travel agency. These agents keep all the commissions they earn from the sale but pay a fee to a travel agency that issues tickets for them or provides support services.

The largest association for these independent agents is the National Association of Commissioned Travel Agents (NACTA), now part of the American Society of Travel Agents. The members include independent Travel Agents, cruise-oriented agents, home-based Travel Agents, and outside sales Travel Agents.

"Some are booking $1 million worth of travel," said NACTA President Joan Ogg, CTC, MCC. However, this would typically net $50,000 (maybe $70,000 if the agent was able to negotiate a higher split), out of which the agent would have to pay for his or her own expenses such as telecommunications, computer, and office supplies.

Some of the people who are drawn to contracting are agency owners who do not want the overhead, or traditional frontline agents who want to be able to work from home. They don't necessarily work from home exclusively, but may pay "house calls" on customers at home or work.

NACTA membership costs $125 for the first year and $85 a year after. Members get a handbook containing sample contracts and agreements, a list of industry associations and organizations, special offerings to members, and access to educational programs (contact NACTA, 1101 King St. #300, Alexandria, VA 22314; www.nacta.com).

Opening Your Own Travel Agency

In spite of the emergence of mega-agencies, the travel agency industry is still overwhelmingly small business and entrepreneurial. It is still a relatively inexpensive business to start—suppliers even provide your inventory, in the form of brochures. You don't even need to be appointed by the Airlines Reporting Corporation (the mechanism to ticket and receive compensation from the 140 member airlines), unless you intend to do airline ticketing (many new companies get around this by working out a cooperative agreement with an appointed agency). There are "niche" agencies that book only land arrangements or cruises that do not require appointment. Some states, such as California and Florida, do require travel sellers to be licensed.

Even becoming appointed through ARC, however, has become decidedly easier. A publicly accessible office is no longer a requirement—you can host a travel site online or operate out of your basement if you like. You do not even need to have a manager with a minimum of two years' experience in ticketing (a requirement that resulted in raiding of other agencies). Instead, ARC now requires that at least one person (which could be the owner/manager) be a Certified ARC Specialist, which means they have taken some professional training and passed a test.

> **INSIDE SECRET:** The Airlines Reporting Corporation has made it much easier for entrepreneurs and new agencies to become appointed to be able to issue airline tickets.

On the other hand, ARC has introduced some new membership categories that open new entrepreneurial opportunities. For example, ARC has created a new category of corporate travel department, allowing corporations to have their own appointment (an agency must have an appointment in order to issue airline tickets, join the Airline Settlement Plan, and earn commissions). This would enable an entrepreneur to make a pitch to a company on operating such a department for them.

The fees to get an ARC appointment are also reasonable: You need to obtain a bond or letter of credit for $20,000, pay a one-time application fee for a new independent entity (single location) of $860, and pay an annual fee of $125 for agencies linked electronically (through a CRS or even the Internet using a PC). For those who operate manually, there will be a surcharge of $100 each quarter.

Having an airline computerized reservation system adds about $1,000 per month to operating expenses (there are CRS fees when you ticket with an airline).

Travel agencies used to be opened typically by doctors' wives and divorcees, and mainly for the purpose of obtaining free travel for the owners, or for a tax write-off. Consequently, nearly half were operated at a loss. However, the steady increases in commission levels have made the travel agency business at least profitable, if not lucrative. The industry now attracts serious professionals—often people retiring from other businesses.

Travel agencies had been opening at the rate of 9 to 10 percent a year, or about 3,000 new outlets, to the point where there seemed to be travel agencies literally on every corner. In recent years, the rate has slowed—in 1990, the number of retail locations grew by only 2 percent to 32,077. In 1999, reflecting the effects of commission caps and consolidation, the number of agencies declined slightly. "The first to leave were the 'hobbyists,'" commented a spokesman for ARC. "These are people who may have retired from another business and thought it would be fun to be a Travel Agent and get free trips. But the business is infinitely more competitive. They need to streamline and rationalize business. The marginal operators closed down. This business is more entrepreneurial than ever before. But it takes a higher, more aggressive, more skilled, educated individual than ever before…. This isn't a 'hobby' or 'fun'…it's serious business."

The ease of opening an agency dupes many into believing that the business is also easy, particularly those who have been successful in other businesses. Operating a successful travel agency is deceptively difficult; there are nuances to the business that have tripped up some of the mightiest companies who thought they could make a go of it, including the ABC television network.

Consequently, instead of starting from scratch, many newcomers buy an existing agency or purchase a franchise. There are advantages and disadvantages to buying an existing agency. You may in fact be buying an agency with a poor reputation or poor business methods. Look for one where the owner is retiring after a successful career, and retain his or her services on a consultant basis.

Franchises and Consortiums

Travel agency franchises sell for thousands of dollars, and are not of the same value as those in real estate or fast food. Unlike the hamburger, which is standardized from store to store, or the home you buy once in 5 or 10 years, or a lifetime, travel is a service purchased frequently. Business success ultimately depends on personal relationships between the agent and the customer.

When you buy a travel franchise, you are buying a more recognized name, some assistance in site selection, training, hiring expertise, agency appointments, technology, and preferred supplier arrangements (plus overrides), as well as marketing assistance. The franchisor generally charges a royalty of sales plus annual fees.

Franchisors, including Uniglobe Travel (www.uniglobe.com), are also offering new kinds of products, such as home-based, Web-based, and cruise-only agencies. Leading franchisors include the following:

- American Express U.S. Representative Travel Network, New York
- Carlson Wagonlit Travel Associates, Minneapolis
- Etravnet.com/Travel Network, Englewood Cliffs, New Jersey
- First Travel Management International, Saddle Brook, New Jersey
- GTM Travel Management, Fenton, Missouri
- Uniglobe Travel, Vancouver, Canada
- WorldTravel Partners Affiliates, Northbrook, Illinois

Many of the services performed by franchise organizations are available through cooperatives, consortiums, and marketing companies, which enable the agency to preserve its independence but have the purchasing power and clout of a group. Indeed, membership in some sort of network or association has become increasingly essential, both to earn higher override commissions from suppliers and to provide clients (particularly commercial accounts) with the wide-reaching services they require (such as a 24-hour help line). In addition to the value they offer a new agency, managing these multi-agency groups has become a career path in itself.

Among the travel cooperatives, consortiums, and marketing companies are the following:

- ABC Corporate Services, Rosemont, Illinois
- Hickory Travel Systems, Saddle Brook, New Jersey
- Protix Agent Support Network, Hudson, New York
- Synergi, Inc., New York
- Thor Inc., Louisville, Colorado
- Travelsavers, Oyster Bay, New York
- Woodside Travel Trust, Bethesda, Maryland

Contacts, Sources, and Leads

The leading trade associations that can provide information about the industry and contacts include the following:

- **The American Society of Travel Agents (ASTA),** P.O. Box 23992, Washington, DC 20026; 703-739-2782; www.astanet.com.
- **Association of Retail Travel Agents (ARTA),** 1745 Jefferson Davis Hwy, Ste. 300, Arlington, VA 22202; 703-553-7777; www.artaonline.com.
- **Airlines Reporting Corporation,** 1530 Wilson Blvd., Ste. 800, Arlington, VA 22209-2448; 703-816-8000; www.arccorp.com.
- **International Airlines Travel Agent Network (IATAN),** 300 Garden City Plaza, Ste. 342, Garden City, NY 11530; 516-747-4716; www.iatan.org.
- **Institute of Certified Travel Agents,** 148 Linden St., P.O. Box 82–56, Wellesley, MA 02181; 800-542-4282; www.icta.com.
- **National Association of Commissioned Travel Agents (NACTA),** 1101 King St. #300, Alexandria, VA 22314; 703-739-6826; www.nacta.com.
- Leading travel industry publications: *Travel Weekly, Leisure Travel News,* and *Travel Agent Magazine.*

CHAPTER 2

CORPORATE TRAVEL MANAGEMENT: THE BEST OF TWO WORLDS

Corporate travel management has been described as "the art of simultaneously serving the disparate needs of the company's travelers and its management." An emerging profession growing more complex with the pressures of business globalization and revolutionary changes in technology, corporate travel management gives practitioners the advantages of working with the exciting dynamics of travel and the people who collectively make up the industry, but in a non-travel, corporate setting.

Snapshot: Corporate Travel Management

This is still an emerging profession. In many companies, even Fortune 1000 ones, the responsibility of overseeing travel is usually left to the purchasing, operations, or personnel departments or put under the Controller's office, and sometimes under the purview of an Administrative Assistant (who often emerges as the Corporate Travel Manager).

However, the status of the job has catapulted, along with salaries. This is because of the spiraling increase in travel expenses, the recognition that travel is the third-greatest controllable expense (after personnel and data processing), and a new appreciation of the vital role travel plays in positioning a company in the marketplace. No longer a mere accommodation made for employees, corporate travel management is becoming appreciated as a means for a company to achieve its business goals and reduce departmental costs. Increasingly, especially where companies are setting up their own in-house agencies or operating incentive programs, it can serve as a profit center. Moreover, with more and more businesses going global, and in the aftermath of such crises as the Persian Gulf War and incidents of terrorism, corporate travel managers have become recognized as critical advisors on safety and security concerns.

INSIDE SECRET: Corporate travel management offers the best of both worlds, affording an opportunity to combine a "corporate" atmosphere, with comparable salary and benefits, with the dynamics of being involved with the travel industry.

Corporate travel department staff members are generally employed by the company itself, and receive comparable salaries and the same benefits and pensions as other employees. They are responsible for arranging travel for the company's employees; arranging meetings, conventions, and incentive programs; and managing travel budgets that can amount to millions of dollars. Increasingly, they are responsible for negotiating contracts with airlines, hotels, railroads, car rental and limousine service companies, conference centers, credit-card and payment system firms, computer services and software, and even travel management services companies. Because they may be responsible for choosing venues for meetings, conventions, and incentive programs, they are heavily wooed by convention and visitor bureaus.

Best Bet

- Information Technology

Companies may employ a single individual to be responsible for setting up a travel budget, establishing policies for employees to follow (such as who can travel first-class), and acting as the liaison with an outside travel agency that actually handles the arrangements. Or, there can be an entire staff organized and functioning much like an in-house commercial travel agency. Sometimes an outside travel agency establishes an "in plant" on the company's premises, operating like a branch office of the travel agency to handle the company's travel arrangements exclusively, but staffed by the company, the agency, or a combination of both. Corporate Agents do not have the reduced-rate travel privileges of travel agency personnel, but their salaries and employee benefits are the more lucrative ones of a nontravel business.

On the other hand, the corporate travel department (because it is typically perceived as a service and not a profit center) is one of the first to be pruned during business downturns. And mobility can be limited (but is improving considerably): Within the department there are generally few senior positions and only one Corporate Travel Manager. Corporate Travel Managers tend to rise by moving to a higher position in the corporate travel department of a larger company.

Responsibilities of the Corporate Travel Manager

The responsibilities of corporate travel management go well beyond booking flights, hotels, and car rentals for executives. When corporate travel management is part of the personnel department, the task may also include personnel relocation, corporate housing, and coordinating training programs. It may involve planning and organizing meetings and conventions, setting up "team-building" exercises, arranging trade shows, and coordinating an incentive travel program. Many

corporate travel departments also administrate corporate aircraft, the car pool, and possibly group recreational trips or vacations for employees. The Manager may also negotiate barter deals and discounts with travel suppliers.

A strong business background is necessary for a Corporate Travel Manager (who may also be called a Travel Administrator or a Transportation Specialist). The Manager has to oversee staff and forecast budgets, handle accounting and reconciliation, choose preferred vendors, coordinate the Request For Proposals (RFP) process, and negotiate contracts for rates on airlines, railroads, hotels, and car rentals. They devise, implement, and enforce travel policy; select a travel agency through a competitive bidding process; acquire computer reservations systems; implement complex Management Information Systems (MIS), a global distribution system, or an Intranet travel site; handle online booking; administer cellular phone contracts; manage a travel data warehouse; and manage electronic expense reporting.

The Corporate Travel Manager has to understand travel industry jargon, read the trade press, keep up with travel industry trends and forecasts that change daily, and be alert to myriad issues that could have an impact on company travelers, such as an impending airline strike or new service, a change in oil prices that could affect fares, or a hint that a vendor might be headed for bankruptcy and could leave your employees stranded.

Corporate Travel Managers have had to keep up with the dizzying pace of changes in the travel industry, the most dramatic being a shift from agencies relying on airline commissions to fee-based management contracts. The technology revolution and the explosion of online booking tools and technology geared to business travelers also have had a direct and monumental impact on Corporate Travel Managers. At the same time, Corporate Travel Managers have to accommodate the equally mind-boggling pace of changes in their own industries and companies: the effects of globalization, of new marketing alliances, and of new products and distribution channels, not to mention the impact of dramatic growth in their own company that may be recruiting and relocating employees as well as sending legions of sales, marketing, operations, and training people to far-flung places.

These days, Corporate Travel Managers also have an unprecedented number of decisions to make in terms of whether they should contract an outside travel agency, to operate on-site or off-site, and what management fees to pay. They also must decide whether they should assume the whole function themselves using the new designation of Corporate Travel Department from the Airlines Reporting Corporation (the same coordinating body that travel agencies use). Should they centralize or decentralize reservations and services or adopt a "rent-a-plate" strategy, where the company uses its own personnel but pays an agency a fee to use its airline ticketing plate?

Besides being an intense business enterprise, corporate travel management is very much a service business. "You have to be someone who gets self-gratification and not live for pats on the back," said Mary Kay Dauria, who was the Director of World Travel Services for a global insurance company. In this position she was responsible for $100 million in travel and a massive global consolidation program that reduced the number of agencies the company worked with from 100 to 1.

She reflected, "You don't hear from people except when there is a mistake. You need to be a self-starter, someone who is hardworking but likes change. You can work for months on something, and then something changes. You need excellent communications skills, a 'calm spirit,' and the ability to be diplomatic."

Why Choose Corporate Travel Management?

"Corporate travel tests your business acumen," said Dauria. It is a fast-moving, changing specialty area of business. It is fun, because the people are fun. People in the industry have open minds; they are well traveled. They help each other, even if they don't know somebody. It is a tight network," said Dauria, who

started out in urban planning and got into corporate travel management "quite by mistake."

The disadvantages are that someone in Dauria's position can spend 80 percent of their time on the road. "It is *not* fun. It is *not* a vacation. When I am on the road, I am working from 8 a.m. to 8 p.m. It is a misunderstood industry—and you have to be able to explain it" and continually fight the perception that you are out sightseeing when traveling.

> **INSIDE SECRET:** Corporate travel management affords the greatest amount of variety and responsibility in the travel industry.

There is tremendous growth opportunity ahead because so many companies have yet to designate a Corporate Travel Manager, and because other avenues for mobility are opening up.

"You have access to every department and access to the highest offices. There is high visibility, great contacts," Dauria noted.

Salaries in Corporate Travel Management

The heightened recognition of the growing professionalism and responsibility is reflected in the fact that salaries have almost doubled in the past decade. In 2000, Travel Managers reported an average compensation of $66,400, compared to $35,000 in 1990, while the ranks of those earning between $60,000 and $89,999 swelled significantly to 38 percent, according to a survey by *Business Travel News*. The salaries are greatest for Corporate Travel Managers in the largest companies, with oversight for the largest travel budgets and greatest number of employees traveling, but also those with a solid command of technology. Those earning under $40,000 are responsible for $3.1 million in airline volume. Those earning $50,000 to $69,900 have responsibility for $11.7 million in airline budgets. Those earning over $90,000 are responsible for $29 million in air volume, on average, and tend to be older. Twenty-seven percent of those earning over $90,000 have a Master's degree.

Indeed, the titles reflect the range in responsibility as much as salary: Corporate Travel Managers can be called Supervisors, Coordinators, Planners, Directors, and Vice Presidents.

Corporate travel management has been an excellent field for women. According to *Business Travel News,* 72 percent of Corporate Travel Managers are women. However, there remains some disparity in earnings, possibly reflecting the educational background and career path into corporate travel management (for example, from the role of an executive secretary versus the Controller's office) as well as the size of company and travel budget that women, versus men, are responsible for. As a result, 15 percent more men than women earn more than $90,000, although a roughly equal percentage of men and women are in the lowest category, earning $40,000 or less (14 percent of women compared to 11 percent of men).

As an example, the Manager of Corporate Travel and Fleet for a Boston-based technology company earned $80,000. Over the course of five years, she created the company's first travel program, managing rapid expansion of air volume from $5 million to $25 million. She presided over the selection of travel services providers and obtained company-wide support for travel initiatives. She also developed and implemented travel policy; negotiated vendor agreements for airline, car rental, hotel, charge cards, and vehicles; globalized programs in Europe, Asia, and Latin America; integrated eight divisions into a consolidated travel program; conducted travel seminars; and published an internal newsletter. This manager came to the position with 10 years of experience in travel administration.

Similarly, a man became Corporate Travel Manager for a $3.5 billion manufacturer with 22,000 employees worldwide, after working for six years with a corporate travel management services company. His background at the travel management services company included

serving as Account Manager for a global company, supervising a staff of 13, and producing $1 million in annual savings by developing, implementing, and enforcing corporate travel policies. As Corporate Travel Manager, earning $65,000, he was responsible for more than $22 million in travel and entertainment spending. His initiative to consolidate travel among designated vendors and enforcing travel policies saved his company $12 million. He also created new communication channels to increase employee awareness of travel programs.

Both these individuals demonstrate a career path into the Corporate Travel Manager position from among National Account Managers of corporate travel management services companies (corporate travel agencies), often the same ones that provided services to the company. A National Account Manager typically has the same responsibility as a Corporate Travel Manager, overseeing very large travel budgets, ensuring quality customer service, negotiating for various travel services, and typically bringing a knowledge of the bidding process and service issues. Generally, people are lured from the agency side by the higher salaries, better benefits, and greater responsibility afforded on the corporate (client) side.

Your Ticket into Corporate Travel Management

Companies used to promote people from other departments into Travel Manager positions; however, that is becoming less common as corporate travel management is becoming an increasingly specialized profession. There are more and more training programs, particularly through the National Business Travel Association, which represents 1,200 corporate travel managers. Corporate travel managers are moving among the various companies rather than staying within their own.

INSIDE SECRET: In the emerging corporate travel management profession, there is still opportunity to write your own ticket—create your own job by assuming responsibilities within your present company for making travel arrangements for the sales force and coordinating meetings and conventions.

Roadmap to the Top

Typically, Corporate Travel Managers rise up by moving to larger companies with bigger budgets, more employees to move, and more responsibility. Many wind up crisscrossing the country, but many seem content to spend most of their careers at one company, seeing increases in salary, responsibility, and compensation as their own companies grow and become more successful. Other career paths are into consulting, into large corporate travel agencies, or with vendor companies like airlines.

Contacts, Sources, and Leads

- The trade association for corporate travel managers is the **National Business Travel Association,** 1650 King St., Alexandria, VA 22314; 703-684-0836. The Web site, www.nbta.org, provides listings for member companies and a members-only job bank. NBTA offers a Certified Corporate Travel Executive program at Cornell University, as well as education programs. It also offers a new site, www.biztravelers.org, with helpful information for business travelers. The regional chapters are great at providing networking assistance.

- **Association of Corporate Travel Executives,** 515 King St., Ste. 330, Alexandria, VA 22314; 800-ACTE-NOW; www.acte.org.

- Leading trade journals for corporate travel include *Business Travel News, Corporate Travel,* and *Travel Weekly*.

CHAPTER 3

TOUR OPERATORS: DREAM-MAKERS OR MERCHANTS?

Whale-watching in Antarctica; digging for dinosaurs in Argentina; ballooning across the chateaux country of France; riding a wagon train through the Badlands of South Dakota; climbing the Himalayas; camping in a Mongolian yurt. These are no longer wild fantasies. Nor are the Pyramids of Egypt, the Great Wall of China, the Incan city of Machu Picchu, the North Pole, or even outer space beyond the reach of ordinary people. The dream-makers who make these fantasies realities are tour operators—a small, highly specialized segment of the $541 billion travel and tourism industry.

Snapshot: Tour Operations

Typically tour operators are people who have been bitten by the travel bug themselves. Possessed by an insatiable desire to see and experience new places, new cultures, and new ideas, they bring their entrepreneurial talents, creativity, "gamesmanship," and love of travel together in the business of designing, producing, and marketing trips for other people.

Tour operators put together all the elements of a trip—transportation, accommodations, meals, sightseeing, and the like. They work with other segments of the industry—hotel companies, airlines, car rental firms, bus companies, cruise lines, local ground operators, government tourist offices, attractions, and restaurants. They negotiate rates and block space, coordinating all the intricate details of an itinerary that travelers themselves probably take for granted,

accounting for every moment of time. Then they "package" the product (the tour) in the form of a brochure and sell it through retail travel agents or direct to the public. The tour operator (who creates as well as markets the package) or wholesaler (who does not "operate" the program, but distributes it) then markets the product, generating awareness and brand-name identification among retail agents and the public.

Tour operators used to be virtually dependent on travel agents to sell their products to the public (making it very difficult and expensive for a newcomer to compete, particularly when agents had negotiated preferred supplier agreements). Now, however, the Internet has made it possible for even specialized, niche operators to find their target market. Consequently, the industry is poised for a new golden age of creativity.

Travels Far and Wide

The tour operations industry is ever evolving. Tour companies developed in the era of the Grand Tour of Europe, and there has always been and still remains a core of deluxe group escorted tour companies. But the packaged tour business really took off in the Jet Age. Operators devised the Group Inclusive Tour (the "group" was only in the sense of many people buying the same air departure) as a device to qualify for a low airfare. The land portion may have been a "throwaway"—some isolated inn for 10 nights. Thus, the mass travel business was born. Then, when the airlines introduced low fares that did not require a tour package, the price-oriented operators had to come up with packages that people really wanted to use.

"The idea of a package tour evokes a mental picture of a group of geriatric dodderers in rimless glasses and cast-iron permanents getting on and off a tour bus," quipped one operator (who worked for a British tour company). Then there is the other popular image, which arose when a trip to Europe was considered a "once-in-a-lifetime" event, so travelers tried to cram as much as possible into a single trip. Tour-goers were treated to what seemed to be seven countries in eight days, giving rise to the expression, "If it's Tuesday, it must be Belgium."

> **INSIDE SECRET:** Tour operations is one of the most creative areas in the travel industry and affords some of the best opportunities to fulfill one's dream of traveling to exotic locales and doing exciting things.

But tour products have changed immensely since then, catering to every style, interest, age group, and income level; group or independent; off-the-shelf or customized. Although the escorted tour market has remained a relatively small percentage—3 percent of the total travel industry, but still $28 billion worth—the packaged tour industry (that is, independent travel in which various travel services such as transportation and lodging are bundled together) is still the lion's share. Packaged tours account for about a fifth of all person-trips of five nights or longer.

Indeed, the packaged tour market has gotten added impetus from travel agents, as the last safe haven for agents to earn commissions for all the components of a traveler's trip: airlines (if that is a feature), hotels, included meals, and attractions.

Most of those who take escorted tour packages want the security and convenience of having everything done for them—transportation, accommodations, and meal arrangements. Another group of people look to a different sort of package, which offers economy because of the buying power of the packager. Still others take tours because they provide access to places and sights that individuals cannot easily visit (China, Antarctica, and Eastern Europe, for example) and are led by experts in a field. The fastest-growing category is

programs that cater to travelers' sophistication, desire for independence, special interests, and need for adventure.

Adventure for Every Taste

The market for the tours is growing along with the expansion of the product offerings. There are tours for every budget, taste, interest, age group, and lifestyle: A journey by covered wagon; a mystery tour by bus, where the destination is a surprise; a "Flight Through Fantasia" in the American Southwest; ballooning in France; archaeological expeditions; dog-sledding in the Arctic; bicycling through Vietnam; gastronomy; women-only adventures; travel for the disabled; New-Age and self-discovery travel; ecological adventure; health and fitness; joining a scientific expedition; tours for the young and the mature; and even companies catering to the booming category of "grandtravel," in which grandparents take their grandkids on a tour.

There are religious and pilgrimage tours; professional development tours; ethnic tours; reunions for veterans; tours for musicians; and tours for artists, writers, photographers, runners, students, gardeners, nudists, and people who collect dollhouses, study caves, or want to try dog-sledding.

There are companies that specialize in the more exotic, adventurous, and cultural programs, such as Lindblad Special Expeditions, New York; Society Expeditions, Seattle; Abercrombie & Kent, Oak Brook, Illinois; and Mountain Travel–Sobek, El Cerrito, California (two famous adventure companies that merged). There are companies focused on ecotourism (so-called "green travel") that are oriented around and concerned about protecting the environment, such as Geostar Travel, Santa Rosa, California.

Even outer space is not out of the realm: Space Adventures (Arlington, Virginia), founded by astronauts and adventure travel pioneers, has partnered with leading rocket companies in the world to begin actual flights into space within the next few years.

Indeed, famed guidebook author Arthur Frommer has targeted a "second revolution in travel" (the first, mass travel to Europe, was launched with his book *Europe*

On $5 A Day). The new revolution is oriented around "cerebral" and experiential travel—travel for ideas, learning, and people. Travel that "shakes you up, introduces you to lifestyles, philosophical viewpoints." In his book *Arthur Frommer's New World of Travel,* Frommer lists 1,200 companies offering programs to places such as personal growth centers, utopian villages, and centers for alternative teaching.

These are enormous markets. The Travel Industry Association of America estimates that half of U.S. adults, or 98 million people, have taken an adventure trip in the past five years, including 31 million adults who engaged in hard adventure activities like whitewater rafting, scuba diving, and mountain-biking. Also, one-fifth—30.2 million adults—have taken an educational trip to learn or improve a skill, sport, or hobby in the past three years.

> **INSIDE SECRET:** "Green" travel—companies that are sensitive to the environment and culture they bring people to and consciously "give back" to the locality—is one of the fastest-growing segments of tour operations.

A Crowded, Diverse, and Changing Market

There are literally thousands of companies that operate packaged tours, but only about 350 that operate on a nationwide basis and sell their product chiefly through travel agents (although more and more are also moving to direct bookings on the Internet). Fewer than 50 of the companies handle as many as 20,000 passengers a year and only about a dozen handle more than 100,000 passengers a year. This is in marked contrast to Europe, where massive travel organizations move hundreds of thousands of tourists a year; some carry 1 or 2 million travelers a year.

Tour companies differ markedly in their style and structure. They may specialize in certain destinations (Europe, the Caribbean, Asia), an activity or special interest (river rafting, museums), or a certain market (singles, youth, women, retirees, families). Their tours

may be geared to the deluxe, middle, economy, or budget market.

Because it is an intensely competitive industry, tour operators work on a very low mark-up (about 20 to 25 percent, compared to a clothes retailer, which marks up 100 percent). After expenses, pretax profit averages 3 percent. This is a business in which volume really pays off, yet ironically, the rising costs of advertising, printing, and postage had been factors keeping operators within small, specialized niches. But that is all being transformed by the Internet and e-commerce.

The variability of airfares, volume-based pricing, market segmentation, and rising costs of marketing and selling tour products, along with the volatility of key suppliers like airlines, is forcing radical changes among tour operators. One aspect of this is a shift away from small, entrepreneurial, family-owned companies to "big businesses" with specialized functions. However, the Internet is enabling specialized operators to reach their potential market in a cost-effective way. For companies big and small, a technology revolution is changing the makeup of the professionals inside the industry.

"This is the Electronics Age," declared Robert E. Whitley, CTC, president of the U.S. Tour Operators Association (USTOA), a membership association of about 55 of the largest tour companies. "The industry is hiring more and more technical people—computer specialists, telephone salespeople, marketers."

"We used to create a tour and then worry about operating it," reflected Ray Cortell, whose family founded Europacar Tours. "It was magical, creative then. Now we first have to consider whether the tour is operable from the computer end, or whether the cost of writing the software would exceed the profit potential. The criteria are changing for everything. Years ago, we would put out a 'dream' tour. Now it is all boiled down to airfares and body counts. We're not selling dreams anymore. We create a product we can operate the best—one where we can handle a booking in four minutes or less."

In Cortell's view, the focus has shifted from operating the tour to distribution and delivery—that is, marketing and sales. "The challenge today is the cost of getting the message out to the people and still make a profit," he said. However, today, the Internet is providing the means for operators to deliver their "dreams" to those in the public who may have an interest in a cost-effective way to achieve these same dreams.

Indeed, the "magic" is very apparent in some of the newest offerings. Space Adventures is one company formed to offer civilians a trip into space, partnering with private companies that are building their own rockets. There are countless other examples of small companies bringing to life the creative imaginings of their founders. There is a trip that re-creates the voyages of Jules Verne; another that enables people to hike at both North and South Poles on a 10-week expedition (Polar Travel Company); another that sails up the Grand Canal through China; and another that enables you to dive down to the *Titanic* (Zegrahm Expeditions).

Risky Business

Tour operations is one of the riskiest businesses in the travel industry. Operators deal with the most perishable commodity possible. Their product is space in time: a seat on an airline flight or a room in a hotel on a particular night. But whereas the airline or the hotel might have many different market segments to utilize their product, the tour operator is much more focused. There is no storing the product on the shelf for a mark-down sale after the departure. They deal with foreign currencies that are subject to rapid and wide fluctuations. They are vulnerable to strikes, political upheavals and policy changes, natural disasters, economic swings, the weather, and simple changes in the tastes of the traveling public. Every item in the newspaper has potential impact on the demand for a tour. The closest comparison for risk and change is the commodities market.

"The business is more nerve-wracking than people realize," Whitley said. "It is a constant condition of management by crisis. You have to make quick decisions. It is difficult to plan ahead, yet you have to plan ahead. You need to be able to change plans at a moment's notice."

You could be a Hawaii operator, for example. Things are going great and you staff up and advertise. Then the biggest airline into Hawaii goes on strike for three months. Or you specialize in Russia and plan for the 1980 Olympics. You go through the negotiations, print the brochures, advertise, put down deposits to hold space, and buy event tickets. Then the U.S. government boycotts. Or, you put together your program to Europe or to the Middle East, and then the Persian Gulf War erupts and no one is traveling abroad at all. You have to cope with the economy of this country and the rest of the world. You have to anticipate what will happen to currency and political events.

"You have to have patience and be able to handle details," Whitley said. Nonetheless, tour operations is the heart of what people associate as the glamour and lure of the travel industry. It is so compelling that few people who enter tour operations leave the field.

The Evolution of a Tour

A basic schedule for a ship or some major event, attraction, or theme may serve as the "embryo" of a tour package, with the rest of the itinerary organized around it. (A trip to Machu Picchu, for example, involves plugging in extra days in various cities in order to acclimate before going up to such a high altitude, and then taking into account limited departures of small airplanes that tend to be canceled due to weather.) The schedule might next go to the tour development manager, who fills in the spaces, accounting for virtually every moment of time. Negotiators, who typically spend a considerable amount of time traveling through the destination, then negotiate for space and rates from suppliers (airlines, hotels, ground transportation and sightseeing companies, and restaurants) based on an expectation of how many passengers the program will carry.

Then the material goes to the production department, which creates a brochure—the actual "product" that goes out to retailers for sale to the public—and to marketing.

Once the tour is available for sale, it comes under the aegis of the operations and reservations departments.

Reservationists take orders from travel agents and from the general public. The operations department gathers necessary documents and mails them to passengers; keeps track of tours as they are sold out or over-booked; and sends out passenger lists (manifests) to hotels. Tour escorts are assigned.

The visa department gathers the documents needed by foreign governments in order for the passengers to be admitted.

Just creating the tour product is not enough (as too many would-be entrepreneurs have learned). Tour operators need sales, marketing, and public relations specialists who are responsible for promoting the program to travel agents and the public. As in other aspects of travel, this often entails negotiating preferred supplier relationships (which is why it is so difficult for a newcomer), partnerships with other vendors, and creative efforts to get the product noticed in a crowded, highly competitive field, in the most cost-effective way.

Your Ticket into Tour Operations

Tour operations is one of the most creative areas in the travel industry and affords some of the best opportunities to fulfill one's dream of traveling to exotic locales or doing exciting things. If there were any facet of the travel industry that had an impact on changing the world for the better, this is it. Tour operations literally brings the world closer together, encourages an exchange of ideas, plants seeds for new ideas, and brings jobs and injects capital to fund progress. Nothing overcomes prejudice better than meeting people face to face.

However, job opportunities are relatively limited and mobility is much more restricted than in other areas, largely because most of the companies tend to be small, entrepreneurial, or family-run; and even in the largest companies, relatively few people handle enormous volumes of passengers.

A company that sends some 20,000 people abroad may have only six to 10 people in any position of real power. The vast majority of jobs are in reservations

and tour escorting. The smaller companies afford the best opportunity to take on the responsibility for a range of tasks and to move more swiftly into the most desirable positions in product development and tour management.

 INSIDE SECRET: One of the most eclectic fields in travel, tour companies employ people of just about every background and specialty.

Moreover, tour operations is one field that utilizes virtually every type of professional—all experience is applicable. Doctors and nurses (especially those who get burned out and change careers) are involved in coordinating professional tours or assisting with programs for the disabled. Former journalists handle public relations and marketing functions. Artists and musicians create and lead tours to the major art and music events of the world. Former educators organize trips for teachers and students as well as alumni, or become the experts leading tours.

Salaries tend to be low (decent for senior management positions), but this is somewhat compensated for by the opportunity to take the trips the company offers and the opportunity to have responsibility.

"The whole industry is highly mobile," noted one executive. "It's a matter of being in the right place at the right time, being motivated, intelligent, and capable. You have to be flexible and willing to move. Success doesn't depend so much on your education as your perseverance and ability to capitalize on opportunities. Anyone that shows promise always finds positions at mid-level."

From a Lake to a Global Enterprise

The international Globus & Cosmos group, which has its North American headquarters in Littleton, Colorado, began as a small, family company in Switzerland. More than 70 years ago, Antonio Mantegazza bought a rowboat to transport commercial goods across Lake Lugano. Antonio's frequent trips across the scenic lake led him to consider opportunities in a different market:

(continues)

(continued)

tourism. His entrepreneurial instinct pushed him to gradually acquire some motorcoaches to transport tourists around the Lake Lugano area. In 1928, Antonio opened a company specializing in motorcoach touring called Globus Viaggi. The company began with a fleet of 12 coaches that operated local excursions for European tourists in Switzerland. By 1950, Globus Viaggi had grown to a fleet of 33 coaches and featured overnight excursions to Rome, Venice, the Dolomites, and the French Riviera. Gradually, these became regularly scheduled tours and grew longer to cover more ground.

Later that decade, under the leadership of Werner Albek, Antonio's business partner, Globus pioneered the concept of Grand European Touring by offering first-class European tours to North Americans. By 1961, the company launched its Cosmos arm, which featured affordable, budget-priced European touring for the cost-conscious British traveler.

The coach tours were so successful that Cosmos soon introduced another form of travel for the British market: air holiday packages to the sunny destinations of southern Europe. By 1968, Cosmos' air holidays became so popular that the company formed its own airline, Monarch Airlines. Monarch Airlines started out modestly with two used Britannia aircraft and eventually blossomed into one of the most successful European charter companies, with a large fleet of modern jets and its own engineering division.

Under the flagship of Sergio Mantegazza, current president and son of Antonio, Globus & Cosmos began expanding its markets beyond Great Britain and North America. Since 1974, tour packages have been sold in Australia, New Zealand, Canada, and most recently Southeast Asia. Starting in the 1970s, the company also aggressively expanded its tour offerings, introducing travelers to more countries than any other tour operator, with packages to Africa, Antarctica, South and North America, Europe, the South Pacific, and Asia.

Today, the Globus & Cosmos group of companies consists of more than 30 tourism and aviation businesses, serviced by a group of more than 5,000 professionals. Globus & Cosmos escorted and independent tours offer more than 12,000 departures of more than 350 different itineraries, covering more than 70 countries on seven continents. Globus & Cosmos together carry about 500,000 passengers a year, making the company the largest operator of escorted tours worldwide.

The company prides itself on a humanistic corporate culture. The head of human resources has the distinguished title of "Executive Director of People & Change."

The company is generous with its benefits, including a significant amount of time off (16 days earned during the first full year of continuous employment, 21 days for the 2nd through 9th years, and 26 days beginning with the 10th year, plus 7 scheduled holidays and 3 "floating" paid holidays). Two "fam" weeks are provided during the career, and employees can use the company's education allowance toward trips or educational programs.

Associates who work a minimum of 20 hours weekly and have an annualized salary of $5,000 are eligible to register with IATAN. After six months, they can get an IATAN card, which is accepted by many travel suppliers for professional discounts.

As is typical of tour operations, Globus & Cosmos has positions in reservations, MIS, marketing and sales, customer service, group sales, product development, administration, and human resources. (For more information, see www.globusandcosmos.com.)

Jobs in Tour Operations

Tour operations employs people of just about every professional background and specialty. For the near term, at least, there will be greater opportunities in operations (particularly information technology/Internet/e-commerce, reservations, customer service, and quality control) than in sales and marketing, but here there is great demand for direct-marketing and loyalty-marketing professionals. Emerging titles include Tour Cost Analyst, Market Research Manager, and Web Site Programmer.

- **Product Development Manager:** Creates the tour package starting with researching destinations; conducting site inspections; planning the logistics and creating an itinerary; negotiating for space and rates with hotels, restaurants, attractions, ground handlers, and airlines; and doing costing that results in the price that will be charged to passengers. May also participate in marketing, brochure production, and advertising. In some cases, also conducts off-site training of agents and supervisors at destinations to improve sales skills. Keeps track of sales and client comments in order to make changes for future tours. Tour companies look for three or more years of experience working for a tour operator; destination knowledge; personal contacts with hotels, attractions, and ground handlers; plus excellent follow-through on details, creativity, and sensitivity to what travelers want.

- **Tour Product Manager:** Manages a product line (a particular tour or geographic area) much like a business unit and is responsible for making sure the tour programs operate properly, efficiently, and profitably. This person usually is responsible for assigning tour escorts, troubleshooting when things go awry, handling customer service, monitoring competitors' programs for quality and price, and recommending changes to make the product sell better, operate more efficiently, or be more profitable.

Best Bets

- Web Designer
- Web Programmer
- Quality control
- Marketing

- **Airline Specialist:** Assists in negotiation of airfares, interfaces with operations and airlines.
- **Sales Agent** (Tour Consultant, Reservationist): Books tours, generally with travel agents but sometimes with group organizers or individual travelers, usually by telephone. Must communicate effectively and be able to ask questions to elicit proper information in order to make correct recommendations and assist the agent/client in booking the most appropriate product. Also assists in designing suitable pre- and post-tour extensions. Recommends ways to combine tours, bridge

nights, and air routings. Accurately costs the program, including airfares and extras, and communicates deposit requirements and cancellation policies. The sales agent must communicate with relevant departments regarding inventory changes, cancellations, and flight details, and assist the customer service department in handling complaints. This position requires travel school or equivalent experience, two years as a travel agent, or one year in wholesale; excellent communications skills and a personable manner on the telephone; knowledge of geography; computer literacy; ability to handle many details at once; and excellent follow-through.

- **Group Sales Representative:** Specializes in processing requests for groups; plans, packages, and sells air and motorcoach tours to groups and individuals. Duties include assisting the client in designing and costing a suitable itinerary; working with overseas offices and third-party vendors in designing and operating the group; establishing costs; sending a written proposal to the client and following up by phone; booking services after the client books the program; maintaining timely communication with the client; assisting the client in creating a brochure, if necessary; working with the operations coordinator on invoices, credit memos, and documentation; and booking/ticketing airline flights. The job also involves preparing a profit/loss analysis for each program and liaising with customer service regarding complaints. Qualifications include travel school or the equivalent, four years in the travel industry or two years in a tour operation, excellent verbal and written communication skills and a pleasant telephone manner, an understanding of geography and time zones, and the ability to work in a "team" environment.

INSIDE SECRET: Salary levels vary widely but are most closely related to size of the company, number of passengers carried, price of tours, international versus domestic, and geographic location.

■ **Tour Director** (also called Tour Manager or Tour Escort): Conducts tours within a specific geographical area; responsible for organization, timing, logistics, and commentary. The job requires intensive research of history, geology, geography, culture, flora and fauna, and the social and economic circumstances of the destination and its people. You must be intense, highly responsible, and able to handle any emergency that may arise. Tour Directors are on call 24 hours a day for long stretches of time. Ideally, the individual comes with hospitality industry experience involving customer contact, or comes from another travel-related customer service. The employer may also look for specific educational background (such as history, art, or literature), language skills, and intensive knowledge of the destination. These positions are very often freelance; only a few tour companies maintain a full-time force (such as Tauck World Discovery). Companies often recruit from specialty schools such as the International Tour Management Institute, San Francisco.

■ **Director of Tour Guides:** Supervises a staff (which can be dozens) of full- and part-time tour guides. Hires, trains, schedules, and briefs guides on all facets of the tours. Prepares and organizes reservations and instructions for each tour departure. Writes tour manuals, guide instructions, and routings for tours. Must be on call 24 hours a day for assessing and resolving emergency situations. The Director of Tour Guides is usually someone who has spent years in the field as a tour manager and has management ability.

■ **Quality Assurance Manager** (Quality Control Coordinator): Troubleshoots when there are passenger complaints or problems. Incorporates corrective measures in tour products. Improves quality awareness within the company. Implements the customer evaluation process and improves procedures to promote customer service and operating efficiency. (Quality Assurance is more preventive; Quality Control is after-the-fact.) A relatively new specialization within tour

operations, the career paths to this position are from reservations or customer service.

■ **Creative Director:** Oversees development and creation of brochures, advertising, sales literature, and the company image. Interfaces with outside agencies.

■ **Operations Director:** Oversees product managers, tours, and supplier relationships. May direct or assist in the strategy and development of new tours.

Other positions include

■ Programmer/Analyst

■ Customer Service Specialist

 # Salaries in Tour Operations

Salaries are tremendously divergent, even among comparable companies, and do not always reflect the level of responsibility. Salaries generally depend on the size of the company (the number of passengers carried, the product pricing, the geographic location of the company, and the number of people managed) and prior experience. International operators and in-house operations of airlines generally pay better than domestic travel companies.

Sample Tour Operations Job Titles and Salaries

Title	Salary
Product Development Manager	$50,000–$90,000
Tour Product Manager	$30,000–$48,000
Airline Specialist	$19,000–$35,000; $29,000 average
Tour Director	$76 per diem, plus tips and expenses
Director of Tour Guides	$35,000–$75,000
Quality Assurance Manager	$55,000

Title	Salary
Creative Director	$36,000–$75,000; $53,000 average
Operations Director	$55,000–$93,000; $78,000 average
Programmer/Analyst	$23,000–$75,000
Customer Service Specialist	$19,000–$30,000; $25,000 average

Sales Agents

Title	Salary
Reservationist (entry-level)	$17,000–$21,000
Sales/Account Representative	$31,000–$54,000; $41,000 average
Group Sales Representative	$45,000–$55,000

Senior/Executive Positions

Title	Salary
Director of Marketing	$44,000–$150,000; $86,000 average
Senior Sales Executive	$45,000–$110,000; $75,000 average
Chief Financial Officer	$45,000–$149,000; $85,000 average
Controller	$50,000–$76,000; $64,000 average
Chief Executive Officer/President	$55,000–$500,000; middle range $66,700–$359,000; $194,000 average
Chief Operating Officer	$42,000–$450,000; $143,000 average

Contacts, Sources, and Leads

- **U.S. Tour Operators Association (USTOA),** 342 Madison Ave., Ste. 1522, New York, NY 10173; 212-599-6599; fax 212-599-6744; www.ustoa.com. Represents some of the most prestigious and best-established tour companies, mainly international, in the industry. Stringent membership requirements, including bonding. Publishes a membership listing; Web site offers great links.
- **National Tour Association,** 546 E. Main St., P.O. Box 3071, Lexington, KY 40596-3071; 606-253-1036; www.ntaonline.com. Has a directory of 600 tour operator members.
- **American Society of Travel Agents,** 1101 King St., Alexandria, VA 22314; www.astanet.com. Publishes a list of tour operators participating in its bonding program.

Publications

- *Specialty Travel Index,* 305 San Anselmo Ave., Ste. 217, San Anselmo, CA 94960; www.specialtytravel.com.
- *The Educated Traveler Newsletter,* P.O. Box 220822, Chantilly, VA 20153.
- *Leisure Travel News.*
- *Travel Weekly.*
- *Travel Agent Magazine.*
- *Condé Nast Traveler.*
- Also check consumer travel publications and Sunday travel sections in the newspaper.

Domestic Tour Operations

Just as there are tours for every taste and lifestyle for those going abroad, there is an extraordinary range of options for domestic trips—everything from a journey by covered wagon (Wagons West, Afton, Wyoming), to digging for dinosaurs in Colorado (Dinamation International Society, Fruita, Colorado), to a mystery tour where the destination itself is a surprise. Though much the same as the international tour operations, domestic group tour companies package destinations within North America (Canada, the United States, and Mexico). Typically, they have different origins, usually from a motorcoach company, and have evolved differently. They tend to have an atmosphere that is more conservative—even provincial—one that is more oriented to serving a local community or special interest rather than a national market.

Most domestic tour operators have their origins as "tour brokers" of motorcoach travel, which at one time was heavily regulated by the Interstate Commerce Commission Act of 1939, which imposed such cumbersome and archaic rules as to squelch competition and innovation. Deregulation of the motorcoach industry in the 1980s has opened the way to innovation and made it possible for operators to creatively fashion programs that appeal to contemporary lifestyles and needs. Deregulation vastly eased entry into motorcoach operations, charters, and tours. The result was literally hundreds of new companies opening almost overnight and a dramatic increase in the numbers of passengers traveling on motorcoach tours and charters. No longer "tour brokers," per se, the companies evolved into "group travel" operators, usually specializing in North America, but some offer international destinations as well.

INSIDE SECRET: Tour operators are not the only companies that create tour products; travel agencies, hotels, and cruise companies often also have tour departments.

The National Tour Association (the largest domestic travel organization, with 4,000 members including 650 tour operators, 2,700 suppliers, and 650 destination-marketing organizations) estimated that in 1992 the industry carried 56.3 million passengers and grossed $5.6 billion. The passengers are not only American travelers seeing their own country, but international visitors as well.

Although the industry had its origins in escorted travel by motorcoach, programs now encompass various modes of transportation. Tours range from one day to several weeks' duration, and prices can range from $35 (for a day-trip) to nearly $10,000. The most popular length is five to seven days and costs $400 to $500. Group tours, which used to be these operators' sole offering, now account for 85 percent of total volume, with independent trips accounting for the rest.

Great Growth and Career Opportunities

Domestic tour operators may be smaller scale and more narrowly focused than international tour operators, but in many cases they offer greater growth and more career opportunities. In many respects, domestic tour operations affords greater creativity—there are so many more markets for domestic tour products than for international, and the industry has really only begun to tap them. Indeed, domestic tour operations has in a sense been reborn, and newcomers to the field have a chance to be in on the ground floor.

INSIDE SECRET: Domestic tour operations can allow for more creativity than international operations, because the industry has just begun to tap its many markets.

Tour participants still tend to be senior citizens, but the age is coming down as new tour products are introduced to appeal to a younger, more active market, as well as to families and multigenerational groups. The emerging specialties include programs oriented around ecotourism and cultural tourism (art, music, museums, and cultural events), sports and adventure, family travel (particularly "grandtravel," where grandparents take their grandkids on a tour), and such innovations as "hub-and-spoke" itineraries, where passengers stay in one place but take day-trips to visit a region.

A typical domestic package might be a six-day fall foliage trip through New England, but new products range from hunting alligators in Florida to hunting bargains in New York City; from whitewater rafting adventures to leisurely sightseeing by boat. The elements of domestic tour operations are essentially the same as in tour operations generally: product development (creating new products), sales and marketing, reservations and operations, and distribution.

The industry is made up of a few large firms with a substantial number of employees, and hundreds of smaller enterprises with fewer than 10. Most tour companies are relatively small: The majority have annual gross sales of less than $2 million. Nearly one-fourth are midsized, with sales in the $2 to $8 million range. Less than 10 percent have sales of $10 million or more.

> **INSIDE SECRET:** The domestic tour industry is made up of a few large operators and hundreds of small companies that employ 10 or fewer people.

The average company employs fewer than 10 people and handles 2,500 customers a year. The largest companies employ more than 200, operate 10,000 departures, and handle 100,000 customers a year.

In most of the tour companies, the owner is mainly responsible for tour development. Then the program is given to a tour-planning department to find hotel rooms, negotiate rates, and decide what attractions or sightseeing to include.

The field is becoming more professional, less mom-and-pop, along with most segments of the travel industry. In the domestic tour business, too, there are some consolidations into larger corporations, but not to the same degree as in other segments. There is also greater sophistication in business operations and more automation. Technology—information systems—is

playing a growing role, making management more efficient by enabling managers to keep track of reservations, how tours are selling, and load factors.

Domestic tour operations is also becoming more sales and marketing oriented, utilizing field salespeople to call on travel agents (some travel agencies have in-house group tour departments) and groups (senior citizens' clubs, church groups, and schools).

> **INSIDE SECRET:** Domestic tour operators are beginning to look abroad for new products to offer their customers; this will mean opportunities for product developers.

Moreover, the focus of the traditionally domestic companies, which may have marketed their tours to an international audience, is turning global. Many are emerging as full-scale international operators, giving these businesses a third dimension beyond domestic (within North America) and receptive (that is, handling inbound visitors from abroad).

High Mobility, Low Pay

Although there tends to be little staff turnover, there is considerable mobility within companies, probably more so than in international tour companies. This is mainly because domestic tour operators tend to be generalists rather than specialists. It is common for tour escorts (the people who lead tours) to rise within the company to the highest levels.

This is still a field where people can get in with relatively little experience; however, salaries reflect it. Consequently, people can stay in a company, taking on enormous responsibility, and still earn modest salaries. The rewards, however, come in having considerable responsibility, the diversity of tasks, the unlimited aspects of the tour product, and the people you deal with.

What compels people to stay? "In the tour business, you work with all components of tourism—hotels, restaurants, events, attractions, destination-marketing organizations," said one tour professional. "You never get bored!"

Contacts, Sources, and Leads

The National Tour Association has a listing of members and further details about the domestic tour operations industry. It provides some placement assistance via notices in its "Tuesday" newsletter (for a fee).

The National Tour Foundation (NTF) assists students with internship placements in the tour business. NTF also manages the Certified Tour Professional (CTP) program—the premier certification for tour professionals. It offers professional development seminars at its conventions.

- **National Tour Association, Inc.,** 546 E. Main St., Lexington, KY 40508; 606-253-1036; 800-755-TOUR; www.ntaonline.com.

- Major trade publications: **Courier** (NTA's magazine), **Leisure Travel News, Travel Weekly,** and **Travel Agent.**

Inbound, Reception Services, and Sightseeing Companies

People generally think in terms of outbound travel and rarely realize that there are people at the other end to service the travelers with transportation, sightseeing, and other facilities. Operators that handle incoming visitors by coordinating their stay and escorting them about are called *inbound* or *reception services* or *ground handlers.* In the U.S., most travel agencies are solely involved with sending visitors out from their areas to other states or countries; abroad, however, most travel agencies handle both outbound and inbound services. In this country, reception services are usually carried out by specialists, although many travel agencies are moving into the field.

Reception Services

Handling reception requires some specialized skills and services—multilingual guides, for example, and contacts with travel agents abroad—for handling foreign groups. But groups also come from other parts of this country. The key ingredients are a thorough knowledge of your locality and contacts with local attractions and facilities. A Coral Gables, Florida, agent, for example, handled a group of Norwegian zoo owners who were visiting to learn about facilities for captive animals in southern Florida. Besides arranging visits to such facilities, the agent also had to coordinate matters concerning passports, visas, lost luggage, and sickness among the tour members.

The reception service works in concert with the tour packager or the travel agent sending the group; frequently, the travelers are completely unaware that they are being handled by an agent for the tour company with which they booked.

Many large companies, particularly motorcoach operators, specialize in reception services (sometimes known as Visit U.S.A. operators). Among them are Allied Tours and T Pro, both of New York. But there are many small companies, including travel agencies, that are getting into this area.

Convention and visitor bureaus are an excellent source for names of companies operating in your area. NYC & Company (the convention and visitor bureau; 810 Seventh Ave., New York, NY 10019), for example, publishes the *Official New York City Travel Planner*, a directory geared to travel professionals that includes a listing of reception companies.

In addition to full-service sightseeing and transportation companies, there are specialized reception services. One company specialized in a "shopping extravaganza" in New York's garment district and department and specialty stores. Another provided behind-the-scenes tours of Broadway shows. Still another provides entree to the world of art, architecture, fashion, theater, and music. Yet another specializes in visiting the Hassidic Jewish community, while Harlem

Spirituals is one of several companies specializing in tours of that celebrated district.

Cary Frederick, a Hoosier from Indiana who made his home in New York, knew what it was like to be an out-of-towner in the Big Apple—the fears, confusion, expense, wonderment, and delight. So he set up his own personalized guide service, appropriately named Rent-a-New Yorker, to help visitors to the city, individually or in small groups. He drew upon his skills as a trained librarian to research and plan itineraries, and prearrange hotel accommodations, restaurants, theater and events tickets, and sightseeing. He even stood in line at the TKTS booth to obtain Broadway theatre tickets at half price for his clients. "Everyone talks about personal service," he said. "I am like a friend in town."

As companies like Frederick's expand due to repeat business and referrals, they generally take on associates or add staff.

Reception companies cater not just to incoming tourists, but also to conventions, meetings, and corporate, professional, and academic groups and individuals as well as their spouses (and, increasingly, their children, by organizing supervised activities when parents are in functions).

The American Society of Travel Agents (ASTA) has been actively working to help its member travel agencies to cultivate reception services, and several hundred have already entered the field, with several hundred more moving in the same direction. This usually involves adding staff.

ASTA member Rex Fritschi, President of Rex Travel, Chicago, launched a reception service two decades ago, providing sightseeing programs in Chicago. His company, Chicago Welcomes, handles groups mainly from overseas, including England, France, Germany, and Switzerland.

"It's a completely different ball of wax from the travel agency," said Fritschi, "different selling, marketing approach, and different handling. The wants, needs, expectations of foreign travelers are different."

INSIDE SECRET: While foreign-language skills are not necessarily a prerequisite in reception services, they certainly help. Primarily, you need to have a good knowledge of the area, as well as maturity and patience.

It takes several years to become established in reception services, to develop the contacts abroad and the name recognition. Skills that are excellent assets for reception services are knowledge of foreign languages, experience living abroad, contacts with travel companies abroad, knowledge of a locality or special interest, good planning and organizational skills, and high creativity.

Reception services also offers a means of entry into the travel business without even giving up your current job. Many of these reception companies need part-time help as escorts, guides, or associates to plan and coordinate trips. These companies afford much of the excitement and sense of traveling without ever leaving town, because the clients are from faraway places.

A job as a professional guide can be an excellent entree into the travel industry and can be a challenging, creative, and financially rewarding position. Guides can work freelance for travel companies, developing relationships with tour operators, travel agents, reception companies, and hotels. Guiding provides an opportunity to maximize one's knowledge of foreign languages, art, history, architecture, clothes, music, theater, entertainment, and virtually any other special interest. Some areas may require licensing (New York City's Department of Consumer Affairs administers a test that qualifies an applicant to become a professional guide). There are several entities in New York that place guides, such as the Guides Association of New York City.

Reception services is a highly entrepreneurial field. If you are considering opening your own reception service, consider what your locality has and doesn't have. Talk with local convention and visitor bureau or chamber of commerce people. There is tremendous opportunity in this area, particularly because of the continued growth in travel into the U.S., fueled in part by exchange rates that have made the U.S. such a bargain. But it's also because of the appeal of the U.S. as a destination.

"Foreigners have 'done' Disney World and New York and want to see what more the U.S. has to offer," said Fritschi. "There is great, great potential."

There are so many reception services and ground handlers that one of the greatest needs for individual companies is marketing. American Sightseeing International was formed to meet this need. ASI is an association of sightseeing and tour companies in more than 100 major tourist markets (40 U.S. cities and 60 countries). Gray Line is another.

Sightseeing Companies and Ground Handlers

Sightseeing is probably one of the more limited occupations in the travel industry. In sightseeing companies, most people in positions of prominence have come up through the ranks of a bus company. Rather than travel industry professionals, they tend to be bus industry specialists.

The appeal of the sightseeing business is that it is intensely people-oriented—escorts, ticket sellers, and bus drivers all are in constant contact with the public. Also, deregulation has forced everyone to be more creative and innovative in terms of product and marketing, because there is so much more competition.

"This is a growth area—any city can have a sightseeing company," said Richard Valerio, ASI president. "There are new hotels, convention centers opening all over the place. Call the convention and visitor bureau to see what is happening."

Ground transportation companies don't just handle sightseeing. They may also handle transfers, from the airport to hotels or to sites for special events. They are used to a great extent in conjunction with conventions and meetings (even for "spouse" sightseeing and shopping programs while meetings are going on).

Why go into the ground transportation/sightseeing business? "The excitement of being part of a worldwide community," declared Valerio, "of hosting visitors, conveying civic pride, being creative."

Contacts, Sources, and Leads

- **American Sightseeing International,** World Headquarters, 490 Post St. #1701, San Francisco, CA 94102; 415-986-2082; www.americansightseeing.org.
- **Professional Guides Association of America,** 241 S. Eads St., Arlington, VA 22202-2532.
- **Travel Industry Association of America (TIA),** 1133 21st St. NW, Two Lafayette Centre, Washington, DC 20036; 202-293-1433; www.tia.org.
- Local convention and visitor bureaus.

Travel for the Disabled

There are an infinite variety of tour companies that specialize in some interest, activity, or demographic group and fall into the category of "special-interest operators."

In recent years, however, the travel industry has became mindful of a huge market of people who had a deep desire to travel but because of some disability were unable to take advantage of conventional programs. According to some experts, there are about 43 million Americans with disabilities, with the potential to generate about $60 billion in travel sales. A whole new industry has sprung up catering to these travelers. It is potentially so large and so specialized that handicapped travel is actually a separate field of tour operations.

Edna Davis, a former travel agent, was brought into the field quite by accident when her son, the captain of his school football team, was tackled and didn't get up.

"In the year that he spent at the hospital, people would hear I was in the travel business and ask me for help arranging travel for them. I realized no one knew anyone to help them. I handled groups, then tours, now reception services, also." Even Disneyland has called her for assistance.

The disabled "are not content to fit into the mold," she said. "They seek freedom of movement. They won't be content sitting still. Disability does not mean inability."

Society for Accessible Travel & Hospitality

In 1976, the late Murray Vidockler launched a major movement on behalf of disabled travelers. After 30 years in the travel industry as a travel agent, international tour operator, and airline executive, he "realized that there was one Final Frontier which had not been recognized as an important goal by our industry as a whole—namely, the enormous, untapped market of the then 40 or so millions of Americans with disabili-

ties who were largely excluded from the possibilities of tourism."

"The industry was growing fast and much new investment was available for the expanding infrastructure," Vidockler said. "At the same time, Civil Rights and Equality of Opportunity were in the air. Changing lifestyles and medical advances were increasing the life expectancy of the population as a whole, but people who were unfortunate enough to have a disability were being excluded from much of the benefit this new society had to offer."

Vidockler, together with a few people who thought as he did, decided that they had to do something to redress the situation. He founded SATH—Society for Accessible Travel & Hospitality—and began a massive crusade to educate the travel industry as to the economic possibilities of this underdeveloped market. At the same time, he began a campaign to inform the population with disabilities that they could join the mainstream in travel, as well as in other aspects of their everyday life. "We offered them dignity and opportunity, not charity or welfare. Our mottoes were 'No Discounts for the Handicapped,' 'Charity No, Services Yes,' and later, 'Jobs by Ability not Disability,'" he said.

Two laws, the Air Carriers Access Act of 1986 and the Americans with Disabilities Act of 1990, forced widespread improvements in access for the disabled and spurred many travel-oriented companies to cater to this market. The law specifically prohibits discrimination in transportation and public accommodations, including hotels, restaurants, theme parks, and attractions.

"The result was that airlines and other forms of transportation made millions of dollars, people with disabilities were able to expect to travel with dignity, and the market in travel expanded exponentially with each increase in the rights of persons with disabilities to be considered as normal travelers," Vidockler said.

In 1996, the American Society of Travel Agents (ASTA) at its World Congress in Bangkok inducted Vidockler into the Travel Hall of Fame and announced its sponsorship with American Express of SATH's World Partnership in Awareness. This group will meet annually at the ASTA World Congress to address problems of participating nations in their receptive services for travelers with disabilities and mature travelers, fostering new initiatives around the world to open tourism to all.

Opportunities for Health-Care Professionals

This is a field of travel that offers special opportunity for people trained in physical therapy, nursing, medicine, and psychology, and for people who are themselves handicapped. Travel agencies, for example, are becoming very involved in serving disabled travelers, on both a group basis and an individual basis, and may be very amenable to hiring someone who is familiar with serving the disabled traveler.

As an example, a registered nurse, Pam Erickson, set up a business called Professional Respite Care (Denver, Colorado) to provide nurses as medical travel companions for the disabled and seniors.

According to Davis, getting into the handicapped travel market requires a knowledge of particular details and meticulous efficiency in anticipating every need and making arrangements for them. "Introduce yourself to a wheelchair," she advised. "See how it works."

She added, "There is no one easy source of information. No two disabled people are alike. All are individuals. Each must be counseled individually—their needs, desires."

"Always discuss with a carrier and check and recheck. Leave nothing to chance. Don't be timid; ask direct questions. They know they are disabled—they live with it. Their problems need to be discussed openly."

Contacts, Sources, and Leads

Other companies active in the field include the following:

- **Flying Wheels Travel Service,** 143 W. Bridge, P.O. Box 382, Owatonna, ME 55060; 800-535-6790; www.flyingwheelstravel.com. Has specialized in disabled travel since 1970, offering escorted tours to international destinations, as well as customized individual travel arrangements.

- **Wilderness Inquiry,** 1313 Fifth Street SE, Suite 327, Minneapolis, MN 55414; 612-379-3858; www.wildernessinquiry.org. This nonprofit group provides outdoor experiences that combine people with and without disabilities from diverse backgrounds. Trips include a canoe trip on Maine's Moose River, a Grand Canyon rafting adventure, and kayaking in the Queen Charlotte Islands.

- **TKTS-N-TOURS TRAVEL, Inc.,** 397 Sawdust Rd., The Woodlands, TX 77380; 888-866-3810; www.ticketsntours.com, www.traveloutlet.org. This travel outlet specializes in physically challenged travel for individuals and groups.

- **Travel Aides International** provides medical companions, a travel agency, and travel products for handicapped, disabled, and seniors. http://members.tripod.com/~Travel_us/index.html.

A prime source of information and leads for potential employers:

- **SATH (Society for Accessible Travel & Hospitality),** 347 Fifth Ave., Ste. 610, New York, NY 10016; 212-447-SATH; www.sath.org. Publishes *Open World* magazine.

Tour Managers

Many expect they can start their career in tour operations as a Tour Manager (also called Tour Escort or Tour Director). In many companies, these jobs are relatively easy to get; in others, some very sophisticated background and skills are needed. For example, those who lead China tours may need to speak Mandarin, have strong academic backgrounds as Sinologists, and be highly knowledgeable about the culture.

Most tour operators contract Tour Managers on a freelance basis since the work is so highly seasonal; Tauck World Discovery, a premier escorted tour company, is unusual because it hires its own (paying salary and benefits) and tries to keep as many as possible working year-round.

Tauck's Manager of Tour Directors is responsible for hiring, and the number can go as high as 250 in peak season (about 80 are employed year-round). This position is a key spot because at Tauck, positions in middle or upper management are often filled from the escort staff. As Peter Tauck, the co-president (formerly director of reservations), explained, "We organize the tour here and sell it to travel agents, so the only way one would see the product is to be a tour escort. Then you see the hotels, how they function. You are more able to handle the day-to-day decision-making. It is hard to teach the product by showing someone the brochure. You have to experience it." Even Peter Tauck, the third generation at Tauck Tours who rose through the ranks and is now co-president, has been a tour escort.

"A Strange Lifestyle"

Though tour escorting is often a steppingstone, it is emerging as a career in itself, albeit one that is hard to keep up after marriage and children.

"Things have changed," reflected Dick Sundby, a tour escort for 12 years, who served as Tauck's tour director supervisor for a while before returning to being a tour escort. "People are beginning to look at tour directing as a career. Many are writers and musicians. They want to work for five or six months and have their own thing to do in the off-season."

Still, "It's a strange lifestyle for a married person or parent," noted Durband. "It's like being a professional athlete—does anyone question whether Bo Jackson should be on the road? But it gives you very little opportunity for parenting. Most who do this who are married just do it in the summer."

Tauck has an intense training program in which escorts (who range in age from 21 to 60) learn how to deal with potential problems and emergencies. A "rookie" is put together with a more experienced driver and escort. Also, Tauck maintains special telephone lines in case escorts get into difficulty along the way.

A few of the tour escorts are married, but this arrangement generally does not work out well for long. Married couples will sometimes work the same itinerary but different groups (but still don't get to see each other more than once a week).

The work is emotionally and physically demanding: 15 to 25 weeks straight working seven days a week with no days off and only a limited amount of free time, little chance to sit down, and having to help lift out luggage and run around keeping everyone happy.

Despite this rigorous schedule, Tauck has a fairly low attrition rate. People either leave after one season or stay a decade. "It suits your personality and lifestyle or it doesn't," said Durband.

It can be a lonely job. "You develop camaraderie with the hotel people," remarked Sundby. "You develop friendships in the towns you visit and it is like going home each time."

Normally, a tour escort will run one itinerary exclusively for one year; the next year, two itineraries; the next, three. With seniority comes more choice of itineraries, but selections are made by performance.

Qualities of a Good Tour Escort

No specific skills are required, but there are many things you have to be. "Like the Boy Scouts, you have to be honest, cheerful, brave, courteous, reverent," said Sundby. "You have to have the understanding and patience to deal with clients. You have to be able to go the extra mile to take care of people on an individual basis—that is equally important to knowing dates and places. It takes a special person to do a complete tour during the day and then handle individual requirements in the evening. You have to be a leader and be a friend."

Tour escorts need to be good communicators, diplomats, detail oriented, well organized, and highly responsible because they frequently have to manage through emergencies as well as handle considerable sums of money.

The guides do a complete narration. "Clients expect a guide to know everything," Sundby said.

A tour escort needs to have a deep curiosity and desire to keep learning, and also the inner desire to do a better job than the time before.

Getting In

Out of 500 resumes, Tauck may hire 20 or 25 escorts. So many resumes come in unsolicited, Tauck does not have to do any active recruiting. "Persistence is the key," Sundby noted. "I tried to get into Tauck four or five times before I got in."

Because so many resumes come in, "It's difficult to tell a good candidate," Sundby advised, "so try to make personal contact." Friends who work in hotels or who are escorts can provide leads. It is also important to demonstrate some kind of familiarity with the product (the tour) and the destination.

> **INSIDE SECRETS:** Tour companies are deluged with resumes for escort positions. To stand out, you need to network and make personal contacts.

Some companies may require a Master's degree in botany or some other specialty. "But for most tours, good general knowledge suffices," said Sundby. "I became an expert in wildflowers and trees just by doing the same tour over and over, and researching the questions the passengers asked."

Most tour escorts are freelance, working for such companies as American Express and Trafalgar and the like. Tour directors can make anything between $40 and $192 a day, but the industry average is $76 a day before tips (but tips can amount to two-thirds of the escort's income). Companies that employ tour directors full time also provide benefits, such as health insurance.

The International Association of Tour Managers (IATM) has 2,000 members worldwide, of which only 100 are in the U.S.—mainly because most domestic tour companies employ local guides rather than escorts (who accompany a trip throughout its itinerary). Membership also requires that the tour manager spend 180 days on the road and that escorting be the primary source of income. The vast majority of tour managers in the U.S. do it part-time; only about 1,000 are professionals.

Dom Pasarelli, who served as the main contact for the IATM in the U.S. for many years, noted that this is a highly specialized field—and one that is fairly elite. The membership roster includes people who have doctorates, speak various foreign languages, and specialize in architecture, art, culinary arts, and so on. Among the IATM members are three barons, two counts, and a prince.

"We're all crazy, eccentric," commented Pasarelli, who holds a doctorate in foreign cultures and has been a tour manager since 1962. "There is tremendous responsibility; you have the lives of 48 people in your hands. You have an awful lot of power: like a ship captain, you can put someone off the tour. I've had to ship some home, including one in a body bag. And people end up in hospital or lose a passport."

Though some passengers may initially regard the tour escort as a kind of lackey to help with the luggage, that changes. "You live with them for many days; they get up when they are told, eat where and when they are told; listen and learn. You function as an interpreter, a Big Sister, and their 'bridge over the cultural gap.' It's fun, and you get paid for it."

Tour managers can also be held liable, and some have been sued.

Contacts, Sources, and Leads

- **International Association of Tour Managers (IATM),** 397 Walworth Rd., London, England SE17 2AW; 071-703-9154.

Training programs include the following:

- **International Tour Management Institute,** 625 Market St., Ste. 810, San Francisco, CA 94105; 415-957-9489. The first and the biggest school (also in Boston and Los Angeles) and the one where most tour operators do their recruitment.

Starting Your Own Tour Company

The ability to market specialized tours to a targeted audience in a relatively inexpensive way through the Internet has created unprecedented opportunity for entrepreneurial tour companies. Most tour companies start in a small niche and grow slowly. A small company can be set up with about $150,000. A company that aims to reach a national market needs about $3 million to start, primarily because of the expense of advertising and promoting the product. Web-based companies also have to have a substantial budget for marketing and sales: You need to promote the site and also pay for links from other sites. Tour companies also need a good deal of capital to tide them over until consumer deposits and payments come in.

Breaking In

Tour operations has been a very difficult field to break into: Chances are, there are bigger, stronger, better-financed, better-known competitors, with preferred supplier arrangements with retail travel agents, effectively blocking new entrants. And there have been failures even among big, household-name companies, such as Rand-McNally, the famous map-maker. They failed in their venture into the market because they tended to underestimate what tour operations is all about, tended to throw money into the trappings, and failed to give enough attention to winning the loyalty of travel agents. Moreover, companies from outside travel, such as J.C. Penney, are accustomed to much higher profit margins and are not willing to hang in

when acceptance takes longer than anticipated (usually two to three years).

 INSIDE SECRET: The Internet is making it possible for a niche company to compete with the biggest operators.

More worrisome is the closure of some of the most famous names in tour companies, which had a great following among travel agents and consumers; for example, TWA Getaways, the in-house tour operation of the airline, which was one of the biggest and most prominent in the industry. Their demise demonstrates the difficult financial waters tour operators must navigate; they simply couldn't survive the multiple assaults of a declining economy cutting demand for travel, spiraling costs, and the fear of terrorism that caused Americans to cease traveling abroad.

Five Key Considerations

To start up your own operation, there are five key areas to consider:

- Product
- Customer target
- Promotion
- Distribution
- Pricing

Product means the destinations chosen; suppliers selected; type of travel, such as cruises, educational, or fly/drive; and class of product, such as deluxe or budget.

Customer target means that a product must be tailored to a demographic characteristic such as income and geographic location (a trip to Hong Kong can be a weekend shopping spree to a West Coast traveler, but a two-week exotic Orient adventure to someone from Boston). Consider the "psychographic" characteristics of the potential customers: Are they retired? Yuppie? Single? Parents?

Promotion means that you have to plan not only the theme and execution, but also the dollar amount in relation to the size and frequency of the program. You also must plan the method of promotion, such as advertising, direct mail, or personal sales calls.

Distribution means that you have to get your product out to consumers. Among the considerations are the physical aspects of your folder or brochure—4 × 9 versus 8½ × 11, for example—and the kinds of distribution channels you plan to use, such as travel agents, clubs, direct to consumers, or the Internet.

Pricing can relate to where you want to position your product in relation to both the "psychographic" characteristic and your competition. The idea is to maximize profit without crossing the "price breakpoint," at which you price yourself out of the market. Pricing is critical to marketing strategy. The price must be one of the key decision factors for the consumer to take your product. The difference in price must be substantial enough to capture the target market's attention, and strong enough to motivate a shift in sales, and still leave enough margin to make a profit. You must also be able to sustain the price over a period of time.

Setting up the tour program—plotting out the itinerary and negotiating for space and rates—is only one aspect. How you will handle reservations should not be underestimated. You have to consider the kind of telephone system and computer system as well as who is taking the reservations. This is such a strong factor that many companies are moving their reservations centers to the interior of the country—places like Tulsa, Indianapolis, St. Louis, and Las Vegas—where there is availability of cost-effective staff.

From an Interest to an Enterprise: Backroads

Many people who launch tour companies do so because they have some special interest (or passion) and want to build a business around it. Tom Hale, for example, "jumped in head over heels" when he set up his own tour company, Backroads Bicycle Touring, in Berkeley, California, in 1979. He was in environmental planning "and just decided I didn't want to do it anymore." He took a 5,000-mile bike ride through the West and then started Backroads. "I had an interest in doing something different and an interest in bicycling and just decided to do it."

Operating a tour company proved to be more expensive and harder to get off the ground than he thought it would. He sells the tours nationally and has to advertise. But the company has grown steadily, with the rate faster now than at the beginning.

Now the company handles more than 16,000 customers a year and has a staff of 100 people in the headquarters, including a Trip Development team of 20, complemented by leader trip specialists in the field. Together, they are responsible for the creation, fine-tuning, and smooth operation of 147 different itineraries to such far-flung destinations as Costa Rica, the Galapagos Islands, Argentina, New Zealand, Thailand, and Vietnam. The remaining staff are in reservations, marketing, accounting, human resources, leader development, logistics, transportation, and now, Web development. Hale still plans many of the itineraries.

"I really like what I do," Hale asserted, but recommends starting up a tour operation to only a small number of people. "There are obstacles at every corner. It takes someone with a fair amount of long-term outlook to get over the short-term frustrations. You have to plug away. There are financial obstacles. You don't make any money for a long period of time—until you get to a size of customer base to support the operation. Like any business, you've got to pay your dues."

(For more information, contact Backroads, 801 Cedar St., Berkeley, CA 94710-1800; 800-GO-ACTIVE [462-2848] or 510-527-1555; www.backroads.com.)

You can also get tripped up with distribution. Just getting a brochure into a travel agent's hands does not ensure that the agent will sell it, particularly when the agency may be hooked up with other "preferred vendors" who can afford to pay a higher override. More importantly, with so many companies failing, agents are skittish about linking up with an unknown, unproven supplier. And the cost of advertising direct to the consumer in order to drive customers to the agent can be prohibitive.

Tour operators are experimenting with alternative forms of distribution, such as a fax linked to a computer database and also e-commerce through the Internet.

Newcomers can surmount many of the obstacles by focusing in on specific niches—special interests—where the main purpose of the trip is not the destination but a particular activity or interest. Specialty markets are more defined, easy to reach (through clubs and specialty publications), and more committed to travel.

Contacts, Sources, and Leads

■ The best source for information on specialty travel companies is *Specialty Travel Index* (www.specialtytravel.com).

CHAPTER 4

INCENTIVE TRAVEL: WIN-WIN-WIN PROGRAMS BRING REWARDS

Disney, General Motors, Aetna, Norwegian Cruise Line, Merrill Lynch, Proctor & Gamble, Mary Kay, Club Med, Continental Airlines, and the Irish Tourist Board. What do all these companies have in common? They are all in the incentive business. In fact, it's probably more difficult find a company or an organization of any size that is not.

Snapshot: Incentive Travel

Incentive travel is the corporate version of tour operations. It involves the use of a trip as a prize or premium connected with some action performed by the winner. Incentive travel is among the most creative fields in the industry; the most demanding and complex in the amount of detail and responsibility; the most interesting in that it combines expertise in marketing, advertising, and promotion as well as travel; and fascinating and sophisticated in terms of the dynamic achievers that you come into contact with. Moreover, for the practitioners, it is the most lucrative, providing compensation on par with advertising and marketing agencies, which are the most similar companies in structure and purpose.

Incentive travel also is one of the fastest-growing segments within travel, offering some of the best opportunities for jobs. Yet incentive travel is one of the least-known and least-understood facets, probably because most of the major incentive companies do not con-

sider themselves part of the travel industry at all. Rather, incentive travel, amounting to $8.4 billion worth, is considered part of the larger, $23 billion motivation industry. Travel, along with the merchandise, cash, and other prizes, is only a means to an end, a small element in a much larger motivational program.

> **INSIDE SECRET:** Incentive travel is the most sophisticated, high-pressure, and high-paying field in the industry; it is more like advertising and marketing than travel. This is the best place for MBA-types.

"I don't sell toasters. I don't sell travel," said an Account Executive for Carlson Marketing Group (formerly E.F. MacDonald), one of the giants in the field. "I sell ideas. We sit down with the Vice President of Sales and the marketing people. They tell us what their problem is, such as to increase their share of market or move some item before the new inventory comes. Then we sit down with our people and design the program."

A Winning Situation

The beauty of incentives is that it is a "win-win-win" situation: The sponsoring company pays for the awards out of incremental revenues (money it would not have had, were it not for the incentive campaign). The winners get a priceless trip, a fantasy come true, for free, not to mention peer recognition and the status that comes with being a "winner." And the incentives company clears about 12 to 15 percent of the total bill. What distinguishes an incentive program is that it starts off with a specific objective and is designed to achieve specific, measurable results.

Incentives can be used to solve any number of marketing, sales, or operational objectives, such as to increase sales, recognize performance, increase market share, build morale, build customer loyalty or trust, improve customer service, introduce new products, foster teamwork, develop contacts, recognize performance, or build traffic. Programs can be directed at an internal sales force, external distributors, consumers, or employees.

For example, a modest-sized small-appliance manufacturer, GEE, has 100,000 ice-cream makers it must sell by December to make room for new inventory. Solution: Rather than spend $100,000 on an ad campaign to inspire consumers to buy the product, the company undertakes an incentive travel program for its 200 distributors. The retail price of the ice-cream maker is $30 and GEE makes $2 on each item. The payback to GEE, then, is $200,000 if all 100,000 units sell. The contest is designed so that each of the 200 outlets has to sell 500 units. If the manager hits this target, he or she wins the trip. The incentive travel planner has a budget of $110,000: $1,000 to spend on each winning couple and $10,000 to spend on the promotional campaign. The $1,000 per couple includes the incentive company's commission of $125. The planner expects 100 to win the prize, but will allow a buy-in (whereby people who do not meet the quota are allowed to pay the difference, thus enabling the operator to fill the blocked space) for the unsold units, at $2 a unit. GEE sells off the units, makes $90,000 profit, and, in the bargain, boosts the loyalty of its distributors.

In addition to solving specific marketing problems and building goodwill among the sales force, distributors, retailers, employees, or consumers, incentives also provide measurable results that an advertising campaign does not.

Maritz

Maritz Performance Improvement Company is part of the Maritz Inc. family of companies headquartered on a 210-acre campus in suburban St. Louis, Missouri. It is the largest single source of integrated performance improvement, travel, and marketing research in the world, employing over 6,000 people and generating annual revenues of more than $2.2 billion. Of these, about 2,000 are incentives professionals within the motivation and travel companies.

Among the incentives professionals are program administration personnel who develop administrative procedures, issue standings reports, send Award Credit checks to participants, and handle all other details of the program; computer programmers and operators who are responsible for sales reports for clients and assist with the program administration; direct-mail specialists who process and mail all communications material; and customer service personnel.

The Project Management group includes Account Managers who essentially sell the motivation/incentive programs to clients. These tend to be mature people, even if they are only in their 30s, with 8 to 15 years of experience in the business world, though not necessarily experienced in incentives. They need a business or marketing background to best understand how products load a market and how a company is organized, and to determine what the client's need is all about.

Maritz maintains sales offices around the country, but nearly all the creative work is done out of the St. Louis headquarters.

The company has a policy of promoting from within, and according to the executive, there is lots of movement inside. "We want our people to enjoy upward mobility," which can mean within divisions and to other divisions.

(See www.maritz.com for more information and job listings.)

Travel is just one of the incentives and premiums compelling millions of people each year to exert themselves to hit some target, exceed some quota, meet some goal, or fulfill some specified requirement in order to win. Cash, big-screen televisions, DVD players, automobiles, radios, computers, digital cameras, and, these days, points that can be redeemed with catalog companies or online retailers are only a few of the rewards in a long list of items.

But ever since the 1950s when companies began to use travel regularly as an incentive, it has proved to be the "ultimate" motivator. More people will work harder and exert more effort to win an incentive trip than any of the cash or merchandise items. The reason is that travel plays on more of the psychological forces that go into motivation—status, peer recognition, dream-fulfillment, and the desire and need to get away. Moreover, unlike a color television, which anyone can purchase from a store at an established price (and probably already owns) and possess for years afterward, an incentive travel program is a unique experience that cannot be bought at any price, cannot be stored on the shelf, and must be renewed each time.

Selecting Destinations

Selecting the destination is a critical aspect of the program because the destination itself has to be the primary motivator. The destination needs to have a certain status and excitement. But it must also meet practical criteria—most companies do not want their key producers away long, so the traveling time is a consideration. Also, the destination must be within the budget and have the necessary space. It must also be relatively safe and secure, because incentive programs are usually decided on two or more years in advance. The destination name must be very promotable, even if the participants do not know precisely where it is.

Top incentive destinations are London, Paris, Hawaii, and Las Vegas, but incentives companies have also done programs to such far-flung points as Hong Kong, China, and the Soviet Union.

Incentives are a vital source of tourism for many destinations, and many tourist bureaus frequently become actively involved in helping incentive planners recognize the appeal of their locality. Australia, although a long distance away, is working hard to entice incentive movements, as is the Montreux, Switzerland tourist

board. They invite incentive planners and decision-makers to make inspection tours.

For the traditional incentive companies, travel is only an incidental in the overall marketing campaign, which can last 12 to 18 months. The program starts and ends with marketing. It kicks off with that first encounter with the Vice President of Marketing, when the incentive Account Executive says, "You've got a problem, and I can solve it, and it won't cost you a dime." It ends with the sales results being tallied and the kickoff of the following year's campaign.

A Winning Campaign

The compelling allure of travel as a prize was proved in an award-winning incentive travel promotion organized by The Meeting Architects for its client, Internet technology company BroadVision. According to the Society of Incentive & Travel Executives (SITE), the program demonstrated the essence of an incentive program: a campaign designed around specific business objectives that achieves measurable results. In this program, top achievers could win a trip to Tahiti and Bora Bora. The campaign was built around the demographics of the company's sales force—25 to 40 years old, married, with an average income of $250,000—who would find Polynesia sufficiently alluring.

The campaign began with custom-designed collateral materials sent to the 300 sales professionals in 60 offices worldwide. Beginning with the design of a custom logo showcasing Polynesia's flora and fauna, campaign items were designed to stimulate all the senses. Throughout the year, BroadVision's sales executives received promotional information at home (which is calculated as being more effective than receiving the promotions at work) every 45 days. Each mailing used tactile elements that stimulated the senses while reinforcing the campaign's Polynesian theme. A pearl theme was carried throughout the campaign, culminating with the presentation of an authentic Tahitian pearl. Desktop teasers reflected the casual elegance of the South Pacific, serving as a daily reminder of the reward that was in store for qualifiers who achieved 100 percent of their sales quota during the 12-month campaign. E-mails augmented the communications campaign, while a custom-designed Web site was established that was accessible only to campaign qualifiers.

The campaign had specific objectives and measurable results: The objective was to motivate the sales professional to meet or exceed sales targets. The result was that forecasted participation nearly doubled because of the effective promotional communications campaign, which increased participants from 40 to 78 and contributed to a 57 percent increase in revenue and record sales for the client.

The Special Difference: Each Traveler Is a VIP

The incentive trip is different from the typical packaged tour. Indeed, although many travel agents are expanding into incentive travel as an extension of their corporate, groups or conventions, and meetings business, the trips are intrinsically different in their make-up and must be specially created.

"Incentive travel is a party, a celebration," said one incentives company executive. "It is about 'making it' in the business world. It is an extraordinary event. It shouldn't be predictable. It should be full of surprises. And the source should appear to be the sponsor company and not the travel coordinator."

Often, incentive programs feature team-building activities. The Walt Disney World Resort has become an incredible incentive venue because it can pull together distinctive settings, theming, and new group activities. For example, at its Wide World of Sports complex, one of these team-building exercises is "Pit Stop Challenge," in which each team designs and races its own car. One automotive-industry incentive group of 400 (which included 200 children) started out an evening at the Atlanta Braves spring-training stadium, where the attendees were greeted by "trainers" who made them feel as if they were baseball stars.

Indeed, a key distinction of incentive trips is that you are not dealing with travelers at all, but winners, each a VIP. The trip is always first class and sometimes ultra deluxe—a chauffeured Mercedes to drive couples

around Switzerland for a day, for example. Generally, the incentive trip is structured so that the winner will not have to reach into his or her pocket at all—not for a tip, not for a taxi. Some programs even provide postcards and stamps.

A Growth Industry

Incentive travel has burgeoned in recent years, yet is still only a fraction of what it could potentially become.

"Productivity is the name of the game today, and productivity and incentives fit together," declared one veteran incentives executive, predicting continued growth in the industry. "We have historically been involved in white-collar travel, and white-collar is the growing portion of the workforce. At banks, fast-food restaurants, and the like, we can help develop good work habits, apart from just boosting sales."

National Cash Register Company (NCR) of Dayton, Ohio, was the first to use incentive travel. In 1906, the company awarded diamond-studded pins and a free trip to company headquarters to 70 salespeople who qualified for its 100 Point Club. In 1911, winners got a trip to New York.

The first regular use of incentive travel began in the 1950s, with the advent of mass travel and the airplane. In one year, 45 companies awarded top producers trips totaling $50 million worth. By 1990, businesses were spending $2.6 billion on incentive travel awards. Less than a decade later, the total spent on incentive travel burgeoned to $8.4 billion.

In the early years, incentive travel was limited to a few incentive "houses" that specialized in handling massive groups and were prepared to take the financial risk of chartering whole aircraft. With airline deregulation, incentives were no longer restricted to using charter movements and whole planeloads; instead, operators could purchase small blocks of seats on regularly scheduled aircraft. This brought down the size of incentive groups from the hundreds to perhaps 50 or even an individual couple—a number that a travel agent or meetings planner could easily handle—and minimized the risk.

Indeed, the burgeoning growth in the incentives industry is because of the huge numbers of small incentives groups. Now, 48 percent of all incentive trips are arranged by travel agents rather than incentive companies, according to *Incentive* magazine.

Apart from travel agents, the number of incentive travel companies is small—perhaps only 100. There are only a few companies that are considered major, full-service incentives houses. Among them are the following:

- Maritz Performance Improvement Company (St. Louis County, Missouri)
- Carlson Marketing Group (formerly E.F. MacDonald, Minneapolis)
- BI Performance (Minneapolis)

The Flow of an Incentives Program

The "theoretical flow" of the incentives program process starts with the Account Executive in the field (in Los Angeles, New York, Chicago, and so on) who talks to a potential client about its "challenge" (usually regarding the sales of a specific line). Based on the problem, the Account Executive brings in the marketing department, which takes that input, couples it with what they know about the industry and what has worked in the past, and makes a proposal that represents the "solution" to those problems. "Everybody has a different problem; every program is different," said an Account Executive. The solution may encompass a combination of merchandise, travel, and other recognition items.

The presentation may involve anything from a flip chart to a "dog and pony show" of live actors to give the potential client the feel of how the agency would kick off their program.

Years ago, travel was reserved for the very top producers—"the sizzle and the steak, the icing on the cake," an incentive expert said. "It was highly promotable, highly visible, but reserved for the elite group." Now travel is commonly used, challenging the incentive company to come up with new destinations and a

broader range of travel categories. "We're stretched. Many clients take two trips a year. We have to give more emphasis to theme parties, new and exciting things to do, such as renting a limo to go across Europe, renting private homes and condos for the top winners."

Once the concept is sold, the motivation program is designed, consisting of communications or promotion; rules and administration; and awards.

There is considerably more detail involved in coordinating an incentive trip than a regular trip. Some are intimidated by the size of the movements—500 to 1,000 people are not unusual. One meeting involved an overnight trip to Atlanta for 2,400 people, "scary to do just from the point of lost luggage," the organizer quipped. Other programs may involve a series of 10 one-week back-to-back trips, with 1,000 "winners" in each. However, the trend today is to smaller programs, and even individual awards, or even points that can be applied toward a trip or a prize.

It is vital to have measurable results so that the company can demonstrate a return on investment to the client.

Get Clicking

Entrepreneurs have adapted incentive planning services as well as promotions sales to cyberspace, setting up new Web sites. For example, from its Hoffman Estates, Illinois, base, Motivationonline.com offers planners and human resource executives online incentive program administration and performance improvement programs that can be used to achieve objectives such as rewarding salespeople for the way they fill out reports, or telemarketers for the number of calls they make. (The prize is points that can be redeemed with brand-name online retailers.) Salesdriver.com is another company, founded by two former Proctor & Gamble product managers who applied their knowledge of running incentive programs to the online service.

TravelAwardsOnline is one of the new breed of Web-based incentive companies, offering program design, tracking, and administration, plus reward redemption and fulfillment. Rewards feature individual incentive travel prizes: Winners can redeem points to be a Fighter Pilot for a Day and fly with Air Combat USA; or win certificates for cruises on Carnival and Holland America, air travel on Delta, or car rentals with Avis. (For more information, contact TravelAwardsOnline, St. Louis, MO 63021; 800-237-5469; www.travelawardsonline.com.)

Why Choose Incentive Travel?

Who should go into incentives? Someone who loves challenge, problem-solving, someone who is excited by being on the edge of a crisis. "There is always the panic moment," one executive said. "We all like that challenge of feeling we can't resolve the problem, and then we do."

"Someone who is achievement-oriented," said Robert Guerriero, President of The Journeymasters, Salem, Massachusetts. "This isn't a job. It is a way of life. This business is not for everyone. There are constant emergencies, constant challenges, constant excitements, and constant rewards. Everyone is divorced whose spouse is not also in this business, because they can't understand the demands. We sell achievement. We sell joy."

"This is a high-pressured business," said one executive. "You have to make decisions on the spot. You need good business sense."

Other important criteria: good communication skills, creativity, imagination, self-confidence, and good listening skills.

Jobs in Incentive Travel

Jobs in the incentive travel field can be found among the following types of companies:

- Incentive houses, which handle all facets of motivational programs, including travel.
- Specialty incentive travel companies.

- Destination-management companies (which put together the travel program for an incentive company).
- Travel agencies.
- Suppliers, including airlines, hotels, and resorts.
- Cruise lines, which regularly incorporate motivation programs into their marketing and sales strategies as well as serve as a coordinator.

Convention and visitor bureaus as well as government tourist offices also have incentive travel specialists on staff to promote the use of incentive programs to their destinations and to facilitate them.

Incentive Specialists are in heavy demand at companies that are the biggest users, particularly among the leading industries that incorporate incentives, including automotive, insurance, financial services, the electronics and appliances industries, as well as nonprofits.

Incentives companies are organized much like advertising or sales-promotion agencies in that they have **Account Managers** who generally are business and marketing specialists and sell the incentives program to companies and act as the liaison between the incentive company and the client. The creative department consists of **Writers, Artists, Audiovisual Specialists,** and **Graphic Arts Specialists.** The travel department consists of people who scout new destinations and facilities, **Trip Planners,** and **Coordinators.**

Best Bets

- Client Services Manager
- Account Executive
- Quality Control

The entry-level position is typically the **Account Coordinator,** who is involved with coordinating the elements of the campaign. This position provides a locus for learning the whole incentives process: conception, operation, and servicing. On a major promotion, the coordinator may even participate in the trip. The Account Coordinator manages transportation, works with the pre-trip department on mailings, and funnels information to the client and Account Executive.

The **Account Executive,** also known as a **Business Development Manager,** is a key position in an incentive company, capable of earning six figures. This is a high-level selling and account-management position, generally operating out of a sales office in a territory. The position draws on the business understanding of an MBA, close contacts and relationships within an industry, the ability to forge relationships, and a consultative style of selling. You have to be able to make presentations to the highest-level decision-makers and be able to land and nurture multimillion-dollar contracts, which are delivered over a 12- to 18-month period.

"I'm not only involved in our business, but all the others—Chevrolet, Avon, Merrill Lynch—and how they go to market," said an Account Executive. "We know the motivation business, the travel business, and our clients' businesses."

For someone who has reached the level of an Account Executive, the business also "gives me freedom," said one who held the position at Carlson Marketing. "You're your own boss, with your own accounts. This isn't monotonous."

Other jobs at a major incentives house include data processing, administration, customer service, purchasing, graphics, art, marketing, print buying, accounting, transportation, and mailroom. "The types of jobs are everything you can imagine."

Because the emphasis in incentives is on marketing, the industry draws more heavily on business executives than on travel professionals. At Maritz, even the so-called "Travel Director," an entry-level job, generally requires a college degree and business experience. Travel Directors also tend to be "bright, attractive, generally youthful, and comfortable with more mature individuals" because they are the client-contact people who actually go out with the incentive groups and are onsite, coordinating sightseeing trips and troubleshooting.

For example, the supervisor of a major car company account was responsible for strengthening relationships with key decision-makers at three different divisions. He participated in negotiations to secure a five-year, $15 million account; increased business volume from the accounts; negotiated supplier contracts; and developed, priced, and presented profitable, bid-winning proposals. His first job out of college was as Senior Travel Director for another major incentive house, where he was the primary contact and liaison between airlines, hotels, and ground suppliers for client companies. In this capacity, he directed all audio-visual, food and beverage, recreational activities, transportation, and VIP requirements. He maximized "add-on billable opportunities," managed budgets of over $1 million, and directed international programs ranging in size from 30 senior executives on an African Safari to a worldwide sales meeting of 2,400 participants.

 ## Salaries in Incentive Travel

The field can be lucrative as well, especially compared to other travel industry jobs. "The salary grows with your bottom line," said a former Carlson Account Executive. The structure is generally a base salary plus commission. "It can pay well, but it takes a bit of luck in addition to skill and creativity. You have to be there at the right time, when the client is ready for a new idea. I sell ideas."

Positions on the operations side, which pay in the $50,000–$80,000 range, call for product-development people to negotiate space and rates and design "fantasy-come-true" travel programs. A planner likely juggles four to seven different incentive travel programs at one time, in various stages.

 ## Your Ticket into Incentive Travel

The largest companies, like Carlson Marketing and Maritz, have the greatest number of entry-level positions and best training programs, but the competition for these jobs is also tough, and you are likely to be relegated to a narrow specialty. The 50 to 100 smaller companies may offer a better opportunity to get in and take part in a greater scope of the business; rising through the ranks may be faster, although how far you can go is more limited than in a large company. Still, smaller companies can be steppingstones to the larger firms.

INSIDE SECRET: Smaller companies are easier to get into and offer a broader view of the business than you could get at a large company.

In addition to jobs at incentives companies, travel agencies, corporate travel management services companies, and conventions and meetings planners with incentives divisions, there are incentive travel specialists at hotels, cruise lines, airlines, car rental companies, and tourist offices. This is a field where you can literally create your own job because the opportunities to apply incentives are unlimited.

The Journeymasters

There are perhaps 100 smaller incentive companies, which consider themselves the "boutiques" of the industry.

The Journeymasters, Inc. of Salem, Massachusetts, is probably one of the most creative incentives houses around. The company's client list is small but blue chip: General Electric, Tupperware, General Felt Industries,

Toshiba, Mita, Sherwin-Williams. Yet the staff numbers fewer than two dozen.

"We're massively elite," commented Robert Guerriero, President. "We do things the big guys can't do. We don't do anything less than 100; a typical group for us is about 200."

The operations department, with about five people, is "the factory—they create the details of the trip, prepare the costing, work with the hotels and airlines," Guerriero said. Two others make up the advertising and sales department. "We do all our own copy, including the letter shop, printing, typesetting and paste-up, and creative portions." Freelancers are also employed.

One of the most exciting incentive programs he operated, he recalled, was billed as the "Rally to the Renaissance" and involved a road rally by Mercedes through Italy for a top-of-the-line furniture manufacturer.

Guerriero maintained that it is not necessary to actually know the client's business; but the incentives specialist must know how to familiarize the client with the value of incentives as a marketing tool. "We'll never know their business as well as they do. But what we can do is show how they can operate a $250,000 contest and it won't cost them a thing."

The Journeymasters believes that a travel incentive needs to have "poetry" and that the company offers "poets of imagination."

(See www.journeymasters.com for more information.)

Contacts, Sources, and Leads

■ **The Society of Incentive & Travel Executives (SITE)**, 21 W. 38th St., New York, NY 10018-5506; 212-575-0910; www.site-intl.org. This is the main trade organization for incentive travel. SITE conducts excellent training programs and seminars. It also publishes job openings in its newsletter and offers a free, confidential employment service. A membership directory is available free to members, for a fee to nonmembers.

Trade Publications

■ *Incentive* **magazine,** www.incentivemag.com.

■ *Meetings & Conventions* **magazine,** www.meetings-conventions.com.

■ *Successful Meetings* **magazine,** www.successmtgs.com.

CHAPTER 5

CONVENTIONS AND MEETINGS

"Show business" is how one meetings consultant described his field. Putting on conventions, meetings, or trade shows offers the technical and logistical challenges as well as the thrill, excitement, and creative fulfillment of a theatrical production. Indeed, some conventions are quite literally "show business," incorporating Broadway-quality entertainment into their program—the sizzle to the meeting's steak.

Snapshot: Conventions and Meetings

Meeting planners work for individual companies, associations and trade groups, government, and educational and religious organizations. They also work in independent consultancies, incentives houses, tradeshow and exposition organizers, travel agencies, hotels, resorts, conference centers and convention bureaus, and tourist offices and associations. The field is mushrooming in people as well as influence. Collectively, meeting planners arrange more than 1 million meetings a year, put on by more than 100,000 corporations and associations, generating $100 billion in spending (almost double the level in 1990). Indeed, conventions, expositions, and meetings generate more than one-third of the hotel industry's annual revenue, and attendees account for 22 percent of airline industry operating income.

Meeting planners are the producers, directors, writers, and ticket-takers of every event. They have to plan for every detail and every eventuality so that everything flows perfectly. They have to solve problems and deal with the inevitable crises that crop up, such as airline strikes, power failures, lost freight, and impending hurricanes.

"This is an artistic business, as well as a scientific one," said Phil Lee, president of California Leisure Consultants, Inc., a San Diego–based meetings company.

 INSIDE SECRET: Convention and meeting planning is very much a networking-style business.

"You work six days a week, 18-hour days, and get paid lower than the legal minimum wage," asserted Ann Raimondi, President of The Raimondi Group, New York. "You have to be tireless, because you need a lot of physical stamina, and have commonsense, which gets you through a lot of unknowns."

The Functions of a Meeting Planner

Meetings Professionals International, the major trade association for meeting planners, has identified no fewer than 25 main functions of a meeting planner:

- Establishing the objectives of the meeting.
- Selecting the site, hotels, and facilities.
- Blocking space and negotiating rates.
- Setting budgets.
- Making reservations for airlines and hotels.
- Arranging air and ground transportation.
- Planning the program.
- Choosing speakers and entertainers.
- Planning food and beverage functions. ("You have to know what people are eating these days, and not to overfeed them at lunch because they fall asleep, and not to serve chocolate at the coffee break," advised one planner.)

- Arranging for all facilities, such as audiovisual and computer equipment.
- Providing necessary security.
- Meeting registration.
- Support services.
- Coordination with the convention center or hall.
- Planning with the convention services manager.
- Preconvention meeting.
- Shipping.
- Function room setup.
- Exhibits and trade-show planning.
- Promotion and publicity scheduling.
- Guest and family programs. (Increasingly, this can also mean supervised children's programs.)
- Meeting materials.
- Gratuities.
- Post-meeting evaluation.

You also have to do budgeting, know how to use computers, have excellent communication skills, have leadership qualities, be able to manage people and handle high pressure, be flexible to change plans, and above all, be diplomatic.

In the past, meeting planners functioned much like a travel agent—merely taking orders of how many people would need transportation and accommodations at a specific site. But increasingly, instead of merely handling the logistics, planners are more crucially involved in negotiations that save the organization enormous sums of money. The planners also play more of a role in the corporate image and public relations aspects and are becoming more involved in setting goals and objectives of meetings, giving advice and counsel on how to make a meeting more productive and cost-effective.

Planners have a key responsibility for site selection, a decision that might be made as much as eight years in advance, and so have to be aware of world affairs and economic trends in order to make judicious decisions. Many special events, shows, and conventions also require extensive skills in direct marketing and promotion aimed at boosting paid-attendance and trade-

show exhibits, as well as promotions to bring in sponsors. They also require public relations to create goodwill or exposure for the organization.

Meeting Planning Comes into Its Own

Not long ago, the task of planning meetings and conferences typically fell to a person holding some other job, like the Assistant to the Director of Sales or Vice President of Marketing. Even now, corporate meeting planners may also be responsible for education and training, while meeting planners attached to associations are frequently also responsible for membership services.

But as the cost, intricacies, options available, and technical knowledge involved in arranging meetings have escalated, the function has emerged as a profession in its own right. Whereas meeting planners of a decade ago might have learned through "trials by fire," now it is more necessary to have some formalized training. Meeting Professionals International offers extensive training programs as well as its own certification process.

In many meeting planning offices or departments, a single individual sees a meeting through from beginning to end, but there is growing specialization and expertise in such areas as negotiations, logistics, programming, food and beverage, even direct-marketing and data warehousing aspects. Often, the travel arrangements are separated out entirely and handled by an outside travel agency, but this still requires oversight and coordination.

 ## Why Choose Conventions and Meetings?

Meeting planning is negotiating, planning, and management. It is very much a people business, involves creativity, and affords considerable (even too much) opportunity to travel. There is an element of glamour and enormous challenge. It is also a business of problem-solving and crisis management.

A meeting planner has to have excellent organizational skills, and more importantly, the ability to manage a project. "Loving people is basic, but everybody does," said Phil Lee. "You need the experience of handling a project that might have started as an idea on a cocktail napkin, progressed to a meeting, and come back into your lap. You have to procure services, harness them, and make sure everything performs where hours and minutes and seconds are critical, and then move on and start all over again. You only need to know half of all the information in the Encyclopedia Britannica.

"It is not quite the entertainment industry," said Lee. "But it has the excitement of the entertainment business. Each meeting is a production. There is excitement that emanates from the stage. There is an audience. You get a little depressed when the show ends. It is just like show business, but you have to be more responsible."

Meeting planning is not for everyone. "You have to have the calling," said one meetings professional. "This is a group communications process. People who are successful are those who understand the components, who pay attention to details." You have to be sensitive to what people are going to want and need, in terms of the environment you create for the meeting, convention, or conference and the creature comforts you provide. "No matter how good the program, it is not going to work if the environment is not conducive and the expectations of attendees have not been met."

A person who becomes a meeting planner, cautioned Ann Raimondi, must be someone "who enjoys doing a job for which you get no thanks. You can't expect your ego to be fed all the time. You are the unseen and unsung hero. After all, you don't make money for the company; you save it."

Good communications skills and excellent organizational skills are critical. Meetings planners also have to be extremely adept at handling people, and be diplomatic. A sense of humor also helps.

A meeting planner may travel two out of every four weeks, choosing sites, making pre-convention inspections, and finally, attending the major meetings or conferences he or she arranged to make sure everything goes smoothly and to troubleshoot or problem-solve glitches.

The frequent travel and the fact that meeting planners are wooed by hotels, airlines, and destinations all the time create an aura of glamour that is hard to dispel. "People perceive the job as fun and games—being wined and dined," one planner remarked. "But it is hard work. All the hours of work that go into putting on a meeting, the worry about every little detail that becomes second nature, and the miles and miles of travel wear thin."

"People want to come in because they want to travel and they like people," said Raimondi. "But after one or two years, you become disillusioned with travel. It loses its appeal. You do it so much (50 to 80 percent of the time), it becomes a chore and kills your social life."

Nonetheless, she added, "It is a fascinating industry. I knew I wanted to stay in it. It is hard to get in, but then you can make your own opportunities."

Apart from the energy, excitement, creativity, and responsibility that are part and parcel of the job, the growth of the field means that advancement opportunities are excellent.

 # Salaries in Conventions and Meetings

The average annual base salary was $60,650 (almost double that of 1990), with 20 percent earning a base of more than $80,000, according to a 1999 survey by *Meetings & Conventions* magazine (October, 1999). However, although more meetings planners are women than men, men earned an average of $27,719 more than women, averaging $76,079 while women averaged $48,360. Indeed, 22 percent of men earned $100,000 or more (8.5 percent earned $150,000 or more), while only 3 percent of women earned six figures. The disparity reflects the fact that men tend to come from executive positions (and their title reflects it) while women tend to come from administrative positions. It also reflects that men averaged 15.5 years as a planner and a median age of 49, while women averaged 10.5 years as a planner and a median age of 42. This survey also pointed to a high degree of job satisfaction: 91 percent said they were satisfied with their jobs.

INSIDE SECRET: Dot-coms are seeking meeting planners, paying $10 to $20K more than other industries, according to *Successful Meetings Magazine* (April, 2000), not to mention potential stock options. But you need to be technically savvy, hip to the culture, okay with constant flux, and, oh yes, know the ins and outs of organizing conventions and meetings.

Your Ticket into Conventions and Meetings

People typically come into meeting planning through the hotel side, where they gain experience in dealing with meetings and meeting planners, negotiations, and the fundamentals of handling the logistics and groups. There are kind of "apprenticeships" in the form of "Assistant Meetings Manager" or "Meetings Coordinator." Large corporations or associations that hold many meetings probably offer the best opportunities for entry, but getting in is tough. There are legions of people drawn to the field by the opportunity to travel, deal with people, and have the kind of responsibility that a meeting planner has. Larger corporations and associations offer more routes into meeting planning, such as through secretarial or some other capacity.

INSIDE SECRET: You can get leads for potential employers from key Web sites for convention and meeting planners.

"Meeting planning has finally come into its own as a profession," stated Ann Raimondi, who was the Corporate Meeting Planner for a major accounting firm until she set up her own consulting company.

"Hoteliers are now used to dealing with professional people expert in negotiating." Deregulation of airfares, making that segment also subject to negotiation, is also a factor in the greater acceptance of the profession.

A recent ad in *Meeting News* defined the position very well: "Meeting Planner Wanted: Some of what you'll handle are: food and beverage, hotel issues, contracts, air, attendees, registration, reservations, ground transportation, and more. You should have the ability to think on your own, use the tools given, be organized, have good mathematical skills, and complete tasks efficiently. Must be able to travel extensively and work long hours, if needed. Macintosh System. Bene-fits. Salary commensurate with experience."

INSIDE SECRET: Meeting planning is such a ubiquitous function, you can be proactive in finding your job: Isolate the geographical area you want to be in, choose the industry, narrow down a list of employers you want to work for, and make your pitch.

An ad for a Conference Manager for an Internet company described the position as "managing all aspects of conference and special-event production, including researching and assessing conferences; working with PR to assess speaking opportunities; promoting the company's presence at trade shows; determining sponsorship levels; hiring and managing contracts; scouting venues and suppliers; and establishing objectives and messaging; as well as overseeing production of conference literature, signage, and artwork. The conference manager will also work with the database manager to collect and organize lead information. This position requires five years' overall experience, with two to three years' hands-on experience in conference planning and management. Candidates should have a strong desire to pursue a career in an Internet company and be willing to go the extra mile. They should be self-motivated and results-oriented with a strong attention to detail, determined to exceed company expectations."

Titles can be deceptive, however. People who are responsible for meetings and convention planning can have titles as diverse as Director of Special Events, Marketing Services Manager, Senior Program Consultant, Group Travel Planner, Director of Education, and Manager of Meeting Services.

 # Roadmap to the Top

Meeting planners can rise to the head of their departments in a corporation or association—with titles such as Corporate Vice President in charge of meetings and conventions—and also increase responsibility and salary by moving up to larger companies and organizations with greater demands, larger budgets, and bigger staffs. Some become very involved with the management of major corporations and associations. Those who harbor higher aspirations generally wind up setting up their own meetings and convention planning consultancies, like Raimondi.

There are about 700 to 800 consultancies. The largest of them might have seven people, and many are solo operations.

MPI reported that 18 percent of its members were "independents," drawn by the opportunity to be in control and creative. Although starting up a business is not difficult (and very often, new consultants have their old company as a client), you need the marketing, sales, and administrative skills of an entrepreneur, as well as starting capital.

The hottest entrepreneurial area is electronic site selection companies, such as Passkey.com (a Web-based group housing service), EventSource.com and PlanSoft (www.plansoft.com), and b-there.com (an event registration system providing online planning).

Middle-level corporate meetings planners who do not aspire to have their own companies are being hired by travel agencies to head up new conventions and meetings divisions.

Meeting Professionals International conducts a number of educational programs, including one-week institutes geared to entry-level, intermediate, and advanced professionals. MPI also publishes various resource books and maintains a resource center, which also can provide "career packages," consisting of information on how to get into the field. MPI works with the Convention Liaison Council, which provides a program toward becoming a Certified Meeting Professional. Several local chapters offer a job bank for members, and MPI is compiling an online employment bulletin board (for members only).

Contacts, Sources, and Leads

- **Meeting Professionals International,** 4455 LBJ Fwy., Ste. 1200, Dallas, TX 75244-5903; 972-702-3000; www.mpiweb.org. The Web site has an active public job board, articles, statistics, and industry news.
- **Society of Corporate Meeting Professionals,** 2965 Flowers Rd., Ste. 105, Atlanta, GA 30341; 770-457-9212; www.scmp.org.
- Local **convention and visitor bureaus** and chambers of commerce can provide excellent leads, along with the business sections of newspapers and industry trade publications.

Trade Publications

- *Meetings & Conventions* **magazine;** www.meetings-conventions.com.
- *Meeting News;* www.meetingnews.com. Its "Meeting Planner's Handbook" has collections of checklists and ideas, as well as an "Ask the Experts" section.
- *Successful Meetings;* www.successmtgs.com.
- **www.meetingsnet.com** is an excellent online source for six meetings-oriented trade publications, including *Corporate Meetings & Incentives.*
- **Meeting guide directory;** www.mmaweb.com/meetings/Directory/.

Destination Management Companies

Very often, meeting planners rely on destination management companies based in the locality to handle the logistics of a convention or meeting. These professionals know their communities, know the unique venues to host a themed event, have clout and purchasing power with local vendors, and specialize in the design and delivery of events, activities, tours, staffing, and transportation. The DMC acts as the meeting planner's local representative, providing such services as arranging transportation, guides, theme parties, entertainment, airport greetings, spouse programs (shopping, sightseeing, and cultural activities during the meetings programs, and sometimes even arranging child care), VIP gifts, hospitality room staffing, registration services, and housing services (that is, booking sufficient hotel accommodations). They are organized much like receptive tour operators, and in many cases are the same companies.

Contacts, Sources, and Leads

■ A key source for locating DMCs is the **Association of Destination Management Executives,** 3333 Quebec St., Ste. 4050, Denver, CO 80207; 303-394-3905; www.adme.org.

Convention Services Management

An increasingly important professional is the Convention Services Manager (CSM), who is expected to create a partnership with the meeting manager, in addition to coordinating details and services at the site. The CSM is responsible for the organization's satisfaction before, during, and after the event. CSMs can be found in three types of facilities: convention and visitor bureaus, hotels, and convention centers.

The CSM in a convention and visitor bureau works with the specific group to bring its meeting to the locale; assists the meeting manager in planning and conducting a successful meeting by becoming an extension of the meeting staff; educates the meeting manager on local policies and procedures; helps keep expenses down; uses knowledge of discounts, amenities, local speakers, and themes that will be interesting to the attendees; and may be responsible for handling housing and assigning registration personnel.

 INSIDE SECRET: Like organizing parties? Convention Services Management is the job for you.

The CSM of a hotel coordinates all the hotel services for the meeting. On the other hand, the CSM of a convention center serves as the liaison between the clients and departments, provides logistics, and fulfills the service requirements needed for the event.

Convention Centers

In essence, a convention center provides the space and facilities; individual show managers provide their own creative people, interior designers, audiovisual technicians, and the like. Most convention centers operate much like a private enterprise but are generally owned by state or local government. Political contacts can come into play in getting jobs.

The Jacob K. Javits Convention Center

If working as a meeting planner is like show business, working for one of the hundreds of convention centers throughout the country is like "opening a Broadway show every day"—especially if that convention center is just across from New York City's Great White Way.

Of the 1,000 jobs at the Jacob K. Javits Convention Center in New York City, 700 are part-time or daily workers (principally people to move equipment in and out) and 300 are full-time. Of the full-time workers, half are electricians, plumbers, and guards, and about 125 are actually the core management staff, consisting of marketing, public relations, personnel, administration, finance, and operations people.

Rachel Dahbany, Director of Administration and Personnel, draws a parallel between convention center management and real estate management, the area she worked in before going to the convention center. "This is a great big corporation that manages a building but also does marketing and public relations." But there are some important differences: The convention center, unlike most office buildings, never closes. After the day's activities conclude or a trade show closes, teams come in to break down one show and set up for another on one floor, while on another a grand banquet may be going on.

Convention center management involves extremely complex logistics. The New York City center is as big as the Empire State Building would be on its side. In any one day, some 70,000 people can be going and coming.

"There is nothing more exciting," Dahbany said. "Tens of thousands of people scurrying about every day. There is madness at night. This building is alive."

Jobs in Convention Center Management

Among the positions that are fairly unique to convention center management are the Director of

Transportation, who is responsible for getting the convention-goers from their hotels to and from the center, trafficking trucks in and out of the building, working with the city to make sure street lights are working and there are enough police on hand when necessary, and dealing with the city's Taxi and Limousine Commission to make sure there are adequate services for the center. Another unique position is Director of Public Safety, who is in charge of the safety of the people and the equipment. There is also a Director of Fire Safety and an Events Coordinator, who is something like a meeting planner but at a much higher level. A center the size of the Javits Center has six or seven Events Coordinators working under a Director of Event Services.

Best Bets

- Convention Services Manager
- Event Manager
- Direct Marketing
- Information Technology

Entry-level jobs for the "white-collar" positions in management might be in reception, mailroom, messenger, and secretarial. New centers tend to hire only experienced people in key positions—generally from hotel convention sales, meeting planning, show management, and convention and visitor bureaus because there is little time to train.

Contacts, Sources, and Leads

- **Professional Convention Management Association,** 2301 S. Lake Shore Dr., Ste. 1001, Chicago, IL 60616-1419; 312-423-7262. This trade organization with 5,000 members offers facts and figures, tools, a listing of college programs, a job bank, and information on meetings technology. It also publishes student resumes online at its site, www.pcma.org.
- Contact local **convention and visitor bureaus** for further information.

Conference Centers

Apart from the convention centers (which are generally stand-alone structures that do not provide accommodations onsite), there are hundreds of conference centers. According to the International Association of Conference Centers, these are complexes that combine accommodations (up to 300 rooms) and food and beverage facilities with meetings facilities.

Conference center management essentially couples hotel and resort management with convention center management, usually with separate categories of professionals.

An executive conference center has a median staff size of 15 in the conference service department; a corporate conference center has a median staff size of seven, while a resort conference center has a median of six.

Professionals who work in conference centers consist of "high-impact" positions (involving face-to-face contact with attendees, such as those on the front desk and those who pick up the attendees at airports and terminals). Also, there are Conference Service Coordinators, who are involved with anything having to do with the conference itself, from booking the meeting to servicing it to following up with a post-meeting evaluation; an assistant manager; and a general manager. In addition to operations positions, conference centers employ a battery of sales professionals.

A path can be drawn from the front desk to the assistant coordinator to conference coordinator and up. How fast one rises depends greatly on the size of the center.

In the past, many entered conference center management from education (former teachers, for example, who become involved in coordinating educational programs), from hotels, and from meeting-planning departments at corporations. But this field, as virtually every other in travel, is becoming more professional. The association is working with a university to create a curriculum for a conference-center management program.

Contacts, Sources, and Leads

- **International Association of Conference Centers,** 243 N. Lindbergh Blvd., St. Louis, MO 63141; 314-993-8575; www.iacconline.com. The Web site offers a job board.
- **International Association of Exposition Managers,** 5001 LBJ Fwy., Ste. 350, Dallas, TX 75244; 972-458-8002; www.iaem.org. The Web site has a career center.

Trade Publications

- *Convene,* published by PCMA (www.pcma.org provides a link).
- *Tradeshow Week* (www.TradeshowWeek.com).

TRAVEL SUPPLIERS

CHAPTER 6

HOSPITALITY: HOTELS AND RESTAURANTS

It was only a 300-room hotel in a metropolitan area with hundreds of hotels. Nonetheless, the opening of the Charles Hotel at Harvard Square in Cambridge was cause for (then) Massachusetts Governor Michael S. Dukakis and Speaker of the House Tip O'Neill to come to officially cut the ribbon, and for the movers and shakers from Boston's political, financial, and real estate elite to turn out in their finery.

Hotels are more than a bed and a hot meal. They are frequently a linchpin for commerce. They literally put a destination on the map as a commercial center or a distinctive place people should visit. Invariably, hotels are a key element in a community's economic base because they generate jobs and draw visitor spending to the area (bringing in new money). They also support many other businesses: the grocer who supplies the hotel's restaurants, the laundry that cleans the sheets and tablecloths, and the taxi services, shops, restaurants, local attractions, and sightseeing companies frequented by tourists and business travelers. Indeed, through the ripple effect, economists estimate that every dollar spent by a visitor multiplies 2½ times through the local economy.

In many parts of the world, a hotel has been the foundation for a tourism industry that turned a depressed area into a vital one, such as Kyong-ju in Korea and Khajuraho in India. Closer to home, in Lake George, N.Y., the reopening as a year-round resort of The Sagamore, a grand summer resort built in the Gilded Age and the largest single employer in the area, was a major event for the community.

 ## Snapshot: The Hospitality Industry

Offering some 1.9 million jobs in 52,000 properties, the lodging industry, which earned a record $99.5 billion in 1999, offers the greatest opportunity for jobs of any single segment of travel in terms of numbers, future growth, and advancement. That is sizeable, but lodging combined with food service makes up the $460 billion hospitality industry, which created 300,000 new jobs in 1999. By 2010, the industry will need 100,000 more lodging and food-service managers yearly just to keep pace, giving workers a fast track up the career ladder. This is an industry where stories abound of the pot washer becoming the president; where it is common to rise from an hourly wage to a six-figure executive slot.

The lodging industry is expanding for all the same reasons that the travel industry is: the maturing of society into demographic categories that tend to travel, more dual-income families, greater value placed on travel. Other factors come into play: the mobility of society, the fact that children may take jobs and establish their homes in communities at a distance from parents, prompting a lot of long-distance travel. Also, the specialization and globalization of commerce continues to fuel growth in business travel, despite the increase in telecommunications, including videoconferencing. Indeed, technology has become such a vital aspect of society that the Park Hyatt Melbourne has a new position of "technology concierge" to assist guests with services like Internet connections.

Continued growth in the hospitality field, which closed out the century with its fourth year of record results (according to the *American Hotel & Motel Association Lodging Industry Profile*), will accelerate the already-rapid career advancement characteristic of the lodging industry. The lodging industry has a long-standing tradition of hiring people with minimal experience into specific entry-level positions, training them, and moving them up through a hierarchy. It is not uncommon for someone to rise to a General Manager position within 5 to 10 years. Among the success stories are Pat Foley, who started out as a Front-Office Supervisor in Seattle and rose to become Chairman of Hyatt Hotels; and Darryl Hartly-Leonard, who started out as a Desk Clerk and rose to become Hyatt's President.

A "Dire" Shortage of Workers

Indeed, the greatest concern of the hospitality industry at this juncture is that a shortage of workers may prevent companies from realizing their full growth potential.

"We will have to be more flexible in establishing split time and flex-time for our employees, and exert a recruiting effort beyond anything we have seen before, because if we can't service the market, we will lose it," said one hotel executive.

Demographics aren't the only problem. The hospitality industry is perceived as being a low-wage industry. Although this is not entirely accurate, compensation has not been on par with the emerging computer and high-technology industries for those coming into the industry. But this is mitigated by the opportunity to rise to higher-level earnings positions relatively quickly. "The situation is dire," commented Sue Gordon, Vice President of Human Resources for Radisson Hotels. She is a member of a high-level 20-person committee—the Experience Lodging Task Force, headed by Curtis Nelson, CEO of Carlson Hospitality—that was pulled together as a result of severe problems in recruiting and retaining workers, to try to come up with programs to introduce people to the lodging industry.

This is a far cry from when 4,000 people stood out in the snow to be interviewed for 200 jobs at a new Four Seasons Hotel (at a time of high unemployment). With a booming economy, particularly among technology companies, "We have heard that hotels have not been able to open because of shortage of people," Gordon said. "We have to have systems and processes in place that not only help us to 'broaden' the net, but broaden the sources to attract people, and the marketing of our hotels."

Companies are stepping up efforts to hire from nontraditional sources, including retirees, the disabled, and people from economically and educationally disadvantaged groups. And they are providing more flexible work schedules to retain working parents.

"Hotels are a 24/7/365 enterprise," said Gordon. "It used to be there was a paradigm that to work in a hotel, you had to be available 24/7/365 days, whenever, wherever we said. That has changed over the last 10 years. The wake-up call came…these people won't work like that. Seniors, college students, women with small children may not be able to work when we want."

To spur people to pursue careers in hospitality, the American Hotel & Motel Association (AH&MA) and the National Restaurant Association (NRA) have combined to create the Hospitality Business Alliance to give motivated high school students a head start on hospitality management careers. The HBA provides high schools with industry-developed hospitality courses that combine classwork with paid and mentored internships. The HBA projects that by 2007, some 100,000 students a year will be taking part in HBA programs nationally (check www.h-b-a.org for more information). Both the NRA Educational Foundation and the American Hotel Foundation provide scholarships and financial aid (www.edfound.org or www.ei-ahma.org/ahf.scholarships).

The New Face of Hospitality

E-commerce, partnership marketing, and yield management have put a new face on what is probably the oldest profession in the world—hospitality—but the essence has remained the same: providing bed and board to travelers, whether they are pilgrims, diplomats, industrialists, artists, explorers, newlyweds, or people looking for R&R.

Long an esteemed profession in Europe, the hospitality industry is just coming into its own in the United States. Innkeeping is probably the oldest "tourist" entity still surviving intact. The tradition of innkeeping, which served pilgrims and merchants thousands of years ago, is still fundamental to the lodging industry. The essence of bed and board is preserved in bed-and-breakfast establishments (which are seeing a new revival), inns, motels, and the "economy" hotel. However, hotels today take many different forms and offer many different services and facilities beyond bed and board. Many hotels are more like mini-cities, offering a full complement of services and a range of professionals to match. Hotels are restaurants, catering services, meeting and convention facilities, and sites for weddings, family functions, and special events. They are sports facilities, retail malls, and tour operators. Many stage live entertainment; some are gambling establishments.

The hotel business is real estate, finance, food and beverage, tour packaging, meeting and convention planning, education and development, engineering, energy management, purchasing, architecture, interior design, maintenance, information technology and management, franchising, administration, entertainment, recreation, telecommunications, and computer systems. It is sales and marketing, administration, and public relations.

The hospitality industry encompasses lodging and food service, and within these two fields is a huge spectrum that spans hotels, motels, inns, resorts and casinos, stadiums and theme parks, cruise lines, national parks, fine dining restaurants, diners, chef-owned bistros, and catering.

INSIDE SECRET: Hotel jobs often provide a springboard to other segments of the hospitality industry, such as destination marketing organizations (convention and visitor bureaus).

People are most familiar with the chain properties because they are the most visible. Most of the chains,

however, do not own all their properties, but manage them for private or even government owners, or franchise the name. Still, it is the chains that generally set the tone and establish the trends and standards for the industry.

The Dynamics of Bricks and Mortar

The distinctive dynamics of the hotel industry derive from the high capital requirements, the time between planning and the hotel opening, and the fact that a hotel is bricks and mortar and cannot be moved if the destination or location falls from favor. Location is nearly everything in the hotel business.

The location will largely determine whether a hotel is geared to business or pleasure travelers and which time periods are busiest. Every hotel has the problem of leveling out peaks and valleys of occupancy—a task of the marketing department. For example:

- A suburban hotel and conference center introduces summer vacation packages and opens a major spa facility.
- A city-center hotel catering to midweek business travelers creates resort-type packages for the weekends.
- A resort that traditionally relied on summer travel cultivates incentives and meetings, spa programs, and family-activity packages to boost business in the fall and winter.

Although demand has continued to increase for commercial lodgings, so has competition, forcing hotel companies to wage more aggressive marketing campaigns and expand their sales and marketing forces.

Segmentation, or product differentiation, is another trend that will continue, as hotels seek to expand their market shares by offering new products, such as high-end accommodations, all-suite hotels, and a variety of new inns and motels. New specialized companies are springing up, such as Holiday Inn Family Suites Resort (the prototype is in Orlando, Florida), which caters to family travelers. Meanwhile older, established chains are diversifying, such as Marriott, which is applying its expertise in hospitality to operate assisted-living complexes for senior citizens as well as timeshare (vacation ownership) resorts.

Proliferation, competition, consolidation, market segmentation, diversification, and increased utilization are the key issues facing the lodgings industry.

Why Choose the Hospitality Industry?

The hospitality industry offers the best opportunity for jobs of any single segment of the travel industry, a fast track up the ladder, and may be a steppingstone into many other areas. For those seeking to work abroad, hospitality is the best bet.

People who work in hospitality are drawn by the opportunity to take on a high degree of responsibility early, and to rise up pretty much as far as they desire; the opportunity to use creativity and to engage in an extraordinary variety of tasks; and to be in a "people" business. Hospitality also affords the best opportunity of any profession to work in a global arena—that is, not only hosting people from everywhere in the world, but having the opportunity to live and work anywhere in the world.

"This is such a dynamic, high-energy business," commented L. Antoinette (Toni) Chance, formerly Vice President of Personnel for Omni/Dunfey Hotels and now an industry consultant. "Opportunities in the hotel industry are unlimited," she said. "There is no more exciting industry, or more opportunities available in any other industry in the country, including high tech. The variety of positions one can have, the flexibility, the freedom to test your wings in other areas with few restrictions. The high status of certain positions."

Chance was Vice President of Human Resources in another industry before coming to Omni/Dunfey, and reflected, "I would be bored working for a widget manufacturer. The hotel industry offers a dynamic quality unlike any other. I can't see myself in any other business. I've seen people leave for a nine-to-five, weekends-off job, but wind up coming back later.

They miss the energy and excitement. Once you get into the hotel business, you're in it for life."

"Hotels are theater," stated John Beier, Regional Vice President for Loews Hotels, New York. "In fact, a lot come to hotels with a theater background. You can live a lifestyle that you couldn't otherwise afford."

The lodging industry offers considerable glamour; the chance to mix and mingle with the powerful, successful, and rich; an opportunity for enormous responsibility at an early stage; and tremendous advancement prospects. Few industries offer as much chance to live and work virtually anywhere in the world; in fact, a career in the lodging industry almost necessitates frequent relocation. Each type of property and each location presents its own challenge and distinct atmosphere.

"Whether you graduate from a hotel school or learn from the ground up," an industry executive observed, "the skills are equally as valuable in Seattle as Miami Beach or Bangkok. If you want to pull up stakes and move, you can. It's not like working in aerospace or in automobile manufacturing, where the key companies are concentrated in only a few places. Hotel skills are in demand everywhere, and if you like to travel and see new places, you can."

The lodging industry also offers a chance to do many different jobs in the course of a career—you are not pigeonholed in any one area. Indeed, wide experience is encouraged for anyone aspiring to a General Manager position.

INSIDE SECRET: If you aspire to be a GM, amass experience in all the major departments—rooms, front desk, food and beverage, sales and marketing, housekeeping. Also, take certification courses or get a degree in business administration and management, and be available to relocate often to take steady promotions.

This is very much a people business—with constant interaction with guests and co-workers—and very literally a service business. "It's a service business—not servitude," stated Beier. "But Americans generally don't understand service."

Career Progression

The hotel industry remains very traditional and very hierarchical, in keeping with its European heritage. There is a definite value placed on "paying dues."

"Being a Bellman or a Front-Desk Receptionist is okay, but there is the nagging feeling that 'I should be doing more,'" said Beier. "But you have to systematically learn the business. No one doubts what a Chef has to go through, the training in all the positions, but too many people in other positions in hospitality think, 'If I'm not the General Manager within the year, I failed.'"

Though patience is a virtue, there is relatively fast progression toward accountability and the higher-paying positions. "You can be accountable for millions of dollars by your mid-30s," said the Human Resources Vice President of a major chain. "There is power and responsibility at a relatively early age," even with relatively little supervisory experience. Within only two years, you can find yourself overseeing 40 people.

A common career path might be the following:

- Beginning in a "line" job at an hourly wage of $6 to $8 plus benefits, for 12 to 18 months.
- Promotion to Supervisor, at $8 to $12 per hour plus benefits, for 12 to 18 months.
- Promotion to Manager, earning $25,000 to $40,000 per year plus benefits, for two to three years.
- Promotion to Director at $37,000 to $68,000 per year, plus benefits, for three to seven years.
- Promotion to General Manager, earning $45,000 to $100,000 per year plus benefits.

Got What It Takes?

The lodging industry demands dedication, sacrifice, and sheer hard work. Hotels do not shut down at 5 p.m. or even midnight—they are open 24 hours a day, weekends, and holidays. The hours can be long—

a Group Sales Coordinator, for example, might have to be at the hotel at 3 a.m. on a Sunday morning to greet a group and stay until 8 p.m. to resolve a problem. Given the number of hours that mid- and senior-management positions require, the hourly rate is not that great. Moreover, there is no such thing as a totally protected holiday.

The hospitality industry is literally a service business, and it demands far more of employees than merely "liking people" and enjoying people contact. "We're looking for people who have warm, outgoing personalities, who see a dignity in serving others and are not resentful of providing service," said a Human Resources executive.

> **INSIDE SECRET:** Personnel people are looking for a take-charge person who wants accountability and autonomy early on, yet can be a team player, is service and people-oriented, flexible, adaptable, adventurous, hard-working, and self-disciplined. The work is physically demanding, so they are looking for energy and stamina.

"Everyone puts such emphasis on technical expertise," commented Jim France, who was the opening General Manager of the Charles Hotel in Cambridge, Massachusetts, in describing what he looks for when hiring. "That is the last thing you need. You can have the most brilliant hotel man, but if he can't handle people—the staff or the guest—then he should be an auto mechanic.

"A hotel may have lovely appointments, but it is essentially brick and mortar. The only thing that makes one hotel better than another is the staff. I would fire an employee who is rude to a guest faster than one who makes a mistake. We can teach a person not to make a mistake, but rudeness to the customer destroys the business," said France.

People looking for a career (not just a job) in the hotel business should also be willing and able to physically move to new cities frequently and not mind doing so. France's own career proves the point: In his first 20 years in the business, he moved 13 times. The need to uproot the family, leave friends, and relocate frequently in order to rise up the career ladder can strain relationships.

The hotel environment can be extremely disciplined, if not autocratic. Front-Desk Clerks, Bellpeople, and Waiters are drilled in techniques, their movements choreographed, their remarks rehearsed. The Charles Hotel in Cambridge, for example, had an 84-page operating manual describing every detail about what Bellmen and Doormen would say to guests; how to present the restaurant check to patrons; what the menu would be like.

At the same time, as one General Manager noted, a hotel must operate democratically, involving individuals in the operation. "We don't want automatons," added Chance. "We want to see 'scenarios,' but we don't inhibit personal style."

Jobs in the Hospitality Industry

Work environments, advancement potential, and even job categories differ greatly in the hotel field, depending on whether the property is a center-city hotel, a highway motel, a vacation resort, a conference center, a country inn, or an all-suite; whether it is full-service or "economy" class; and even whether it is a chain or independent property.

Best Bets

- Guest Services Manager
- Group Sales Manager
- Convention Services Coordinator
- Executive Housekeeper
- Front Office Manager

The AH&MA lists 223 different hotel job titles, from Accounting Supervisor to Yard Cleaner, Potwasher to President, and Security Guard to Systems Analyst. Depending on the size of the property, functions can be separate jobs or combined into one.

- **Front office staff:** Responsible for direct personal contact with the guests, handling reservations, special needs, and check-in and check-out. Positions include Front Office Manager, Assistant Manager, Room Clerk, Reservations Clerk, Cashier, Information Clerk, and Telephone Operator.

- **Service staff:** Greet guests, handle baggage, and assist with travel plans. Positions include Superintendent of Service, Concierge, Lobby Porter, Bell Captain and Bellperson, and Doorperson.

- **Accounting:** Track financial information. Positions include Controller, Assistant Controller, Credit Manager, Purchasing Agent, Food and Beverage Controller, Income Auditor, Food and Beverage Auditor, Cashier, Accounts Payable, Accounts Receivable, Payroll Supervisor, Night Auditor, ADP Systems Supervisor, and Secretary. The Controller can play a key role as a financial advisor along with the General Manager and professional staff; the Assistant Controller serves as Office Manager.

- **Food service:** Positions include Food and Beverage Director, Catering Manager, Maitre d'Hotel, Captain, Waitperson, Busperson, Bartender, Wine Server, Food Checker, and Dietician. A Food and Beverage Manager for a hotel doing $10 million in annual volume, for example, is responsible for keeping a cap on costs by controlling inventory and obtaining better prices, serving as the liaison between the company and outside contractors and unions, determining how to upgrade restaurant operations, achieving staff "harmony," planning work schedules, overseeing accounts payable and receivable, and ultimately having responsibility for profit and loss.

- **Food preparation:** Positions include Executive Chef, First Assistant, Second Cook, Fry Cook, Roast Cook, *Garde Manger,* Vegetable Cook, Pastry Chef, Butcher, Pastry Supervisor, and Steward.

- **Housekeeping:** Positions include Executive Housekeeper, Floor Supervisor, Room Attendant, Serving Specialist, and Houseperson.

■ **Sales and marketing:** This department is responsible for promotions, handling special arrangements for groups such as meetings, banquets, special events such as weddings, selling to the travel trade (travel agents, tour operators, car rental companies, and airlines), setting rates, and making decisions regarding products and services. Positions include Marketing Director, Sales Director, Sales Representative, Group Sales Coordinator, Banquet Manager, and food-service staff.

■ **Maintenance and operations:** Positions include Chief Engineer, Air-Conditioning Engineer, Plumber, Carpenter, Electrician, and laundry and kitchen equipment service personnel. The Director of Engineering does not necessarily have to have a degree in engineering; rather, this position requires experience in building maintenance and equipment. The Director of Engineering usually supervises five or six people and maintains a $75 million building.

Hot Trends

By 2010, the hospitality industry will need 100,000 more managers each year just to keep pace. But demand for particular specialties—such as food and beverage, marketing and sales, housekeeping and operations, and finance—flows in cycles.

"Demand runs in spurts because turnover runs in spurts," said Sue Gordon, Vice President of Human Resources for Radisson Hotels and a member of the AH&MA's Human Resources Council. "The Executive Housekeeper position comes and goes; also Controller, Director of Sales, and Food and Beverage Director. All positions are opportune areas for people wanting to make careers in lodging."

Growing sophistication, specialization, and greater service-orientation among the properties is also producing new positions and shifting emphasis. For example, there is substantial growth in concierge positions as part of an industry-wide push in the guest services area. Convention services has come into its own as more and more properties are appreciating the potential of the groups and meetings business.

Director of Catering has also become a key position, with a new emphasis on promoting banquet sales (much like room sales). The popularity of health spas, golf courses, tennis courts, and other sports facilities as well as entertainment at properties makes the lodging industry an important employer of these kinds of professionals, as well.

Computers have become an essential tool in hotel operations, used in reservations, accounting, energy management, and sales; and most hotel companies have MIS departments. Hotels are now embracing computers as a guest amenity, as well. Moreover, e-commerce is transforming the way hotels and lodging companies market their properties and book their rooms (some $6 billion in bookings were recorded in 1999, with $20 to $30 billion forecast in 2001), putting a premium on Internet specialists. Some 90 percent of hotel companies now have Web sites, some offering "virtual tours" of rooms and services.

The marketing and sales arena has changed significantly with growing involvement in frequent-guest (loyalty) marketing programs and collaborations with airlines and other travel and non-travel partners. Best Western International has a Director of International Development, charged with helping chart the company's growth in strategic ways, seeking out properties in areas of the world that need a well-recognized, global brand. Club Med also employs someone to scout out potential sites for new resorts. A large, heavily segmented chain such as Marriott has a Vice President of Brand Marketing, while most of the chains now have some kind of frequent-guest/loyalty marketing program that is likely linked with other partners (partnership marketing), under the heading of customer acquisition and retention.

The hospitality industry is also a great place for people who want to pursue careers in tour operations—many individual hotels as well as chains offer their own packages, involving negotiations with local attractions and transportation companies and possibly wholesalers—as well as incentive and meetings planning.

Because of their distinctive quality, hotels may also employ some unique specialties:

- The Peabody Hotels in Memphis and Orlando employ a "Duck Master"; twice a day, they lead a "march of the ducks" from their penthouse home, down the elevator, and over a red carpet to the lobby fountain.
- The American Club in Kohler, Wisconsin, employs a Shepherd.
- The historic Williamsburg Inn at Colonial Williamsburg has a Wildlife Steward.
- The Ojai Valley Inn & Spa in Ojai, California, has a Bird-Wrangler.
- The Hotel del Coronado in Coronado, California, has a Director of Heritage.
- Historic hotels like the Brown Palace in Denver; Mohonk Mountain House in New Paltz, New York; and La Fonda in Santa Fe employ artisans to restore art, furniture, and architectural structures.
- Club Med Columbus Isle has a "G.O.," who is responsible for maintaining a $2.5 million collection of art objects.

General Managers

Shifts in emphasis and changes in services and management techniques directly affect the position of General Manager. General Managers are much like mayors of a city in that they have the ultimate responsibility for perhaps thousands of guests and employees. But they are also chief executives of large, complex businesses. They must be responsible for financial management and provide leadership.

Not everyone working in the hotel industry aspires to the General Manager spot, and with the expansion in the numbers of properties, there is actually a shortage of talent. Becoming a General Manager is a very attainable career goal. But, warned one hotel executive, "People don't have a realistic view of the demands. They see "Hotel" on television, and the glamour side of wining and dining celebrities. But that is only a very, very small part of it. Being a General Manager is

a demanding, highly responsible job, 24 hours a day, seven days a week. There are a lot of nitty-gritty, dirty types of things that need to be done to meet guests' needs."

INSIDE SECRET: Not everyone is cut out to be a General Manager, which entails the same sense of responsibility as being the mayor of a city—a city that never sleeps.

Finally, chains and hotel networks have positions in regional, national, and international offices, although these are relatively few. A major international chain with hundreds of properties worldwide might have about 200 such positions, which include marketing, sales, public relations, personnel, business development, and franchising.

$ Salaries in the Hospitality Industry

Although entry-level jobs are relatively low-paying, mid- and upper-management positions pay well. Salary levels are directly related to the size, price segment, and revenue of the property. For example, the median salary for General Managers (GMs) in properties with more than 175 rooms is $85,000, compared with $32,000 for GMs in properties with fewer than 75 rooms. The median salary for GMs in the luxury segment is $112,000, versus $34,000 for GMs in the budget/economy segment. And the median salary for GMs in properties that yield more than $4 million in revenue is $64,000, twice the level for GMs in properties that earn less than $1 million. The following table gives a sampling of median salaries in different hotel job categories.

INSIDE SECRET: Hotel salary levels are directly related to the size, price segment, and revenue of the property.

Median Hotel Salaries, 2000

Title	Salary
Administrative	
Director of Human Resources	$55,000
General Manager	$47,000
Resident Manager	$35,000
Assistant Manager	$26,000
Director of Information Technology	$42,000
Accounting	
Controller	$51,000
Payroll Clerk	$23,800
Accounting Clerk	$21,000
Front Office	
Rooms Division Manager	$31,400
Front Office Manager	$31,400
Reservations Manager	$28,200
Front Office Clerk	$16,800
Telephone Operator	$16,200
Bell Captain	$15,100
Lobby/bell staff	$12,400
Food and Beverage	
Food and Beverage Director	$60,000
Executive Chef	$48,000
Restaurant Manager	$36,700
Sous Chef	$36,600
Sales and Marketing	
Director of Sales and Marketing	$47,400
Catering Sales Manager	$39,700
Sales Manager	$36,600
Conference Planner	$35,900
Housekeeping	
Executive Housekeeper	$29,000
Maintenance Employee	$20,600
Assistant Housekeeper	$15,000
Engineering	
Chief Engineer	$39,000
Security	
Security Director	$37,600
Security	$19,500

Source: American Hotel & Motel Association.

Your Ticket into the Hospitality Industry

Entering hospitality can be the most difficult part. Although this segment of the travel industry offers the greatest number of entry-level positions, applicants at prime properties can outnumber openings by 200 to one. But once you're inside, it is fairly easy to move up or over.

Many hotel companies recruit directly into management training programs from major colleges with four-year degree programs in hotel management (including Johnson & Wales, Cornell University, Michigan State, and Florida International), as well as other disciplines including business, engineering, marketing, and accounting.

The American Hotel & Motel Association, representing about 10,000 properties nationwide, has established a junior organization called Future Hoteliers of America, aimed at those enrolled in vocational, hotel school, or college programs, in order to involve people in the industry early on.

"The number one thing I look for is whether the school has an internship program and the student has worked each year in the industry in various capacities," said the Vice President of Human Resources for one hotel company. "A Dishwasher gets equally good experience as a Front-Desk person. I look for a grasp of the realities of our industry. And the reality is, there is a tremendous amount of hard work."

 INSIDE SECRET: Although a hotel's corporate headquarters receives many resumes, most personnel directors advise new entrants to contact directly the hotel at which you want to work.

Every hotel has entry-level positions—such as Sales and Reservations, Front-Office Clerk, Cashier, Convention Services Manager, and Floor Manager in a convention services department. The second level is a Team Leader supervisory position, perhaps in housekeeping. From there, one can become an Assistant Manager in housekeeping or rooms, or a Front-Office Supervisor.

Because commercial lodgings operate around the clock, it is usually possible to work in at least a part-time job to get a taste of what the work is like, get valuable experience, and get your foot in the door for a full-time position.

When a new hotel opens, management generally tries to hire as many people locally as possible and therefore will not be as likely to insist on prior experience as a well-established property would be. Although experience is helpful, it is not always necessary; it is more important to demonstrate willingness to work and ability to learn. A major hotel company may interview 6,000 to 8,000 candidates to fill 400 positions.

"What I look for," said Jim France, the opening General Manager of the Charles Hotel in Cambridge, Massachusetts, who filled most of the 341 positions locally from among inexperienced people, "is personality, attitude—the guy who smiles and is friendly, is guest-oriented." France's method is to have candidates go through several screening processes—personnel, the department head, the division head, and finally the General Manager.

Opportunities in the Chains

Chain properties in general offer better opportunities for new entrants. They have the most sophisticated training and development programs, as well as the best chance for advancement within a single organization. Companies such as Omni, Hyatt, Marriott, Westin, Sheraton, Hilton International, and Radisson have excellent programs.

INSIDE SECRET: Chain properties tend to offer better entry-level opportunities. However, positions in small operations could entail greater responsibility, move you up the ladder at a faster pace, and put you in position to accept a higher position at a larger property.

Snapshot: Marriott Hotels

Marriott Hotels, which exploded in growth during the 1980s when it grew from 100 to 600 properties worldwide, does most of its hiring for properties locally. The personnel office usually opens three months ahead of the scheduled hotel opening and begins advertising for positions.

"We have a profile of a 'Marriott' person, whether they come to us as a housekeeper or front-desk person. We look for people who are energetic, like people, problem-solvers, people who are interested in an opportunity to grow to their fullest extent, who work to their maximum ability." On average, the hotel hires one employee per room, so a 400-room hotel would have 400 openings.

When the staff is put together, rather than send neophytes to "school," Marriott forms a task force of the "best of the best" from around the world, including Operators, Waiters, Housekeepers, and Doormen. Someone might be taken from Torrance, California, and sent to Hong Kong to help train and work side-by-side with the "new kids on the block" for a two-month period to teach them "the Marriott way."

For the vast majority of employees who start in entry-level jobs, those jobs are precisely that: steppingstones to higher positions. Fully 40 percent of Marriott's management started out as a Housekeeper, Waiter, or Doorman. Moreover, people can move from any position in Marriott to any other.

Marriott Hotels is only one unit of Marriott Lodging, which operates several different brands (Renaissance, Residence Inn, Courtyard, TownePlace Suites, Fairfield Inn, SpringHill Suites, and Ramada International), which in turn is a unit of Marriott International Inc. (MAR on the New York Stock Exchange). Marriott International is a leading worldwide hospitality company with more than 2,000 operating units in the United States and 57 other countries and territories, generating $10 billion in revenue. The company also develops and operates vacation ownership (timeshare) resorts under the Marriott, Ritz-Carlton, and Horizons brands; operates executive apartments and conference centers; and provides furnished corporate housing through its ExecuStay by Marriott division. Other Marriott businesses include senior living communities and services, wholesale food distribution, procurement services, and The Ritz-Carlton Hotel Company, LLC. The company is headquartered in Washington, D.C., and has approximately 145,000 employees worldwide, including 3,500 at headquarters.

The company has a superb Web site at http://careers.marriott.com/ (job listings are posted at http://jobsearch.marriott.newjobs.com/).

A major growth area for the company has been the development of senior living resort communities, employing an average of 150 people at each location. The company so far has 100 of these facilities in 30 states.

Marriott International has an active college recruitment program as well as internships. The company has also set up a foundation to help people with disabilities find rewarding jobs. Marriott Foundation for People with Disabilities and "Bridges…from school to work" provide stepping stones for youth to fulfilling employment, and links for employers to a rich and underutilized applicant source. (For more information, contact the Marriott Foundation for People with Disabilities, One Marriott Dr., Washington, DC 20058; 301-380-7771.)

Small Properties, Big Opportunities

Do not overlook small operations. Although there are fewer entry-level positions and a lower "ceiling," positions in small operations could entail greater responsibility and greater personal satisfaction, move you up the ladder at a faster pace, and put you in position to accept a higher position at a larger property. At Balsam House, an inn in upstate New York, a Busboy became a Chef and a Front-Desk person assumed the position of a Marketing and Promotions Specialist without the usual years and tiers of experience.

Smaller, independent properties may also be a better starting place because they cannot afford the same recruitment programs and high salaries to draw graduates of hotel-management schools. But although there may be an opportunity to rise to mid-management or gain diversified experience, there is a limit to how high one can rise in smaller properties because positions at the top tend not to turn over frequently, if at all. In contrast, positions in upper management turn over every few years at a major chain.

Another consideration is the mix of properties in a chain or hotel group. A major chain such as Hyatt or Radisson has excellent management training and tracking programs that literally keep track of people as they acquire more experience and responsibility and then tap them for promotion. Chains with a variety of property sizes and locales can give people opportunities very early to take on responsibility as a General Manager or a Food and Beverage Director. In other companies that have only large hotels, the General Managers tend to be older and it takes longer to attain the required seniority.

 INSIDE SECRET: Chains with a variety of property sizes and locales can give people opportunities very early to take on responsibility as a General Manager or a Food and Beverage Director.

Other points to look for:

- Where the hotels are located largely determines the clientele, product mix, and how fast the company is expanding (if it's a chain).
- The reputation of the hotel and its professionalism.
- Its track record in retaining people.
- The hotel's financial record.
- The philosophy of upper management.
- Human resource policies, particularly those concerning promotion from within.
- Training and development programs.
- Salary and benefits.
- The degree of specialization/generalization of function and tiers of hierarchy.

Roadmap to the Top

The lodging industry has some of the best computerized systems for tracking, tapping, and training employees for advancement. Radisson Hotels, for example, uses a "Person-Power Planning System" for human resource development. It maintains data on the individuals who are currently in management positions, and those who are "high-potentials"—either those who are either in management positions but could be in more senior positions, or individuals who are not yet in management positions, but perhaps are first-line supervisors. The database includes a skills bank inventory, which includes assessments by supervisors and a career statement by the candidates as to what they want, their educational background, and positions they have held over the past five years. Each hotel has the data for its own use, but the data is also collected centrally in order to maximize the opportunities for people across hotels that are managed and owned by Radisson (not franchise organizations).

Such systems will come in handy at Radisson, which is slated to triple in size in the next few years. Presently it has 12 luxury hotels. The company plans to expand to 30 by 2003; and the company that presently employs 3,500 people in its hotels and corporate organization will grow to 10,000.

"People are not bottlenecked," said Sue Gordon, Vice President of Human Resources. "They are cultivated to move up. Every aspect of work is valued." The President of Carlson Hotels (Radisson's parent company) started as a Bellman at age 19 and went on to become President of Starwood Hotels before coming to Carlson Hotels.

What might be the timetable for advancement? "To be a General Manager is a very individual thing," she noted. "Some people can be GM at age 28 and others not until 38, and not everyone wants to be GM. But the cream does rise to the top. People who are enthusiastic, dedicated, and committed, who put in more than expected, are the ones who will be noticed and promoted."

Sue Gordon elaborated:

Bottlenecks could happen if you had 18 star performers in one area, vying for one position. Usually, though, you have a variety of individuals, and not everyone wants to be head of the department. We need "maintainers" as well as fast-trackers.

Opportunity abounds for individuals who are committed, dedicated, enthusiastic, and have a service mentality. You need skills—computer skills are more important today, financial skills, marketing—backed up by more than nice attitude and a nice smile. There has to be meat on the bones. Education is a certain plus; we still prefer four-year hotel school grads, though individuals without that can make it. When we interview candidates for Vice President, most often, they not only have a B.A. in business or hotel administration or marketing, but they have a Master's.

We are in the service industry. We look for people who have a smile on the inside as well as on the outside. You cannot teach smiling. You cannot teach attitude. It is easier to hire nice people than to train people to be nice.

Because it affords an opportunity to rise up to great heights, hospitality can be extremely lucrative—many GMs are at six figures (some even have equity); such benefits as 401K plans and profit-sharing are also commonplace. It is very demanding, though, a lot of hard work. But if you talk to people who work in hotels, young managers, they are very gung-ho. They like the fast pace, the variety of experiences, the interesting guests; they want to wear more than one hat. We make it exciting by offering cross-training opportunities.

The willingness and ability to relocate are important factors in how far and how fast you rise in a hotel organization. But while in the past a management person might have been "blacklisted" for refusing an appointment, most major chains have become more sensitive to this issue.

When I started in the hotel industry some 20-odd years ago, when the company said you were going to Oshkosh, you only answered, "What time do you want me there?" Now people are considering offers and turning them down because of their families. We as a company have been supportive, liberal. We haven't been dictatorial. We try to work with them. We don't blacklist.

"This industry is one of the last to come to grips with the fact that people prize their personal life," said Toni Chance. "It is only recently that management people feel comfortable in refusing a move."

The traditional path to the General Manager's seat had been through the Rooms Division—Front Desk, Housekeeping, Resident Manager or Executive Assistant Manager of Rooms, and, finally, General Manager. The route is now wide open.

"Career paths are changing," Gordon noted. "Doors are more open. At Radisson, we are encouraging people to 'cross lines.' Technical knowledge can be picked up if you have the basic skills and aptitudes. We are identifying skills and talent needed for the General Manager's spot, so someone can come from Accounting, Rooms, Food and Beverage, Sales. It is good to have experience in other areas. We are no longer pigeonholing people." The necessary skills include leadership, allocation, control, teamwork, and coordination.

She also pointed to a trend among hotel companies to "streamline" positions and "flatten out" layers of management, which means that more decision-making will be pushed further down in the organization—in other words, empowerment.

"Empowerment means more satisfaction for the workforce. There are more opportunities to attract and retain people when more decisions are made at lower levels," Gordon said.

It also means that people will have wider authority and more opportunity to learn different skills within the same hotel. "The more cross-trained you can be, the better for the company," said Hyatt's Director of Personnel. "You progress by moving from hotel to hotel, company to company."

More opportunities have opened for women. Although women were always highly represented in Sales, Personnel, and Housekeeping departments, few achieved the General Manager spot, much less Chef or Department Head. But that has changed; women are General Managers, Food and Beverage Directors, Chefs, even Executive Chefs and Corporate Vice Presidents of Operations.

Rising to the Top

Jim France's rise to General Manager of the Charles Hotel typifies the traditional career path and the lifestyle and dedication a hotel career exacts.

Born in Scotland, "where if you came from a middle-class family on the wrong side of the tracks, you had no way to change," France was the son of a hotelier "and knew that I wanted to be one my whole life."

While attending the renowned Lausanne Hotel School in Switzerland, he took jobs in hotels as Dishwasher, Waiter, Cook, Accountant, Front-Desk Person, and Steward. After graduating, he gained experience in convention services, sales, and food and beverage. He was a Food and Beverage Director for eight years before moving into management.

France, who has since become a specialist in opening new hotels for companies, moved 13 times in 20 years (6 times in 10 years of marriage), and in the course of his career had worked with some of the major chains. He moved to Boston to open the Charles Hotel for a private hotel company, Interstate, that has plans for expanding aggressively.

His wife, Dale, said philosophically, "It is the fate of a hotel careerist—constant moves with every promotion. If you are adventurous, it's okay. You take away a little of every place. But it is difficult when you have children."

France agreed. "The spouse has to be adventurous, willing to give up family ties and friends and be adaptable."

Foreign assignments are particularly difficult—you have to get to know the culture, learn how to communicate in a different language, and learn how to function on a day-to-day basis. Mrs. France had to learn Norwegian during her husband's posting there.

(continues)

(continued)

France recommends that new entrants to the field apply for any job at a new hotel and go through community employment agencies. But he counsels those serious about a career to go to a hotel school. "You get a better grounding. It doesn't mean you will get a job and advance quicker. A streetwise person who comes up through the ranks who is good with people can rise faster. The whole industry is people."

Required and Continuing Education

Even the executives who rose up through the ranks or entered from other fields agree that some schooling is necessary to advance. Although increasing professionalism and sophistication in the industry are one reason, sheer competition for new jobs is the most compelling one. A degree in hotel management can give you the edge in getting a job and put you on a fast track.

INSIDE SECRET: A degree in hotel management can give you the edge in getting a job and put you on a fast track.

"A degree helps you move up quicker, but won't give you a higher position starting out," said John Beier, Regional Vice President of Loews Hotels, New York. "We're not in brain surgery. We're in the job of selling a room, cleaning a bed. It's a simple thing."

In an effort to increase professionalism in the industry, the AH&MA created the Educational Institute, which produces resource materials for the industry and schools, as well as administers its own in-class and home-study program (including online courses). Coupled with work experience, these programs lead to various degrees, including Certified Hotel Administrator (CHA), Certified Rooms Division Executive, Certified Engineering Operations Executive, Certified Food and Beverage Executive, Certified Human Re-

sources Executive, Certified Hospitality Housekeeping Executive, or Certified Hospitality Supervisor.

Course selections include human relations, communications, food-production principles, marketing, energy management, law, accounting, resort management, sales promotion, convention management and service, and food and beverage controls. The program is geared to people looking to enter the hospitality industry or move up from entry level, and to working professionals seeking to advance to higher management.

INSIDE SECRET: For more information, contact the Educational Institute of AH&MA, 1407 S. Harrison Rd., P.O. Box 1240, East Lansing, MI 48826; 800-752-4567; www.ei-ahma.org.

Because the hospitality industry is probably the biggest single segment in travel and tourism and because of the anticipated growth, hotel schools and academic programs are opening widely. The best-known four-year programs of hotel and restaurant management are at Cornell University, Michigan State, Penn State, the University of Denver, and the University of Houston.

The Council on Hotel, Restaurant, and Institutional Education (CHRIE), a nonprofit organization, publishes "A Guide to Hospitality and Tourism Education," which lists colleges and universities across the U.S. that offer hospitality curriculum, a variety of scholarship resources, and key industry organizations. Contact CHRIE, 1200 17th St. NW, 1st Fl., Washington, DC 20036-3097; 202-331-5990; www.chrie.org. (Students and alumni can post their resumes free of charge on the CHRIE Web site.)

Having a degree in hospitality is very helpful in obtaining a job in the industry, since many chains and independents recruit on campuses. Graduates usually enter at a higher level because of the experience gained in the program as well as specialized knowledge. However, you will likely do the traditional entry-level jobs (Dishwasher, Reservationist, Front Desk) during your schooling.

Club Med: Living the Good Life

Club Med is not like any other hospitality company; not like any other company, actually, in the structure of its organization or its approach to staffing. Yet, with 120 resorts in 36 countries on five continents, and with a projected need for 1,000 jobs a year in the North American "zone" alone, it is a significant player.

"The sun is always shining on a Club Med," said Club Med's Chairman and Chief Executive Officer Philippe Bourguignon, who came to Club Med by way of Euro Disney and Accor Hotels. "When it is sundown at Bora Bora in Tahiti, it is at its zenith at Sandpiper, and people at Agadir, Morocco are dancing under the stars."

Club Med is about living the "good life," the "sportif" life, experiencing new things and creating a new kind of culture. The distinctive aspect of Club Med, where the resorts are called "villages," is that the staff, called "G.O.s" (for *gentil organisateurs*, or gentle organizers), live the experience their guests (called G.M.s, or *gentil membres*, or gentle members) do, joining them for meals, for example, but acting as gracious hosts and gentle guides to new experiences, like scuba diving or in-line skating, and "the good life." G.O.s sign on for six-month or one-year contracts and live in the village (the resort). They may specialize in a skill or activity, like tennis, scuba, sailing, circus arts, or yoga, but take part in many different aspects, including the special shows and entertainments performed for the G.M.s. The guy who led you down on your first dive may well be wearing a penguin costume as part of a skit that night, and then dancing at the disco after the show. Since many of the "clubs" cater to families with young children, hundreds of G.O.s are engaged as counselors for the supervised activity programs.

When the contract is coming to an end, G.O.s are given a "dream sheet," to list their first and second choices for their next assignment—perhaps Bali, perhaps St. Moritz, perhaps a club geared to adults or perhaps a family club like Sandpiper in Florida, or the Crested Butte, Colorado, ski resort. Many G.O.s join up to take a year or two off after college, and wind up staying their entire career; others come when they need a break from a career they have chosen. When they marry and have a family, G.O.s who want to continue on either choose a village where they can have their family live nearby, or try for a corporate posting in the Coral Gables, Florida, headquarters

for North America, or the worldwide headquarters in Paris, or perhaps as an outside sales representative in various cities.

Though the pay is modest for a starting-out G.O., it actually works out extremely well, because your bed and board (even your wardrobe), in fact all your living expenses, are completely paid for, even the roundtrip plane ticket to get you there and back home. You can pocket $750 to $1,000 per month, which for a young person is quite a bit of change.

"You don't have a job; you live a lifestyle," said Rod Frankel, formerly director of recruitment, who started as a water-skiing instructor with Club Med 12 years before. His own career typifies that of others at Club Med. Promoted to a Chief of Water-skiing, he later worked snow skiing, became Chief of Sports at a club, spent one season as a Coordinator of Entertainment, and then spent the next 4½ years as a *Chef d'village* (like a General Manager). Every six months (one season), work assignments and locations changed.

"To replenish the energy, spirit, it is important to change your atmosphere," he remarked. Frankel has lived and worked at Club Meds in Paradise Island (The Bahamas), Egypt, Tunisia, Switzerland, Guadeloupe, and Mauritius. Even in his capacity as Director of Recruitment, he did not want to get away from "the field," and was spending the summer heading up a new camp program for youngsters at Copper Mountain, Colorado.

"Though G.O.s are not paid a great salary," he said, "one of the advantages is the opportunity to travel."

Frankel had never intended to spend a career with Club Med. A former chemical engineer who decided to recharge his batteries by teaching snow skiing in Vermont, he felt he was headed nowhere and took a job with Club Med. Many of the G.O.s have also come from other careers, such as law and nursing. Some regard it as a brief interlude, a paid vacation, but an increasing number are seeing Club Med as a career. All of the management positions are hired out of the clubs. Many professionals use their skills in positions.

"We need someone who can work in our bank at a club—that person may need accounting and financial skills. But he or she also needs to be outgoing, to be able to dance a French cancan on stage, to remember the names of the G.M.s and strike up a conversation with them. At a Sheraton, the person working the

(continues)

(continued)

cashier's desk doesn't have to remember the guest's name because he or she won't be seeing him again. At Club Med, the G.O. may be eating at the same table as the G.M. at dinner that night," Frankel said.

"You'd never become a millionaire, but to live the lifestyle of a Club Med if you didn't work there, you would have to be one."

Eric Stewart, the Director of Human Resources, had been a chemist. "I worked in laboratories. I hated being left in the lab. I was happier to be on the management floor. I went to night school for three years to get a certificate in industrial management, in order to change to human resources. I always felt like a square peg in a round hole until I came to Club Med—others say that too."

Now in the role of hiring for the North American zone (which includes Canada, Mexico, the Caribbean, South America, and Asia/Pacific), Stewart looks to hire people who have skills, sure, but more importantly, a "G" quality (like "Emotional Intelligence"). He is also responsible for coordinating the moves of thousands of G.O.s who terminate one contract, designate a choice for their "dream sheet," and move on to another village.

"It's like controlled chaos. You have to fit their needs. A 20-year-old may have energy and like to party, so you don't send him to a family resort; a more seasoned G.O. may want a family village. After a few seasons, those G.O.s who show promise and want to advance are given more formalized training to move up.

Some 16,000 people work at Club Meds worldwide, and with the expansion program planned, that number should go up substantially.

(For more information, see www.clubmed.com.)

Contacts, Sources, and Leads

- **American Hotel and Motel Association,** 1201 New York Ave. NW, Washington, DC 20005-3931; 202-289-3100; www.ahma.com; as well as local chapters.
- **The AH&MA Web site** provides links to major chains, and these sites list career opportunities (www.ahma.com); to check on current salary ranges, visit www.ei-ahma.org.
- Industry references such as the *Hotel & Travel Index* list properties, addresses, and General Managers.
- You can also check local **newspapers, convention and visitor bureaus,** and **chambers of commerce.**
- Keep on the lookout for **newly built properties** and try to contact the General Manager or Director of Personnel.

Trade Publications

Major trade publications point to where new hotels are opening, and which are expanding and opening new services and divisions. These include

- *Hotel Business* (www.hotelbusiness.com)
- *Hotel & Motel Management* (www.hmm.online.com)
- *Hotels*
- *Innkeeping World*
- *Lodging Hospitality* (www.Llhonline.com)
- *Lodging,* published by the AHMA (www.lodgingmagazine.com)
- *Nation's Restaurant News* (www.nrn.com)

- *Restaurant Business* (www.restaurant.biz.com)
- *Restaurants & Institutions* (www.rimag.com)
- *Restaurants USA* (www.restaurant.org)

Employment and Search Firms

There are a battery of employment, placement, recruitment, and search firms that specialize in the lodgings industry. Among them are the following:

- **Travel Executive Search,** 5 Rose Ave., Great Neck, NY 11021; 516-829-8829; TESIntl@aol.com.
- **BSA Hospitality/Bonnie Smith Associates,** 747 E. Green St. #206, Pasadena, CA 91101; 626-432-6620.
- **Executive Recruiters, Inc.,** 1907 Clarks Glen Place, Vienna, VA 22182; 703-556-9580; www.hotelrecruiters.com.
- **Hospitality Recruiters,** www.hospitalityrecruiters.com.

Innkeeping

Innkeeping is probably the most ancient form of lodging, and one that retains a very distinctive character.

Kathi Ransom graduated with an MPS in hotel administration from the Cornell Hotel School, and then became a training supervisor at Westin International, where she had interned. But she left to become an innkeeper at the Lake Placid Manor, a charming, 38-room Adirondacks inn in upstate New York. The daughter of an innkeeper, she saw this as an opportunity to get back to her roots.

An innkeeper has to be considerably more than a General Manager. "There are days I have to make the beds, cook, and do the accounting," Ransom related. "There are a lot of hours."

But there are advantages in working at a small organization compared to a large one. "As an innkeeper of a smaller property, you are involved in all aspects of the operation; in a larger organization, you are more concentrated," she said.

"You do get to meet a lot of interesting people, and it is very satisfying when you put on an interesting dinner. There is a lot of ego involved, but it is fairly internalized—you know when you've done a good job.

"Innkeeping is creative," she added. "It is very much a reflection of your personality. But there are a lot of hours, it is very demanding, and you probably don't make as much as in another profession. You learn to bite your tongue a lot and not to take everything personally. You have to love the work."

Ransom, who had some thoughts about eventually owning her own inn, later left Lake Placid Manor to go back to Westin.

Bed-and-Breakfasts

A variation on the innkeeping theme is bed-and-breakfast. Common in Europe, the concept whereby private individuals open their homes to guests, literally providing bed and breakfast, has become a trend in the United States. Bed-and-breakfasts offer cozy, comfortable accommodations in a homey environment. Some-

times the homes are an attraction; sometimes the hosts are. Barbara Notarius, for example, opened her six-bedroom Victorian mansion as a B&B. She got into the business after she had a baby because she wanted to work from home, and left a job as a psychologist. Besides operating her own B&B, she launched a bed-and-breakfast reservations service.

Many who operate bed-and-breakfasts do so to supplement their income and cover the costs of a large house. But some are operated much like small inns and are the sole income to a family.

Vacation Ownership

Vacation ownership (what used to be called timesharing) is one of the many innovations going on in the lodging industry. Its somewhat-tarnished image has a new gloss thanks to star-studded companies including Disney, Marriott, Starwood, Ritz-Carlton, Hyatt, Hilton, Four Seasons, and the American Skiing Company, which collectively own about 25 percent of the market.

Rising out of the ashes of the 1974–75 real estate recession, timesharing has grown from less than $10 million in sales in 1972 to about $2 billion in 2000. Some 2.4 million households worldwide own a vacation interval in one or more of the 3,050 vacation ownership resorts worldwide.

A zesty combination of real estate, travel, and resort operations, timesharing (also known as interval ownership, fractional ownership, or vacation ownership) allows consumers to purchase the use of a vacation place for a specified period of time—for example, one week in December for 25 years, or one week per season in perpetuity.

There are several variations. In one, the individual actually purchases the property for a designated period of time or in perpetuity, owns the deed, and may resell it or will it. In the second, the individual purchases only the right to use the apartment or condominium for a period of years (typically 20 or more), but does not have ownership interest in the real estate. Disney has a different spin: Purchasers buy points, rather than property, that are applied toward a stay or traded.

Costs can run thousands of dollars per unit, plus annual maintenance fees.

At first glance, one might wonder why anyone would want to commit to spending the same week or two of every year in the exact same spot. But timesharing has proved appealing for a number of reasons, and there is far more flexibility than you might think.

Vacationers are seeking protection from inflation that may put the cost of owning a vacation home or even a traditional resort vacation out of the family's budget. Also, timesharing suits people who are concerned about the shortages of desirable accommodations in the most popular resort areas, like the ski resorts of Colorado and sun resorts of Florida and Hawaii. They like the idea of being an "owner" rather than a transient, and may enjoy the clublike atmosphere. Some vacation ownership projects also provide added benefits for owners that transient guests do not have. Moreover, interval owners are not confined to using their own timeshare property year after year; trading clubs such as RCI (which has burgeoned into a massive travel company) enable owners to trade their right to use their property with another member, and there are members all over the world. Also, in many new formulas, the ownership week floats so that it is not at the same time each year. (This is particularly true in fractional ownership, where you own one week out of a month.) You can offer up for vacation rental the period of time that you own but don't use, through the management company, getting a portion of the fee. Or you can use it to trade for a trip to another resort at a more convenient time.

American Skiing Company gives incentives to its fractional owners not to use their time, but rather, to put it into the rental pool. In exchange, owners get to stay whenever there is a vacancy, paying just the maintenance charges. The skiing company is building Grand hotels at all of its ski resorts, and owners can trade locations and, in some cases, use season lift tickets at the other ASC resorts.

Timesharing is not confined to resort properties, but is being used by city-center commercial hotels. Yachts and campsites are also being offered for interval owner-

ership (there are 580 private outdoor camp resorts in the U.S., with more than 450,000 family owners).

Timeshare is lodging but with a finance component—you are not just selling a vacation destination, but also an equity interest. Because of this, vacation ownership has drawn people from virtually every professional background.

"They come from all over," noted a spokeswoman for the American Resort Development Association, a trade association representing timeshare developers. "It is a multifaceted career, needing broad experience from different fields. Almost everything you learned or know would not be wasted."

There is a need for specific skills, such as finance, resort management, public relations, advertising, marketing, and generating leads.

Companies specialize in various activities, such as

- Planning (accounting, architecture, economic research and feasibility, engineering, environmental and financial analysis, land planning, landscape architecture, legal, marina planning, design and layout, market research and feasibility, and site selection)
- Development and construction
- Marketing and sales
- Financial services
- Publishing
- Tours and travel services

Exchange companies, like Interval International of South Miami, Florida (www.intervalworld.com), and Resort Condominiums International, Indianapolis, Indiana (www.rci.com), are essentially computerized inventory and reservations systems, enabling member timeshare owners to trade their rights to use their properties with other members. These are also emerging into massive retail and wholesale travel companies in their own right; both companies have introduced in-house tour packaging divisions.

Contacts, Sources, and Leads

- **American Resort Development Association,** 1220 L St. NW, Washington, DC 20005; 202-371-6700; www.arda.org.

- **Trades Publishing Company;** 931-484-8819; www.resorttrades.com (publishes job classifieds online).

CHAPTER 7

SKI AND SPA: UPLIFTING EXPERIENCES

Both the ski industry and the spa industry afford an unparalleled opportunity to combine lifestyle with work. Both are specialized facets of the resort industry and present additional career paths for hospitality professionals. Both also draw on professionals from sports, health, and education. Whereas the ski industry is geographically more constricted (basically, anywhere there are mountains), the spa industry is much more widespread, and in many cases, is also an incorporated element of ski resorts.

 INSIDE SECRET: The ski and spa industries afford the best opportunity to combine work and lifestyle.

The Ski Industry

Like riding a lift to the crest of a mountain, most senior executives in the ski industry started at the bottom, literally, and rose to the top of their profession. This is still a field where you can start as a lift operator and rise to the level of CEO, although today you also need sophisticated business skills and professional training.

Those who make the ski industry a career do it because they are passionate about the lifestyle (and living and working among others who share the same interests) and consciously sacrifice more lucrative occupations. Their captivation with the industry is testament to the fact that this industry affords the best opportunity to blend work and lifestyle.

 ### *Snapshot: The Ski Industry*

The up-through-the-ranks rise has continued despite the evolution of ski areas into big-business destination resorts. These mega-million enterprises include many that are now public companies on the stock exchange, accountable to boards of directors and shareholders. Ski areas of a generation ago were characterized by a lift, a ticket booth, a cafeteria, a ski school, and a rental facility. These days, ski resorts have evolved into complex, multimillion-dollar entities with such diversified enterprises as real estate development, hospitality and restaurant management, tour operations and reservations centers, shopping malls, nurseries, day camps, schools, even business centers and convention and meeting sites—kind of a cross between a city, a resort, and a theme park. Nor are they dependent on snow, or even winter sports. They have been transformed into complete mountain resort destinations, specializing in outdoor and active pursuits regardless of season, but with enough to satisfy even those who desire quieter, more leisurely, or cerebral pleasures.

"I run 60 different businesses," said Bill Jensen, whose career rise from Lift Operator to CEO of Vail Resorts is not uncommon. "But what makes this all work is the lift ticket."

Jensen rose to the pinnacle of the industry, but along the way he got his MBA from Stanford Business School. When Jensen was 25, he got a $1,200-per-month job at Sun Valley, and the first person he met had a trust fund. "I realized I never would have that.

It motivated me to continue my career, to have the tools to be successful and still be passionate about this business."

"In life, we all have to have a period—10 years or so—to develop a record of achievement. From 25 to 35, I chose to develop the technical skills in an industry, and then the ability to lead people. I've been skiing my whole life. I am passionate about the sport." When he looks to hire other executives for his management team, he looks for someone who is also passionate about the sport. "I look to someone who knows the customer, why they want to ski. The industry, because of the size of the business, demands business skills of anyone at the executive level. Lots of MBAs work for me, but they all have passion for what they do."

INSIDE SECRET: Increasing diversification at many large resorts enables more professionals to work year-round.

There are still many thousands of seasonal workers; however, these days the ski industry affords many more professionals the opportunity to work year-round, shifting over to other seasonal sports such as mountain biking and river rafting, or on-mountain activities in sales, marketing, and operations. Others follow the snow, working in Australia and South America when the lifts shut down in the Northern Hemisphere.

The dynamics of the industry go beyond sport and play. Every major ski company, Jensen noted, has to work in partnership with the community. "We have to be concerned how to create a relationship with the community so we can move together. One can't move without the other." This means that mountain resorts are very involved in environmental matters, community affairs, and governmental affairs.

Another issue has to do with the big-business aspects of finance and, increasingly, being a publicly traded rather than privately owned company. "Vail was the first pure resort to play as a public company. The challenge is to be a public company in the ski industry. We have an asset, but, like owning Yankee Stadium, the underlying value of the asset isn't reflected in the stock price."

The transition has challenged the ski industry to become more sophisticated in marketing and management, and to forge closer alliances with partners and sponsors. Today, the job titles that are emerging at ski companies include Tactical Marketing Manager, Webmaster, International Sales Manager, Environmental Manager, Resort Services, Resort Planning and Development Manager, and Risk-Management Director. Meanwhile, jobs like Mountain Manager, Grooming Manager, Lift Maintenance Manager, Race Coordinator, Ski Patrol Director, and Ski School Director have become unique specialties.

The Challenge of the Slopes

The greatest challenge for those who want a career in the ski industry is not the vertical of the slope, but managing to live on a relatively low salary compared to the cost of living elevated by a resort area.

"Pay in the ski industry is still significantly lower than others. It is changing, but slowly," reported Dr. Aaron S. "Woody" Liswood, Director of Sierra Nevada College's Ski Business and Resort Management Program. "People still work partially because it is a lifestyle choice and partially because it's a career choice." In only a few instances does the resort company provide some kind of subsidized employee housing; in others, employees have to travel long distances, often in bad weather and difficult roads, to get to work. (On the other hand, ski resorts have proved leaders in making child care available to employees.)

Another element that makes the industry different is the environment the sites are in—typically national forest land or a preserve. Master planning means working with the Environmental Protection Agency and the U.S. Forest Service, as well as working to get the community on board, which typically battles against further development. Liswood further points to the uniqueness of running an on-the-mountain type of business. Unique concerns include

- How you organize and manage the ski patrol, ski school, and grooming.
- How you staff, what you pay, what skills are necessary.

- How many people it takes to run a lift, and the implications of running with more or fewer people.
- What it costs to staff all departments.

"What are the safety implications?" asked Dr. Liswood. "In the ski industry, safety is absolutely critical. People can die easily. You have a life-or-death responsibility on the mountain. You won't find that in a typical resort. Those folks out there make decisions that save peoples' lives all the time. They work in terrible conditions, sometimes. That's one of the attractions of that job."

That is also a key reason why so many people who have worked up to General Manager have come out of the Ski Patrol, such as Ridge Morehead, General Manager of Monarch.

> **INSIDE SECRET:** Working on the ski patrol requires intense dedication and decision-making skills. As a result, many people have worked up from ski patrol to become General Manager of a ski resort.

Another key concern for ski industry managers is that "it is not as capital-intensive as it is labor-intensive," Dr. Liswood said. "Because it is labor-intensive, labor costs are astronomical, even at the rates we pay compared to revenue. We can't keep raising ticket prices—the public has balked." Ski areas are being challenged to find other ways to generate revenue without raising lift prices.

Ski Industry Faces Challenging Landscape

The continual challenge facing the ski industry is that the number of skiers (people who have skied or snowboarded within the past two years)—21 million—is less than 10 percent of the population, and seems to be stuck on a plateau. The ski industry generates nearly $2 billion in revenues on about 52 million skier visits, and pays out $400 million in salaries. The 100 largest ski resorts collectively employ more than 100,000 employees. The 27 members of Colorado Ski Country USA alone attracted 10.8 million skier/

snowboarder visits in 2000 and employed 7,500 people year-round, 12,000 in high season.

There are just over 500 ski areas (10 percent fewer than in 1990); only about 100 of them are true destination resorts—places people come to from outside the immediate area and stay at least one night. Because of the high costs of operating ski areas and the increasing pressure to offer a full complement of ski and non-ski activities to attract the sophisticated, affluent clientele, smaller areas find they are struggling to survive. The trend has been for ski areas to conglomerate and become multipurpose companies—big businesses.

> **INSIDE SECRET:** Four companies—Vail Resorts, American Ski Company, Intrawest, and Booth Creek—own the bulk of the largest mountain resorts and offer the greatest opportunity for industry employment.

Because skiers are discerning—they go where the snow is most consistently the best—ski companies have had to invest enormous sums on snow-making and grooming, and faster, state-of-the-art lifts, which adds an extra technological dimension to this industry. And like most other facets of the travel industry, the demands of sophisticated reservations/computer systems and e-commerce (more and more resorts offer online bookings capability and "virtual" tours in addition to one-stop-shopping reservations centers) put greater emphasis on computer technology, as well.

> **INSIDE SECRET:** Not surprisingly, some of the best opportunities at mountain resorts today are in Internet-related jobs, including Information Systems Management and Webmaster.

Easing Off a Plateau

Despite an investment of hundreds of millions of dollars, the ski industry has had a fairly stagnant base of skiers for the past 10 years, a cause for major concern for an industry that banks heavily on growth. There is an industry-wide effort to "grow" new skiers through "learn to ski" promotions and special events, and family packages and programs to get children on skis. The industry is also working to engage others in snowboarding, snow skates, and other downhill innovations, as well as cross-country skiing and snowshoeing. It is introducing nonski activities such as spas and athletic centers; and programs targeting women, seniors, disabled skiers, and most recently, a renewed focus on "singles." To further diversify, the most sophisticated resorts are moving to develop entirely new markets such as incentive, conventions, and meetings business, and to entice the international market (particularly Europeans, Asians, and South Americans).

The industry has also made a greater effort to reach new skiers through the mainstream travel industry—tour operators and travel agents—resulting in more marketing and sales professionals with ties to this segment. Travel agents can reach potential skiers in their locality and suggest a ski vacation; can overcome objections and obstacles (as they do for cruises); can recommend a suitable ski destination based on needs, wants, and budget; and provide the convenience of one-stop shopping. Tour operators accomplish three critical functions: they bring down the cost of skiing (a major impediment) and reduce the confusion and complication of booking all the different elements of a ski trip (air, ground transportation, lodgings, lift tickets, lessons, and equipment) by packaging all the elements, which they have purchased at negotiated rates; they spend money to promote the ski destinations in local markets; and they help advise travel agents as well as skiers on the best choices for their particular interests.

INSIDE SECRET: Some of the largest of the ski tour operators include K&M Rocky Mountain Tours (www.skithewest.com); Advance Reservations, Park City, Utah; Moguls Ski and Snowboard Tours, Colorado; and Any Mountain Tours, Arlington, Virginia.

More significantly, mountain resorts are forging ties to airlines, which are important ski packagers but also provide the all-important "lift" to these often hard-to-reach areas at a fare that makes the package affordable.

Increasingly, ski resorts have formed their own travel agencies and tour operations in order to better reach consumers with one-stop shopping and competitive rates. They have gone so far as to subsidize direct air services on major airlines, such as American, United, Continental, and Delta, into local airports in the competition to get skiers to the slopes the fastest, most convenient, and economical way.

Children's programs continue to present a huge opportunity for jobs (the idea being to not only make it easier for parents to ski, but to "hook" the little ones on snow sports early so that they will be the skiers of the future). A decade ago, children's ski programs had to fight for recognition within a ski resort; marketing was instead targeted to singles and young executives. More than a decade of concerted focus on families, with the development of outstanding nurseries, day camps, ski schools, and family activities, has successfully shifted the balance, with the result that families are now the biggest single segment of the ski market. Indeed, parents with their children generated 43 percent of 11.4 million visits in 1999 to Colorado ski resorts, by far the largest segment of the skier market. The result is that ski resorts are shifting their focus somewhat back to the "singles" market.

INSIDE SECRET: The emphasis on children's ski programs has increased demand for Infant Caretakers, Activities Directors, and Ski Instructors who can connect with children.

More Than Just Skiing

Back in the 1950s and 1960s, ski areas were precisely that: places people went to ski. Now, more and more are emerging as true destinations with a full range of snow sports as well as nonski activities to appeal to skiers and nonskiers alike, such as world-class spas, jeep tours, llama tours, dogsledding trips, indoor sports facilities (such as tennis, racquetball, swimming, and rock-climbing walls), ice skating, shopping, and dining.

Areas once totally dependent on winter and snow are actively diversifying, developing summer activities and programs to expand the season, keep people employed, and keep money coming in year-round. Many, like Stratton in Vermont, have developed tennis and golf academies. Winter Park, Colorado; Deer Park, Utah; and Mt. Snow, Vermont have established themselves as mountain-biking centers. Telluride, Colorado, opened a golf course and a world-class spa. Attitash, New Hampshire, has alpine slides and waterslides and gives gondola rides. Other areas, such as Aspen, Vail/Beaver Creek, and Telluride, have cultivated music, dance, film, and cultural festivals. Aspen/Snowmass, Colorado, has developed culinary and wine events, while Keystone, Colorado, specializes in conventions and meetings in the summer.

Adaptive Sports Programs

Several major ski resorts, such as Winter Park in Colorado and Windham in New York, offer excellent adaptive sports programs. These programs are not only for skiing; they have expanded to other sports in other seasons, as well. Winter Park is the home of the National Sports Center for the Disabled, which handles 3,000 students a year from throughout the world (47,500 since 1970, when the program was founded), offering instruction to children and adults with almost any type of disability, including visual impairment, paraplegia, mental disabilities, amputation, stroke, cancer, cerebral palsy, hearing impairment, and multiple sclerosis. Winter programs include downhill skiing, ski racing, snowboarding, snowshoeing, and cross-country skiing, while summer programs include whitewater rafting, sailing, therapeutic horseback riding, rock climbing, hiking, adaptive cycling, mountain biking, camping, fishing, and in-line skating. (For more information, contact the NSCD at 970-726-1540; www.nscd.org.)

> **INSIDE SECRET:** If you have an interest in working with the disabled, the adaptive sports programs developed at ski resorts are ideal.

Environmental and Legal Opportunities

Since a formidable obstacle to mountain resort development arises from local environmentalists and the need to work with federal and state authorities, there are important opportunities for government/public affairs specialists. (The President of one ski company was a former Associate Director of the National Park Service.) Planning development departments include Environmentalists, Legal Specialists, and often Community Liaisons.

The ever-increasing cost of insurance and exposure to liability, and the decline in leisure time and discretionary dollars are also challenges to be overcome by the ski industry, and result in demand for Risk-Management professionals.

 # Why Choose the Ski Industry?

The ski industry draws people who are committed, even fanatical, about skiing and the outdoors. "You get to ski, to live and work amid incredible scenery, in the outdoors, in pure air, working with people who tend to be active, outgoing, energetic, and delivering a service that makes people feel happy," commented one industry executive.

"I worked 70 to 90 hours a week for 26 years and there was never a day that I didn't want to go to work," said Jensen of Vail Resorts.

 # Jobs in the Ski Industry

Every ski area has a Marketing Department, Group Sales, Advertising and Public Relations, a General Manager or President, and people in various services, including Food & Beverage, Ski School, Ski Patrol, Guest Services, and Nursery and Day Care.

There is usually a Maintenance Division, including a Director of Lift Maintenance and Vehicle Maintenance, Grooming, a Snowmaking Supervisor, and a Mountain Manager.

Other departments might include Sales or Rental Management of Real Estate, Property Management, Hotel Operations, Retail Travel Agency or Tour Department, and Finance.

There also are usually risk management, retail, and clerical positions. Emerging specialties include community affairs and government affairs, as well as travel specialists.

Best Bets

- International Sales Manager
- Marketing Director
- Corporate Sponsorships Manager
- Group Sales Coordinator
- Environmental Manager
- Resort Services
- Resort Planning and Development Manager
- Risk-Management Director
- Mountain Manager
- Grooming Operations Manager
- Lift Maintenance Manager
- Ski Patrol
- Ski School Director
- Day Care Supervisor
- Webmaster
- Government Relations Manager

And specialties have changed. Food & Beverage used to consist of cafeteria-style arrangements; now many resorts get into elaborate restaurants and functions, such as sleigh-ride dinners. Marketing and Sales now also address corporate, group, and incentive markets, as well as international markets.

Salaries in the Ski Industry

Salaries vary considerably depending on the size of the ski area and its geographical location, but generally are on the low side even for the travel industry.

But benefits abound, including free skiing for the family, reduced-rate child care, health club membership, and (occasionally) free food. A few resorts provide subsidized housing for seasonal employees, but the problem with ski areas is that housing costs tend to be high, or you have a far commute, often in bad weather.

Median Ski Resort Salaries, 2000

Title	All Resorts	Largest Resorts
Administration		
General Manager	$90,000	$142,000
Ticket Sales Director	$35,000	
Shuttle Bus Driver	15,000	
Human Resources Director	$49,000	$60,000
Lodging Director	$61,000	
Sales Director	$51,000	$57,000
Special Events Manager	$27,000	$35,000
Public Relations Director	$44,100	$56,000
Marketing Director	$58,000	$77,000
MIS Webmaster	$30,000	
MIS Director	$54,000	$63,000
Reservations Director	$42,000	
Guest Services Director	$39,000	$63,000
Operations		
Mountain Manager	$47,000	$75,000
Director—Vehicle Maintenance	$48,000	
Grooming Director	$41,000	
Building Maintenance Director	$49,000	

Title	All Resorts	Largest Resorts
Operations		
Food & Beverage Manager	$32,000	
Rental Director	$39,000	$63,000
Ski Patrol (experienced)	$20,000	$25,000
Ski Patrol Director	$29,000	$50,000
Child Ski School Director	$22,000	$35,000
Adaptive Ski School Supervisor	$23,000	
Ski School Director	$40,000	$60,000
Race Manager	$30,000	
Snowmaking Director	$49,000	

Source: National Ski Areas Association: Industry Salary and Benefit Survey, Spring 2000, conducted by Sierra Nevada College/Ski Business and Resort Management Program, Aaron S. Liswood, Director.

Your Ticket into the Ski Industry

Like so many prominent executives in the ski resort industry, Paula Sheridan, Vice President of Marketing for Winter Park, Colorado, started her career as a Ski Instructor. After seven years of that, she seized an opportunity to become the first woman on Winter Park's Ski Patrol. She moved over into "Risk Management"—investigating accidents, interviewing people, and taking pictures. "Then, when I wanted more of a mental challenge versus a physical challenge, I moved over to management as a Communications Coordinator," said Sheridan, who knew she liked to write. Starting out as an Assistant, she anticipated some on-the-job training; but three months later, the Director left and she had the "sink or swim" option of taking over, or facing perhaps 10 years before she had another shot.

Ceci Gordon started out her career in the ski industry answering phones and mailing brochures at Mt.

Cranmore in North Conway, New Hampshire, and in less than five years rose to Director of Marketing.

"You get your foot in the door and then rise up," Gordon related. "Most companies are not as interested in your background as the type of person you are. You can work seven days a week, 20 hours a day for five months. It requires a person with personality and drive; you can learn marketing, management, and how a lift runs."

"The industry isn't that old—only 55 years. So many people who started out with a ski area are now managing it," said Gordon, who has since gone on to a public relations company representing the United Ski Industries Association.

Kent Myers epitomizes the second key path into the ski industry: through Property Management. He started as Director of Property Management for Copper Mountain Resort, Colorado, then rose up by moving from one ski company to another: to Winter Park, where he was Director of Sales and then Vice President of Marketing; then to Steamboat Ski Corporation, where he innovated the first direct-air program into a ski resort; and then to Vail, where, as Vice President of Marketing for Vail Associates, he introduced direct air programs as well as a full in-house tour operation.

Lift operations, ski school, and property management are still key ways to get into ski resort management. Increasingly, however, ski areas are reaching outside—to other industries (from within travel, including hospitality, airlines, cruise lines, and theme parks, as well as from other industries entirely) and to university programs—for marketing, sales and finance, hotel operations, and entertainment professionals.

Roadmap to the Top

Robert Gillen, former Assistant Vice President of Corporate Communications for Crested Butte, Colorado, and now with a public relations company that handles Stowe, Vermont, is one who sees a bright future for the ski industry and for career opportunities for professionals. "The ski bum is on the endangered list. Continued maturation of the ski industry means growing professionalism. There is demand for professionals from business, sales, public relations, advertising, and a lot of flushing out of the hale and hardy ski bums. You have to make a commitment over a few years. You sacrifice income for the view. And you have to work hard—salespeople work 60 to 70 hours a week sometimes," he said.

But you do get to ski. Gillen, who came to the ski industry by way of *Ski* magazine, purchased new ski boots because they were easier to get on, so that he could be out the door of his office and on the slopes in 10 minutes flat. He managed to ski 100 days one season.

"The industry has become more sophisticated," said David Ingemie, President of Snow Sports Industries America. "It's still entrepreneurial, but as the industry matures, business practices are becoming more sophisticated in terms of marketing, accounting, strategic planning, and opening up new specialties and tiers of management. It's still a career path for ski bums, but for the most part, management is chosen from specialized fields such as real estate, accounting, customer service, travel operations, public relations.

"It's the kind of business where you either stay a season or two, or a lifetime," said Ingemie.

Vail Resorts

Vail Resorts is widely regarded as one of the largest and most forward-looking ski companies in the country. Vail Resorts employs some 11,000 people among its four resorts (Vail, Beaver Creek, Breckenridge, and Keystone); 3,350 at Vail in winter and 1,100 in summer.

Like many of the major ski resort companies, Vail has developed a rich array of summer programs to balance out seasonality: It created a music festival and a special children's camp, and introduced a Peak Performance program of customized plans similar to Outward Bound experiences, geared to corporate groups. It does a brisk meetings and conventions business, as well.

Vail is organized in six major divisions: Finance, Administration, Marketing (Public Relations, Advertising, and Sales), Real Estate, Hospitality (and Travel), and Mountain Operations.

Besides operating the ski lifts and other ski-related facilities, Vail manages various hotels, condominium units, and homes; has a large real estate brokerage; and handles time-share management. The company now has a full-scale in-house tour company and travel agency (which in winter has 30 Reservationists on staff, down to 2 in the off-season) that sell only Vail products. The travel company has people on staff who negotiate with airlines, transportation companies, lodges, tour operators, travel agencies, and ski clubs. It also has an online booking capability through its Web site, and now employs 16 people in Internet positions.

As one would expect considering Vail's premier position, it pays on the top of the scale—along with Aspen, Deer Valley, and Killington—but still would be considered low-paying relative to other parts of the travel industry.

Vail employs 1,100 Ski Instructors alone—a career in itself—including 175 that only teach children. In addition there are 185 Children's Caretakers, many who are Child Development Specialists, in the nursery and day camp, who oversee some 73,000 kids in a season.

Hospitality is a developing area—including Resident Managers and office personnel. Indeed, Vail is a community of 30,000 "pillows" plus 15 to 20 restaurants. For these positions, Vail looks for people with hospitality (resort) operations experience.

People involved in the technical area—Mountain Management—because it is the most specialized, have the least turnover. Some internships are available, for lifts and for food service.

Every year, Vail recruits 1,000 new people to replace about 25 to 30 percent of the staff.

(For more information, see www.snow.com.)

Ski Education Programs

Sierra Nevada College's Ski Business and Resort Management Program teaches the nuances of how to run a ski resort—not just how to run lifts, but also how to manage master planning, budgeting, and running every department—including hotels and restaurants. People in the program range in age from 18 to their 30s, and include recent high school graduates, people who have consciously made a decision to have a career in the ski industry, career changers, and people who have had some experience in the ski industry and want to enter management.

INSIDE SECRET: Get a lift up in the ski industry by landing an internship during college. Contact your favorite ski area in early fall, right before the areas start their huge employee search and job fairs.

The following are some of the most prominent ski education programs:

- **Colorado Mountain College,** Leadville, Colorado; 719-486-4229; www.coloradomtn.edu.

- **Lyndon State College,** Lyndonville, Vermont; 802-626-6475; www.lsc.vsc.edu.

- **Sierra Nevada College,** Incline Village, Nevada (Lake Tahoe); 800-332-8666; www.sierranevada.edu. B.S. in Business Administration with a major in ski business or resort management.

- **University of Colorado,** Boulder, Colorado; 303-492-4267; http://bus.colorado.edu.

- **Killington, Vermont,** has become a college town. Green Mountain College, the Rome Family Corporation, and Killington Ltd. formed an alliance to bring the Green Mountain College Center to Killington. The new facility will complement the college's flagship campus in Poultney, Vermont. The new center provides educational services and offerings, including cooperative education opportunities with Killington Resort (www.killington.com).

Contacts, Sources, and Leads

- **American Skiing Company,** P.O. Box 450, Sunday River Rd., Bethel, ME 04217; 207-824-8100; www.peaks.com. (*Vermont:* Mount Snow/Haystack; Killington/Pico, Sugarbush. *Maine:* Sunday River, Sugarloaf USA. *New Hampshire*: Attitash Bear Peak. *Utah:* The Canyons. *Colorado:* Steamboat Ski and Resort Corp. *California/Nevada:* Heavenly Ski Resort.)

- **Aspen Skiing Co.,** 40 Carriage Way, Snowmass Village, CO 81615; 800-525-6200; www.skiaspen.com.

- **Booth Creek Ski Holdings,** 1000 S. Frontage Rd. W., Ste. 100, Vail, CO 81657; 970-476-4030; www.boothcreek.com. (*New Hampshire:* Waterville Valley, Mt. Cranmore, Loon Mountain. *California:* Bear Mountain, Northstar-at-Tahoe, Sierra-at-Tahoe. *Washington:* Summit at Snoqualmie. *Wyoming:* Grand Targhee.)

- **Intrawest Corporation,** 800–200 Burrard St., Vancouver, BC V6C 3L6, Canada; 604-669-9777; www.intrawest.com. **Canada:** Whistler/Blackcomb, British Columbia; Mont Ste. Marie, Quebec; Mont Tremblant, Quebec; Panorama, British Columbia; Blue Mountain, Ontario. **United States:** *California:* Mammoth Mountain. *West Virginia:* Snowshoe/Silver Creek. *Vermont*: Stratton Mountain Resort. *Colorado:* Copper Mountain. *New Jersey:* Mountain Creek at Vernon (formerly Vernon Valley Great Gorge).

  Intrawest is building a four-season destination village at Squaw Valley, California. It has a premier timeshare business in Solitude, Utah. It's also in a real estate joint venture with Vail Resorts to develop a village at Keystone, Colorado. Intrawest has a significant investment in Compagnie des Alpes, the largest ski company in the world in skier visits, and Alpine Helicopters Ltd., owner of Canadian Mountain Holidays, the largest heli-skiing operation in the world.

- **Vail Resorts, Inc.,** P.O. Box 7, Vail, CO 81658; 800-404-3535; www.snow.com. (*Colorado:* Beaver Creek Resort, Breckenridge, Keystone, Vail.)

- **National Ski Areas Association,** 133 S. Van Gordon St. #300, Lakewood, CO 80208; 303-987-1111; fax 303-986-2345; www.nsaa.org.

(continues)

(continued)

- **Colorado Ski Country, USA,** 1560 Broadway, Ste. 2000, Denver, CO 80202, 303-837-0793; www.coloradoski.com; representing 27 of Colorado's major ski resorts, keeps a job bank.
- **SnowSports Industries America,** 8377-B Greensboro Dr., McLean, VA 22102-3587; 703-556-9020; www.snowlink.com and www.snowsports.org.
- **Vermont Ski Areas Association, Ski Vermont,** 800-VERMONT, ext. 763; 802-223-2439; fax 802-229-6917; www.skivermont.com, www.ridevermont.com.
- Each region has its own **ski association,** and each major ski area now has its own **Web site** and usually an online job bank. Also, the major ski companies such as American Ski Company, Vail Resorts, Intrawest, and Booth Creek have their own sites and centralized hiring.
- A really excellent Web site for ski and other outdoor/adventure related jobs is **www.coolworks.com**.
- *The National Parks Trade Journal,* published by Taverly Churchill, features opportunities for more than 100,000 positions in national parks, ski resorts, scenic lodges, outdoor schools, and worldwide environmental organizations. Available for $14.95 postpaid from National Parks Trade Journal, Wawona Station, Yosemite National Park, CA 95389.
- Other related fields incorporating skiing, but not at the resorts, include **tour companies** (SkiTops is a membership organization; 916-452-8456; www.skitops.com), **trade associations** (SnowSports Industries America, McLean, Virginia; 703-556-9020; www.snowsports.org), and **suppliers.**

The Spa Resort Industry

Much like ski resorts, spa resorts have emerged as a subset of the travel and hospitality industry and afford people an opportunity to combine lifestyle (a penchant and philosophical devotion to health, fitness, and "wellness") with work.

The opportunities include major resort properties, which offer world-class spas on site, like The Sagamore on Lake George, N.Y.; Marriott's Camelback Inn Resort, Golf Club, and Spa in Arizona; and The Spa at Doral, Miami, Florida. Other specialized spas include

- The Greenhouse, Arlington, Texas, an elite, women-only spa
- Green Valley Fitness Resort and Spa, Utah
- The Golden Door, Escondido, California
- Canyon Ranch Health and Fitness Resort, Tucson, and its sister resort in the Berkshires of Massachusetts
- New Age Health Spa in the Catskill Mountains of New York

Others are classified as new-age retreats, such as the Shoshani Yoga Spa in Colorado. There are adventure spas, such as the Mountain Trek Fitness Retreat and Health Spa in British Colombia, Canada, and The Peaks Resort and Spa at Telluride, Colorado. Spa resorts are located throughout the country and the world; some of the most famous international ones are the Terme di Saturnia in Tuscany and Brenner's Park Hotel in Baden-Baden in the Black Forest of Germany.

Spa resorts are expanding their markets from the staple of women seeking beauty or weight-loss treatments; many are cultivating programs for men, and positioning themselves as places to find stress reduction and rejuvenation. They are cultivating new marketing initiatives, such as programs geared to bridal parties and incentives, which translate into jobs in marketing and sales.

INSIDE SECRET: Market expansion and incentives in the spa industry are creating more opportunities for sales and marketing professionals.

Contacts, Sources, and Leads

- **Spa Therapy,** a site sponsored by the international spa industry, offers online specialist courses as well as a jobs board (www.spa-therapy.com).

- One of the best single sources to find spa resorts is **SpaFinders,** a quasi wholesaler/travel agency/marketing company that offers one of the most comprehensive reservations services, selling to consumers and to travel agents. The company has been on the leading edge of the spa industry, offering gift certificates, incentive programs, partnership programs, and so on. SpaFinders publishes a superb magazine that is more like a directory to the industry. For more information, contact Spa-Finders Travel Arrangements Ltd., 91 Fifth Ave., New York, NY 11003; 800-255-7727 or 212-924-6800; www.spafinders.com.

Other travel companies that specialize in spa programs:

- **Spa Adventures,** 325 W. 45th St., Ste. 910, New York, NY 10036; 800-955-SPAS or 212-399-0700.
- **Spa Traveler,** 13106 NW Germantown Rd., Portland, OR 97231; 800-300-1565.

THEME PARKS AND ATTRACTIONS: THE BUSINESS OF MAKING SMILES AND MEMORIES

To appreciate the role theme parks and attractions play in the travel industry and in local communities, you only have to fly into Florida's Orlando International airport, which has grown tenfold since opening in 1981 and now handles 30 million passengers a year. Then, ride up International Drive, where many of the area's 100,000 hotel rooms and 50 theme parks and attractions have sprung up to cater to 41 million visitors (vacationers and business travelers, both domestic and international) who spend $19.7 billion a year. Then consider that in 1971, the year Walt Disney opened the Magic Kingdom, all that was here were swampland and orange groves.

Snapshot: Theme Parks/Attractions

Showtime! Fantasy! Fun! Theme parks recreate the world in humans' image—fanciful reconstructions of how the world might be—the ideal, the unreal and fantastical. Theme parks are a magical blending of science and art, education, and entertainment.

"It has often been my pleasure to tell people where I work and watch a slow smile creep across their face," said the Director of Association Relations for the International Association of Amusement Parks & Attractions, Alexandria, Virginia. "Even at the association level, the industry has a unique ability to bring joy, entertainment, distraction, and a certain relief from daily cares and concerns to consumers around the world. This is a very rewarding activity."

The theme park industry, consisting of about 450 major parks, may be fun and play to patrons, but it is big, serious multibillion-dollar business. The number of visitors ballooned from 253 million visitors spending $5.7 billion in 1990 to 309 million visitors spending $9.1 billion in 1999. The industry employs 500,000 people on a seasonal or part-time basis, but full-time, career-oriented jobs (about 50,000 of them) are in relatively short supply and high demand.

INSIDE SECRET: Only about 10 percent of the jobs in the theme park industry are full-time, career-oriented positions.

Even at Walt Disney World, more of a complete city than a theme park, only about 3,300—10 percent—of the 33,000 employees are full-time, salaried employees. Similarly, Six Flags, the largest regional park company, has 3,000 full-time employees but 50,000 seasonal workers in all of its parks.

For those who work full-time in a theme park or major attraction, this can be a fantasy come true.

Out of This World

Career opportunities at theme parks and attractions are virtually unlimited. Theme parks are becoming total multiday destination resorts, with more and more offering on-site hotels, shopping, and entertainment complexes, adding experiential and immersive attractions with creative themes. The trends put emphasis on specialists in Finance, Sales Promotions, and

Marketing; and those specialized in licensing and forging partnerships and marketing alliances, e-commerce professionals, Computer Graphics Artists and Engineers, as well as Artists and Designers (the "Imagineers," to use a Disney phrase).

Kerry Graves, for example, specializes in marketing and sales promotions. He started his career as Promotions/Public Relations Director at a local entertainment center, moved on to become an Assistant Director of Marketing at a hotel, then Vice President of Marketing at the Delta Queen Steamboat Company. Then he joined Anheuser-Busch as Marketing Director of Promotions and Corporate Sponsorships, devising such initiatives as the multipark pass program and arranging for Busch Gardens, Tampa Bay, to be the U.S. Olympic Team "Send Off Site" in 1992. He has applied these same skills to the Grand Canyon Railway and to Adventure Entertainment Corporation, which operates 15 water parks and family entertainment centers.

"Entertainment is the common thread," Graves reflected, "whether you are being entertained on board a cruise, a resort, or a theme park…every day is different from the day before. When you lose a day, that is a day of inventory you will never pick up; once it's gone, it's gone. You are always at the mercy of so many different catalysts—weather, gas price hikes—but once you are aware of a potential problem, you try to set up enough contingency programs so you can implement them at a moment's notice. You have to be proactive rather than reactive."

Wish Upon a Star

Walt Disney, the legendary creator of Mickey Mouse, invented the "theme park." Up until 1955 when Disneyland opened, there had been only amusement parks, consisting mainly of rides in a carnival-like atmosphere. Walt Disney, who had two young daughters at the time, sought to create a place where the whole family could experience attractions together. He created themes, story lines that were woven into the costuming, the architecture, and everything connected with an attraction; instead of just plain roller coasters,

there were "Big Thunder Mountain Railroad," an Old West runaway mine train, and Space Mountain.

The vast majority of the approximately 450 parks and attractions that compose the U.S. amusement industry cater to a local market. Of these, about 50 to 100 qualify as destination attractions capable of drawing visitors from regional, national, and international markets. Often, these theme parks are not just features included on a trip, but are the main purpose for a trip, and they are an integral part of the travel industry.

These destination attractions incorporate many travel-related activities, including hospitality, food and beverage, and entertainment. The attractions may have complete travel departments that work with the tour operators, airlines, car rental companies, and travel agents. Many even package their own programs to groups and individual travelers. A major part of their marketing and sales effort is directed toward inspiring tour operators and group organizers to include their attraction. Many also offer conventions and meetings facilities for corporate functions.

A few companies dominate among the largest destination theme parks:

- The Walt Disney Company, Burbank, California: Draws 86 million visitors to Disneyland, Disney World, and Disney's California Adventure, in addition to managing EuroDisney in France and Disneyland in Tokyo.

- Anheuser-Busch, Oklahoma and New York: Has the Busch Parks and Six Flags, and is the largest regional theme park company, with a total of 37 parks throughout the United States, Europe, and Latin America that host 50 million guests worldwide.

- Universal Studios in Orlando and Hollywood.

- Busch Entertainment Corp., St. Louis: A division of Anheuser-Busch, with 10 parks, including two Busch Gardens, four Sea Worlds, and Sesame Place.

Other major players include Knott's Berry Farm, Buena Park, California; Paramount's Kings Island, Kings Island, Ohio; Cedar Point, Sandusky, Ohio;

Santa Cruz Beach Boardwalk, Santa Cruz, California; Hersheypark, Hershey, Pennsylvania; and Dollywood, created by country singer-songwriter Dolly Parton, in Pigeon Forge, Tennessee.

Walt Disney World

Walt Disney World is probably the quintessential theme park. Actually, it's four parks in one: Magic Kingdom, Epcot, Disney/MGM Studios, and Animal Kingdom. It is both the model and the pinnacle for the industry. The largest theme park in the world, Disney World has been elevated to a vacation destination in its own right (indeed, it is frequently included on lists of the most popular vacation places on the planet), and is intimately connected with the travel industry. Disney World has branched out to encompass even more than rides and attractions; it has the Downtown Disney and Pleasure Island restaurant, shopping, and entertainment complexes; sports centers; the Disney cruise ships; major resort and convention facilities; a vacation-ownership program; professional training programs; and as many retail shops as a major mall. It has a massive travel company that packages its own product and sells it to consumers and the trade, a reservations center, and a retail agency. It has a convention services/incentives and meetings department (an expanded activity since Disney opened its own hotels and can now accommodate large meetings). And because Disney World has become one of the most popular places for honeymoons and destination weddings, it even has a wedding-planning division (you can book the chapel as well as Cinderella's glass carriage).

Walt Disney has become a major resort company as well, operating seven hotels with 15,000 rooms, plus a campground and vacation-ownership villas, at Disney World alone.

The scope of what an attraction like Walt Disney World entails is a little clearer when you consider that on any night, there might be 50,000 people living in the on-site accommodations, as many as 100,000 people in the park a day, and 20 million in a year. Disney World is a self-sufficient city complete with its own energy plant, waste facilities, and transportation system; Epcot even grows most of the food served in the restaurants.

Disney World employs more than 1,000 entertainers, including musicians, performers, and technical support people such as set designers. Because theme parks like Disney employ hundreds, even thousands of entertainers, the theme park industry can be an alternative to struggling for a spot on Broadway. Comedian Steve Martin is just one of those who went on to fame and fortune after working at Disneyland. Disney often sends talent scouts on national tours to recruit entertainers.

There are 1,500 "back of the house" culinary professionals ranging from assistants to executive chefs to serve the hordes of hungry park attendees.

Though the "Imagineering" staff—the people who dream up the concepts for rides and attractions—are based in the Burbank, California, headquarters for the Walt Disney Company, there are many operations people in place in Orlando making sure the concepts are actualized.

Disney has a noncredit college program whereby students can spend a semester working at the park, usually in a job related to their major, such as hospitality. Often, those who start at Walt Disney World as college students working during the summer or a season go on to a career there. Dick Nunis, President of Walt Disney Attractions, is one who started as a college student working during the summer.

Disney offers a management-development program through (what else?) the Disney University.

There's a strong effort to hire from within; occasionally, for jobs that require a certain specialization that would have to be acquired elsewhere, people are hired from the outside.

An example of "hiring from within" is the Executive Chef at Epcot, Keith Kehoe, who started at Walt Disney World in 1971 as a Burger Chef and rose to the highest position in culinary, Executive Chef. Kehoe was put into a culinary development program and learned under some top chefs. Now Walt Disney World has a culinary apprentice program affiliated with the American Culinary Federation (which sets out guidelines for culinary development), so budding chefs can become ACF certified at Disney World.

Other unusual career paths: Disney has nearly 500 people who work in horticulture and landscaping, plus Woodcarvers and Costumers.

Disney approaches personnel hiring as "show business—you are cast for a role." Hence, the personnel office is called the Casting Center. For more information

(continues)

(continued)

on job openings, contact the Casting Center, 1515 Buena Vista Dr., Lake Buena Vista, FL 32830.

Now Disney is being called on to work its magic in Anaheim, California, as it did in Orlando. The opening of Disney's California Adventure theme park, a $1.4 billion expansion to Disneyland Resort, means not only the revitalization for Anaheim, but also some 7,000 new jobs at the theme park, plus the 750-room Disney's Grand Californian Hotel, and a Downtown Disney complex. The new jobs are in categories including Convention Services, Food Operations Engineering, Costuming, Food and Beverage, Resort Transportation/Parking, Information Systems, Security, Recreation, Guest Services, Creative Services, Sales and Marketing, Finance/Business Planning, Nurses, Travel and Leisure, Human Resources, Merchandise, Hotel Operations, Store Operations, Attractions, and Custodial. For more information, check in with Disney Casting, Disneyland Resort Staffing, P.O. Box 3232, Anaheim, CA 92803-3232; fax 714-781-1616; www.Disneycareers.com.

The leader of the design team for the development of Disney's California Adventure, Barry Braverman, is proof of the eclectic quality of professional backgrounds that have a role in theme parks. He started his career as an elementary school teacher working with educationally handicapped students. He brought that background to Disney, developing Disney educational products, exhibits, and a children's activity center. He joined Walt Disney Imagineering in 1977 as a research analyst for Show Design and Business Affairs; in 1980, he took on the role of show producer for Image Works, an interactive art and technology playground in Journey into Imagination at Epcot. Next came leadership on a concept team working on a project creating prototypes of innovative game systems. He left Disney in the mid-1980s to form a consulting company specializing in interactive media for museums, toy companies, and educational publishers (which explains how museums are coming to resemble theme parks), but returned to Imagineering to become the show producer for Wonders of Life, which opened at Epcot in 1989. He became the executive director of the Epcot Design Studio, responsible for creative direction of all design work on Epcot attractions, and was a principal

contact with corporate sponsors (signing major deals with Coca-Cola, American Express, Kodak, Nestle, AT&T, General Motors, and Exxon). All of this put him in a good position to become the "producer" of the new theme park.

(See disney.go.com for more information.)

Theming: An Emerging Industry

Theming has become so important to parks, attractions, and entertainment centers that it has burgeoned into an industry in its own right and is becoming known as *location-based entertainment,* which includes theme parks as well as other forms of entertainment. Theming is being used at all levels, from the most sophisticated theme parks to mom-and-pop operators. The growth in this activity is spawning whole new categories of job titles in areas including technical design, graphics design, set design, scenic design, and engineering. Indeed, it has spawned its own trade association, Themed Entertainment Association, an international alliance of professionals in the location-based entertainment industry: Concept Designers, Writers, Architects, Operations Experts, Filmmakers, Set Builders, Audio/Video System Designers, and full-service companies who can oversee the project.

Positions combine art as well as education. For example, the job of Entertainment Designer encompasses architecture, media technology, and storytelling; projects combine art and engineering, theatrical elements, a sense of guest experience, and the reality of budget requirements.

INSIDE SECRET: Theming is the most significant trend in the industry, affecting every level from the major parks to location-based entertainment centers. It is spawning new job titles in design and engineering, as well as a trade association.

Attractions

The attractions industry is harder to pinpoint than theme parks. There are attractions just about everywhere. Attractions range from natural, like the Grand Canyon, to manmade, like the Empire State Building, to historical, like the Alamo, to supernatural. They can be zoos, caves, historic buildings, national parks such as Yosemite, shopping malls, theaters, museums, even factories—anything that draws visitors. Hundreds of major attractions are members of the National Tour Association or the Travel Industry Association, which brings them together with tour operators that bring in such a large proportion of visitors.

Colonial Williamsburg in Williamsburg, Virginia, for example, draws about 1.2 million visitors a year, and in many ways has become the anchor of an attractions industry centered in Williamsburg much like Disney World has been to Orlando. As Colonial Williamsburg developed and drew more and more visitors, other attractions such as Busch Gardens, Kings Dominion, and even other historic attractions like Jamestown and Yorktown have developed. Today there are 10,000 hotel rooms in the area to cater to visitors.

Williamsburg had been the capital of the Virginia Colony, but after the Revolution, the capital was moved to Richmond, where it languished. Then, in 1926, John D. Rockefeller Jr. sought to restore Williamsburg to the days of its greatest glory. He contributed $68 million for the preservation of 88 original structures that had survived from Colonial times to the present, and the reconstruction of another 50 buildings, and to acquire additional property to create a protected historic area. What he accomplished then would be unaffordable today.

Colonial Williamsburg is not a theme park, but the largest outdoor living history museum interpreting 18th-century American colonial history. It consists of 500 buildings altogether. Indeed, about 100 of the buildings are occupied, rented out to employees, relatives of employees, and visitors.

Some 3,500 people work at Colonial Williamsburg, including its five hotels and 11 restaurants—in 850 job titles that range from typical hospitality specialties (golf maintenance, health and fitness club people, tennis support people, and hotel management) to the historic side. There are 800 people who are historic interpreters (300 of whom are character interpreters) who wear 18th-century dress and basically stay in the character of the Colonial Williamsburg resident they are portraying. Trades people include blacksmiths, shoemakers, silversmiths, and carpenters. Colonial Williamsburg generally recruits these people, such as wheelwrights, through a national search, frequently advertising in specialty magazines. The apprentices are technically "entry-level" and may take six to eight years to learn their craft and rise up to a journeyman.

For the people who dress and live the part of an 18th-century colonist, it's easy to lose track of time; but the bulk of employees are very much a part of the 21st century, wrestling with contemporary issues such as human resources, marketing and sales, information systems, publications, clerical support, educational programming, and special events. Considerable sales, marketing, and public relations activity is directed to the travel market as a source of needed revenue, particularly as contributions from government and other funding sources fall off and overhead increases. Positions in these areas (which are very 21st century) include hotel sales and conference planning.

INSIDE SECRET: Many attractions have their own jobs lines. For example, Colonial Williamsburg's, at 804-220-7129, is available 24 hours daily.

Other living-history destinations include Plimouth Plantation; Old Sturbridge in Massachusetts; and Mystic Seaport, Connecticut; and the Henry Ford Museum and Greenfield Village, Michigan.

Cultural Tourism

Broadway Theater, Radio City Music Hall, the Metropolitan Museum of Art, and Lincoln Center are all in the tourism business. Cultural and Historic Tourism is one of the more popular sectors of the travel industry.

You only have to peruse the Travel Industry Association directory to get a sense of the scope of entities that are part of the mosaic: Bubba Gump Shrimp Co., San Clemente, California; Bloomingdale's, New York; Chicago Symphony Orchestra; Corning Glass Center and Museum, Corning, New York; Jack Daniel Distillery, Lynchburg, Tennessee; Union Station, Washington, D.C.; and Mall of America, Bloomington, Minnesota.

> **INSIDE SECRET:** Cultural tourism is an area where you can be proactive and make your own job; major cultural institutions are relying more and more on revenue from out-of-towners, but are only beginning to put staff in place to deliberately market and sell to the visitor industry.

A recent survey by the Travel Industry Association found that 53.6 million adults said they visited a museum or historical site in the past year and 33 million U.S. adults attended a cultural event such as a theater, arts, or music festival. Cultural and historic travelers spend more, stay in hotels more often, visit more destinations, and are twice as likely to travel for entertainment purposes than other travelers.

Indeed, more than half the summer theatergoers in New York are from out of town; advance bookings from incoming visitors help keep shows going in the early months and sustain it through the run. In New York City, cultural attractions have been found to be a key motivation for making the trip among the 38 million visitors; exhibits like "King Tut," "Impressionist Painters," and "Van Gogh" at the Metropolitan Museum of Art draw tourists from throughout the world. Opera festivals are the basis of many tour programs.

At the same time, cultural institutions, facing critical funding cuts from government and private sources, have looked to the travel industry to help increase their revenues from attendance and have become more deliberate in their dealings with the travel industry. The New York City Opera, the Museum of Modern Art, Carnegie Hall, and the Brooklyn Museum go so far as to have people on staff who are travel industry specialists, responsible for developing packages and marketing programs.

This is a whole new field for a travel professional—promoting tourism at a cultural institution. The importance of the cultural tourism market is demonstrated by a study by the Cultural Assistance Center and Port Authority of New York and New Jersey. It showed that 1,900 arts institutions entertained an annual audience of 64 million people in the metropolitan area, 13 million of whom visited from outside the region. Of the visitor audience, nearly half came to the region specifically for the arts and stayed an average of two days. In addition, another 15.6 percent extended their stay by an average of two days in order to attend cultural events—representing enormous incremental revenue to the localities.

The study estimated that $1.6 billion was generated by the expenditures of visitors who come primarily for, or extend their stay for, arts and culture and from the portion of the proceeds of touring companies that are returned to the metropolitan economy.

Besides employing travel professionals to draw visitors into their cultural institutions, many theater and dance companies and even art shows utilize the services of travel professionals to coordinate their tours.

Why Choose Theme Parks/Attractions?

"There really is something about putting smiles on people's faces," reflected Tim O'Brien, Parks and Attractions Editor for *Amusement Business* magazine. "Whenever you talk to someone who is at the top of a park and ask why they are putting in 18-hour days for six months at a stretch, they point you to the exit and say, 'Look at the smiles on people's faces as they walk out.' The ones who do well in this industry are the people who love it for what it is."

For those who make a career in theme parks, there is great satisfaction that they are creating smiles as well as forging lifelong memories. And there is no small measure of being able to feel like a kid, like a toy maker who is in love with toys.

The work can be an intense, high pressured business—a roller-coaster ride of sorts—assaulted by the strains of a huge capital outlay, demand for seasonal labor, sharp swings in cash flow, and heavy dependence on conditions ranging from the weather to the state of the economy, as well as the overriding concern to maintain a safe facility. Largely because of the preoccupation with safety, most workers (such as the ride operators) have to stick to a strictly prescribed script that includes what to say, where to be, and what to wear or not (like not wearing ponytails or earrings while operating a ride).

On the other hand, theme parks afford an incredible opportunity for people to be creative in everything from designing rides and imaginative menu options, to sales promotions, special events, and marketing alliances. Those who are committed and persist can rise to fantastic heights. Theme parks and attractions afford an alternate career path for rare specialties—everyone from agronomists to animal trainers, engineers to entertainers, and chefs to computer graphics artists.

 # Jobs in Theme Parks/Attractions

Probably the most eclectic category of travel, the theme park/attractions industry employs everyone from Actors, Artists, Agronomists, and Animal Trainers to Web Programmers and Zoologists. General categories of employment include the following:

- General manager
- Operations
- Marketing
- Public relations
- Food service and hospitality
- Purchasing/logistics/inventory
- Maintenance
- Finance

Particular specialties include Engineering, Safety, Security, MIS, Training, and Personnel Management. Some of the more innovative parks are adding Product Development and Market Research Specialists. Other distinctive opportunities are in Licensing, Retailing and Store Operations, and Government Relations. The largest companies also have Site Planners and Developers, and Real Estate Development and Management.

Best Bets

- Global Sales Manager
- Manager of Corporate Sponsorships and Partnership Marketing
- Incentive Sales and Corporate Sales
- Product and Sales Development Manager
- Productivity and Process Improvement Manager
- Financial Planner
- Games and Attractions Manager
- Information Technology Manager
- Technical Designer
- Training and Recruitment Manager
- Director of Employee Experience

Sales and marketing can also include Meeting Planning and Incentives, since some of the major parks also are used as convention sites and for incentive awards. And of course, the industry that owes as much to P.T. Barnum as to Walt Disney makes ingenious use of sales promotions.

Here are detailed job descriptions for several major jobs in theme parks:

- **General Manager:** Has Profit & Loss accountability, cash control, and corporate asset management expertise. Requires excellent staff recruitment, training, team-building, and mentoring background. Proven creative marketing, promotion, and sales skills. Significant large-facility operations management. Able to operate effectively in a multitask environment. Requires strong strategic planning and budgeting skills and independent, confident, and results-oriented management style. Total customer service and quality focus. Requires three years of experience.
- **General Manager** (small park): Responsible for Profit & Loss accountability, cash control, staff

recruitment and training, marketing and sales, strategic planning, and budgeting skills.

- **Director of Employee Experience:** Oversees all Human Resources functions including hiring, training, benefits, employee relations, compensation, and labor laws. An understanding of the industry's cultural issues is also required. Requires five to eight years of experience.

- **Entertainment Technician Supervisor:** Manages the entertainment department's operations from show production to daily operation. This covers recruitment, training, and supervision of all technical staff as well as daily supervision of performer, usher, and costume character staff. Responsible for repair, maintenance, and troubleshooting of all entertainment technical assets. Provides pivotal support in the planning and execution of all special events and activities. Assists in managing the departmental operating budget, with particular attention to managing labor resources and ongoing supply costs. Works closely with performers, ushers, and technical staff, overseeing daily operation and ensuring that the artistic integrity of the shows is maintained at the highest standards possible. Provides leadership and motivation needed to exceed guest expectations of service and professionalism in all areas of the entertainment department. Requires a minimum of three years of experience.

- **Food and Beverage Catering Supervisor:** Responsible for organizing and delivering the food and drink aspect of all banquets and special events within the park. Oversees the Unit Lead and MCs responsible for the catering operation, including the preparation, handling, and service of food and beverage; overall guest service standards; scheduling; and personnel issues. Responsible for implementing and maintaining all park and legislative policies and procedures. May be asked by the management team to take on particular projects. Requires Bachelor's degree or equivalent experience.

- **Food and Beverage Manager:** Responsible for overall management of food and beverage areas including restaurant, snack bar, concessions, and catering. Experience in supervision, training, menu development, food purchasing, Point-of-Sale/computers, and budgeting required.

- **Manager of Admissions and Guest Relations:** Manages the day-to-day operations of guest entry into the park and all related guest services associated with this position. In addition, this individual must be able to maintain an ongoing working relationship with marketing and group sales. Additional responsibilities are to develop and execute departmental procedures for admissions and guest relations, including cash management, admissions transactions, and guest services; develop and implement operational budgets in areas of responsibility; recruit, train, and manage supervisory staff for admissions and guest relations; collaborate with marketing and group sales to ensure ease of entry for groups visiting the park. Required: Bachelor's degree or equivalent and three years of experience.

- **Digital 3D Artist:** Models real-time 3D animated characters, objects, and terrain. Creates concept art, user interfaces, game design, and development. Requires knowledge of 3D Studio Max and PhotoShop, and prior game-development experience; strong traditional drawing skills a plus.

- **Game Programmer:** Requires a minimum of two years of experience in game development and one to two complete game development cycles. Strong C++ and object-oriented design and architecture methodologies required. Win9x, experience in DirectX, 3D games, 3D graphics, AI and network game programming (TCP/IP, UDP/IP, IPX) a plus. Software Engineering or Computer Science degree required. Two years of game-development experience required.

- **Maintenance Mechanic:** Repairs, maintains, and troubleshoots mechanical, electrical, hydraulic, and pneumatic systems and components. Requires three years of mechanical maintenance.

- **Amusement Rides Coordinator:** Oversees the safe operation and maintenance of the amusement rides. Supervises, trains, and schedules amusement rides staff and volunteers. Works with mechanics, vendors, and staff to ensure proper and safe operation of the amusement rides. Oversees a preventive maintenance program. Responds to inquiries and concerns from the public. Assists in the selection of the rides. Handles cash and may act as Duty Supervisor in the absence of the Amusement Park Supervisor.

- **Safety and Security Manager:** Responsible for directing a coordinated safety effort that includes policy and procedure development, staff training, emergency drills, accident prevention, and ensuring compliance for the entire organization. This position ensures that the living and physical assets are secure from unauthorized intrusion or harm. In addition, this position is responsible for the security of employees and guests. Also responsible for hiring, training, and managing two full-time supervisors, five full-time safety and security officers, 25 temporary safety and security officers, and reception/radio dispatch personnel. Requires Bachelor's degree and four years of experience.

- **Training and Recruitment Manager:** Develops programs, helps build a team to deliver guest service, and makes an impact. Develops and administers new recruitment strategies through visiting labor sources (colleges, high schools, churches, and senior centers), Internet job postings, job fairs, publications, creating flyers and other recruitment materials, and interviews. Creates new training programs for line staff and supervisors; develops rewards and recognition program for staff; oversees scheduling process; meets or beats budget. Continually monitors progress through review of financial statements and internal tracking.

- **Maintenance Director:** Responsible for overseeing all maintenance department functions, including rides, facilities, janitorial, RVs, and vehicle maintenance. Responsible for capital and facility construction projects. Responsible for developing and maintaining department operating budgets.

Responsible for developing qualified team members within all areas of the department. Requires leadership and strong management skills; five years of related park experience; and maintenance knowledge in rides, utilities, and construction.

- **Technical Designer:** Designs and develops components for entertainment scenery and machinery design projects. Conceives elegant and profitable design solutions that enhance the artistic as well as functional goals of projects. Requires computer literacy with AutoCAD, Windows, Excel, and Word3D.

Salaries in Theme Parks/Attractions

Yearly salaries for front-line managers range from $10,000 to $50,000, with an average of $27,679 at facilities overall, according to IAAPA's 1998 Personnel Survey. Middle managers receive between $15,000 and $80,000, with an average of $44,519 annually. For top or General Managers, the annual salary averages $64,177, with a low of $18,000 and a high of $100,000. The following table lists salary ranges for some representative positions:

Salary Ranges for Representative Positions

Title	Salary
General Manager	$60,000–$80,000
General Manager, Small Park	$40,000
Manager of Admissions and Guest Relations	$45,000–$51,000
Digital 3D Artist	$40,000–$70,000
Game Programmer	$80,000–$100,000
Maintenance Mechanic	$16–$20 per hour
Amusement Rides Coordinator	$32,000
Safety and Security Manager	$48,000–$67,000

Your Ticket into Theme Parks/ Attractions

The best way into the industry is to start while in school, as a seasonal worker, and through an internship. Because of the eclectic nature of the industry, there are a wide variety of college programs that are suitable preparation, such as Hospitality, Travel and Transportation, and coursework in fairs and exposition management, special events management, and sports management.

Because of the distinctive technical and creative aspects, however, a number of specialized degree programs have been introduced. For example: The Art Center College of Design, Los Angeles, offers Entertainment and Industrial Design; Carnegie Mellon University, Pittsburgh, offers Entertainment Technology; Art Center at Night, Los Angeles, and Pratt Institute, New York, offer Entertainment Design; Oglebay Entertainment Business Institute, West Virginia, offers Entertainment Management.

Although there is stiff competition for management jobs, some markets face serious shortages of seasonal workers, prompting the industry to adopt a variety of innovative programs including incentives (involving contests and merchandise giveaways); bonuses such as free tickets, subsidized transportation, and gift certificates; bussing people in from inner cities; and recruiting retirees. Some of the attractions hold job fairs or go directly into high schools to recruit.

 INSIDE SECRET: The fastest track into theme parks can be through internships or seasonal work.

Many accomplished executives in the field started out as summer workers, such as Gary Story, President of Six Flags, Inc., Oklahoma City, and Dennis Speigel, President of International Theme Park Services, a Cincinnati-based management and consulting company to the industry.

Speigel began his career as a ticket-taker during the summer at Coney Island Amusement Park in Cincinnati, worked his way up to Assistant Park Manager there, and then went to Kings Island. There he supervised general park operations including personnel, rides, food/beverage, merchandise, and games. He then became the Vice President and General Manager of Kings Dominion/Lion Country Safari in Richmond, Virginia. In addition to overseeing the planning and construction of the park, he administered a $60 million construction budget and managed the park. All of this gave him the broad background needed for his consultancy.

The list of functions that the consultancy provides also shows a blueprint for the theme park industry:

- Feasibility analysis, defining the financial and design planning parameters for a project.
- Developing a comprehensive land-use and master plan, as well as conceptual layout and design layout.
- Pre-opening operational planning (administrative procedures, staffing requirements, and training manuals; food service and merchandising programs; information systems; and operations, maintenance, and safety policies).
- And finally, developing sponsorship programs.

"Imagination is only the beginning," is the slogan at his Web site: www.internationalthemepark.com.

 # Roadmap to the Top

The theme park industry is a step behind the ski industry in requiring specialized college preparation. Most people in senior management roles rose up through the ranks of finance, sales, and marketing, and to some extent operations.

To step up the career ladder, begin with a college preparation similar to Hospitality (such as Cornell University's program) with a focus on finance and business management. Add to that professional training through the International Association of

Amusement Parks (which each year offers a middle-management intensive program at Cornell University, and workshops in conjunction with the annual convention in key areas including law, safety, maintenance, food management, and marketing). To get on a fast track, take advantage of internship opportunities while still in school.

Contacts, Sources, and Leads

- **Association for Living History, Farm and Agricultural Museums,** Judith Sheridan, Secretary/Treasurer, 8774 Rte. 45 NW, North Bloomfield, OH 44450; sheridan@orwell.net. The ALHFAM Web site has links to 80 different sites, as well as job listings (www.alhfam.org/alhfam.jobs.html).

- **The International Association of Amusement Parks and Attractions,** 1448 Duke St., Alexandria, VA 22314; 703-836-4800. The Web site, www.iaapa.org, offers job and internship postings (www.iaapa.org/careers/index.htm), as well as industry information and links to member sites (www.disneycareers.com is a careers section for all Disney companies).

  IAAPA offers professional training and workshops and provides an international student exchange program, which sends students from one country to work on a temporary basis at amusement parks in another, provided the student can demonstrate sufficient linguistic skills and meet other requirements of the program. The association also provides a growing number of training and educational materials. It publishes the most comprehensive annual guide to the industry, *International Directory and Buyer's Guide.*

- **National Tour Association,** 546 E. Main St., Lexington, KY 40508; P.O. Box 3071, Lexington, KY 40596; 606-253-1036.

- **Themed Entertainment Association,** Burbank, CA; www.themeit.com. Has industry news, a job board, and an online members directory.

- **Travel Industry Association,** 1100 New York Ave. NW, Suite 450, Washington, DC 20005-3934; 202-408-8422; fax 202-408-1255.

- An excellent consumer Web site that provides links to theme parks is **http://themeparks.about.com/travel/themeparks/**.

Trade Publications

- *Funworld* (published by IAAPA)
- *Amusement Business* (www.amusementbusiness.com)
- *Park World* magazine
- *Splash* magazine
- *Entertainment Management* magazine (www.entertainment-centers.com)

CHAPTER 9

AIRLINES: RISING LIKE A PHOENIX

Airlines were once the most glamorous facet of the travel industry. But after two decades in which airplane travel has become as ubiquitous as buses were 50 years ago, some of the luster is gone from the "silver birds." But the real appeal of the industry is in its dynamics, like a high-powered, high-pressured, jet-paced game of three-dimensional chess. Also, the ability to take off literally on the spur—like flying off to Switzerland for the weekend to buy a cuckoo clock for a birthday present—becomes matter-of-fact, and yet so addictive that people stay their entire careers in the airline industry, leaving only when they are forced by a layoff, and returning when conditions improve.

Snapshot: The Airline Industry

The airline industry affords several unique jobs, such as airline pilot, and a slew of others that revolve around the industry dynamics and high-flying finance that have come to characterize airline companies. Airlines are arguably the biggest businesses in the travel industry because of the capital-intensive combination of airplanes, computer systems, and the supporting infrastructure. In the airline business, even a penny increase in the price of a barrel of oil can bring an airline to the brink of collapse, and the need to protect a hub from a predator can escalate to a price war with few survivors. Today, although the nuts and bolts of operating the airplane itself have remained essentially the same, the skyscape has been transformed by global alliances, telecommunications, and the Internet.

An Air Race of Global Proportions

President Jimmy Carter's signature on the Airline Deregulation Act of 1978 was like a gunshot signaling the start of the most frantic air race in history.

After decades in which the airlines operated much like utilities with protected routes and regulated pricing, they were thrust into a free market in which they could enter and exit routes virtually at will and charge as much or as little as the market would allow. For the first time, the way was clear for new carriers to rush in with innovative services, fares, and corporate structures that might better suit new and changing markets, while those that could not compete effectively were left to fail.

And rush in they did. Bold, innovative carriers took on the entrenched giants like modern-day Davids and Goliaths. The airline industry had always attracted risk-takers and those with a spirit of adventure—the old barnstorming image—but in the new paradigm, risk came not so much from flying, but from the business itself, affecting entrepreneurs and employees alike. New and old carriers have failed or have been swallowed up in periodic waves of consolidation and expansion, while travelers have had to become savvy in the strategies of "hub-and-spoke" and "frequent-flyer miles."

Prior to 1978, there were only 36 carriers certificated by the Federal Aviation Administration, of which fewer than two dozen are still operating today. If all the carriers that have been certificated since 1978 were still operating, there would be 200 carriers today; however, in 2000 there were 94 scheduled carriers operating, including 13 majors (those that take in more than $1 billion a year in scheduled passenger revenue), 35 nationals, and 46 regionals. Nor are the largest and oldest carriers immune, as the demise of famous names like Eastern Airlines and Pan American prove, while continued consolidation may reduce the number further (such as with United Airlines taking over US Airways and American taking over TWA). Indeed, it is estimated that three "mega-carriers"—American, United, and Delta—control the majority of the market, and each virtually monopolizes travel at its major hubs. Other majors include Northwest, Continental, Southwest, Trans World Airlines, America West, and Alaska Airlines. (At this writing, Delta and Continental were reportedly in talks regarding their own merger.)

A Roller Coaster

The airline business can be a roller coaster, one year posting astronomical profits, the next spectacular losses. The U.S. scheduled airlines scored record operating profits of $7.9 billion in 1999. In contrast, between 1990 and 1995, the airlines posted a combined loss of $13 billion (more than all the profits earned by all airlines since the Wright Brothers made their historic flight at Kitty Hawk in 1903), and 120,000 airline employees got their walking papers.

The airline business is not unlike a three-dimensional chess game. You are selling both a service and a price-sensitive commodity. An airline seat is one of the most perishable products in the world: Once that airplane pulls away from the gate, the seat—the airline's product—is gone forever. This fact puts intense pressure on planners to predict demand months or even a year in advance, forcing them to determine how much capacity (how many seats) to offer, and at what price, in order to attract enough people to cover costs and make a profit. (This is called yield management, which is one of the key growth specialties in the industry.) In fact, demand shifts depending on the time of day, day of the week, and season of the year; there could be as

many as a dozen different fare categories on a single flight, with precise allocation of seats in each category.

> **INSIDE SECRET:** Yield management, combining expertise in financial marketing and systems analysis, is one of the key growth specialties in the airline industry.

Just how critical is effective yield management? TWA used sophisticated yield-management computer systems to analyze 3.6 million fares it set for its 300,000 flights in one year. Using the yield-management programs more effectively boosted revenue by more than $1.5 million on just one route.

But that is not enough. Just when you think you have your market figured out, you have to predict what the competition will do, and the competition is changing all the time. Unlike hotels and factories, which take years to plan and build and cannot be moved from place to place, an aircraft can be shifted almost at will, so the competitive environment facing the airlines changes constantly.

But carriers are not completely free to move in or out of markets. They have to work within parameters. There are only so many "slots" available at an airport. An airline may have a fleet of aircraft that work most efficiently on a certain flight length and that have seating capacity that works best for a particular market. So the transcontinental (New York–Los Angeles) market may be critical for a carrier, and the carrier may resort to "kamikaze" pricing (offering tickets below cost) in order to protect the market from predators.

Airlines are vulnerable to any number of conditions. Fuel is the second-highest expense for an airline after personnel; a penny change in the price of fuel can save or lose a major airline millions of dollars. In 1990, Iraq's invasion of Kuwait and the Persian Gulf War sparked an explosion in fuel prices, from 60 cents to $1.40 per gallon. Every penny change in the price cost the U.S. carriers $150 million (airlines spent $7.8 billion on fuel that year) and contributed heavily to the industry's $2 billion loss.

Changes in the value of the dollar against foreign currencies and interest rates also have dramatic consequences for profits and losses. Strikes, accidents, terrorism, and economic declines all seriously impact the demand for the airlines' services. Indeed, the Persian Gulf War, besides sending fuel costs skyrocketing, caused fear of terrorism, and, coupled with a recessionary economy, sounded the death knell for Eastern Airlines, thrust Pan Am into bankruptcy, and caused TWA to teeter.

But all that changed in the second half of the last decade. In 1999, the carriers celebrated a fourth consecutive record year, handling 635.4 million passengers and generating $84.2 billion in passenger revenue (including $17.2 billion on international flights). They earned another $11.2 billion carrying freight, $1.7 billion carrying the mail, and $3.7 billion in charters, a total tidy sum of $118.2 billion.

The Sky's the Limit at Southwest

Anyone contemplating a career in the airlines should look at Southwest Airlines, which has ranked among the top five companies to work for in a *Fortune* magazine survey. The closest competition, Delta and Continental, have made it only as far as the top 100. "Not only is Southwest a great travel industry company, but it is a great company to work for," said Libby Sartain, Vice President of People (the company's term for Human Resources).

Not only is Southwest a great place to work, but it is a growing place, from its present level of 30,000 employees and 330 airplanes operating to 57 cities. With 290 planes on order, Southwest is forecast to grow by about 10 to 20 percent a year for the next five years, essentially doubling in size by 2005.

The airline will be hiring in all its key categories, including Customer Service Agents at airports (those who sell the tickets and greet passengers at the gates), Ramp Agents (load cargo and baggage and mail), and Operations Agents (responsible for load planning, and analysis of flights and fuel). In addition, Southwest anticipates hiring Flight Attendants at the rate of 30 per plane and Pilots at the rate of 10 per plane. However, because Pilots are required to retire at age 60, and beginning in 2002 many SW Pilots will reach retirement age, the airline will be hiring Pilots not only to compensate for growth, but to replace retirees.

In addition, Southwest will be hiring Reservation Agents in various reservations centers, regional and field sales positions, and at corporate headquarters in Dallas. Key positions are in Revenue Management (those who determine how much to sell a seat for in order to maximize seats sold on each flight), Schedule Planning (where to put planes and at what optimum schedule), and Loyalty Marketing. There is also a small group of professionals in the emerging Marketing Internet Group, where Southwest has been doing as much e-commerce as the largest dot-com companies, at about $1 billion in bookings (Southwest does not participate in Travelocity and Expedia, preferring to have its own site). These are more likely to be marketing people rather than techies.

Similarly, the Loyalty Program (a Frequent-Flyer Rewards Program) is a direct-marketing vehicle to hundreds of thousands of members. There is a whole sales center that caters just to these members. This group also negotiates with other suppliers to offer benefits (prizes), as well as partnership programs so that points earned in one program (such as with a car rental or hotel) earn miles on Southwest.

What truly distinguishes Southwest is its corporate culture, the creation of its innovative (once known as a "maverick") founder Herbert D. Kelleher. "There are a million wonderful things we offer our employees—benefits, social functions. But that's not what makes people love working here," said Sartain. "What makes them love working here is that they feel they make a difference as an individual. Their work is valued. We are very employee-oriented and employee-centered." This includes building in flexibility in setting hours. "Once you get seniority, you can work as much or as little as you want."

Southwest also provides for free, unlimited travel on Southwest for employees and their families (there are employee companion passes, up to four a year, for single employees and for nontraditional families); Southwest employees can also travel on other airlines by paying a nominal charge.

There are some misconceptions about working at an airline. "We have had Flight Attendants get hired and then quit because they said, 'I didn't know I would have to

(continues)

(continued)

travel so much.' The airline business may not be quite 24/7, but it is 20/7. Not many Flight Attendants are home at night (the exception are small, regional carriers). They get on at one place and go home four days later, but then they are off for three days. And working a schedule means you might not be home for Christmas or some special event. You have to work when you are needed."

Salaries are modest to start with, but become good after four to five years and "excellent" after 10 to 15 years. But what is special about Southwest is the profit-sharing program. "With over $1 billion in assets, we are retiring people as multimillionaires who were Flight Attendants and Ramp Agents because our stock has done well."

When hiring, "Southwest looks for unique people: team players; people who are customer oriented, fun-loving, have a good sense of humor, a positive attitude. Skills are important too, but we look for the kind of person who will do well in our environment."

Though many people are content to stay in a particular position for their career, the sky is the limit for someone who aspires to management. "One great thing about Southwest is we have a 'promote from within' policy—all our supervisors and managers are promoted from within. There are dramatic, exciting stories: our new VP of Inflight Services started as a Res Agent 20 years ago and moved through the system; a Maintenance Quality Assurance Supervisor was promoted to VP Maintenance within four years."

(For more information, see their Web site, www.southwest.com, or call 800-SWAJOBS.)

Seesaw in Jobs

There were 330,000 employees working for U.S. scheduled airlines in 1978, just prior to deregulation. By 1999 the number of employees at U.S. scheduled airlines had climbed to 650,000. Of these, 68,200 were Pilots, with 5,500 Pilots hired each year; 14,300 were other Flight personnel; 105,366 were Flight Attendants; 73,675 were Mechanics; 294,549 were Aircraft and Traffic Service; and 100,000 were office and other employees, according to data supplied by the Air Transport Association. Total compensation averaged

$65,341. The scheduled airline industry added a total of 25,300 employees in 1999 to handle increasing traffic and aircraft operations. (In addition to airline employees in passenger-carrying airlines, another 250,000 are employed in the major cargo carriers, including Federal Express, with 150,000; DHL with 53,000; and UPS, with 338,000.)

Despite the growth of the industry, competition for jobs is probably more intense in this segment of the travel industry than any other, so finding a job takes considerable resourcefulness.

Deregulation opened up career opportunities with the scores of new carriers and new types of services that were spawned. And, by radically changing the structure and economics of the industry, deregulation also changed the volume, nature, and even location of employment. Competition brought a sudden demand for Marketers and Revenue and Yield-Management experts, and further spawned Frequent-Flyer Programs, Loyalty Programs, and Customer Relationship Marketing and Data Warehousing. Proliferation of fares and services, all changing at mind-boggling speed, forced a shift toward computerized information and reservations systems—global distribution systems, as they were called before the birth of the Internet and e-commerce. This created demand for computer experts to operate what had become the most sophisticated computer systems ever devised for civilian use. (Such computers were needed to cope with the frantic pace of change; for example, ticket price changes were averaging 70,000 a day, but when Iraq invaded Kuwait, the rate of fare changes soared to as many as 2.5 million a day.) The profit/loss quagmire the carriers found themselves in fostered a need for a new breed of financial whiz.

Cost efficiency became the key to survival in the new environment. The major airlines (carriers doing more than $1 billion in revenue a year), which essentially had always flown point-to-point (city to city in a line), found they could operate more cost-effectively with a hub-and-spoke system, funneling traffic from secondary cities to a central station (hub) for connecting flights. Almost overnight, cities that previously had only limited air service became major hubs—St. Louis,

Dallas, Atlanta—vastly increasing the number of Reservationists, station personnel, and Maintenance people located in these centers. The hub-and-spoke system also proved a windfall for regional and commuter carriers, particularly those that entered into partnerships with the major carriers.

Business or Leisure?

The market for airline travel divides into two roughly equal parts:

- **Nondiscretionary travelers**, primarily people who have to travel for business purposes, who may not be able to book well in advance and are much more concerned about convenient schedules and good service than they are about price.

- **Discretionary travelers**, people traveling for vacation or pleasure or to visit friends and relatives, who are very much swayed by price, can alter their schedules to take advantage of a better fare, and, if they cannot find a fare they like, can choose not to travel.

By balancing out these two markets—discretionary and nondiscretionary travelers—through calculated use of fares, schedules, and routes (an activity called Yield Management), airlines can increase their load factors (the percentage of seats occupied by paying passengers) and maximize the utilization of their fleets, both critical for achieving profitability.

Air Travel Continues to Soar

Despite periodic reversals and the consolidation process going on among airlines, the airline industry as a whole continues to expand. Once air travel was a luxury. Today, airlines are the largest common carrier (that is, commercial transportation). With improved technology, the rise of low-cost airlines, and the proliferation of discount and promotional fares, the cost of airline travel has come down dramatically over the decades, and now competes with bus, rail, and even private automobiles in terms of all the expenses associated with a trip. More than 90 percent of all transportation on common carriers (air, bus, or rail) is on airlines.

Air travel is also expected to increase because of demographics (particularly, the maturing of the Baby Boom generation into their peak earnings and travel years), migration of family members to other parts of the country, a higher standard of living, and increased leisure time. A growing, increasingly global economy means more business travel, as well. (There is even a plan being tested by NASA and Embry-Riddle Aeronautical University in Florida for personal jets that would operate somewhat like cars and use a Small Aircraft Transportation System into smaller, more dispersed airports around the country.)

Hiring Trends

The major forces affecting the travel industry—deregulation, consolidation, technology, and globalization—are nowhere as apparent as in the airline industry and directly affect hiring trends. Deregulation reshaped airline economics and put pressure on marketing and sales; competition then fostered consolidation—mergers, acquisitions, failures—putting emphasis on finance. Now, globalization is producing alliances and outright ownership of airlines by airline companies from other nations. More sophisticated computerized reservations systems give airlines an edge in managing their product and delivering it to the user, increasing demand for computer specialists. The intense scrutiny of the airline industry by the U.S. Congress prompts the need for government affairs and legal specialists.

The roller coaster of profits and losses in the airline industry against a backdrop of economic cycles is reflected in the hiring (and firing) patterns. Between 1980 and 1982, a period of back-to-back recessions in the U.S., the airline industry hired only 1,860 Jet Pilots and only 8,000 Flight Attendants. Then, with the economy rebounding and expanding in 1983 to 1985, the industry hired 14,700 Jet Pilots and more than 30,000 Flight Attendants, according to Airline Economics, Inc. Hiring dwindled again in 1990, when only 7,700 pilots were hired. During the recession of 1991–1994, 120,000 airline people lost their jobs; since then, however, there has been a steady rebound.

In 2000, a total of 19,000 pilots were hired, and the figure is expected to continue on a strong path for the next five years, according to AIR, Inc.

 INSIDE SECRET: Pilot hiring rates are expected to continue on a strong path until at least 2005.

Computer Reservations Systems and E-Commerce

Perhaps the most significant change in the airline industry is computer technology and the employment opportunities the computer has generated.

Because airline seats are some of the most perishable commodities, the ability to sell seats in real time has proved critical. This was accomplished through computer reservations systems. These systems were created in the 1970s, and the direct links they forged between the airlines and their distribution system (travel agents) were at the essence of a dealership type of relationship with agents. In their day, airline reservations computers were the most sophisticated nonmilitary computers in existence.

Several carriers also own outright or have stakes in sophisticated computer reservations systems marketed to travel agents and used by other airlines and travel suppliers (hotels, car rental companies, and tour companies). These include Sabre (which American Airlines has spun off as a separate company); Galileo (formerly Apollo, owned by United); and Worldspan (Delta and others). These operations have become profitable businesses in their own right, with huge computer centers manned by computer programmers, technicians, and sales and marketing people.

However, airline seats—essentially space in time—prove exceptionally well suited to cyberspace, and airlines have been a major beneficiary of the Internet and e-commerce. Several airlines now also have major stakes in e-commerce sites, booking directly with consumers, including Travelocity.com (American),

TravelGalileo.com (United and partners), and Orbitz (Continental, Delta, Northwest, United, and American).

 INSIDE SECRET: Airlines used to depend on travel agencies as their retail outlet; now they are going it alone, using cyberspace to sell air space. As a result, they are hungry for Web-smart professionals.

The Frequent-Flyer Business

Launched in the 1980s by American Airlines, frequent-flyer programs like American's AAdvantage were originally aimed at instilling loyalty, particularly among business travelers, so they would not be lured away by the competition's price cuts (the premise being that air travelers regarded plane seats as commodities, rather than a distinctive service, and would travel on whatever airline offered the cheapest price). The programs worked so well that they have created a new business-within-a-business. Now the airlines sell miles (at two cents a mile) to credit-card companies and others, who repackage them into incentive programs, making air miles the "Green Stamps" of the millennium. Members have accumulated so many miles that, ironically, the airlines have resorted to "auctions" so they can use them to purchase fantasy trips and nontravel items. The airlines rack up more than $1 billion in revenue from the sale of the miles—not too bad considering that the miles can be redeemed only for seats that would otherwise go unsold. These programs now employ Direct Marketers, Customer Service Agents, Customer Relationship Management Specialists, Partnership Marketers, Account Managers, Data Processors, and Incentive Specialists.

 INSIDE SECRET: Frequent-flyer programs provide job opportunities for Direct-Marketers, Customer Service Agents, Partnership Marketers, Account Managers, Data Processors, and Incentive Specialists and are at the center of an emerging field of Customer Relationship Management.

Why Choose the Airline Industry?

"There is an aura to the airlines, a special feeling you have even after you join, even among the administrative and accounting people that never see an airport," said Don Preston, who was US Airways' Director of Personnel Services.

Despite the glamour and the free travel, however, there are cautions. "People interested in the airlines must be aware that it is an extremely volatile business," asserted Fran Hamilton, Manager of Central Employment for TWA. "With deregulation, companies come and go; jobs come and go. This isn't the place for a person who needs security."

Being successful in the airline business, she advised, depends on a lot more than "love people, love travel." She said, "A person must be flexible and resilient; someone who can handle nonroutine and unpredictable situations. There are a lot of technically qualified people who don't succeed because they can't handle the environment. The cultural environment is more significant than technical qualifications."

 INSIDE SECRET: To succeed in a career in the airlines, you need to be flexible, resilient, and willing to relocate.

Employees are frequently asked to relocate. "An airplane can go anywhere," Hamilton explained. "In deregulation, airlines have to respond to keen competition. There is no way of anticipating how long the carrier will be in a market. Routes, schedules, fares, capacity are all shifting fast, and individuals are affected."

Despite the insecurity, there is no shortage of people wanting to plunge into the airline business. One of the reasons jobs are hard to get is that few people leave the airlines voluntarily. Many jobs in the airlines are unique to the airlines, such as Pilot, and salaries are largely based on seniority. A Pilot earning six figures at one airline would face a substantial drop in salary by moving to another.

 # Jobs in the Airline Industry

Though deregulation has created new demand for Marketing, Computer, and Financial professionals, it is still the Pilots, Flight Attendants, Customer Service Agents, Reservationists, Mechanics, and Engineers that account for the vast majority of positions.

Individual airlines vary tremendously in terms of the management style, work environment, and career opportunities they present.

Best Bets

- Customer Service Agent
- Partnership Marketing Manager
- Manager of Internet Distribution
- Global Sales Manager
- Manager of Yield Management
- Manager of Quality Assurance
- Training Manager

Some of the newer positions reflect the growing importance of the Internet and e-commerce, and partnerships and global alliances: Continental Airlines, for example, has a Vice President of Multinational Sales and Revenue Programs and a Vice President of Distribution Planning and Revenue Decision Support.

There are three main categories of personnel:

- Flight operations
- Maintenance and engineering
- Administration, sales, and marketing

Flight Operations

- **Captain:** Commands the aircraft and is responsible for the safety of its passengers and cargo.
- **First Officer:** Assists or relieves the Captain in the operation of the aircraft.
- **Second Officer:** Assists in flight operations and sees that the mechanical and electronic devices of an aircraft are in perfect working order.

These positions require FAA certification.

Jobs are extremely limited and competitive. Often, the carriers' requirements for flight time and equipment necessitate a military career, or may be earned by working with private or corporate aircraft; in addition, airlines prefer a college degree or equivalent. Newer, smaller carriers generally do not require the same amount of experience as the major carriers.

INSIDE SECRET: Embry-Riddle and AirNet Express have a "new-hire bridge" program whereby university graduates become Pilots at AirNet Express.

The cockpit jobs are the most glamorous (although the flying assignments to exotic points like Europe and Asia are few and far between, and short hops around the U.S. are more typical) and well paid (salaries can go to nearly $200,000), but they are jobs that exact heavy demands on lifestyle. "You get up early, wait around the airport, sleep in midday in a strange hotel," said a spokesman for the Air Line Pilots Association. "Pilots tend to be health-conscious: You have to take medical exams once or twice a year and your career can end with a wrong squiggle on an EKG."

Seniority is precious—it not only gets you the highest pay and preference for aircraft, routes, and schedules, but also makes you highest up on the totem pole when a carrier has to furlough Pilots. Consequently, people tend to stay at an airline until their mandatory retirement age of 60. This is not a burnout field; Pilots are passionate about flying and tend to stay their entire careers unless they are forced out for medical reasons or layoffs.

INSIDE SECRET: It is no longer necessary to fly in the military to land a job as a commercial Pilot. Airlines today are also hiring Pilots with requisite hours logged from private services, air taxis, regionals, and commuter airlines.

The military used to be the primary source of airline Pilots, but less so today. Today, many start as private Pilots and become Instructors in order to log the hun-

dreds and hundreds of hours needed to qualify for an air taxi operation, then a regional or commuter airline. After a couple of years and accumulated flight time, they go on to bigger regional airlines and finally to the majors. The path is made easier because there are strong alliances, even ownership relationships, between the majors and regionals (American Airlines, for example, owns American Eagle). Many women now are among the ranks of Pilots.

Cockpits are increasingly computerized, but flying has not gotten any easier. Automation reduces a lot of the workload, but this was mainly to enable airlines to eliminate the third person in the cockpit, the Flight Engineer. On the other hand, flying has become more stressful because of overcrowding at the airport and in the sky and pressure by the company to increase efficiency.

INSIDE SECRET: The best source for cockpit jobs is Aviation Information Resources, Inc. (AIR, Inc.), 3800 Camp Creek Pkwy., Ste. 18–100, Atlanta, GA 30331; 404-592-6500; 800-JET-JOBS; www.jet-jobs.com.

■ Another key flight crew position is the **Flight Attendant**, who is responsible for the safety and comfort of passengers during a flight. Most travelers fail to appreciate the great responsibility for passenger safety Flight Attendants have and the intense training these crew members must undergo.

American Airlines, for example (which looks for public contact work experience and an educational background in English, psychology, public speaking, first aid, language, and home economics when evaluating candidates), gives a five-week training program at American's Learning Center in Fort Worth, Texas. Immediately following training, new Flight Attendants are assigned to a U.S. city (such as New York City or Chicago). Seniority determines flight assignments.

■ **Operations Agents:** Compute the weight and balance of the aircraft so that baggage and cargo can be properly loaded to balance the aircraft. They also schedule aircraft work crews and coordinate information for the passenger-service employees, the provisioning department, and the flight crews.

- **Flight Dispatchers:** Authorize all takeoffs of aircraft and monitor the flight's progress to the destination by radio. They help control the entire daily flight schedule of an airline, taking into consideration weather as well as problems with aircraft, flight crews, destination runways, and passenger, cargo, and fuel loads. Prerequisites for training positions are college mathematics, physics, and meteorology.
- **Meteorologists:** Prepare weather reports for flight personnel and for airline operations and traffic departments.

Maintenance and Engineering

Maintenance is another huge category for the airlines. Maintenance jobs include the following:

- **Airline Maintenance Inspectors:** Check the work done by Mechanics and other specialists and must give final approval before the aircraft is released for operation.
- **Air Frame and Powerplant (engine) (A&P) Mechanics:** Work with skin and frames, engines, propellers, brakes, and wheels, and are responsible for the proper mechanical functioning of the aircraft.
- **Instrument Technicians:** Install, test, repair, and overhaul all aircraft, engine, and navigational instruments; a certificate is required.
- **Radio Technicians:** Install, maintain, repair, and test all aircraft radio equipment.

If you have an interest in electronics, you may choose to specialize in avionics: aircraft navigation and communication radios, weather radar systems, autopilots, and other electronic devices. This field is becoming more interesting and challenging as the technology expands. In the past, avionics were added to an airplane almost as an afterthought; today's digital aircraft depend on sophisticated avionics systems as part of their design.

Industry observers say there is a demand for avionics specialists who are prepared to master the intricacies of the aircraft and work shoulder to shoulder with A&Ps. Because of a shortage of technicians and the complexity of aircraft systems, the industry needs more people who are cross-trained. They want A&Ps who can troubleshoot the black boxes, as a time server in the maintenance operations. Avionics technicians with the licensing that enables them to work on the airplane, either removing or reinstalling equipment, are especially in demand.

Skills required for certification may be developed at privately owned and operated schools. You can get an approved list of such schools from the Department of Transportation, Federal Aviation Administration, Washington, DC 20591; www.faa.gov.

- **Airline Engineers:** Work closely with aircraft manufacturers to develop equipment suited to the airline's particular type of operation. Such engineers are often involved in the design of aircraft and aircraft accessories and in improving maintenance and overhaul procedures.

  Airlines also have an engineer responsible for safety oversight, typically a Vice President or Director position.

Administration, Sales, and Marketing

Administrative, sales, and marketing departments offer some of the best entry-level positions with the least requirements for education and prior experience or accreditation. However, those who have completed a travel and tourism program at a college or vocational school generally have a better chance at jobs such as these:

- **Reservations Agents:** Book and sell the tickets. May sell other travel products, such as tours, hotel accommodations, and car rentals. They may also operate computer reservations equipment and assist passengers in solving their travel needs. There are about 54,000 airline Reservationists in the U.S. (mostly in massive call centers in the Midwest) who occupy the better part of a day sitting in front of a computer screen with a headset on, talking over the telephone to passengers and travel agents, making and changing reservations.

- **Ticket Agents:** Sell tickets to airline passengers at the airport and city ticket offices. They give air travel and tour information, make flight and tour reservations, compute fares, prepare and issue tickets, route baggage, and prepare cash reports.

- **Airport Operations Agents:** Perform agent duties in airport operational areas. Meet and dispatch flights, take tickets from passengers as they board the plane, administer seat selection, coordinate boarding and post-departure procedures, handle baggage service, and maintain a high level of customer service with passengers.

- **Passenger Service Agents:** Provide service to passengers primarily at the ticket counter, passenger boarding, or baggage claim areas. Assist passengers by providing information, arranging for ground transportation, and giving directions to passengers. May fill in for reservations or ticket agents.

- **Ticket Agents:** Work at the airport ticket counter selling tickets and giving information on flights, giving passengers seats, and tagging luggage.

- **Fleet Service Employees:** Load and unload air cargo and baggage on the aircraft and make certain baggage gets to the proper destination. Good physical condition and outdoor work in every kind of weather is required; previous experience with equipment (belt loaders, container lifts, heaters, aircraft pushback tractors, and de-icing equipment) or freight handling are plusses. "Ramp agents really love their jobs. Ramp agents tend to be outdoorsy, physical people, enjoy working outside, weightlifters, into sports and football; they like the camaraderie, the challenge of getting the plane loaded," said Southwest's Libby Sartrain.

- **Sales Representatives:** Promote and sell an airline's various passenger and cargo services, mainly to travel agencies and to corporate accounts.

- **District Sales Managers:** Administer city ticket and reservations offices and promote and develop airline passenger and cargo traffic in the district, in accordance with the company's goals and policies.

- **District Operations Managers:** Are in charge of ground and flight operations at an airline station and supervise all the people involved.

- **Freight Airport Operations Agents:** Process routing and rating of shipments, contact customer on arrival of shipments, and arrange for delivery.

- **Freight Telephone Salespeople:** Quote rates and patterns of service and complete necessary shipping documents.

- **Fleet Service Clerks:** This group includes the following: cabin service (clean cabin interiors and replenish cabin supplies); line cargo (handle the loading and unloading of baggage, freight, and mail on passenger aircraft); and air freight (handle the loading and unloading of freight in specialized equipment on jet freighters).

Headquarters and regional sales offices employ people in public relations, personnel, accounting, insurance, and finance, as well as Administrative Assistants and Receptionists.

The marketing department also employs Research Analysts who prepare detailed statistical analyses and reports that may relate to the rate structure and tariffs, traffic problems and trends, or the amounts of passengers, mail, and freight carried.

Other positions include Crew Scheduler, Executive Secretary, Foreman, Industrial Engineer, Inspector, Instructor, Passenger Service Manager, Personnel Representative, Programmer/Analyst, Purchasing Agent, Statistical Analyst, and Supervisor.

These broad job categories mask the diversity and range of specializations. For example, within the sales function may be specialties including Incentive Sales (specializes in working with coordinators of travel prizes), Travel Industry Liaison (works with travel agents), and Interline Sales (coordinates with other airlines on mutual exchange of tickets and is responsible for reduced-rate travel of airline and travel agency personnel). Other specialties include Aircraft Purchase and Sales, Charters, Freight/Cargo, Insurance, Properties and Facilities, Purchasing, Labor Relations, and Community and Environmental Affairs.

Several airlines also have their own Tour Operations, such as American Airlines' FlyAAway Vacations. These entities employ many of the same kinds of professionals as tour companies, including Product Development, Operations, Marketing, and Sales.

Salaries in the Airline Industry

For most airlines, entry-level salaries are modest, but then rise significantly. "After four or five years, you are making good money, after 10 or 15 years, you are making great money," said Southwest's Vice President of People, Libby Sartain. "Flight attendants have made six figs, but $50 to $60K is common." On the other hand, the benefits can be fabulous, starting with the coveted free travel on their own carrier and 90 percent off on other airlines. If you happen to be lucky enough to be at a carrier like Southwest, which has profit-sharing and has made profits, you may be like the Southwest retirees who retire as millionaires.

Annual compensation per airline employee (including salary) ranges from about $20,000 for a new Flight Attendant to well over $100,000 for a Senior Airline Captain.

Salary rates for pilots vary with experience and also the equipment flown: A first-year flight officer on the smallest aircraft averages $32,604; a fifth-year flight officer on a medium aircraft averages $84,744; a 10th-year captain of the smallest aircraft averages $136,536; and a captain of the largest aircraft averages $176,964, according to AIR, Inc.

Senior management executives are also well compensated compared to other travel counterparts. Some examples:

Median Airline Executive Salaries, 2000

Title	Salary
National Account Manager	$60,000
Manager of Agency Sales	$48,000
Resident Sales Representative	$40,000
International Pricing Analyst	$60,000
Supervisor, Passenger Services	$45,000
Manager, Customer Service	$50,000
Leisure Market Development Manager	$60,000
Regional Marketing Manager	$55,000
Director, Yield Management	$75,000
Vice President, Cargo Marketing and Sales	$90,000
Vice President, Passenger Sales	$100,000
Regional Vice President	$120,000

Your Ticket into the Airline Industry

Each carrier presents a different work environment (work conditions range from plush to World War II–era salvage bunkers) and very different outlook for advancement opportunities and security. The age and size of the carrier are not necessarily indications of future stability.

Salary is important, but these days, many airlines offer employees stock options and profit-sharing. Consider, also, the benefits package. If travel is important to you, find out what the travel benefits are and whether the airline has interline privileges (entitling personnel to travel on other airlines at very little cost) with other carriers.

INSIDE SECRET: The best opportunities for breaking into the airline industry are at regional carriers.

Examine the job itself and opportunities the company offers for advancement. Look at the background of the company (particularly its human resources policies and past record on layoffs) and what is planned for the future. Find out how many cities it serves, what cities, what kind of fleet, its fleet purchase plans, who is backing the company, whether the airline has joint marketing arrangements with other carriers, and its relationships with other travel entities, particularly travel agencies. Consider whether the airline is having difficulty with unions or staff and if a strike is looming. Look at the airlines' share of market and whether its share has been growing. Consider its profitability.

The most active job categories for entry-level jobs are reservations, secretarial, and airport.

For Reservationists, airlines generally look for people with travel and training acquired at a travel school, a travel agency, or another airline. They seek some kind of relevant experience, particularly some familiarity with the airline computer reservations system. Reservations people have been known to move throughout the company, primarily to automation support, sales, customer service, training, and marketing.

And, although it is common to think of jobs like Reservationist and Passenger Service Agent as steppingstones to other positions, the majority of people employed in these positions, as well as clerical, Fleet Service Agent, and Ticket Counter Agent, are content to spend their entire careers in those jobs.

There are 200 applications for every opening. "We get 1,000 per month from Flight Attendants alone," said one airline's hiring executive. "One year we saw about 8,000 candidates for Flight Attendants and hired 330, or 4 percent. This is the most selective area."

One way in is to start part-time; indeed, a significant proportion of jobs throughout the airline industry are part-time, perhaps 15 to 25 percent, because there is such fluctuation in schedules and traffic and

part-timers are more cost-effective for the airline. (We met one Flight Attendant on a charter carrier who was a New York City detective during the week and flew only on weekends.) Often, part-time, weekend, or nightshift jobs lead to full-time positions. And once you are inside the company, opportunities to rise to supervisory positions are in reach.

INSIDE SECRET: A key strategy is to be alert to where airlines are expanding and adding hubs. Don't wait for a classified ad to appear; contact the airline directly.

 # Roadmap to the Top

Largely because the attrition rates are so low, advancement at an airline depends on how swiftly it is growing—in routes or fleet. Hamilton noted that at TWA, "It is possible to jump into a responsible position, but that's not likely to happen fast. The competition in the organization is keen. Movement in management ranks is slower." An up-and-coming carrier, or even a strong regional or commuter airline, may well offer a faster track up the ladder.

Regional Carriers Offer Faster Advancement

Regional airlines like JetBlue present excellent career opportunity. These carriers—about 100 of them including Piedmont, American Eagle, Continental Express, Comair, and Air Wisconsin—provide scheduled, short-haul air transportation between small and medium-size communities and the nation's hub airports. Traffic on the regional airlines more than doubled during the 1990s, to 78 million passengers enplaned in 1999. Because of "code-sharing" arrangements with major carriers, you may not even be aware of flying on a regional airline on one or more legs of a trip into a hub airport.

Over the past decade, regional airlines, which employ about 75,000 people, have been growing and cutting into the nationals' share of traffic; they now account for about 13 percent of all domestic traffic.

JetBlue

JetBlue, a start-up airline with a hub at JFK International Airport in New York, was launched by a 41-year-old David Neeleman. Neeleman had created another discount airline, Morris Air, initially to compete with Southwest, but it was subsequently bought by Southwest. He worked with Southwest for a while but was driven by his entrepreneurial spirit. Neeleman went on to help start Canada's successful new entrant WestJet and develop Open Skies, the world's simplest airline reservation system. It is no accident that JetBlue has much of the same people-oriented culture of Southwest: Ann Rhoades, JetBlue's Executive Vice President of Human Resources, headed and named the People department at Southwest and solidified Southwest's reputation for retaining and hiring the best people, despite its rapid growth at the time. She has also worked for Mbank and Promus Hotel Corporation. This airline is another growth opportunity. (For more information, see www.jetblue.com.)

An advantage of working at a regional airline is that there is more opportunity to be a "jack of all trades." Said one executive, "You're more likely to have hands-on experience. The majors are more specialized." Also, because the regionals tend to serve smaller communities, you have the opportunity for a better quality of life.

Getting in can be more than just being in the right place at the right time; you can "make it happen." By being alert to when carriers enter a market, or when they are about to be certificated, you can approach them before they get flooded with applicants. Call on people you might know within the carrier.

Though there are many entry-level positions, getting a job at a regional, as at the other airlines, is easier if you have some experience or training in the travel industry—such as an airline or travel school that teaches reservations systems.

"Occasionally, when we enter a new market, we will hire locally," said an executive, "but generally you need some skill or training or have to know somebody."

Some regard the regionals as a steppingstone to the major carriers, but many are content to spend their careers with a regional carrier, taking advantage of the opportunity to rise higher in the organization than they might have at a major carrier.

Most regionals also have interline arrangements with other carriers (enabling personnel to travel at little cost on those carriers), so they may offer privileges such as being able to fly free on domestic as well as international airlines.

Salaries are decent, though somewhat lower than the majors.

New Twists on Charter Air

The marketplace has produced a new innovation that bridges the gap between private jets and scheduled commercial air transport. New charter companies and fractional ownership providers are appearing on the scene, including Skyjet.com, a Web-based provider of real-time business aircraft reservations; also BidJetCharter.com, a service of Quincy, Massachusetts–based Aviation One Management; and Ejets, Aliso Viejo, California (www.ejets.com). A company called JetOne, in Waterford, Michigan, is offering fractional ownership.

Foreign Flag Carriers

Foreign flag carriers offer more limited opportunities, but some of the best opportunities to work in a global arena.

International carriers offer positions in middle management, but most of top management is composed of foreign nationals, with the exception of the second-in-command, who is usually an American (because he or she knows the market).

Department heads, except for public relations and personnel, also tend to be foreign nationals; but all departments usually have U.S. nationals under them.

Station heads may be from the carrier country or American. Reservationists and sales and marketing staff are typically American (however, foreign-language capability may be required). Relatively few Americans are employed by the foreign airlines abroad.

It is not imperative, but it is definitely beneficial to know the language of the foreign country in order to rise; however, some positions may require foreign language (such as in reservations).

At the Center of Glasnost and Geopolitics

One of the more fascinating aspects of working at an international flag carrier is being caught up with geo-politics and geo-economics.

Jonathan Hill, for example, personally lived *glasnost*. Joining Aeroflot as marketing manager, U.S.A., just as relations between the U.S. and Soviet Union were reaching an all-time high, he also suffered when the government cracked down on regional independence movements, prompting a renewed chill in relations.

An airline is a country's lifeline and its pipeline to the world. It is not only a mark of prestige, but integral to its independence and defense. Consequently, Hill's position was a vital one and he met with people at the highest rungs of government. "It was a priceless experience," he declared.

Hill, whose father worked for Sabena and United and whose mother worked at American Airlines (they met fighting over a passenger), had the distinction of being the lone capitalist in an organization struggling along in that direction.

Required and Continuing Education

In general, all positions that are onboard aircraft or working directly with the aircraft (such as mechanics and machinists) require certification or licensing.

Some colleges offer excellent preparatory background, especially for the positions that require certification or licensing, and are on well-trod paths for industry recruiters. These include the following:

- **Embry-Riddle Aeronautical University,** 600 S. Clyde Morris Blvd., Daytona Beach, FL 32114; 800-94-EMBRY; www.embryriddle.edu. The University offers more than 30 degree programs. These include undergraduate programs in engineering, communications, physics, computer science, professional aeronautics, business administration, aviation, experimental psychology, and science, technology, and globalization. Graduate programs are offered in engineering, business administration, human factors and systems, and software engineering. The university also offers an Executive MBA program. It also offers a distance-learning program: 800-359-3728.

- **FlightSafety International,** 100 Moonachie Ave., Moonachie, NJ 07074; 800-480-8623; www.flightsafety.com.

- **College of Aeronautics,** La Guardia Airport, 86–01 23rd Ave., Flushing, NY 11369; 800-PRO-AERO; www.aero.edu.

Further information about education programs and which aviation jobs require licenses or certification is available from the Director of Education, Department of Transportation, **Federal Aviation Administration,** 800 Independence Ave. SW, Washington, DC 20590; 202-366-4000; www.faa.gov.

Contacts, Sources, and Leads

- You can get leads and insights about airline companies from the **trade press** (*Aviation Weekly, Travel Agent Magazine, Travel Weekly*).

- Check the **financial pages** of newspapers and magazines, and business publications such as The *Wall Street Journal*.

- Review **annual reports** and literature by and about the company.

- The directories published by **AIR, Inc.** are also helpful.

Major Airlines

- **Air Line Pilots Association,** Herndon, VA; 703-689-2270; www.alpa.org. Publishes *Airline Pilot* magazine.

- **Air Transport Association,** 1301 Pennsylvania Ave. NW, Washington, DC 20004; 202-626-4000; www.air-transport.org. Has a listing of members; industry statistics.

- **Aviation Employee Placement Service (AEPS),** P.O. Box 550010, Ft. Lauderdale, FL 33355; 954-472-6684; www.aeps.com. Provides an interactive database for pilots, flight attendants, mechanics, management, and other aviation positions for commercial carriers, corporate, charter, freight, and FBOs (free to companies; candidates pay a subscription fee of $12/month or $59–99/year). Also hosts Aviation Career "airfairs" nationwide. A sister company publishes an online *Aviation Career* magazine: www.aviationcareer.net.

- **International Air Transport Association,** 800 Place Victoria, P.O. Box 113, Montreal, Quebec, Canada, H4Z 1M1; 514-874-0202; www.iata.org. Represents 272 members worldwide. The site lists career opportunities at IATA and member airlines and links to other aviation sites.

Regional Airlines

- **Regional Airline Association,** 2025 M St. NW, Ste. 800, Washington, DC 20036; 202-367-1170; www.raa.org. Has addresses for U.S. regional airlines, plus statistics.

- **Aviation Information Resources (AIR Inc.),** 3800 Camp Creek Pkwy., Ste. 18–100, Atlanta, GA 30331; 800-JET-JOBS; www.jet-jobs.com. Lists regionals, commuters.

- **Trade publications** include *Commuter Air International, Commuter/Regional Airline News,* and *Regional Aviation Weekly.*

CHAPTER 10

CAR RENTAL: AT A CROSSROADS

"Once car rental gets in your blood, it stays. There are a lot of 'retreads' in the business—people who go from company to company," declared one car rental executive.

Like many in the car rental business who are not otherwise driven by some fascination with the automobile, Robert Coffey stumbled in but soon found himself caught up in the dynamics of the industry and never left.

Coffey had been working for a major international airline for five years when he found himself one of the casualties of the "bloodbath" in which thousands of airline personnel lost their jobs in one of the periodic industry downturns. But his boss at the airline had a buddy in top management at Avis who offered him a position.

"I was complacent," Coffey related. "I thought the airline business so dynamic—a fleet of 150 airplanes going to hundreds of points all around the world. You knew where they were going. Then I realized that Avis had 65,000 cars in its fleet, and that customers may tell us they will return a car to one place and wind up in another. The whole prospect of keeping track became exciting." (The Avis fleet has since grown to 220,000 cars and 1,600 locations.)

"I found the car rental business one of phenomenal change—the capacity of the product changes daily in each city. There are new cities to open, new marketing opportunities, new people to meet, new places to go." Coffey, who went on to become Vice President of Market Planning at another car rental company, finished by saying "and it is more exciting every day."

Snapshot: The Car Rental Industry

Car rental does not have the glamour (or prestige) of the airlines; however, many come to it from the airlines. But people who are contemplating a job in the travel industry fail to appreciate the dynamics and the challenge of the car rental business and tend to overlook the opportunities available. Indeed, the car rental industry offers much the same people-contact, high technology, and exciting airport activity as the airlines, and, indeed, is an integral part of the travel industry. Car rental companies are typically linked with airlines, hotels, and tour companies.

INSIDE SECRET: Car rental companies offer much the same dynamics, but not the travel benefits, of the airlines.

The car rental industry exploded in growth during the 1970s and into the 1980s, when there was a frantic scramble for car companies to obtain coveted on-airport locations. The airport was where the real growth of the business was taking place: Airline deregulation was pushing down airfares and driving in new entrants, persuading people to leave their personal cars at home and take airplanes, instead. That left passengers needing rental cars at their destinations. The car rental industry doubled in size during the decade, growing at an average rate of 10 percent a year and outpacing most other segments of the travel industry.

The car rental industry now generates about $25 billion in business and employs about 250,000 people.

The top 10 car rental companies generated $21 billion in business and together operate more than 25,000 locations. The top 10 companies are the following:

- Enterprise Rent-A-Car (St. Louis)
- Hertz Corporation (Park Ridge, New Jersey)
- Avis Group (Garden City, New York)
- Budget Rent a Car (Lisle, Illinois)
- National Car Rental System (Minneapolis, Minnesota)
- Alamo Rent-A-Car (Ft. Lauderdale, Florida)
- Dollar Rent A Car (Tulsa, Oklahoma)
- Thrifty Car Rental (Tulsa, Oklahoma)
- Advantage Rent-A-Car (San Antonio, Texas)
- Payless Car Rental (St. Petersburg, Florida)

Car rental companies differ markedly in style, position in the market (market share), market niche (whether they are focused on business travelers, budget market, or insurance replacement), and to some degree in the kind of services they offer. Kemwel Group (based in Harrison, New York) and Foremost Euro-Car, Inc. (based in Van Nuys, California), specialize in arranging lease/purchase deals for Americans in Europe. Other companies specialize in fly/drive programs in Europe. Some companies (such as Cruise America) specialize in renting recreational vehicles. In some highly competitive leisure markets, car companies can become extremely creative; for example, the Budget franchisee in Hawaii devised a discount coupon book for restaurants and attractions to get a competitive edge in attracting customers. Still other companies specialize in car and driver arrangements, such as Carey International.

Intense Competition

Like the hospitality industry, the car rental industry has huge growth prospects and affords excellent advancement opportunities, as well as the chance to take on tremendous responsibility early in a career. But unlike the hotel industry, where buildings take years to plan and construct and capacity is fixed, car rental companies (even more so than airlines) can shift their supply and adjust prices to meet demand virtually at will. This flexibility allows them to react quickly to competitive threats. Profit margins tend to be razor-thin; as an industry, a margin of 4 percent is considered high. Car rental executives complain that in a perfect world, the price of renting a $20,000 vehicle would be on par with renting a hotel room, but it is not.

Consequently, car rental is one of the most intensely competitive of all travel businesses. Every detail is shrouded in secrecy—executives do not divulge, for example, the number of cars in any one location because it would betray valuable information to the competition. This is a commodity business where the commodity—the car—can be moved instantly to tap into demand.

Service, price, and, increasingly, loyalty and partnership programs rule here as with the airlines, but the two key elements that contribute to the special nature of the car rental business are fleet and finance.

INSIDE SECRET: The two key elements of the car rental business are *fleet* (how many cars, what kind, and where they are located) and *finance* (the extremely high capital investment of new vehicles each year, franchising, and stock values).

Fleet utilization is the name of the game in car rental, and this means logistics. "There is a substantial logistics problem in getting the fleet to the right place at the right time," a Hertz executive stated. Contributing to the car rental dynamic is the possibility that a company may not have gauged demand correctly and either placed not enough or too much of its fleet in a location.

For example, when Hertz was faced with the problem of moving cars out of Florida and back into the Northeast after peak season, it solved the problem through substantial price incentives: Floridians were offered a car for a week plus two return air tickets to Florida for only $129. Avis accomplished the same objective by creating a new tour company to offer value-added packages.

Fleet also means the kind of car the rental company offers. The car company has to anticipate the design, size, and fuel economy of cars people will want to *rent* (for example, if fuel is plentiful, people want to drive bigger, sportier, faster cars; if scarce, they shift to smaller vehicles). But they also have to anticipate what people will want to *buy* 18 to 24 months out, because rental companies also have to sell off the used cars.

"There's so much to consider," asserted Coffey. "You even have to figure the impact of such things as teleconferencing [satellite transmissions that enable meeting participants to be in different locations, which could cut down on the amount of airline travel and therefore car rental business], or will people want cellular phones, and how the cost of airfares may or may not stimulate air travel." Their fortunes are intimately linked with the economy, which affects the pace of business travel and the ability of vacationers to take long-haul trips requiring car rental, rather than economizing by going a driveable distance in their family car.

"If you're positioned properly and have read from the crystal ball correctly, you make money," an Avis executive quipped.

Whereas the battle used to be waged in terms of on-airport locations, now the battlegrounds are local neighborhoods—suburban and rural—to go after the lucrative insurance replacement market (that is, where homeowners need to use a rental car when their own car is being repaired or replaced) that Enterprise had claimed as its own.

INSIDE SECRET: Biggest growth segment for car rentals: suburban neighborhood locations and the lucrative insurance replacement business.

The newest competition among car rental companies is in three areas: service, marketing, and distribution. Car rental companies are competing now about who can better incorporate technology for onboard services, including cell phones and wireless Internet access, and global positioning systems (Hertz features NeverLost, "the in-car satellite navigation system that shows and tells you how to get wherever you want to go!"). They are marketing more aggressively, partnering with airline and hotel frequent-traveler programs, and utilizing these memberships for direct marketing. They also are aggressively negotiating preferred supplier deals with resellers (travel agents, corporate travel managers, wholesalers, and tour operators).

Car rental companies also are looking to tap into new technology in order to get their product out to the travel industry and business and vacation travelers directly, by linking to global distribution systems (GDS) and e-commerce sites. (Budget formed an alliance with Homestore.com, the largest home and real estate network on the Internet, to sell truck rentals online, while Dollar linked up with Thetrip.com to launch a full-service travel Web site, www.dollartravel.com.)

The car rental booking systems, which the companies call "global distribution systems" (comparable to the airlines' computer reservations systems), are vital. "Increasingly, this is becoming a technology-based industry with global computerized data communication networks," commented an Avis executive. "The only way to survive is to be quick and accurate."

Increasingly, though, the dynamics of car rental reflect the surprisingly complex finance issues, which relate not only to financing the purchase of the fleet, but also to franchising and stock values.

A highly leveraged, capital-intensive business, car companies borrow heavily each year to finance a new stock of cars. If interest rates change by just a point, it can mean multimillions of dollars to the bottom line of a major car rental company. The intense competition among companies has also put pressure on pricing, which means equal pressure for raising productivity.

The car rental companies have tended to be popular plums for takeovers. Since Hertz was founded in 1918, it has had several owners, including RCA and United Airlines. Avis has been owned by ITT, then publicly owned, then acquired by Norton Simon, which was bought by Esmark, then by Beatrice, then by Westray Capital; then in 1987, it was acquired by employees in one of the nation's largest ESOPs (employee-sponsored ownership plans), then acquired by HFS, which in turn was acquired by Cendant.

Major car rental companies have a second business that is equally important as the rental side: Reselling the cars. The companies have to predict two to four years in advance what customers will want to rent as well as to buy; frequently, the two wants are not the same. A change in gasoline prices can render a whole fleet obsolete. Not surprisingly, therefore, the nation's largest auto retailer, AutoNation, now owns National Car Rental, Alamo Rent-A-Car, and CarTemps USA.

But over the past decade, major car manufacturers, including Ford, General Motors, and Chrysler, have stepped in to take substantial ownership interest in several of the major car rental companies, changing the complexion of the car rental industry. Usually there is a buy-back arrangement, reducing the risk of disposing of used cars and making it possible for renters to have new cars each year (which gives the rental company a competitive edge). But in exchange, the rental companies have had to acquire car models of the manufacturers' choosing, which may or may not be the sort people want to rent as opposed to own.

Car rental companies are also in the franchise business, which adds yet another dimension to business operations.

A Business of Balancing Business and Leisure Travelers

The backbone of the business is the commercial renter—the business traveler. Signing up commercial accounts and enticing them with corporate rates and frequent-traveler programs and other incentives are key activities.

The growth side of the business, though, has been the leisure renter, particularly with the increase in popularity of the fly/drive travel package. Key responsibilities for marketing and sales departments include negotiating with airline, hotel, and tour operator partners to be included in their packages, and currying the loyalties of travel agencies through incentives and promotions.

INSIDE SECRET: Job titles created as a result of increased interaction with tour packagers and travel agencies include Director of Travel Industry Sales and Director of Partnership Marketing.

The leisure business is likely to expand markedly because of the growth of airline travel (particularly when discounts and low fares abound) and the maturation of the Baby Boomers into family units, because fly/drives have more appeal than taking very long trips with the family car.

A large portion of the car rental company's business, however, does not come from the renter at all; instead, the "customer" is the travel agent or the corporate travel manager who has to be presold to choose that car company.

The growth of travel agency bookings has been exponential, from 10 percent of the industry's total sales to 60 percent in a 15-year period. But today, car companies, like airlines, are beginning to plug into the Internet to directly reach corporate travelers as well as vacationers. The growing importance of distribution is reflected in the growth specialties.

INSIDE SECRET: Car rental companies are trying to directly reach corporate travelers and vacationers through the Internet, creating positions such as Manager of Internet Partner Sales and Interactive Marketing Manager.

Why Choose the Car Rental Industry?

The car rental industry affords an alternative path for people attracted to the dynamics of the airline industry, an opportunity to be part of major global companies. It is suitable for people who like an intensely competitive environment, and who are intrigued by the challenge of dramatically changing distribution systems.

> **INSIDE SECRET:** The car rental industry has huge growth prospects and affords excellent advancement opportunities, as well as the chance to take on tremendous responsibility early in a career.

This is an industry in which it is fairly easy to get an entry-level position without the same certification or licensing requirements of the airline industry. Once inside, it is relatively easy to rise up the ladder by showing commitment, motivation, and leadership.

The industry is ripe for innovation and is being transformed by marketing, service, and distribution, making for new job titles, particularly in Internet distribution, partnership marketing, global sales, and yield management.

Jobs in the Car Rental Industry

The biggest concentration of people power is among the Rental Sales Agents, who work the counter and have considerable responsibility.

Handling people proves to be the challenging and even creative aspect of the job. "Someone who has been on an airplane for six hours has not had control of his life—where he sits, where his bags wind up, what he eats, who sits next to him. The first time he retakes control of his life is at our counter, where he asserts himself," said an Avis executive.

The second biggest category is the Service Agents, who clean and prepare the cars. If "love of cars" is a motive for entering the car rental business, this is the position that can best realize that objective. But Service Agent positions are more of an assembly-line nature, with repetitive tasks and little decision-making.

The third-largest category is the "Shuttlers"—people who move cars from one location to another.

Best Bets

- Customer Service Agent
- Director of Partnership Marketing
- Manager of Internet Distribution
- Director of Global Sales
- Manager of Yield Management
- Manager of Quality Assurance
- Training Manager
- Manager of Fleet Utilization

Other positions in a rental outlet include Bus Drivers, Service Mechanics and helpers, and Clerical Support workers. The number of positions in the offices varies largely by location; all of these are entry-level positions.

Then there are the Shift Managers (the outlets are open 24 hours a day), the Assistant City Manager, and the City Manager, who is in charge of the facility. The City Manager also has marketing responsibility. Every city develops its own marketing contacts—with the airline managers, local travel agents, tour operators, hotels, and convention centers. They try to get group business and may participate in sales blitzes throughout the country (for example, the Miami City Manager may come to talk with New York City travel agents).

Aspiring to a management position is a realistic goal for rental agents, as well. A typical career path might be the following:

1. Rental Agent
2. "Lead Agent" (who answers customers' questions), or Quality Assurance Supervisor (who talks to customers to find out how the car performed and assists customers generally)
3. Shift Manager
4. Station Manager
5. City Manager, who has responsibility for sales and marketing initiatives as well as management and operations

From City Manager, a person can move to Division Manager, Regional Sales Manager, or Director. From there, the path can go to Division Vice President or into headquarters.

Headquarters positions include Operations (Personnel, Car Control, Fleet Control, Fleet Utilization, and Operations), Fleet Administration (making deals to buy and sell cars), Sales and Marketing, Reservations, and Finance (including Accounts Payable/Receivable and Data Processing).

The marketing function, which is responsible for planning, forecasting, designing the product, pricing, and physically selling the product, generally is consolidated at the national level, but there usually are Marketing Managers in each region. Marketing specialists are the ones that will try to negotiate alliances with airlines, tour companies, and hotels.

INSIDE SECRET: Marketing is generally consolidated at the national level, but there usually are Marketing Managers in each region.

Sales programs are also established at the national level, but companies usually maintain sales offices in major markets, which have Sales Representatives to call on commercial accounts and travel agents.

Technology is a growing part of the car rental business. Avis, for example, a company that made early inroads into computer systems, has 400 Computer Specialists and maintains a training department just for this "special breed of cat."

Among the top management positions for a car company are the Fleet Acquisition/Positioning Specialists, Fleet Coordinators, Accounting people, and Controller. There are also individuals who negotiate with airlines and tour companies.

INSIDE SECRET: Technology is transforming car rental companies, from the way cars are booked to the cell phones and global positioning systems on board the rental cars.

Although there is a long list of these senior management specialties, there are not a lot of positions compared to the legions of lower-level jobs, which is why many people at the management level move from company to company, or city to city, in order to advance.

INSIDE SECRET: The small percentage of management jobs means that people seeking advancement must move from company to company or city to city to advance.

Salaries in the Car Rental Industry

Salaries at entry level are slightly better than minimum wage, but there are bonuses for everyone in the field based on performance.

Some examples of salaries and specialties:

Median Rental Agency Salaries, 2000	
Title	Salary
Automation Training Manager	$50,000
Director of Sales and Marketing	$65,000
Regional Vice President of Sales and Marketing	$75,000
Vice President, Travel Industry Marketing	$120,000

Your Ticket into the Car Rental Industry

The car rental industry is one of the least demanding in terms of educational background and qualifications. To rise up, however, companies will look to business management preparation along with industry experience.

The largest car companies, including Enterprise, Hertz, and Avis, are considered training grounds.

The oldest and largest car rental company, with 6,000 outlets worldwide, Hertz is also considered one of the training grounds for the industry, since there is a lot of movement from company to company. Hertz employs some 19,000 people in the United States. Although most of the hiring is done at the local level, the company does have training and development programs at the corporate level.

Avis has a "new hire program" for incoming rental sales people, involving training at one of seven major training centers for two weeks. The training familiarizes the individual not only with the computer, but also on how to rent a car without it, and even more importantly, knowing how to handle situations: qualifying the customer, computing a rate manually, dealing with travel vouchers, and figuring travel agents' commissions. The myriad details are what make the job interesting, as well as the people contact and the airport activity.

What does a car company look for when hiring? Counter Agents (or Rental Sales Agents) need to have good communications skills, need to be adept at dealing with people, should enjoy challenge, should not be timid, and need to be capable of making judgement calls. "You have to determine whether or not a customer is fit to take possession, however temporary, of a $20,000 vehicle."

Enterprise Rent-A-Car, the largest car company with $4.7 billion in revenue and nearly 4,000 locations, has an unusual approach. The company hires people straight out of college, grooms them to become Station Managers, drills them on providing extraordinary customer service, pays them an incredibly low base salary ($30s), but offers an enormous incentive (bonus), so even an Area Manager can earn six figures. Such people rarely leave because they cannot match the compensation elsewhere.

To find your way into the car rental business, it is best to apply at the district office or head office for the area in which you want to work. You can also check the company's Web sites, which usually list job offerings by location.

> **INSIDE SECRET:** Car rental companies' Web sites usually list job openings by location. See the end of this chapter for the addresses of the top 10 companies' job-listing Web pages.

Roadmap to the Top

In a typical Enterprise experience, a fellow was hired straight out of college and promoted to Representative after only 60 days (90 days is average). Within eight months, he was promoted to Assistant Branch Manager. Over the course of the next 12 years, he became Branch Manager, growing a new location to more than $1 million in revenue, building the fleet, and managing staff; was promoted to Area Rental Manager; and then was relocated to another city as city Rental Manager, where he was charged with developing a new territory. From there, he was promoted to Group Rental Manager, overseeing 33 locations and supervising 120 employees and $24 million in sales.

Hertz, the largest car rental company in the world with 6,000 locations and $4.7 billion in revenues, has a very different structure.

Walter Seaman's rise to Staff Vice President, Worldwide Fleet, Maintenance and Car Sales operations for Hertz, illustrates a different career path. In this position, Seaman is responsible for the company's worldwide fleet operations, which includes the acquisition of all new vehicles, fleet maintenance and repair, and fleet disposal, including manufacturer/dealer repurchase and lease vehicles, and retail and wholesale sales. This gives him oversight of a fleet of 525,000 vehicles in 6,500 locations in 140 countries from the company's worldwide headquarters in Park Ridge, New Jersey. Seaman has more than 25 years in the automotive management field. He rose to this position from Division Vice President, Fleet Maintenance and Car Sales Operations, where he was responsible for Hertz's fleet, maintenance, and the retail and wholesale sales of daily rental vehicles. In addition, he was responsible for the development of programs to enhance the marketing, sales, and profitability of nationwide car sales programs.

Contacts, Sources, and Leads

- To get leads for jobs, start with the local **Yellow Pages.**
- Follow industry **trade publications** such as *Auto Rental News, Travel Agent, Travel Weekly,* and *Business Travel News.*
- **American Car Rental Association,** 1125 Roger Bacon Dr., Ste. 8, Reston, VA 20190-5202; 703-234-4148; mainly a lobbying group.

Rental Company Web Sites

- **Advantage Rent-A-Car:** www.advantagerentacar.com/cgi-bin/employ.cgi
- **Alamo Rent-A-Car:** www.alamo.com
- **Avis Group:** www.avis.com/company/employment/
- **Budget Rent a Car:** www.drivebudget.com
- **Dollar Rent A Car:** www.dollar.com/company_information/employment_opportunities.asp
- **Enterprise Rent-A-Car:** www.erac.com/recruit/
- **Hertz Corporation:** www.hertz.com/company/hr/index.cfm
- **National Car Rental System:** www.nationalcar.com
- **Payless Car Rental:** www.800-payless.com/CareFrameSet1.html
- **Thrifty Car Rental:** www.thrifty.com/careers.asp

CHAPTER 11

GETTING ON BOARD THE MOTORCOACH AND RAIL INDUSTRIES

Two other facets that along with airlines complete the picture of common carrier transportation are the motorcoach and passenger rail segments. There is little similarity between the two in terms of the industry dynamics and the issues they are facing, except that both distribute and sell their product/services through the travel industry, both are chugging reluctantly into the new millennium, and both are underappreciated fields of the travel industry and are generally overlooked by job seekers. Both can be characterized as unglamorous, even folksy, and yet essential services.

Motorcoach Operators

The motorcoach industry, though one of the most uncelebrated areas of travel, is poised for some exciting changes and expansion. Still wrenching itself from under the weight of unflattering stereotypes of a smoke-spewing bus, the motorcoach industry affords unlimited creativity afforded by a marketplace freed from regulation and is a vital element in the group travel and transportation industry.

Snapshot: The Motorcoach Industry

Languishing in the decades after World War II as the nation's resources went toward building a highway system to support the private automobile and the airlines skyrocketed in popularity, the motorcoach industry was revitalized with the energy crisis of 1973. The crisis reminded the nation about the essential service, fuel efficiency, flexibility, economy, practicality, and ubiquity of the good, old-fashioned bus.

When gasoline supplies returned, attention all but turned away again until the federal government, in 1983, lifted the constraints that had been imposed since the Interstate Commerce Commission Act of 1935. The industry became free to address the problems of an archaic product, and could develop new products to fit current needs.

When the bus business was regulated, existing companies operated under a kind of government protection, their routes like franchises and profits virtually assured. Without competition, the companies could charge customers pretty much what they liked. And although they usually had authority to operate both point-to-point (scheduled) service and charters, long-haul scheduled service was the mainstay of the business.

Consisting mainly of family businesses, many companies were operated by third and fourth generations of the founders with little incentive to innovate or respond to changes in the marketplace. Immediately following deregulation in 1983, however, thousands of new companies obtained operating licenses. There were 1,500 companies in 1983. Today, 4,000 private companies employing about 60,000 people and operating 44,000 buses currently offer service in one form or another. Of these, only 50 bus companies are large enough to have more than 100 coaches in the fleet, and altogether these carry 56 percent of the passengers.

Nearly two-thirds of the industry are small carriers operating fewer than 10 buses, which collectively carry 97 million passengers. However, this is changing, with a few giants such as Greyhound Lines and Coach USA gobbling up independents (which can work out to the benefit of the company as well as employees by providing the benefits of bigness). Only 12 percent of the companies provide scheduled service, operating some 10,000 coaches and accounting for 50 percent of the motorcoach mileage. Today, the gravy for the motorcoach companies is in charters and tours, which have become a critical component of the business, accounting for half of all bus passengers and revenue.

In the 1940s and 1950s, the heyday for the bus operators, relatively few families had a car; air service was nonexistent or prohibitively expensive, and even the railroad served limited numbers of communities. Things have changed dramatically; cars have become ubiquitous, air travel has become a lot more available and affordable, and rental cars fill in the gaps. Consequently, the bus industry has been fighting an uphill battle to maintain its customer base for scheduled service.

Nonetheless, the intercity bus industry, which serves 13,000 communities compared to only about 200 airports for scheduled service, still serves more communities than any other common carrier, and its use has been back on the upswing. In 1999, the industry carried 774 million passengers in the U.S., dwarfing the 568 million carried by commercial air carriers and 377 million by commuter rail and Amtrak.

Buses still perform a valuable service in providing low-cost, point-to-point transportation, particularly from the thousands of communities not readily accessible by air. But it is difficult for bus lines to compete with the airlines in speed and competitive rates, and, particularly, personal automobiles. For the industry to survive, it must find ways to provide a widespread, comfortable service at low fares.

Greyhound: Rising to the Challenge

Greyhound, still the largest single bus company and the only one providing a truly nationwide network of regular-route passenger service, epitomizes the challenge facing the motorcoach industry. Greyhound serves more than 3,700 destinations with 20,000 daily departures across the continent, and carries some 22 million passengers a year. In addition to providing scheduled transportation, it also provides package and courier express service, charter and tour services, and food service at certain terminals. A new unit, Greyhound Travel Services, has returned the company to the tour business after a hiatus and is operating vacation packages in the United States and Canada.

Two thousand of the 13,000 employees are Managers. "The Greyhound Manager must be a very strong, nonbureaucratic, broad-based Manager who can deal with all kinds of customer service, bus control, and driver issues," said one executive. "Airlines are encumbered by more levels of specialization; our Managers are generalists—people with practical, hands-on, general management experience."

With a fleet of more than 2,400 buses, a significant number of positions are in the maintenance department. The maintenance department consists of 14 maintenance centers and 29 service island locations nationwide. This department employs more than 900 people, including Managers, Assistant Managers, Supervisors, Technical Trainers, Mechanics, Parts Room Personnel, and Clerical Staff. Among the positions are Transportation Management/Supervision, Fleet Management, Technical Training/Development, Diesel Mechanics, Transmission Troubleshooting and Repair, HVAC Controls and Repairs, Electronic Engine/Transmission Controls, Preventative Maintenance and Inspections, Body and Frame Repair, Parts Purchasing.

Not surprisingly, the bus company has substantial needs for Information Technology professionals—Programmers, E-Commerce Developers, and Project Managers.

"It's more challenging and interesting than I had imagined it would be," commented one manager.

(For more information, see www.greyhound.com.)

Tours and Charters

Tours and charters has proved to be one of the more profitable areas of the bus industry. Virtually all the companies now offer charter service (in which the motorcoach is hired for exclusive use by a preformed group), which now accounts for one-third of motorcoach mileage. Eight percent of motorcoach miles are logged on tours and sightseeing, to such popular places as Atlantic City, Branson, Chicago, Las Vegas, Los Angeles, New York City, Nashville, Orlando, and Washington, D.C.

The growth of charters and tours is vastly changing the professional make-up of the industry, shifting the emphasis from operations to sales and marketing. "Companies are going outside the family unit," an American Bus Association veteran noted. "They are hiring people with hotel sales experience who know how to package and sell tours." Many are coming into the tour and charter side of the business from travel agencies as well as hotel sales.

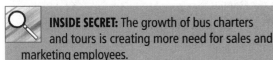

INSIDE SECRET: The growth of bus charters and tours is creating more need for sales and marketing employees.

The National Motorcoach Marketing Network (www.motorcoach.com), born in 1983 from deregulation, epitomizes the new direction the industry is heading, and the new emphasis on marketing and sales. A consortium, or marketing alliance, of 80 member companies collectively operating 2,000 buses, the National Motorcoach Marketing Network represents one of the largest charter networks in the country. Essentially, it provides one-stop shopping for anyone who needs to charter a bus from anywhere. Although up until now the company had focused on North America, it is now expanding internationally. The network is able to wage marketing efforts that independent companies could not afford on their own. In so doing, they have been able to tap into new markets for coaches beyond the mainstay senior-citizen market. These include military personnel, student bands and sports teams, festival groups, inbound visitors, travel agency–generated groups, corporations, and associations. The network also publishes an in-bus magazine, *Byways,* which is similar to the airlines' in-flight magazines.

High-Tech Equipment, Unpretentious People

The word "bus" hurts the image of the business. People tend to think of a rumbling, smoky, dirty bus rolling out from a dingy terminal in a decrepit inner city. But the present reality is vastly different from the worn stereotypes.

New, slick, high-tech buses incorporate many of the amenities of airline compartments and go beyond the airlines in terms of wide windows and roomy seats (some even offer in-bus movies; and some are executive coaches, rolling business suites, for a small group of VIPs or politicians campaigning for office). Tours are being designed to appeal to every interest and degree of travel sophistication (see the section on domestic tour operations in chapter 3). Innovations in fares, negotiated programs with other travel suppliers, and distribution (computerized reservations and ticketing) are also making the business more interesting as well as profitable.

Why Choose the Motorcoach Industry?

The industry itself tends to attract people who are "very unpretentious, warm, and friendly," commented one veteran. "There is camaraderie—people enjoy the business. Some owners think nothing of taking tours out themselves."

People who are attracted to the motorcoach industry tend to be mechanically oriented, enamoured more of the vehicle itself than the notion of travel (much the same as airline people who are in love with a silver bird).

One of the special appeals of working in the bus business is that because the businesses tend to be small (many are family owned and operated), they are more personal. "For somebody who wants to work in the travel industry, the bus business may be one place to fulfill what you want to do," said one veteran. "It may not be as glamorous as the hotels, but it is another way to fulfill one's dream."

The motorcoach companies also tend to be located in many different locales—urban, suburban, and rural—so people can get comfortable working in their own community (much like the regional airlines).

The newest trend in the motorcoach industry is that smaller, independent operations are being gobbled up and consolidated into large companies, like Coach USA, making the operations more professional and providing employees more of the benefits of a big business.

Jobs in the Motorcoach Industry

Jobs in the motorcoach industry are much like those in the airlines, but with less specialization. Entry-level positions include Driver, Escort, and Customer Sales or Service.

Positions in operations include Mechanic, Maintenance, Supervisory, Parts, Purchasing, Driver, Dispatching, Scheduling, and General Manager.

Administrative positions include Payroll and keeping track of different states' bus regulations. The motorcoach companies also employ Tour Directors, Sales Managers, Advertising Executives, Tour Planners, and people to prepare the company's brochures.

Best Bet

- Customer Service Agent

The bus industry, like the airlines, is focusing on innovations in marketing and sales, yield management, customer service, computerized reservations, and fleet-management systems, which spells new professional opportunities in information technology and e-commerce.

INSIDE SECRET: New opportunities in the motorcoach industry are opening up in information technology and e-commerce.

Salaries in the Motorcoach Industry

In general, jobs in the motorcoach industry pay on par with those in tour operations (see chapter 3).

Drivers are paid an average salary of $30,000 before tips (which can be substantial). A General Manager can earn $60,000 to $75,000, depending on the size of the company. A Vice President–Sales for a major bus company can make $135,000.

One bus industry executive's career path is illustrative. Starting out with a B.A., he joined a bus/sightseeing company, rising to Director of Sales and Marketing, where he supervised 100 staff and branch offices. There he was responsible for product development, analysis, supplier negotiations, pricing, and tour brochures. After a long tenure, he left to become the Director of Operations of another company, where he established a regular route service to Atlantic City; then he went on to another bus company as General Manager before establishing his own bus business. He merged his bus business with a larger one, and, as Chief Executive Officer, supervised a staff of 65 employees (45 Drivers, 4 Managers, 6 office staff, and 10 people in the shop) and operated 26 charter buses. He sold this company to a bigger bus business and served as a Consultant for Fleet Utilization and Operations. Along the way, he earned his MBA.

Contacts, Sources, and Leads

- **American Bus Association,** 1100 New York Ave. NW, Ste. 1050, Washington, DC 20005-3934; 202-842-1645; www.buses.org (has a link to job classifieds in the industry, plus links to member companies and industry data). Publishes a monthly magazine called *Destinations* as well as an annual report, and conducts annual conferences that can be sources of job leads.

- **National Tour Association,** 546 E. Main St., Lexington, KY 40508; 800-682-8886; www.ntaonline.com.
- **National Motorcoach Marketing Network,** 10527 Braddock Rd., Ste. C, Fairfax, VA 22032; 703-250-7897 (www.motorcoach.com).
- **Greyhound Lines, Inc.,** P.O. Box 660362, Dallas, TX 75266-6196; www.greyhound.com. The Web site posts job openings and has an interesting FAQ section.
- **Coach USA, Inc.,** One Riverway, Ste. 500, Houston, TX 77056-1921; 713-888-0104 or 888-COACHUSA; www.coachusa.com.
- Check local **convention and visitor bureaus.**

Passenger Railroad: The Little Engine That Could

Railroads opened up America, transforming the frontiers into commercial and cosmopolitan centers. They played a critical part in the industrialization process and made it possible for the nation to grow as big as it did and still remain united. Whole communities depended on the railroad; in the age of the horse and buggy, the train was like the jumbo jet today. Tiny stations developed into terminals, and terminals into commercial hubs.

But it is not mere nostalgia that keeps what is left of the passenger rail service operating. America's passenger rail service, embodied in the National Railroad Passenger Corporation, universally known as Amtrak (a blending of the words "American" and "Track"), is a quasi-governmental entity and remains a vital, if often unappreciated, element in the nation's transportation system. Though waging a constant struggle for survival against the budget-slashing of the federal government, Amtrak has in many ways been reborn, as it rekindles an interest in rail travel.

Snapshot: The Passenger Railroad Industry

Many of the 24,000 people who work for Amtrak come to the line for the same reasons that many of the 22.2 million passengers who ride it do: the sheer love and fascination for trains and rail travel.

In 1929, during the heyday of rail travel when the great and legendary lines were still running, the nation's railroads operated 20,000 passenger trains and carried 77 percent of intercity passenger traffic by common carrier. By 1950, more than half the passenger trains had disappeared, as the railroads' share of intercity passenger traffic declined to 46 percent. By 1970, rail passenger traffic had dwindled to a mere 7 percent, and the trains still operating numbered fewer than 450. Of these, 100 were in the process of being discontinued and many were operating with only one or two passenger cars.

The private automobile, which ballooned to about 82 percent of all intercity traffic, was a key factor in the decline of the railroads, while the airlines had come to dominate the common-carrier market.

By this time, many began to feel that the excessive reliance on the private automobile and airplane during the previous four decades had left the nation with a serious imbalance in its transportation. Many feared that unbridled expansion of highways and airports would strangle the nation's central cities, produce environmental problems such as air and noise pollution, take up excessive amounts of land, and result in the dislocation of people. The Arab Oil Embargo of 1973–1974 was a clear demonstration of the danger of being overly dependent on petroleum-driven modes of travel.

The creation of a national rail passenger system was viewed as a means of saving an alternate form of transportation that possessed a priceless asset: existing tracks and rights-of-way into the nation's major population centers. Upgrading these rail facilities was economical compared to the costs of constructing new highways and airports.

Amtrak was created by the Rail Passenger Service Act, enacted October 30, 1970 (service began May 1, 1971). But from the beginning, the struggling line seemed to be trudging uphill. It inherited an antiquated business; with passenger losses steadily increasing, the railroad operators had no incentive to maintain or modernize equipment or facilities.

International Rail Services

Outside the United States, passenger rail systems are considered national treasures. Indeed, the spirit of the "Orient Express," with its aura of romance and adventure, survives in a recreation of that famed line using some restored cars.

Thousands of people travel the world just to ride such renowned trains—the Orient Express in Europe (with new services that extend into Asia and Australia; www.orient-express.com), the Siberian Express through Russia, and the Blue Train in South Africa. In India, there is a train with cars like a maharajah's palace. In China, one of the world's last steam-powered trains plies the Gobi Desert to Mongolia.

Many of the foreign rail systems have an active presence in the United States for marketing their services under the Rail Europe (www.raileurope.com) umbrella. Starting well before World War II as a commercial representation of the French railroads, the Rail Europe Group was created in its present form in 1991 when the wholly owned U.S. subsidiary of SNCF, the French National Railroad, merged with the North American arm of the Swiss Federal Railways. While it is still a subsidiary of the SNCF and the CFF (Swiss Federal Railways), Rail Europe is also the official North American representative for 60 European railroads, the latest addition being the 25 Train Operating Companies of Britain.

Over the past decade, Rail Europe has evolved into the largest distributor of European travel-related products, catering to both the leisure traveler and the business traveler. Each year, more than 1 million American leisure and business travelers use one of their products.

Although there are very limited opportunities for Americans to work for national rail services abroad, many Americans work for the marketing, sales, and distribution centers of the foreign rail companies here in the U.S.

For the first two years, Amtrak was almost totally dependent on the private railroads, leasing equipment and using their facilities. An Amtrak customer could make a reservation, buy a ticket, and take a trip without ever coming into contact with an Amtrak employee (indeed, when it opened for business in 1971, there were only 25 employees in the whole company). Further, Congress had allocated only a two-year experimental term, so planning future improvements was impossible.

With echoes of "The Little Engine That Could," Amtrak has made extraordinary strides considering the obstacles, and has become one of the largest public carriers in numbers of passengers carried.

Amtrak now operates an average of 265 trains a day over a 22,000-mile route system and serves 500 station locations in 45 states (plans are underway to serve Maine, and Wyoming is served by Amtrak Thruway Motorcoaches). At 2,768 miles, the Sunset Limited between Orlando and Los Angeles is the longest Amtrak intercity passenger train ride.

Along the bustling New York–Washington corridor, Amtrak carries enough passengers to fill 121 airline flights per day, and handles 1.8 million riders per month system-wide. In 2000, Amtrak served more than 22.5 million guests (61,000 a day).

The railroad has dramatically improved its equipment and facilities, bringing on the Metroliners, Superliners, luxurious bilevel cars, sleepers, Amfleet cars, Heritage cars (refurbished and reconfigured cars), Turboliners (which operate at 125 m.p.h.), Vista Dome coaches (with an elevated dome permitting 360-degree viewing), and self-propelled cars. Engineers are developing prototypes for new kinds of locomotives and passenger cars, and Amtrak is testing the first three-phase alternating current traction-drive system for a diesel locomotive in this country.

Amtrak operates 2,188 railroad cars plus 343 locomotives (278 diesel and 65 electric). The line owns three heavy maintenance facilities in Wilmington and Bear, Delaware; and Beech Grove, Indiana; as well as other maintenance facilities in Boston; Chicago; Hialeah, Florida; Los Angeles; New Orleans; New York City; Niagara Falls; Oakland; Rensselaer, New York; Seattle; and Washington, D.C. It owns 18 tunnels and 1,165 bridges.

The passenger railroad has devoted about as much of its resources to improving the marketing and distribution of its services as to the fleet and track. Amtrak installed a highly sophisticated computerized reservations system, now linked to travel agents through several airline reservations systems. It also created a "Teletrak" telemarketing program, whereby Amtrak sales agents service smaller travel agency accounts by telephone.

Amtrak has also become innovative in attracting more of the longer-haul (that is, vacation) traveler, introducing an air/rail program with United and a rail/sail program (take the train to a port, cruise, and then return by rail) out of Miami, Montreal, New Orleans, San Diego, and Vancouver; and a cooperative program with VIA, Canada's passenger railroad. Such programs are devised by the marketing and tour departments.

The line has been under constant pressure to reduce deficits and eventually become profitable. Toward this objective, Amtrak has expanded into contract work—doing track renewal, assembling subway cars for the Washington, D.C., Metrorail system, and developing the first cogeneration plant (designed to produce steam and electrical power for both Amtrak and others). It also hauls mail and packages for the U.S. Postal Service. The line now is looking to introduce some new routes.

Improvements like these help bolster the employees, who frequently feel the frustration of working for a private company that is publicly subsidized. Amtrak has been moving to become self-sufficient by bringing on more passengers and decreasing costs. With improvements in services, innovative products, and growing disenchantment with traffic on roads and in the sky, the goal seems attainable. Indeed, ridership has steadily increased, and the gap between revenues and subsidies has steadily declined.

Amtrak is a quasi-governmental entity, an operating railroad corporation with the U.S. government, through the Department of Transportation, as the sole stockholder. Consequently, it has many of the political hassles of a government agency, felt most intensely every two years when Congress must approve a new allocation. However, it is operated as a private corporation. Although workers are not civil service, about 90 percent of the more than 25,000 employees are union members. The remaining 10 percent (about 2,500 people) are management.

Scenic Railways

Train travel is such a special experience for many people that historic and scenic lines are major tourist attractions. These provide all the gritty jobs of operating a railroad (many are coal-burning steam trains or vintage cars) as well as the operations, marketing, and sales positions of a tourist attraction. Often, people who work at these are also history buffs and devotees of the old railroads.

Why Choose the Passenger Railroad Industry?

Perhaps because of the special qualities, the romance and excitement of railroading, and the feeling of being under constant siege, many at Amtrak speak of a "family-like" atmosphere. "There is a common goal, a dedication. You get the idea that the number-one priority for everyone is to move trains through a territory," an Amtrak veteran related.

Jobs in the Passenger Railroad Industry

Many of the jobs at Amtrak are common to most major businesses (particularly transportation companies), such as sales and marketing, finance, and administration and personnel. But there are many jobs, such as in engineering, passenger and operating services, and operations, that are unique to railroading.

Among the 25,000 employees, there are

- Onboard service personnel (such as Porters, Dining-Car employees, and onboard Chiefs who supervise long-distance trains)
- Station personnel
- About 500 Reservations and Information Agents at five central reservations offices who handle requests from the general public and travel agents
- City Ticket and Station Ticket Agents
- Workers at maintenance facilities and yards

A new emphasis on training and development, including management training and development and an employee safety education program, has produced new jobs in these areas. Sales Representatives call on travel agents and other major clients (such as tour operators) and attend travel industry trade shows.

Train operating crews, such as Engineers, Conductors, Trainmen, and Brakemen, are employed by Amtrak as well (but have to be qualified by and generally come from the freight railroads that operate on the routes).

The marketing area is getting as much emphasis today as operations. In the past, the Marketing department also contained Tour Planners who help create about 400 national tours (another 400 tours were created locally); this function has been relegated to a tour operator, which creates "private-label" tours for Amtrak.

Salaries in the Passenger Railroad Industry

Salaries are "very competitive with the travel industry." Union positions have a salary scale that pays 80 percent of full salary in the first year; 90 percent in the second; and 100 percent in the third. Benefits are "outstanding," but the packages differ for union and management, generally including health and life insurance and rail-travel privileges.

Your Ticket into the Passenger Railroad Industry

Although rail travel is increasing, the number of openings is not increasing as much because the carrier is under such pressure to reduce costs by increasing productivity.

Many of those who apply for jobs had parents who worked for a railroad. "It gets into the blood," one veteran said. And there is considerable movement back and forth with freight railroads.

The headquarters personnel office in Washington, D.C., is responsible for hiring upper management and people for administrative positions; field offices recruit for all the union positions, track, maintenance, and commissary. There is a 30-day probation period, after which a worker usually joins a union. Railroad jobs are known for their excellent security.

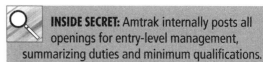

INSIDE SECRET: Amtrak internally posts all openings for entry-level management, summarizing duties and minimum qualifications.

Roadmap to the Top

There is a policy of promotion from within that is enforced by the technical nature of most jobs. Most management positions require experience that can be acquired only from a union position. About the only entry-level management position that Amtrak has to go to the "street" for is computer programmers.

As in so many travel businesses, rising up through the ranks frequently means being moved around to where job opportunities are.

Amtrak has a career-development program, but mobility is hampered by the fact that "there is so much talent and only 10 percent of the positions are in management."

Contacts, Sources, and Leads

■ **Amtrak National Railroad Passenger Corporation,** 60 Massachusetts Ave. NE, Washington, DC 20002; www.amtrak.com.

■ Another excellent general source for leads is http://dir.yahoo.com/Economy/Transportation/ Trains_and_Railroads/.

Rail Travel and Tour Companies

For more of these, check the *Specialty Travel Index* or visit www.specialtytravel.com.

■ **Copper Canyon Tours,** Sierra Vista, AZ; 800-499-5685; www.ss-tours.com.

■ **Premier Selections Inc.,** Harrison, NY; 800-234-4000; www.premierselections.com.

■ **Rail Travel Center,** St. Albans, VT; 800-458-5394; www.railtravelcenter.com (a great site for anyone who loves trains).

Scenic Railways

■ **The Durango and Silverton Narrow Gauge Railroad,** Durango, CO; 303-259-0274.

■ **Grand Canyon Railway,** Williams, AZ; 800-THE-TRAIN.

■ **Cumbres Toltec Scenic Railroad,** Chama, NM; 800-426-5279.

■ **Mount Washington Cog Railway,** Mt. Washington, NH; 800-922-8825.

CHAPTER 12

CRUISES: FULL SPEED AHEAD

Until recently, those who would have quested after the glamorous life aboard ship as depicted on the popular television show *The Love Boat* might have found opportunities extremely limited. But all that is changing. The cruise industry, still technically in its adolescence, is undergoing phenomenal growth as more and more people discover this vacation alternative.

 ## Snapshot: The Cruise Industry

The cruise industry grew by 1,200 percent between 1970 and 2000, from fewer than 500,000 to 6 million passengers. Since 1970, an estimated 77 million passengers have taken a cruise.

The cruise lines achieved this growth largely by repositioning the concept of "cruise" away from a mode of transportation to a destination/resort product, and away from an "elitist" activity to a mass-market vacation. Scores of new packages, programs, and styles of ships and cruising are successfully tapping new cruise customers.

The cruise industry has had a vital impact on the economy, generating more than 176,000 jobs throughout the U.S., and an economic impact of $11.6 billion (taking into account all the related jobs that are created to support the cruise industry). Because of growth, it is forecast that the cruise industry will generate almost 275,000 jobs in 2002, for a total of $18.3 billion in U.S. spending.

Not too long ago, great ships like the *Queen Mary* were the main form of intercontinental transportation. Fortunes sank when "high society" (the mainstay of the cruise-going public) became the jet-setters. The industry struggled along until the aura of *Now Voyager*,

featuring Bette Davis as a debutante who falls in love while on a long-distance sail to South America, gave way to *The Love Boat*, where it seems whole boatloads find their true loves. It was then that vast new groups of people began to see themselves cruising, too.

Instead of competing with the airlines, the cruise lines have become their partners, and compete instead with destinations, resorts, and other styles of vacations. Moreover, cruise ships have become a venue for conventions and meetings, and cruises have become an incentive reward for a job well done, giving cruise companies a whole new corporate market to pursue.

The Tip of the Iceberg

The industry believes its phenomenal growth in the past 25 years is just the tip of the iceberg, so to speak. Only 11 percent of Americans have ever cruised, yet industry analysts claim that nearly 60 percent of adults (75 million North Americans) say they are interested in cruising in the next five years, and more than 41 million say they definitely or probably will. Moreover, historically, people who have tried cruising once are extremely likely to cruise again, and many cruisers take at least one cruise a year.

In dollar terms, the Cruise Lines International Association (CLIA) estimates the cumulative market potential for the cruise industry over the next five years at $85 billion.

Key reasons why the cruise industry is not reaching its full potential are lack of awareness of the range of products and prices available, anxiety, and other misconceptions about cruising.

The stereotype is that cruises cater to wealthy senior citizens. But key markets for potential cruise-goers are younger people (the average age of "hot prospects" is

42), baby boomers, people with moderate incomes (nearly 60 percent of all cruise passengers earn between $20,000 and $59,000 per year), couples with children (the family market), friends or relatives of current cruise clients, and clients who have taken a resort vacation in the past.

All American Line: American Classic Voyages Poised for Growth

American Classic Voyages Co., based in New Orleans, may not be the biggest cruise line in the world, but as the largest American-flag–carrying line poised for a dramatic expansion, it affords the best opportunity for Americans who want to work on board a cruise ship.

The line has four mainland riverboats, among them the famed historic landmark the *Delta Queen,* which evoke the era of Mark Twain, plus one cruise ship, the S.S. *Independence,* which operates under American Hawaii Cruises in Hawaii. The line has an ambitious fleet-building program: In four years, it will expand to a nine-vessel company, building two 1,900-passenger cruise ships for service in Hawaii in 2003 and 2004, under the famed name of United States Lines; plus a new fleet of intimate 226-passenger ships to operate as Delta Queen Coastal Voyages along the Eastern Seaboard, Great Lakes, Caribbean, and Mexico. And eventually it will also operate in Alaska and the West Coast. The first two of these ships, the cv *Cape May Light* and cv *Cape Cod Light,* will begin service in 2001.

The line will effectively triple in size, from 1,500 to 4,500 employees (of which 3,800 will be on board vessels), and quadruple in business. As a result, the line is hiring the full gamut, from entry-level to seasoned sailors, from customer service to navigation engineering. The ms *Patriot* (formerly Holland America's *Nieuw Amsterdam*), which carries 1,200 passengers, typically has 477 positions on board. This number includes 100 positions in the marine navigation side (the deck), of which some are licensed and some are unlicensed (working your way up from a Deckhand is not uncommon). Every ship also has a "hotel" side, with about 350 positions, everything from Bartenders and Dining Room Servers to Pursers (comparable to working the front desk in the hotel industry). The onboard staff is supported by 400 people ashore, including 40 staff at the Honolulu office, plus about 30 regional sales-people who work out of "virtual offices."

Because AMCV flies the American flag, it is crewed by Americans (even Carnival Cruise Lines flies a foreign flag and hires its onboard staff abroad, so only about 10 to 15 percent of the staff are Americans).

AMCV recruits from hotel schools and from people in hospitality, pays competitive wages, and complies with American labor laws. In the galley, First Cooks earn $120 per day for a 10-hour day; a Junior Cook earns $76 (the smaller vessels have 35 Cooks and the larger ones have 50). Bartenders can earn $70 per day plus tips; Waiters get $47 per day plus tips (which can work out to $700 to $900 per week). Laundry people get $75 per day. And deck-engine jobs, including Maintenance, get $100 per day.

AMCV's biggest ships will operate seven-day cruises in Hawaii (where the line is doing its heaviest recruiting). The crew experience provides a shorter rotation than most of the blue-water competitors—three months at a time (12 to 13 weeks on and 6 weeks off) versus eight or nine months of the time. The crew members are not contracted for six to eight months, as on other lines, but are full-time employees with an annual schedule (working toward a pension), although there are limited opportunities to work a six-month schedule in Hawaii (but you have to pay your own way to Hawaii).

The riverboat operation is somewhat different. Here the crews work shorter rotations, six weeks on and two weeks off.

"People have to accept the adventurous lifestyle," said Craig Keller, Vice President of Human Resources. "It is not for everyone. You have to be honest with yourself about living away from home (we provide room and board for 6 to 12 weeks at a time). Our 'day' in Hawaii is a 10-hour day (you get overtime if you work longer). You have to be comfortable living and working in the same place."

Because AMCV is growing, there will be greater upward mobility, as well as the chance to transfer vessel to vessel, itinerary to itinerary, and experience different brands and different adventures.

There is some movement between the boats and shore-side positions. "All three recruiters in H.R. have worked two to three years on the riverboats," Keller said. "They wanted to get their feet dry. We have people who come ashore and then go back. A lot don't come ashore because they like the extended time off; if someone is comfortable with a 12 and 6 rotation, they normally don't like the five days a week, 50 weeks a year type of job."

Onboard, the line is doing more of its own entertainment (instead of subcontracting it), which includes historians known as *koumus* in Hawaii and *riverlorians* on the riverboats. There are also some children's programs in summer.

One benefit is that employees can cruise standby (that is, at the last minute, and if space is available), which can be a $5,000 perk. Another perk is that the line is publicly traded and there is an employee stock-purchase plan.

To work onboard, you have to have a realistic expectation of your living quarters. On a historic ship like the *Delta Queen,* the bathroom is down the hall and you will be assigned a roommate. On the newer ships, there are two people to a cabin, with bunk beds and a private bath. "It's more like a college experience rather than military, but not like a fraternity/sorority lifestyle. We don't tolerate rudeness to a co-worker, or anti-social, aggressive behavior."

"This is not a paid vacation. It's a 10-hour day and people will work hard," Keller said. "Nobody gets a day off. But after three months, you have extended time off and lots of earnings to pocket.

"We look for people who have a bit of an adventuresome spirit," Keller said.

(For more information, see www.amcv.com.)

"Let's Make a Deal"

CLIA's 25 members operate about 125 vessels, ranging from super yachts to super-liners, and claim to account for 90 percent of all the cruise business.

As it is, though, the industry has experienced tremendous increases in cruise capacity that far outstrip the increase in passengers. During the 1980s, some 40 new ships were built; in the 1990s, nearly 80 new ships made their debut; between 2000 and 2005, the cruise industry is forecast to introduce at least 52 new ships, among them mega-liners that can accommodate more than 3,000 passengers, as well as smaller, more intimate luxury vessels.

Carnival Cruise Lines (www.carnival.com), one of the fastest growing, was faced with the problem of virtually doubling the number of passengers it had been carrying just to keep up with the increased capacity it brought on with its newest mega-liners.

This phenomenal growth has fueled the continuing evolution of the cruise industry product. Cruise companies have expanded itineraries to include more exotic ports of call, and have introduced more innovative onboard facilities, such as ice-skating rinks, cyber-cafes, rock-climbing walls, multiple themed restaurants, state-of-the-art meeting facilities, and world-class spas.

The growth in capacity has not been just from the existing lines. Several new lines have been launched, such as Disney Cruise Line (www.disneycruise.com), Seabourn Cruise Line (www.seabourn.com), and Crystal Cruises (www.crystalcruises.com; Los Angeles). One of the newest lines, Windstar Cruises (www.windstarcruises.com; now part of Carnival Corporation) has a fleet of four-masted ships with computer-directed sails.

The cruise business is further complicated by the extremely high overhead expenses attached to the ships. "This is a capital-intensive business," stated Bob Dickinson, President of Carnival Cruise Lines. "All costs are fixed except food—the fuel consumption is the same for one passenger as 1,200." Whereas a hotel can break even with only 55 to 60 percent occupancy, and airlines at 60 to 65 percent, the ships have to go out 80 to 90 percent full just to cover costs.

Pricing is key to drawing in new cruise passengers. "We are very price-sensitive. If you have 1,000 passengers, you can spread the fixed costs and make a profit. If you expect only 80 percent occupancy, you have to take the fixed costs and spread them over the smaller number and charge more.

With that kind of pressure to produce passengers, passengers will be produced," said an industry expert.

Always deregulated, the cruise lines' zeal to stimulate new passengers and take a greater share of the existing market has produced a discount-pricing situation much like the airlines, and frequently has seemed like *Let's Make a Deal.*

The lines are responding to the problem with new products and facilities to appeal to virtually every age bracket, taste, and budget—singles, married couples, families, retirees—as well as becoming extremely aggressive in their marketing and sales strategies.

A decade ago, a wider spectrum of the public began to picture itself cruising. Cruise lines instantly responded with more trips of shorter duration, lower-cost trips that would appeal to a more youthful, active market, and across more income levels.

Cruises were introduced ranging from an overnight "cruise to nowhere" for as little as $69 per person, and wide selections of three, four, and seven-day itineraries.

Onboard amenities were also changed: lighter dining selections, health clubs, computer rooms, video game rooms. Cunard went so far as to install an entire "Golden Door" health spa on the *Queen Elizabeth II.*

The lines also added more ports to itineraries and developed theme and special-interest cruises to further tap into specialized markets—big band music festivals, opera performances, financial planning seminars, weight-loss clinics, lectures about the movie industry, and University at Sea (on Holland America Line, with accredited programs for professionals) are but a scant few of the diverse subjects featured on cruises.

These efforts have been enormously successful in broadening the market. A recent study showed that 48 percent of all cruise passengers earn less than $25,000 annually, nearly half are under 45 years old, and 10 percent are younger than 25. The great surge in singles and families has helped expand the cruise "season" to year-round.

Although most of the effort in the industry is being focused on positioning cruises as a floating, all-inclusive vacation, the industry is also aggressively pursuing commercial business in the form of conventions, meetings, and incentives (travel awards won by people who meet a sales target or some other preset goal).

These changes have enormous implications for the kinds and quantities of jobs available in the industry. In contrast to the airline industry, which offers a very limited and specific kind of service, cruise lines have a very diversified and dynamic product, which makes for an excitement that is distinct to this segment of the industry.

 # Why Choose the Cruise Industry?

People in the cruise industry love being involved in the pleasure side of the travel business, and sense the thrill of anticipation and the excitement of seeing new places that their passengers experience. They also like being part of a global community—both the cruise industry and the travel professionals who sell the cruise product.

For those who work in headquarters, the business is sufficiently diverse (hotel operations, tour operations, and being involved with everything from airlines to visitor bureaus). It's also competitive, but the competition among cruise lines is friendly, not cutthroat, so cruise industry people feel like part of a community.

Onboard jobs take you to faraway places and away from home; you get to meet interesting people among the passengers and crew, as well as in port. But it is hard work.

"The average American sees *The Love Boat* and thinks that working on a ship is an adventurous idea," said Michael Trubenbacher, Manager of Hotel Operations for Regency Cruises. "The reality is 12- to 13-hour workdays, no days off for a six- to eight-month contract, living four to a cabin where you live and breathe your fellow worker. It's not glory and glamour."

Jobs in the Cruise Industry

Most of the career opportunities available in cruise lines are in corporate offices in the following departments: Air/Sea (they coordinate passengers' travel into ports, usually negotiating special airfares); Finance and Administration; Human Resources; Information Technology; Marine Operations; Marketing; Reservations; Sales; and Vessel Operations. As in the airlines, there are many positions involving engineering, maintenance, safety management, and coordinating with government regulations and authorities.

Best Bets

- Counselor
- Sales Representative
- Incentive Sales Specialist
- Conventions and Meeting Services
- Manager of Partnership Marketing
- Revenue Management Analyst
- Webmaster
- Reservations Agent

The marketing and sales side is actually quite complex, combining airline/transportation with hospitality. The dynamics of the industry demand strategies that encompass direct marketing, loyalty marketing, sales promotions and incentives (think about all the contests that use a cruise as the prize), and partnership and relationship marketing. Cruise lines also do not sell just to the leisure-travel market (travel agents and consortia), but have a business-travel component as well, in terms of incentive programs as well as onboard meetings and conventions.

Some examples of job titles and descriptions include the following:

- **Sailing Coordinator:** Requires at least one year of experience as an Airline Reservationist or Travel Agent with airline computer experience, strong organizational skills, and a strong command of the English language, both written and verbal. Must

also be able to work in a multitask, fast-paced environment and work overtime when necessary. Responsibilities include making all travel accommodations for air/sea passengers (airline, rail, hotel, transfers, and so on) and maintaining and updating activities relating to air/sea passengers.

- **Supervisor, Fleet Health and Safety:** Requires at least two years of experience coordinating maritime safety programs and a Bachelor's degree in Safety Management or equivalent work experience. Responsibilities include implementing safety programs throughout the fleet, including all associated training, assisting with vessel record-keeping, and complying with the company safety-management system. Ability to speak Spanish or Italian is a plus. Must be PC proficient and able to travel when necessary.

> **INSIDE SECRET:** The cruise industry does not afford as much upward mobility as other segments of the travel industry. Senior management positions, although among the highest paying in the industry, are relatively few and there is relatively little turnover.

- **Analyst, Pricing Operations:** Requires a minimum of two years of experience with pricing concepts and a demonstrated proficiency in project management plus a Bachelor's degree in a similar discipline or equivalent work experience. A Master's degree is a plus. Responsibilities include ensuring the integrity of the pricing structure and developing pricing system enhancements to maximize yield improvement and efficiency.

- **Analyst, Revenue Management:** Requires a minimum of two years of strategic planning and revenue analysis experience and a Bachelor's degree in Finance or Marketing or equivalent work experience. Responsibilities include developing, interpreting, and implementing complex pricing and inventory-management actions to maximize revenue yield.

There are relatively few positions onboard ships because most of the lines are of foreign registry and employ crews from Greece, Italy, Portugal, the Philippines, and Indonesia. Positions that are available to Americans onboard include the areas of entertainment, Social Director and staff, Shopkeepers, casino staff, spa staff, Children's Counselors, medical staff, Photographers, Onboard Newspaper Editor, Shipboard Information System Manager, and business office.

> **INSIDE SECRET:** Relatively few positions are available to Americans onboard the ships themselves; most of these are in the business office, entertainment, Social Director and staff, Children's Counselors, Shopkeepers, spa services, and casino workers.

Apart from the conventional areas of marketing, sales, and operations, "the industry is extremely eclectic in terms of its [hiring] needs," one expert declared. "There are many different kinds of people getting involved."

Jim Flynn, a former golf pro, for example, became a cruise director for one cruise line. He started doing golf lectures onboard the ship and went on to organize all of the line's programs.

The industry also hires entertainers to perform onboard, people to publish shipboard newspapers, training specialists to conduct seminars for travel agents, and doctors. Child-care professionals are much in demand as many of the lines reach out to the family market. The trend toward themed and special-interest cruises has also vastly expanded employment opportunities. One line has a series of celebrity cruises such as a Basketball Hall of Fame Cruise, a News Cruise, a Chocolate Lover's Cruise, and a Halley's Comet Cruise. In addition to the extra people who are hired to fulfill the theme or special interest, there are entire staffs devoted to dreaming up new ideas and booking the entertainers and celebrities.

> **INSIDE SECRET:** Themed and special-interest cruises have opened opportunities for employees to think up new cruise ideas and make them happen.

Salaries in the Cruise Industry

Actually, even the onboard positions can pay well when gratuities are factored in. A Waiter can earn $2,500 to $3,000 a month, for example (not bad when you consider that room and board are provided). One position in high demand is the Maitre d', which on a ship is more of a European-style Banquet Manager. The Maitre d' has to organize 400 to 500 people in a dining room, and the position pays well.

Entertainers can earn $500 to $3,000 a week, depending on their reputation and the cruise line.

Once you get into mid-management positions, cruise lines pay relatively well, somewhat better than airlines and hotels (reflecting the size and price point of the cruise line)—indeed, among the highest levels of the travel industry. Many positions afford an opportunity to travel—certainly on the cruise ships and usually in on-shore positions, as well. However, it must be recognized that cruise line management positions are relatively few and therefore are scarce.

Sample Salaries and Specialties

Title	Salary
Hotel Director Assistant	$30,000
Agency Marketing Manager	$40,000
Executive Account Manager	$50,000
Entertainment Manager	$50,000
Vice President—Passenger Service	$80,000
Vice President—Sales	$90,000
Vice President and General Manager	$150,000
President and Chief Executive Officer	$200,000

Your Ticket into the Cruise Industry

Cruise lines have traditionally hired abroad—in Europe, the Mediterranean, and Asia—for most of the onboard positions, which are considered entry-level spots for movement into management, because wages are lower and because of the notion that Americans are unwilling or unable to provide the high level of service. However, with standards of living rising worldwide and cruise lines facing shortages of skilled workers to staff a growing fleet, Americans have more of a shot.

 INSIDE SECRET: The cruise industry is a close cousin of the lodging industry, so there is a natural career path from hospitality into cruising.

Cruise companies recruit many of their people from hotel schools and hotel companies because the businesses are much alike. Indeed, Cunard, which has a hotels and resorts entity, is moving to increase mobility between the two areas. Carnival Cruise Lines has also opened up a resort.

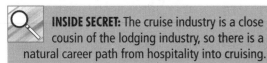

Roadmap to the Top

Entry-level jobs are mainly in reservations and telephone sales. "In the process, you learn product, know product and people, and deal with travel agents from all over the country," said Dickinson.

From a reservations position, "you can move quickly, if you are good, to supervisory positions in sales, in groups, the air/sea department, or marketing. A lot depends on individual attitude, motivation, and ability to grasp new ideas and grow," he said.

Opportunities are greatest at the chief ports of call where ship lines are generally headquartered: Miami, Port Everglades (Ft. Lauderdale), Port Canaveral, Los Angeles, Vancouver, New York, St. Petersburg, Palm Beach, San Juan, and San Diego.

Carnival Cruise Lines

Robert Dickinson is one of the pioneers of the American cruise industry and has probably done more than anyone to transform cruising from transportation to a vacation and popularize this form of travel. Yet Dickinson came to the cruise business by a convoluted route.

Indeed, raised in the Midwest, he reflected, "I had no perspective and no experience," and cruising was hard to learn. Moreover, his background was in finance and not sales and marketing. After many years as one of the most prominent sales and marketing executives in the cruise industry, he has become President of Carnival Cruise Lines, the largest cruise company in the world.

Dickinson, who sold industrial tires while a university student, started his management career with Ford Motor Company, then went to RCA Corporation, and then found himself at American International Travel Service (AITS), a travel company tapping the new field of charter travel. AITS then switched gears and boldly went out and bought its own cruise ship, which became the beginning of Carnival Cruise Lines.

"Cruising has been the fastest-growing segment of travel. It's where the action is. It is still in the embryonic stages. Contemporary cruising has only existed since the 1960s, whereas the hotels, airlines are more established, " Dickinson said.

"The problem in the industry is not over-capacity, it is under-demand. As an industry, we have done a poor job of marketing our product as a vacation. The biggest change in the industry is in the marketing aspect, and also the product."

Carnival has 14 "fun ships" in its fleet, including the 2,758-berth *Triumph* superliner, and was scheduled to add six additional ships by 2004. In addition to Carnival, the line also owns Holland America and Windstar.

The growth at Carnival, like the industry as a whole, directly translates into jobs. When Carnival Cruises had only the *Festivale*, it employed 17 people in sales. Seven years later, with five ships in the fleet, it had 39 salespeople in the U.S. and 12 in Canada. Having again nearly doubled in size, the number of salespeople has nearly doubled, as well.

Carnival has 1,100 "shore-side" staff at its Miami headquarters. The basic categories of jobs are sales and marketing, passenger service (works with passengers after they have sailed), group sales, group reservations, individual reservations, an air/sea department that works with the airlines, a travel department that develops the air tickets, and a marketing department that develops pricing. An in-house sales service department works with travel agents (because travel

(continues)

(continued)

agents book 95 percent of all cruises). There are an accounting department, computer/data processing programmers, and system analysts. Quality assurance specialists fine-tune reservations procedures.

Carnival employs more than 6,070 people in operations who work on ships, from 35 to 40 different countries, including Americans. These are Pursers, Entertainers, Casino Dealers, Shopkeepers, Waiters, Busboys, Chefs, Cruise Directors, and Crew (the *Ecstasy* has a crew of 920, including Captain, Chief Engineer, Staff Captain, Staff Chief Engineer, Chief Purser, Chief Steward, and Ship's Doctor).

There are Sales Representatives working in the field all over the United States and Canada, as well as some that are responsible for international sales. They earn salary plus travel expenses, and have a company-owned car and two bonus plans, which can more than double their salaries. "They can earn six figures," Dickinson said.

Dickinson noted that Carnival is different in terms of its human resources. "We are one of the few cruise companies that is American-owned. We don't have the international, cultural problems of other lines. It makes a big difference—the mores of different cultures are sometimes difficult to reconcile. European owners have a hard time understanding the marketing techniques that are successful here, or those successful in Europe don't necessarily work here. The tendency in a foreign-owned cruise company is that the American marketing company is just a marketing company."

At Carnival, though, all the cruise ships and everything on the ships is owned and controlled by Carnival—even the casino. Other lines farm out catering, casino, photography, and concessions. So overall, there are more jobs for Americans in this line than in most others. (Carnival also has moved into the resort/casino business, which provides even more opportunities for Americans.)

Most American companies tend to be inland waterway lines. But to operate an oceangoing ship under the U.S. flag, the ships have to be built in the United States. Carnival's ships are built in Scotland and England; and though they are American-owned, they fly a foreign flag.

There is a mystique about the ships, Dickinson reflected, "a magic which comes over me whenever I see one of the babies come in and out of port. I didn't have it at the start, but I have developed a love affair with the ships.

"You position yourself in the vacation business, make a lot of people happy. This is a people business, and it is creative."

Opportunities in the cruise industry had been somewhat restricted for women, particularly as the cruise industry tended to be a tight club. But that has changed considerably, with Carnival leading the way. Several lines now have women as Presidents or in senior executive positions.

Carnival is one of the largest cruise lines in its own right, but now is only one part of Carnival Corporation, which owns Holland America Line and Westours (a leading tour operator in Alaska and the Canadian Rockies), as well as Windstar Cruises, a specialty cruise operator composed of four computerized sailing vessels. It also owns the ultra-luxury Seabourn Cruise Line, which has a pair of 208-passenger all-suite vessels, the *Seabourn Pride* and *Seabourn Spirit*, plus the *Seabourn Legend*. The venerable Cunard Line, operator of the famed *Queen Elizabeth II*, and its five ships were merged with Seabourn's three vessels to form the new Cunard Line Limited, the industry's largest luxury operator. Cunard plans to build a new ship, *Queen Mary II*, which at nearly 150,000 gross registered tons will be the largest cruise ship ever constructed.

In recent years, Carnival Corporation has embarked on a number of ventures designed to increase its presence internationally. It has an equity stake in Airtours plc, a vertically integrated British-based travel supplier composed of hotels; cruise ships; charter airlines; U.K., Scandinavian, and Canadian tour operators; and retail outlets in the U.K., Scandinavia, and Finland. It also has a stake in Genoa, Italy-based Costa Crociere, Europe's leading cruise company, which currently operates a fleet of seven ships on worldwide itineraries primarily in Europe and North and South America, with three more ships on order.

(For more information, see www.carnivalcorp.com.)

Alternative Career Paths

Apart from the more traditional cruise lines, those who want to make a career on the water can consider the following:

- Yachting companies, particularly in the Caribbean (such as Windjammer Barefoot Cruises, Miami Beach, Florida)

- Private yachts that operate out of most port cities (such as World Yacht Enterprises, New York City, which specializes in entertainment and dining on short sails from New York harbor)

- Specially designed exploration ships, such as those operating in Alaska and the Galapagos Islands (Salen-Lindblad, New York; World Explorer Cruises, San Francisco)

- Barge trips up the Thames, Rhine, Nile, and other waterways (Floating Through Europe, New York)

- Riverboat companies (The Delta Queen Steamboat Co., New Orleans)

- Sightseeing boat companies (Maid of the Mist Boat Tours, Niagara Falls, New York; The Circle Line, New York City)

There is even a vacation market among the freighter lines, which rent out a few cabins for cruises of unspecified length and destination (suited for the really adventurous, people who like to spend a lot of time reading, and people with lots of time on their hands). Freighter World Cruises (800-531-7774; www.freighterworld.com) is an agency that specializes in booking passengers on such ships.

There also are companies that specialize in booking cruises, such as International Cruise Center (Mineola, New York) and Victory Tours & Cruises (New York City). There are also online reservations companies, such as ExpeditionTrips.com (877-412-8527) and EWaterways.com (B&V Associates; 800-546-4777).

One innovative company, ResidenSea, is believed to be the first to offer a luxury residential community at sea—people purchase apartments on the ship and travel around the world without leaving home. There are even accommodations for home-based businesses on board. In addition to the 110 apartments, there are 88 guest suites, which are marketed and managed by Silversea Cruises (ResidenSea; 305-264-9090; www.residensea.com).

Cruise-Only Agencies

Cruising is the fastest-growing segment for travel agencies, especially as agents have shifted their businesses to leisure and vacation travel and away from airline bookings. Travel agents continue to book about 95 percent of the cruise product. The report that the cruise industry is potentially $30 to $80 billion means that there is potentially $3 to $12 billion in commission. The success agents have had in tapping into the cruise market has spurred many agencies to set up cruise-only divisions, and for others to open cruise-only agencies.

INSIDE SECRET: Because there is little regulation of cruise-only agencies, many franchisors are in the market selling these, even as home-based businesses. You need to evaluate these offers carefully; check the reputability of the company and what they are promising before you hand over your money.

There are several franchisors who specialize in setting up cruise-only agencies (even home-based ones), but *caveat emptor* should be your rule of thumb if you are thinking of purchasing a franchise. Check their track records and references carefully. The cruise-only agencies are not subject to the same oversight as agencies that sell airline tickets.

Contacts, Sources, and Leads

- **Cruise Lines International Association,** 500 Fifth Ave., Ste. 1407, New York, NY 10110; 212-921-0066; www.cruising.org.

- **International Council of Cruise Lines,** Arlington, VA; www.iccl.org. Can be a source of background information regarding the cruise industry. It does not handle employment requests.

- **Trade publications** include *Leisure Travel News, Travel Weekly,* and *Travel Agent* magazine.

- **American Classic Voyages Company,** Robin Street Wharf, 1380 Port of New Orleans Place, New Orleans, LA 70130-1890; 800-423-JOBS; www.amcv.com.

PART III

PUBLIC-SECTOR AND NONPROFIT ENTITIES

Chapter 13: Destination Marketing
Organizations

Chapter 14: Airport, Aviation, and
Port Management

DESTINATION MARKETING ORGANIZATIONS

Travel is not only big business, it is the principal business of countless counties and countries. Travel and tourism is a gigantic generator of tax revenues for federal, state, and local governments and a major employer, particularly of women, minorities, youth, seniors, and people with disabilities. Indeed, the travel industry is the first, second, or third largest employer in 29 states, according to the Travel Industry Association (TIA). It has become so important that it has spawned a new quasi-political profession of destination marketing organizations. These include local tourist and convention and visitor bureaus, state travel departments, and national tourism promotion offices.

Snapshot: Destination Marketing

The $541 billion in expenditures by domestic and international travelers supported 7.8 million jobs ($158 billion in wages and salaries), and indirectly supported another 9.4 million jobs. In effect, one out of seven people is either directly or indirectly employed because of travel to and within the United States.

What's more, the travel industry is an incredibly efficient engine of employment growth. Even during periods of recession, the travel industry has shown an uncanny ability to generate new jobs. In areas where heavy industries have become outmoded or obsolete, travel and tourism has frequently been a salvation. Moreover, travel and tourism is a "clean" industry—it does not pollute or eat up the countryside—and is

generally as politically popular and noncontroversial as "motherhood, apple pie, and the flag."

Employment directly generated by travel has grown 27.7 percent in the past 10 years, almost one-and-a-half times as fast as the more modest 19.6 percent increase in total nonagricultural U.S. employment, and it is projected to grow another 21 percent between 1996 and 2006. Looking at it another way, unemployment in the U.S. would have been an unsatisfactory 10 percent without the new jobs added to the economy by the influx of travel and tourism dollars, more than twice the actual rate of 4.5 percent. Think of the difference it would make to localities to have to make up those lost jobs and income taxes.

INSIDE SECRET: Want a job where you get to travel? Promoting a destination can be the ticket.

Tourism affects every business in a community. It is estimated that each dollar spent by a traveler ripples through the economy 2½ times because of all the goods and services needed to meet the needs of the traveler either directly or indirectly.

The important role travel and tourism plays in local economies has become clear to many political entities, as reflected in the allocations to state tourism offices and local convention and visitor bureaus to develop and promote tourism.

The budgets have become substantial—$644 million worth at the state level alone in 1999, according to TIA. As a result, what used to be a popular dumping ground for political patronage is becoming a professional career: destination marketing organizations.

Politics and Private Enterprise

Public-sector travel promotion is a spicy combination of politics and private enterprise. There is an exhilarating sense of being in on almost everything that happens in a locality because virtually everything impacts a destination's ability to draw travelers for business, pleasure, or convention purposes.

You can see how tourism is used to breathe life back into city centers and ports where the commercial base has shifted. In Providence, Philadelphia, Baltimore, Boston, Memphis, Cincinnati, St. Louis, Miami, and New York, abandoned factories, warehouses, shipping ports, and railroad terminals have been converted to chic complexes of boutiques and cafes as magnets for visitors and their dollars. The decisions to make the conversions were political ones, and they intimately involved the tourism officials in the community. Very often, the local convention and visitor bureau people act as a catalyst and a facilitator in developing and attracting investments for tourism infrastructure (attractions, hotels, transportation), and then promote and market the destination.

Destination travel promotion is sales and service—selling meetings and conventions planners, tour operators, and wholesalers on the idea of choosing your destination for their program; servicing individual travelers (and their travel agents) with information and products that will make their business or pleasure trip more satisfying. Destination marketers have to be as expert at beating out the competition as any private company, but they work on behalf of their constituency. Unlike the private enterprises on whose behalf they sell, they generally do not complete the sale, "just whet appetites," passing the leads to the companies that will then turn the profit.

The field is becoming more competitive: More and more cities, towns, and hamlets are opening up convention centers (half of all convention bureaus in the U.S. were established after 1980). And the competition is becoming global because the marketplace for

travel and meetings is becoming more international in scope.

The rewards can be great. There is a great deal of satisfaction in destination promotion that derives from having a "tangible impact on the economic well-being of an entire community," said George Kirkland, president of the Los Angeles Convention and Visitors Bureau. Doing a good job means more jobs for the community. Destination marketers are at the center of the action. The work is constantly stimulating because instead of selling only one product or working in only one industry, they become involved with countless products and business entities. An emerging profession, destination promotion is becoming a fairly well-paying field, as well.

Moving Up by Moving Down

Interestingly, this is a field where moving up can mean moving down the hierarchy. Someone who had a position as the Commissioner of Tourism for a state may opt to become the Director of a city's convention bureau. Although there may be more prestige in presiding over the state's tourism department, local convention and visitor bureaus tend to be more sophisticated about tourism promotion than the states, which have come to the activity much more recently. The city CVBs also tend to be higher paying than the state. Jobs are much more plentiful—particularly since new convention bureaus and tourism offices are opening everywhere—and generally longer lasting than at the state level, where politics still comes into play.

The typical career path is to start at a hotel sales office or in marketing or public relations and move into a convention and visitor bureau. From there, a person could move into a state travel office and perhaps back down again to a convention and visitor bureau, but at a level of greater responsibility and authority.

For example, Marshall Murdaugh has had an opportunity to compare work at a state travel office with a convention and visitor bureau. After 13 years as the State Travel Director of Virginia (where he takes credit for developing the "Virginia is for Lovers" campaign), he accepted a position as President of the Memphis

Convention and Visitors Bureau—a post that paid better and offered some new challenges. In the three years he spent in Memphis, he put into place a new marketing program and helped implement a new funding initiative, which provided a five-fold increase in the budget and expanded the staff from 6 to 23 employees. Result: Tourism revenues grew from $600 million to $1 billion.

Murdaugh next moved on to become President of the New York Convention and Visitors Bureau—a plum position in the field. But immediately upon accepting the post, the city government eliminated its budget commitment to the bureau, forcing massive layoffs, the closing of the visitor center, and the elimination of many marketing programs. In response, Murdaugh developed a legislatively dedicated tax plan that more than doubled the bureau's budget and provided for 20 more key marketing and sales personnel and the establishment of offices and sales throughout Europe and Asia.

Murdaugh came to destination marketing from marketing and communications. He had been a public affairs officer in the Navy, worked in local government as a research and public information officer, and was working as the Public Relations Manager for Reynolds Metals when a friend who worked in the Virginia Governor's office informed him that the Director of Tourism for Virginia was retiring. He encouraged Murdaugh to pursue the job, which essentially involved marketing communications. "But instead of a product, I was selling a service. Selling travel is not unlike selling a commodity, but the difference is the specialness of the experience and people's expectations. Travel is an emotional kind of thing."

For Murdaugh, promoting tourism to Virginia was a chance to "make a mark." He believed firmly in the role of travel and tourism in promoting global understanding and peace. "Tourism is the social, political, economic fabric of society and a heck of a lot of fun. The products are so diverse in travel—there are so many components and so many businesses. The number-one task anyone faces is to significantly increase business through tourism expenditures and ultimately increase jobs in the community," Murdaugh said.

 INSIDE SECRET: Destination-marketing opportunities are greatest at convention and visitor bureaus.

Murdaugh advises people who aspire to destination promotion to take college programs in tourism development, hospitality management, commercial recreation, or liberal arts, and to study marketing, public relations, or advertising.

"Tourism is the business of providing goods and service to travelers. Motivation of the traveler is paramount, and the answer is found in marketing."

Convention and Visitor Bureaus

The greatest opportunities in destination promotion are at convention and visitor bureaus. Bureaus or destination marketing organizations are opening all over the country, in virtually every town, hamlet, and region. Even Harlem now has a tourism promotion association (formed with a grant from Citicorp to the Uptown Chamber of Commerce). And areas that do not have full-fledged bureaus usually have some kind of tourism information or promotion office, perhaps as part of local government or the chamber of commerce.

Some bureaus are attached to local government, but most are nonprofit organizations backed by the private sector (who are members) and funded in part by local government. A few are operated as private nonprofit companies. Consequently, even though the executive director or chief executive officer of the bureau might not actually be a political appointee, politics is very much a part of the process because the bureau must be responsive to a broad constituency.

Working for a bureau usually entails being on the inside of the political process, mixing and mingling with the movers and shakers in a community. It combines some of the power of politics with the dynamism of private enterprise.

INSIDE SECRET: Destination marketing organizations are great for people who are politically savvy and like to move among the movers and shakers.

The chief executive officer of a bureau, particularly, has to be able to get along with people. "You have to be sensitive, have to have a strong back to take the slings and arrows and withstand the pressure," said Charles Gillett, who was the President of the New York City Convention and Visitors Bureau for 25 years and the spearhead to the "Big Apple" campaign. A sense of humor and conviction are other important requisites.

"It's an interesting job, but not an easy one. It is frequently frustrating, particularly fund-raising, which goes with the territory of a nonprofit association. You work for thousands of people."

Convention and visitor bureaus are very much a career. It is not uncommon to find people who have spent their entire working lives at bureaus, rising up through the ranks generally by accepting higher posts in other cities.

George Kirkland, for example, the President and Chief Executive Officer of the Los Angeles Convention and Visitors Bureau, and former President of the International Association of Convention and Visitor Bureaus (IACVB), has spent more than 25 years working in bureaus. He started in Oakland, California, as Sales Manager in a chamber of commerce with a small convention and tourism department. Then he went to Anaheim for five years as a Convention Sales Manager, then to the Hawaii Visitors Bureau as the Vice President of Sales for 3½ years. Then he went to the Kansas City, Missouri, C&VB as President and Chief Executive Officer for 2½ years before spending six years as Executive Director of the San Francisco C&VB. He next served as President and CEO of the Miami Convention and Visitors Bureau before moving back to California.

One of the principal advantages of pursuing a career in convention and visitor bureaus, Kirkland pointed out,

is the advancement potential due to the growing professionalism and increased sophistication of tourism marketing and promotion efforts. There are also a greater appreciation of the economic importance of tourism at the local level, more funds being allocated, expansion of bureau staffs with specialization of functions, and the opening of new bureaus all over the world.

The growth in destination promotion, he said, "is part and parcel of the emerging trend that travel will be the number-one economic activity in the world in the millennium."

There are 480 member bureaus of the International Association of Convention and Visitor Bureaus (IACVB) in 30 countries—twice the number from 1984. The bureaus vary considerably in size and scope of activities. Some function with as little as $100,000 and three to four staff members; the largest have budgets of tens of millions of dollars and staff of 100 or more.

Essentially, all convention and visitor bureaus have four main activities:

- **Convention sales** (which could be a whole division, a department, or a single individual's responsibility and is usually the largest component)
- **Pleasure travel promotion** (involving tourism marketing to the trade, such as tour operators, motorcoach companies, and travel agents, as well as the public)
- **Administration** (financial management, possibly membership services, and fund-raising)
- **Public affairs**

 ## Why Choose Convention and Visitor Bureaus?

People skills have become vitally important, since, between government sponsors in city agencies, private membership, and the public, "there are multitudes of people to service and satisfy." This can also be a source of frustration and a challenge. "Bureau staff are on a public stage more than in private enterprise," Kirkland noted. "While not necessarily a government agency, bureaus work in concert with local government and use public money."

Unlike the state travel offices, which have until recently gone outside the field to private industry to recruit professionals for upper management, larger bureaus look for a successful track record with a public-sector promotional organization. "Native sons may get some preference in small communities."

Destination marketing requires an extraordinary commitment of time and energy. Many of the positions entail considerable travel for sales calls, conventions and meetings, trade shows, promotions—and not necessarily to glamorous destinations. The thrill of travel can wear thin when you are on the road one or two weeks out of every month. Still, for those who love hard work and can tolerate the detail involved, working for a convention and visitor bureau can be very gratifying.

"Within a hotel, the product is reasonably narrow, well defined," said Kirkland. "At a convention bureau, you are selling the entire community. There is a lot of excitement. You can make a tangible impact on the economic well-being of an entire community."

Kirkland, ever the pioneer in the industry, created two new entities within the Los Angeles CVB that will probably serve as a model to others: First, a Department of Cultural Tourism, presently with four staff members, aimed at cultivating visits for cultural purposes (it offers various itineraries to visitors). Second, a separate nonprofit entity, the Los Angeles Sports and Entertainment Commission, aimed at drawing major sports and entertainment events such as the Grammy Awards and Super Bowls. Such events not only generate significant income to the city, but also enhance the image for people to come for visits or to do business.

NYC & Co.

"We don't sell anything, in one way. In another, we sell everything," said the former Vice President of Tourism Development at the New York Convention and Visitors Bureau, which was reorganized as a private entity, NYC & Co.

A private, nonprofit marketing organization, NYC & Co. represents some 1,300 separate entities ranging from the Empire State Building to Macy's Department Store. It is largely through the bureau's efforts that the city draws 39 million visitors a year (19 million who overnight), who spend some $16.7 billion in the city and make tourism the city's second-largest industry, supporting 277,000 jobs.

Funded with $12 million (almost half from the city), NYC & Co. has several key departments: Visitor Information Counselors; Membership (solicits new members and services existing ones); Convention and Tourism Sales (sells New York as a total convention product; reaches markets through programs in conjunction with agents, operators, airlines, and carriers); Convention and Tourism Services (develops sales leads and referrals and coordinates all the resources); Conference Express (a service to event planners who need assistance with placing small meetings and special events); Communications (promotes the city and products and services of members); Audiovisual Services; Publications; Web Site; and Research. In addition, the agency operates a Visitor Information Center and satellite offices in London, Munich, Chicago, and Washington, D.C.

Convention sales is a key area. Sales staff go after thousands of possible conventions, trying to get them to commit to coming to the city. This is a critical enterprise because convention business usually is booked five to eight years in advance and gives the destination an economic cushion for its tourism enterprises. Each convention has to be solicited in a different way—even to the point of knowing whether the spouse of the association's decision-maker likes New York City or not. The convention sales manager has to know everything about the association or industry, its leadership, and the time of year it holds its meeting. "You have to know the peccadilloes of the convention manager."

Tourism development involves going after travel agents and tour operators, and working with hotels, tour and agency sales managers, and airlines on promotional activities. It is easier, in some respects, to sell the travel trade on the idea of bringing their groups into New York, so the bureau's marketing goals include leveling out the peaks and valleys in visitor flows, getting more people to visit the boroughs outside of Manhattan, motivating more foreign visitors into the U.S., and getting Americans on their way out to stop over in New York before

(continues)

(continued)

going on to other places. "Once you know the program and the tour operators personally, you have to be at the right place at the right time, such as sitting face-to-face with them at a trade meeting."

The Tourism Development Manager spends a lot of time in face-to-face meetings with customers and at trade shows and conventions, conducting seminars and promotions, and traveling about one-third of the year to cultivate business during these off-periods. "It is both wonderful and tedious. We identify some important markets, arrange radio and television appearances, rack up free exposure, talking about New York, inviting people to send for the catalogues and brochures." In fall, she pushes winter; in spring, she pushes summer.

The job is "wonderful and rewarding," she declared, "because some people promote and sell stuff they can't get excited about—widgets. But if you are selling and promoting something you can identify with—a city you live in and love—it's an ideal job. If you like to deal with people and not numbers or papers or computers all day, if you like to get out, this is great. This is a people-oriented business."

There are advantages, too, over working in a hotel, or airline, or other travel company. "Then you are selling just that hotel, airline, or sightseeing attraction. But 'selling' the city, you are dealing with all levels of the industry—Saks Fifth Avenue, the Museum of Modern Art. You are meeting with big tour operators on one day, going around with the deputy commissioner of traffic and parking on another, trying to identify where tour buses might encounter problems. One week I was abroad with the 'I Love New York' state promotion; the next, welcoming three different familiarization trips. The job is not Monday to Friday, 9 to 5. The hours are long. But then, no key job in the travel industry is 9 to 5."

(For more information, see www.nycvisit.com.)

Jobs in Convention and Visitor Bureaus

- **Convention Sales Manager:** Opens new markets for meetings, conventions, and trade shows, typically targeting key industries in a geographical area that have potential; develops leads and assists in closing group business on behalf of a local convention center or convention bureau and the local hospitality industry. To achieve this end, the CSM makes sales calls, attends trade shows, and implements sales blitzes, necessitating a high degree of travel. The CSM also is responsible for the marketing budget and maximizing the effectiveness of marketing dollars, and also serves as liaison between members (such as in the local hospitality and attractions industries) and meeting planners. The CSM needs to be able to make presentations to high-level decision-makers, provide a high level of service, and be creative in finding leads. People coming from hotel sales typically fill these positions.

Best Bets

- Convention Sales Manager
- Convention Services Manager
- Leisure Travel Specialist
- Tourism Marketing Manager
- Market Research Analyst
- Director of Public Relations
- Advertising Manager
- Manager of Information Technology

- **Convention Services Manager:** Works with the organizers of conventions and meetings that have been booked to come (anywhere from a couple of months to years away). Finds out what they need, then serves as a liaison, notifying CVB members which vendors may be appropriate to bid for the business (such as hotels, restaurants, ground transportation companies, attractions). The manager uses expertise in keeping costs to a minimum; makes recommendations for amenities, unique venues, local speakers, and themes; may be responsible for handling housing and assigning registration personnel; and makes sure that all contractual agreements between the CVB and the organization are fulfilled.

- **Group Tour Specialist/Group Travel Coordinator:** Locates and sells to travel agents, tour operators, civic and religious organizations, social clubs, and senior groups that generate group travel. Once the group is sold on the destination, the specialist hands the booking over to hospitality industry members. This specialist may also create packages and itineraries that agents or operators can sell, in order to stimulate tour business to an area. Sales, hotel, or travel industry experience is usually required.

■ **Senior Staff Assistant:** Provides administrative support while learning the fundamentals of the department (such as sales, tourism, and communications). Works on special projects such as helping to coordinate familiarization trips for travel agents, tour operators, and media. This is an entry-level position.

■ **Tourism Marketing Coordinator:** Coordinates the bureau's participation in domestic and international trade shows (registration, shipping materials, follow-up). Coordinates with the private sector; helps arrange familiarization tours to the destination by media and the travel trade; arranges seminars; sends invitations and notices. This is an entry-level position.

■ **Public Information Officer:** Develops public relations and marketing programs designed to increase visitor traffic and enhance and protect the destination's image. Functions include planning, writing, and disseminating information through various media; preparing flyers, brochures, and other resources; designing and producing official publications distributed to residents, tourists, businesses, and media representatives. This position may involve organizing media events and familiarization trips. Prior experience in public relations or marketing is usually required.

■ **Special Events Coordinator:** Develops, prepares, and manages the implementation of events and related promotions and programs designed to increase tourism for a destination. Though this is often an entry-level position, prior experience in putting together events—such as at a hotel or meeting-planning company—is desirable.

■ **Market Research Analyst:** Designs market surveys, planning and organizing research projects with outside research companies that the analyst has selected as appropriate for the project, usually after a bidding process. Then analyzes results and publishes and disseminates information. The analyst's objective is to derive the information to help the marketing department identify markets that should be promoted more aggressively, help determine market strategies and campaigns, and get the best results with limited promotional dollars. May also assist the private tourism industry in developing products, services, and pricing strategies to better suit the travel market. You need a degree (in math or statistics) and some professional experience in research or statistics.

■ **Director of Advertising:** Plans and implements multimillion-dollar consumer and trade advertising campaigns, supervises the advertising agency account team, and directs the development of advertising RFPs and vendor selection. Qualifications include senior management experience in development, execution, and evaluation of consumer advertising campaigns; managing a full-service advertising agency account team and budget; and experience integrating Web-based and direct marketing strategies.

Other distinctive titles:

■ National Sales Manager/Religious and Education Market

■ Manager of Housing Services

■ Film Commissioner (promotes the destination for shooting films, commercials, and so on)

■ Director of Finance

■ Director of Computer Operations/Management Information Services

■ Director/Manager of Membership, Membership Services

Salaries in Convention and Visitor Bureaus

Working at a bureau is more of a career today, and the pay (beyond entry level) reflects that change. While salaries at the lower level are more typical of nonprofit organizations and are generally comparable to the hotel industry, salaries for chief executive officers of the largest bureaus run into six figures.

"Remuneration for chief executive officers of a destination marketing organization has become quite good," stated Kirkland, because of the need to attract highly qualified individuals who can handle the increased responsibility of managing a bureau. "The biggest demand is for managing an organization in such a way as to show a solid return on investment."

Your Ticket into Convention and Visitor Bureaus

Although there are vast opportunities in convention and visitor bureaus, you must be tenacious because there are far more applicants than jobs, particularly at the larger bureaus in the more desirable cities.

The field is becoming more and more professional and there are fewer and fewer jobs open to those lacking experience except at an administrative level, but there

is still an element of luck. You can increase your chances of getting a job by taking college courses in business management, marketing, and communications; getting an internship with a bureau; working in hotel or convention sales offices or for a convention center; and cultivating contacts in travel and other industries.

 INSIDE SECRET: The best way into destination marketing is through hotel sales departments or straight out of college.

Smaller bureaus tend to have only a few very experienced people, but there may be openings at the administrative level that can afford you an opportunity to learn the business and work into an important position, particularly as the bureau expands. Larger bureaus may have more entry-level positions, but these are harder to get because of greater competition, and may not offer the same opportunity to learn—the jobs are more specialized.

Entry-level positions are generally filled from hotel convention and sales offices. But frequently, the way to get in is to create your own position. Getting in at entry level may entail some financial sacrifice because these positions are low-paying (comparable to hotel positions), but there are greater growth possibilities. People can also come into the field with a business-to-business sales, marketing, public relations, or promotion background.

Contacts, Sources, and Leads

- The best leads are through local convention and visitor bureaus, tourism promotion offices, or chambers of commerce.
- An excellent link to local CVB Web sites is through the **Travel Industry Association of America (TIA)** site, www.tia.org, and through TIA's **National Council of Destination Organizations.**
- Another helpful Web site is **Tourism Offices Worldwide Directory,** www.towd.com.
- **The International Association of Convention & Visitor Bureaus,** 2025 M St. NW, Ste. 500, Washington, DC 20036; 202-296-7888; www.iacvb.org. Has an excellent job-posting site.

Sports-Marketing Commissions

An emerging trend among destination marketing organizations is the creation of sports-marketing commissions. Functioning much like convention bureaus, sports-marketing commissions are charged with bringing sports events to an area. These could be school teams, training centers, national and world-cup, and even Olympic trials and events. In addition to sales and marketing strategies to bring in such groups, the commissions even serve as facilitators, coordinators, and liaisons after the event is won, helping to organize local hospitality and transportation. They may assist in marketing the event to generate an audience and bringing in sponsors. When the event takes place, they may have an active role in making everything work smoothly. This part of the industry is closely aligned with the sports/entertainment and media business.

INSIDE SECRET: Have a passion for sports? Get on the ball and score with a local sports-marketing commission; more and more of these are opening around the country with an aim to lure major events and training programs to a locality.

Major events like the Olympics, Super Bowl, Goodwill Games, and national championships not only bring a significant media spotlight that results in millions of dollars worth of advertising. But such events also bring enormous numbers of visitors, including athletes, coaches, family members, and spectators who stay in hotels, dine in restaurants, shop in stores, and visit local attractions. An event like the New York City Marathon is estimated to bring $120 million in revenue to the city.

Indeed, the TIA Travel Poll found that 52.7 million adults who traveled 50 miles or more from home participated in a sports event, competition, or tournament in the past year. For a significant percentage, the sports event was the main reason for the trip.

Florida has about 20 local sports-marketing commissions all around the state; Long Island established a Long Island Sports Commission, which was successful in bringing the Goodwill Games and other major events and spurred the building of world-class sports training facilities.

State Travel Offices

The activity may come under many different titles—State Tourism Division, Department of Economic Development, Department of Commerce, Recreation Department, Parks and Recreation and Tourism, Department of Local Affairs, Department of Industry and Trade, Commerce and Community Affairs. But all state travel and tourism offices are in business for the same reason: to promote visitor business within the destination, whether for pleasure, business, or convention purposes, and from within or from outside the state.

Some of the offices hold cabinet status; some are commissions or agencies or divisions within other departments in state government. A few are privatized, such as the Hawaii Visitor and Convention Bureau, a private, nonprofit corporation contracted by the state and run by a professional manager as President; or a public-private partnership such as the not-for-profit Florida Tourism Industry Marketing Corporation, which was formed by the Florida Commission on Tourism and the tourism industry. The titles of the Chief Tourism Officer are equally diverse—State Travel Director, Commissioner of Tourism, Deputy Commissioner of Tourism Development, Director of Marketing Services Division, and, in the case of the privatized commission, President and Chief Executive Officer.

Invariably, though, the state travel office is very much a political entity within the government structure. The director's position may last only as long as the governor's administration.

Those who work for the state travel office also have to contend with the frustration of the budgetary process and the bureaucratic rules and regulations governing purchasing services for the department. New York State, for example, went from a peak of $17 million to $6.6 million. "It is part of reality; we are a government entity. Politics always applies," an official said.

Toward More Professional Recruitment

Nonetheless, working in the state travel offices is becoming more of a profession and more of a career. Though the offices are still caught up in political tides, there is more of a trend toward mounting recruitment programs to tap talent nationwide, instead of hiring native sons or political hacks. This is in contrast to the recent past, when "Governors believed if you could promote the candidate, you can promote the state," as one State Travel Director put it. But as states gained more of an appreciation and healthy respect for the social and economic importance of tourism, and began to allocate huge sums toward tourism development and promotion, they sought out professionals to manage elaborate, targeted marketing campaigns.

Many state travel promotion budgets have been rising at double-digit rates. And many of the states have budgets exceeding $10 million (Hawaii has a $60 million budget; New York State has $21 million). "When you get to that level," asserted one State Travel Director, "they are not just putting in political hacks anymore. They are hiring people who may have some loyalty or allegiance to the administration but who are marketing professionals, and they are hiring people from other states."

Although it is possible to make a career in state travel offices, particularly as assistants to the Director, the top spot still has no guarantee of longevity. But even those who do not see the Director's position as the cap to their career are willing to undertake the challenge and tolerate the inevitable frustrations and modest pay because they see the high-visibility job as an invaluable springboard toward other opportunities in the private sector, to other destination-marketing positions in other states or local convention and visitor bureaus, or even to other government offices.

"I find myself learning the travel industry," said one State Travel Director, who was a former teacher brought into the department to create recreational and naturalist programs at state resorts and parks and then moved into the marketing slot. At the state level, "you get a much larger perspective here that you can't get in a more narrow job in the private sector. Contacts, knowledge of the industry, involvement at the national and international level. Most regard the position as a springboard to something bigger and better. Though the state travel offices will become more career-oriented, it is still looked at as a springboard, now."

This Director had 66 people on his staff. But for him, the job was not about power; it was about influence. "You are a top executive in the state as it relates to travel and tourism," he said. "You carry the prestige. The position makes heavy demands on your time—you are the spokesman for the state's tourism. There is considerable responsibility—I won't say power. You have influence."

While marketing, promotion, and advertising skills necessary in private enterprise are needed to promote the state, there is a difference between the two that frequently makes the jobs incompatible. "The private sector is freer, there is more flexibility and latitude to advertise and promote. The state travel office has to contend with strict purchasing laws, follow strict procedures, and promote the area in a businesslike way. There is strict accountability. Frequently, the person from the private sector [coming over to the state] gets frustrated," he explained.

Politics and Poker

Stephen Richer had always been interested in politics, but also became active in travel very early on. While in college, he escorted tours overseas. After college, he worked briefly for a company, decided he was "too issue-oriented," and preferred a less corporate atmosphere. So he went back to work for the travel agent, escorting tours to Europe for three years. Meanwhile, he became active in politics—specifically, Brendan Byrne's campaign for Governor of New Jersey. When Byrne was elected, the governor asked Richer to take on the Bicentennial celebration effort.

That was in 1975. In 1977, Richer moved over to the Governor's office, and in 1979, at age 32, he became the state's first Director of Tourism after the state created a full-fledged separate tourism commission. (Before that, the state had a small office within the Department of Labor headed by a former union official.) Atlantic City had just won its controversial campaign for casino gambling and Richer became involved in promoting the re-born destination.

As the new head of tourism for the state, Richer undertook a research project and decided to target the drive-in market. He created an advertising campaign and developed a vacation guide, a calendar of events, and other literature and created the first tourism regions in New Jersey, which interfaced with private businesses.

His staff ranged in size from 10 to 20, depending on the budget. Some were newly hired, "referrals from the governor's office."

"It was fairly political," he related. "Things can change pretty much as the administration and the legislature's budget change."

Richer subsequently won a job as Nevada's State Travel Commissioner over 100 other applicants in an open-interview process. Richer knew gaming and, from his involvement in national travel trade organizations, knew some of the people, such as then-Nevada Congressman James Santini, and he hit it off well with Nevada's Governor.

In Nevada, where tourism is the state's largest industry (one-third of the population is employed in tourism), the state was "more business oriented" when it came to hiring. All 10 staff people in the office were selected for their talent; there were no referrals from the governor's office.

"In New Jersey, I was expected to be involved in politics," said Richer. "In Nevada, I was expected not to be in politics."

Richer, who eventually moved back to New Jersey to head up Atlantic City's Convention and Visitors Bureau, advised someone who aspires to a government travel office position to "get other jobs first. Find a niche in the government travel bureaucracy. But if you aim for the Director's job, realize that though the field is more professional, politics will always be there.

"You have a chance of getting things done," said Richer, "but there is a lot of bureaucracy. It is a good field. You get to do something really fun, and for a short period of time, you can be in the middle of things."

Where the Jobs Are

Jobs are relatively low-paying compared to the private sector, and even compared to convention and visitor bureaus, but the salaries are getting better at the top. The salaries for state travel directors reach six figures.

Essential qualities for the job include "a high level of adaptability to the political system, willingness to take risk, willingness to take a job knowing it will not last forever, and planning skills," noted Richer.

The chief assistants to the Director generally last longer than the State Travel Directors (who average 3.5 years), particularly if the post comes under civil service.

State travel offices vary widely in the size of their staffs. The staffs range from 5 to over 100 full-time employees, with an average of 32 per office. Many also employ part-timers. The size of the office, particularly the number of management, marketing, and sales professionals, usually is tied to the size of the budget, which in turn reflects the economic importance of tourism to the state.

A key activity for the state travel office is advertising, and almost every state has at least one person on staff who is responsible for the development of a travel advertising program. Almost half of the states employ someone to take charge of art, design, and layout of advertising materials. Most states also have a matching funds program for cooperative advertising, which is managed by a staffer. Other key activities include promotion, public relations, and research.

A new initiative is in Web site development; collectively, the states spent $5 million in one year for Web site design, development, and maintenance.

More than half the states also operate in-state welcome centers, designed to extend visitor stay by informing them of attractions, activities, and events. Most states also mount annual travel conferences to bring together travel sellers with buyers.

Most states have programs devoted to package tour development, many with a staff member responsible for tour packaging. In order to promote more tours to the state, the states also host familiarization tours for tour operators and travel agents.

Contacts, Sources, and Leads

- States occasionally advertise positions in the trade press *(Leisure Travel News, Travel Weekly,* and *Travel Agent Magazine).*

- A source of leads, short of contacting your own state travel office, is the **National Council of State Travel Directors of the Travel Industry Association of America,** www.tia.org.

National Tourism Promotion

The United States is presently the only major industrialized country without an official government tourist office. In 1996, Congress voted to cease funding the U.S. Travel and Tourism Administration (USTTA), which had been part of the U.S. Department of Commerce, and has failed to fund the U.S. National Tourism Organization (USNTO), a public-private partnership organization supported by the travel industry, which was supposed to replace USTTA. The task of promoting the U.S. now falls to a nonprofit association of state and local travel offices and private entities, the Travel Industry Association of America (TIA).

In a recent initiative, the largest one-year increase in program activity in nearly 60 years of its history, TIA is spending about $4 million on international programs and increasing staff by 10 to 17 people. TIA plans to establish offices in the United Kingdom and Japan, and an in-country presence in Brazil. Eventually, there will be six offices (as the USTTA once had). The offices will represent TIA at trade shows, meet with overseas travel agents and tour operators, handle media relations, answer questions from the travel trade, and help organize training seminars to educate travel agents about the U.S. travel product. There will be themed marketing campaigns, aimed to appeal to overseas audiences (such as American music, adventure travel, multicultural tourism, and shopping). TIA is also establishing an international travel research office (www.tia.org).

Indeed, in 1999, 48 million international visitors spent $74 billion in the U.S., $14.1 billion more than Americans spent traveling abroad (according to data supplied by TIA and the International Trade Administration). The resulting trade surplus means that tourism has become a greater export revenue producer than even agricultural goods and chemicals. The money foreign travelers spent visiting the U.S. directly supported more than 700,000 U.S. jobs and generated billions of dollars in federal, state, and local tax revenue.

"There are those in Washington who wonder why we need to promote when we're already [the world's most popular international visitor destination]," declared Rockwell Schnabel, shortly before leaving office as Undersecretary of Commerce for Travel and Tourism. "The answer is very simple: If you don't, you lose by default. This is still the promised land as far as people in most countries are concerned, but we can't afford to assume that they will come without encouragement from us."

Foreign National Tourist Offices

Most national tourist offices hire Americans for specific positions, particularly in marketing, sales, public relations, and clerical support. Americans know the U.S. travel industry and the market, and provide longevity (foreign nationals usually have to rotate every several years). However, the field can be frustrating because there is definitely a ceiling on how far you can go; it is only in rare instances that Americans rise to the top positions. Also, foreign national tourist offices are subject to political tides and fortunes, so there is frequent change in leadership.

INSIDE SECRET: Knowledge of a foreign country and the language are significant assets for working in a foreign national tourist office.

"An American has a better knowledge of the way the travel industry works, and a better understanding of how the American press works, how newspaper travel sections are put together, the individual travel editors' likes and dislikes," said Bedford Pace, who was the Promotion Department Manager for the British Tourist Authority for more than a decade. "My job isn't to know Britain, but to be a contact for a press person." Pace had worked with a major public relations company handling a tourism destination among his other accounts, when he decided he liked tourism the best and would prefer to work for a single destination.

The Promotion Department Manager arranges press trips, supervises a department that puts out its own news and features items to hundreds of newspapers around the country, fields inquiries from journalists, works with television stations that are doing a tourism segment, and arranges for major British personalities to tour the U.S. and promote travel to Britain.

Contacts, Sources, and Leads

■ Consult the telephone directory or **national consulates** for locations of national tourist offices in your locality. Major centers for foreign national tourist offices are New York, Washington, D.C., Chicago, and Los Angeles.

CHAPTER 14

AIRPORT, AVIATION, AND PORT MANAGEMENT

In aviation, most of the attention is focused on the airlines and not on the gigantic, complex system of airports, air traffic control facilities, and governmental bodies that make commercial and private aviation possible. But airports are the linchpin to the aviation system, and the challenging task of managing them falls to a small but elite group of professionals and specialized companies. Similarly, a relatively small group of professionals operate the nations maritime ports, vital for commerce as well as the cruise industry. These professionals have the gargantuan task of operating facilities to provide the greatest economic benefit and also be safe and secure for passengers.

Airport Management

About 750 million passengers traveled on 17 million planes—22,000 scheduled flights a day—through some 17,490 airports in the United States, of which 5,089 are publicly owned. Out of all these, only 680 are certificated by the Federal Aviation Authority, and only 400 have enough volume of flight operations to warrant a control tower. A mere 50 airports account for 82 percent of all air traffic; only about 750 airports employ a full-time manager, according to American Association of Airport Executives (AAAE) estimates.

Snapshot: Airport Management

Airport management is a small area—it employs only about 15,000 people. Until recently, it was also a fairly closed club, a brotherhood, with the vast majority

men, more often than not former World War II pilots. But a new breed of airport manager is coming on the scene, much better equipped to deal with a vastly more complicated environment.

Airport managers must balance conflicting interests: local political entities, which are probably their owners/employers; private companies, which are tenants; airlines, which are both the airport's client and its product; the community, which benefits materially from the airport's services, but pays a price in noise and air pollution; and the airport's customers, the air travelers, who may or may not be from the community.

 INSIDE SECRET: Managing an airport is like managing a city: It involves politics, retail, transportation, police and fire protection, and environmental issues.

There is an intense love/hate relationship with airports, which airport managers feel deeply. Airport management comes into direct conflict with the community when they seek to expand, yet many communities would "dry up and blow away" were it not for the commercial vitality brought by the airport.

An airport is a fascinating mixture of a political entity, commercial venture, and public utility. Managing an airport is nothing more nor less than managing an entire city, with shops, restaurants, hotels, transportation systems, parking lots, fire and police protection, and tens of thousands of people.

INSIDE SECRET: Port management still tends to be a closed club, but the best way in for outsiders is through marketing, sales, communications and finance.

The primary responsibility of the Airport Manager is to operate a safe facility; the primary task is raising funds. Maximizing safety can pit the manager against the community on issues such as noise abatement (the safest take-off or landing may exceed accepted noise levels) and runway obstructions. It can also prove costly, such as maintaining expensive crash-fire-and-rescue (CFR) equipment and manpower when statistics say they will not be needed.

"Airports are like any other municipal entity," said one Airport Manager. "We all compete for dollars.... Everything is a compromise. Grooving costs $2 a square foot and you have a runway 7,000 feet by 150 feet. Do you do that or buy a fire truck, or do you make sure there is adequate drainage? And on and on and on. You put your dollars where they do most good. That's management."

"Airport management always had two basic goals," said another manager, "to be a safe airport facility for the public to use and to be a business and make ends meet. I have always seen a conscientious effort for safety projects—nothing is ever done that would compromise safety. But the definition of safety is elusive. The airport manager knows what is safe."

Deregulation—which gave airlines freedom to enter and exit markets—has added a new dimension to airport management. Airports are now faced with the problem of competing for passengers as well as for airlines. In this new environment, airports are caught in a Catch-22 that forces them to concentrate more on passenger conveniences, such as terminal facilities and parking lots, that make their airport more attractive to passengers. Without passenger numbers, airports would not have the airlines to draw the passengers in the first place.

Under deregulation, airlines also can change their capacity and equipment. This can also be a problem if

an airport is not prepared for the change in the make-up of aircraft that are coming in. The airlines also attempt to schedule flights during the most popular time periods for passengers, making it almost impossible for the airport to operate them on an on-time basis.

The airlines also flock to the busiest markets for air travel, so some airports such as Washington's Reagan National and New York's La Guardia are getting more traffic than they were designed for, while others are underutilized.

Then there are the airport tenants—the shops, restaurants and car rentals, and other services which can generate as much as 75 percent of airport revenues. This is critical, because if airlines have to bear the brunt of the costs and fees are too high for the number of passengers they draw, they can move to another airport.

Landing fees are dramatically affected by the number of landings; the more landings, the lower the cost for each one. An airport that is losing traffic becomes even more uneconomical to the remaining carriers.

A portion of airport operating funds is raised from tax revenues, but a large part comes from the bond markets. Even here, airport managers are becoming frustrated by the competitive marketplace. Bond ratings, which determine how high an interest rate the airport must pay, depend largely on projections of future traffic, how dependent the airport is on any one carrier, whether there is a competitive airport offering cheaper fees or better service, and whether there are expectations of large financing needs.

Hartsfield Atlanta Airport

Some 44,800 people work at Hartsfield Atlanta International Airport, making it the largest employment center in the state of Georgia. However, only about two dozen are responsible for administration (the rest work for airlines and concessionaires). The entire Airport Authority consists of 160 people (not including fire fighters and police), of which 100 are maintenance, most of the rest are in clerical positions, and the others "could as easily be in the insurance business," said John R. Braden, Director of Marketing in the Airport Commissioner's Office.

Airport authorities tend to have more staff and more independence from the local political organization than airports that are operated as a city department. In Atlanta, the airport is operated as a city department. The Commissioner of Aviation, who theoretically has airport experience, is appointed by the mayor. Under the Commissioner is a Deputy, and then a group of Directors: accounting, properties management, marketing and public relations, maintenance, operations, planning, noise mitigation, and community relations. There are a few other staff positions, such as a technical person who acts as a liaison with the Westinghouse Company, which operates the airport's "People Mover" system.

Since the airport is operated as a city department, requests for new staff are filled through the city's personnel department. The department sends over candidates and the Director makes the final choice.

"At a smaller airport, the biggest function of the Manager is to keep enough money in the till to repair potholes. At a big airport, you become a landlord. You build huge facilities and lease them," Braden said.

Atlanta had a tougher challenge. Only a short time ago, Atlanta was only a regional airport. Largely because of its excellent marketing, the airport has become a major hub for domestic and international traffic and a catalyst to the commercial boom in the Southeast.

Despite the fact that the airport generates $244 million in revenue and supports a payroll of $2 billion (which translates into an economic impact of $3.4 billion with an area-wide impact of $16.8 billion) and is the largest single employment center in the city, there is an intense relationship with the community.

"It is more of a hate relationship," Braden declared. "The community thinks more about the noise than the billions of dollars a year income. We spend a lot of time and money to cultivate good relations in the community. Atlanta would dry up and blow away without the airport."

His advice for getting into the business: "People generally get into the airport system at a smaller airport and then move up by getting a lesser job at a bigger airport and moving up slowly. There are a lot of peripheral jobs at airports, with fixed-base operators, such as refueling aircraft, pumping air into tires. You learn a little and move up a bit until you can find an assistant-operator or clerk's job at an airport. You have to stay abreast of new developments. You join AAAE, which

does a lot of work helping airports find qualified applicants, but also keeps the circle closed." (For more information, see www.atlanta-airport.com.)

A Special Breed

Airport management is truly a distinctly different business—challenging, frustrating, but immensely satisfying—as evidenced by the fact that few people leave the field.

There is so much technical expertise involved, problem-solving, and business management. An airport manager has to know as much about concrete, deicers, fire trucks, friction testers, and lighting equipment as he does about how to work with local, regional, and federal government; the community; the press; banks; bond markets; negotiating contracts and leases and developing new business opportunities; and the latest trends in dining and shopping. Then, there is the excitement of the airport itself—constant activity, movement, people of all strata, and cargo coming from everywhere and going everywhere.

"Being an Airport Director is like being the Chief Executive Officer of a multimillion-dollar corporation," said Spencer Dickerson, Executive Vice President of the AAAE.

On the other hand, this is one field of travel where travel has little to do with it. "You don't go in to travel," he said. "You go in because of a love for aviation and the skills that go with it."

 ## Your Ticket into Airport Management

If these challenges are the sort that interest you, the greater challenge is breaking into the field. There are very few entry-level jobs; most of the jobs are in highly responsible areas. And most who come into the field spend their careers in it, to the point where airport management is considered a "brotherhood." Although there is mobility among professionals (moving up mostly by moving on), there has been little turnover and little expansion of new jobs. And because most of the airport authorities are agencies of the local government, salaries are relatively modest compared to the responsibility they carry.

INSIDE SECRET: One of the most technically demanding and diversified fields, the best way into port management is through college programs which provide the necessary certifications and background.

At some airports, top positions change with the political administration; at others, positions are more secure.

Because of the environmental restrictions on the expansion of the major airports (such as Chicago, New York, and Los Angeles) and the obstacles to building new airports of any size, growth in the field is greatest among the so-called "reliever" airports—smaller, secondary facilities that mainly handle general aviation. Also, many of the smaller airports are thriving with the trend toward hub-and-spoke airline route structures.

Poised for Growth: Denver International Airport

Denver International Airport rises out of the Colorado Plain like snowcapped mountain peaks or perhaps the summertime festival tents of Aspen. Built at a cost of $4.9 billion, it is a state-of-the-art airport facility that replaced the highly flawed Stapleton Airport, and now proudly serves as the gateway to the Rocky Mountain region and a catalyst to economic growth in Denver.

"It is the driving force behind one of the most vital economies in the country and a modern-day tribute to technology and design," stated Bruce Baumgartner, Manager of Aviation.

It is reportedly one of the smoothest-running airports in the world, with a record of being among those in the nation having the least delays. Even the baggage system, a bugaboo in aviation that provides fodder for comedians, has been recognized for excellence. It has become Colorado's third-largest shopping center, largely because of an innovative approach to airport concession management: DIA has 42 local business owners providing goods and services at the airport rather than having

one large master concessionaire. This resulted in record-breaking gross sales in food, retail, and services of $115 million in 1999.

But, of course, the real business of DIA is air travel. Each year, 38 million passengers make their way through DIA, the 10th-busiest airport in the world. The airport occupies 34,000 acres (53 square miles), operates five 12,000-foot-long runways, and has a 1.5 million-square-foot terminal with three concourses linked by an underground rail system. More than 100,000 people travel in and out each day on more than 1,300 flights operated by 20 different airlines from 94 gates to 115 cities worldwide.

Air traffic is controlled from the tallest tower in the FAA system, set 327 feet high. Its 33 stories take 20 minutes to climb, but it gives the air traffic controllers an unobstructed view of all runways. The FAA's Terminal Radar Approach Control (TRACON) facility, located about three miles south of the terminal complex, houses highly trained air traffic controllers who coordinate aircraft flights within a 45-mile radius, up to an altitude of 24,000 feet. Final Monitor Aids help the TRACON controllers coordinate triple independent simultaneous landings at DIA, the first airport in the world to have such operations. The FMA system uses radar, computers, and color monitors to give real-time tracking information to controllers who are monitoring the final approaches of landing aircraft. Two Airport Surveillance Radar systems (ASR-9s) provide airspace-tracking information to FAA controllers.

Twenty-nine wind-speed and direction sensors provide crucial wind-shear information to a central computer that reports to the air traffic controllers. There is also a Terminal Doppler Weather Radar system, which tracks storms and locates microburst activities. ASDE-III (Airport Surface Detection Equipment) radar enables controllers to monitor airport ground traffic and is especially valuable when weather obscures part of the airfield. Linking this technology and other FAA facilities and systems is a network of more than 800,000 feet (152 miles) of fiber-optic cable. All of this gives DIA the most advanced aviation technology available.

More than 22,000 people work at DIA, but the airport is operated by 900 Aviation Department employees who keep everything working 24 hours a day, 7 days a week, 365 days a year. The Aviation Department comes under the authority of the city's Career Service Authority.

DIA recently hired a Director of Marketing in the airport's Public Relations and Marketing Division, responsible for developing and implementing an integrated marketing plan to position DIA for expanded domestic and international service. The marketing plan is aimed at developing tactics to reach new markets, as well as providing a platform to develop, implement, and evaluate processes, products, and services to the airport's existing customers.

"We are in a competitive business," said Amy Bourgeron, DIA's Deputy Manager of Aviation/Public Relations and Marketing. "Our goal is to develop an aggressive plan of action to market this facility as a world-class airport that is leading the aviation world in service and efficiency. That will require well-developed marketing strategies that unite our many communication processes into a cohesive action plan which is accountable, measurable, and effective."

DIA is already considered one of the best connecting hubs anywhere, and is poised for growth. Whereas most major airports around the world have limited ability to expand, Denver has the only airport in the nation ready and able to grow. Along with enough space to more than double its passenger capacity (it can add seven more runways, expand the existing three concourses and build two new ones, and add a second terminal building), it has the sound environmental systems to minimize local opposition.

(For more information, see www.flydenver.com.)

Specialized Jobs

"It is certainly not impossible to break into airport management, said Dickerson. "However, it does require initiative, patience, and initial sacrifice in most cases." Indeed, someone running a $400 million enterprise with more than $1 billion in capital programs in the private sector can make four to five times as much as an airport manager.

But as airplane travel becomes more commonplace, airport management becomes more complex, and the financial costs and rewards grow, it would seem inevitable that there will be substantial increases in airport facilities and the staffs to man them. Also, half of the executives are approaching retirement age, while another half are in their 20s and 40s.

 INSIDE SECRET: Half of all airport executives are now approaching retirement age.

While in the past airport managers tended to come out of the ranks of military and commercial fliers, the "new breed" is coming in with business, law, or accounting backgrounds, or out of local or county government, since business and political savvy have become essential skills. Many are coming out of an increasing number of aviation-management programs at colleges such as Embry-Riddle and Auburn University.

 ## Job Titles and Salaries in Airport Management

Job titles, responsibilities, salaries, and requirements vary widely with the range in airport size and facilities. A sampling:

- **Airports Director** for international airport and secondary airport with five years of experience, B.S. in aviation management or public or business administration: $55,000–$65,000.

- **Director of Aviation** for a small airport, responsible for planning and directing all operations, administration, and improvement projects, with five years of experience: $46,780–$54,200.

- **Managing Director of Operations** for a metropolitan airport: $45,900.

- **Director of Operations** for a metropolitan airport to supervise, direct, administer, and coordinate crash-fire-rescue, police, maintenance, and custodial departments; handle construction, design, planning, public affairs, and airport operations matters; required four-year college degree in aviation management, engineering, or business administration and three years of experience: $42,000–$56,000.

- **Airport Manager** for a regional airport, responsible for administration, supervision, and direction of maintenance, security, operations activities, and personnel. Required B.A. in aviation/airport management, business, or a related field and five years of senior airport management experience: $37,000–$56,000.

- **Property Manager** for a large international airport, with two to four years of property management experience for an airport, airline, or aviation concern; degree with coursework in real estate, economics, or business administration (a law degree could substitute for some experience): $46,000.

- **Finance Director** for a mid-sized airport, with five years of financial administration experience and supervisory/direct computer systems administration: $45,000.

- **Business Development Manager** at an international airport to administer accounting systems, contract and leasing activities, and automation of all functions. Required degree in accounting plus five years of experience: $45,000.

- **Airport Facilities Supervisor** for a small-sized airport; required four-year degree in business administration, building construction, engineering, aviation management, or related field and three years of experience in the operation and maintenance of a major facility (airport, hospital): $41,000.

Best Bets

- Air Traffic Controller
- Facilities Manager
- Marketing Manager

- **Airport Manager** for a county airport, required two years post–high-school education in airport management, business administration, public administration, or a closely related field and three years of experience managing or operating an airport: $36,800.

- **Manager of Marketing and Communications:** $30,500–$45,700.

- **Noise Abatement Officer** at a major aviation authority overseeing noise control for two airports. Required degree in aeronautical engineering, airport administration, public administration, public relations, or related field, plus four years of experience with one year in a noise-control–related field: $30,000.

- **Airport Marketing Manager** to implement an aggressive marketing/public relations program to inform the public about various services and facilities available at two municipal airports: $40,000.

- **Aircraft Rescue and Fire Fighting Chief,** Fort Myers, Florida. Responsible for principles and practices of modern crash rescue fire fighting and fire administration. Ability to plan, evaluate, and coordinate activities performed by fire personnel. Responsible for proper development of fire prevention, suppression strategies, and training programs: $54,647–$74,294.

- **Assistant Manager of Administration** for a regional airport: $33,000.

- **Maintenance Supervisor** for a regional airport: $30,000.

- **Airport Operations Supervisor** at a smaller airport to oversee construction, maintenance, and operations activities. Required high school degree and seven years' experience in airport operations (two in a supervisory capacity) or B.S. degree and three years of experience: $23,000.

Contacts, Sources, and Leads

- **American Association of Airport Executives,** 4212 King St., Alexandria, VA 22302; 703-824-0500; www.airportnet.org. AAAE offers an airport-management accreditation program for people who are actively working in airport management. The association's conferences provide valuable education and invaluable contacts, and its newsletter posts some job openings. AAAE also publishes a directory of its 1,500 members, as well as a bimonthly magazine, *Airport.* It also has student chapters.

- Many airports offer internships, as well.

Fixed-Base Operators

Yet another way of moving into aviation management is through a "fixed-base operator" (FBO). Indeed, FBOs were the forerunner of today's airports.

Snapshot: Fixed-Base Operators

Before there were FBOs, there were only "barnstorming," field-hopping, post–World War I pilots with no fixed base of operations. The founder of the first FBOs were pilots, but they were also businesspeople who recognized the need for stable, professional flight and ground services for air customers from a permanent base of operations.

Today, FBOs form the backbone that supports the air transportation industry, providing the ground services and support required by general aviation, and at many locations, for major airlines and military units, according to the National Air Transportation Association (NATA), the trade group for FBOs, commuter airlines, and air taxis. Even if there is no aviation manager, there is most certainly an FBO at virtually every airport accepting transient aircraft. These FBOs provide products and services such as aviation fuels and oils, aircraft repair and maintenance, aircraft sales and rental, flight instruction, air taxi or commuter airline service, hangars and tie-downs for aircraft, pilot and passenger lounges, avionics service, aircraft parts, and pilot supplies.

Because the FBOs are directly responsible for maintaining, servicing, and fueling aircraft and in some instances maintaining runways and taxiways, they have a critical responsibility for aviation safety. Sometimes a single full-service FBO provides all of these services. Many FBOs maintain an air taxi service, making this type of company an integral part of the air transportation system.

There are about 4,000 FBOs, employing 45,000 people altogether. The majority are small businesses with fewer than 500 employees. One fifth have sales of $1 million or less, while 36 percent have sales in excess of $5 million, with the average company at $10 million, according to data provided by the NATA.

Deregulation has vastly increased business for aircraft maintenance and repair facilities, particularly among the new carriers that cannot support the overhead for their own service and maintenance facilities. But most airlines today are also interested in contracting out services, particularly when they go into a new location. Even at large facilities, aircraft fueling and de-icing is done on a contractual basis by the airline and the FBO.

Among the largest FBO companies are Signature Flight Support (Orlando, Florida) and Jet Aviation (West Palm Beach, Florida).

NATA, with about 2,000 members, has taken an active role in government affairs, representing industry positions with the FAA, Environmental Protection Agency, and Internal Revenue Service, among others. NATA members can take advantage of discounted travel (some may offer interline privileges on airlines) as well as 401K programs for member employees.

Salaries and Wages with FBOs

Business size correlates with executive pay levels. The President of a small company ($500,000 or less) received on average $52,092; at the largest, companies doing over $5 million, the average salary was three times that, at $160,692.

Sample Salaries for FBO Employees

Title	Salary
Avionics Manager	$54,000
Maintenance Manager	$52,000
Chief Flight Instructor	$28,800
Chief Pilot	$52,800
Comptroller	$42,000
General Manager	$63,600
Flight Operations Manager	$54,000
Line Service Manager	$36,000

(continues)

(continued)

Sample Salaries for FBO Employees

Title	Salary
Maintenance Manager	$51,600
Marketing Manager	$52,400
Parts Manager	$38,400

Source: National Air Transportation Association.

Hourly wage earners include the following:

- Avionics Specialist
- Dispatcher
- Inspector
- Line Personnel (fueling and directing planes)
- Mechanic with A&P (airframe and powerplant)
- Mechanic without A&P

Contacts, Sources, and Leads

- **National Air Transportation Association,** 4226 King St., Alexandria, VA 22302; 703-845-9000; www.nata-online.org. A membership directory is available to nonmembers for $45.

Some colleges offer excellent preparatory background, especially for the positions in aviation and port management that require certification or licensing, and are on well-trod paths for industry recruiters. These include the following:

- **Embry-Riddle Aeronautical University,** 600 S. Clyde Morris Blvd., Daytona Beach, FL 32114; 800-94-EMBRY; www.embryriddle.edu.
- **College of Aeronautics,** La Guardia Airport, 86-01 23rd Ave., Flushing, NY 11369; 800-PRO-AERO; www.aero.edu.

The Federal Aviation Administration

Another active partner in the aviation system is the Federal Aviation Administration, within the federal Department of Transportation, which acts as both the manager of the airspace and monitor of the system to ensure the public's safety. There is, however, discussion about somehow privatizing the management of the nation's air traffic control system, much as Canada has, financed by user fees. This would result in a complete change in the economics underlying the management of the air traffic control system and open a new chapter in the deregulation saga.

INSIDE SECRET: The air traffic control system, under the oversight of the FAA, is under pressure to be modernized, upgraded, and expanded, which will generate enormous career opportunities.

Some 45,000 people are employed by the Federal Aviation Administration, almost half of whom are engaged in air traffic control. They staff some 430 airport control towers, 23 air route traffic control centers, and about 200 flight service stations. It is their task to manage a system that is expected to handle one billion airline passengers a year by 2010, with most of that funneling through the 28 largest airports. The FAA is charged with dividing 3.5 million square miles of airspace over the continental United States into aerial highways to accommodate some 20,000 scheduled flights a day, not to mention chartered and private aircraft.

Deregulation of the airline industry transformed the aviation system, and the FAA simply has not quite caught up. Airlines schedule flights in order to make them most desirable for their passengers, often overtaxing the system's ability to manage the flights safely. But the FAA has yet to install technology that is up to the task. It is only partway through a $40 billion modernization program that was supposed to be in place by 2004.

About 9,000 technicians and engineers install and maintain the various components of the system, such as radar, communications sites, and ground navigation aids. For example, the system includes more than 275 long-range and terminal radar systems, more than 800 instrument landing systems, and about 950 very-high-frequency omnidirectional radio ranges. The FAA also operates its own fleet of specially equipped aircraft to check the accuracy of this equipment from the air.

Much of the research and development for the National Airspace System Plan came from the FAA's own Systems Research and Development Service and its Federal Aviation Administration Technical Center in Atlantic City, New Jersey. Much of the engineering and development (E&D) projects are done in-house at the Technical Center at Atlantic City and at the Transportation Systems Center at Cambridge, Massachusetts. Aeromedical research is done at the FAA's Civil Aeromedical Institute at Oklahoma City. At the Technical Center in Atlantic City, for example, engineers are looking into safety issues, studying ways to improve the crashworthiness and fire safety of aircraft.

A key responsibility for the FAA is aircraft and airmen certification. There are more than 200,000 civil aircraft in the U.S. and the FAA requires that each be certified airworthy. FAA aeronautical safety inspectors work along with factory engineers. The FAA has a team of specialists to approve airline maintenance programs, license repair stations, and conduct regular inspections.

The FAA employs 3,400 flight standards (safety) inspectors, with starting salaries around $30,000, depending on the position's civil service grade.

Air carrier airworthiness, general aviation airworthiness, and avionics airworthiness inspectors evaluate mechanics and repair facilities for initial and continuing certification, evaluate mechanic training programs, inspect aircraft and related equipment for airworthiness, and evaluate the maintenance programs of air carriers and similar commercial operators.

Manufacturing inspectors inspect prototypes of modified aircraft, aircraft parts, and avionics equipment for conformity with design specifications and safety standards. They assume FAA certificate responsibility for manufacturing facilities, determine the airworthiness of newly produced aircraft, and issue certificates for all civil aircraft, including modified, import, export, military surplus, and amateur-built aircraft.

Getting into the FAA

Applicants for inspectors must have three years of general experience in aviation that has provided familiarity with aircraft operation, or in the aviation industry related to the specialization (advanced education in related fields such as aeronautical engineering or air transportation can be substituted for general experience). In addition, two or three years of specialized experience that provided a broad knowledge of the aviation industry, aviation safety, and the federal laws, regulations, and policies regulating aviation are also required.

To apply, contact the Federal Aviation Administration, Special Examining Division, AAC-80, P.O. Box 26650, Oklahoma City, OK 73126.

The FAA, which employs about 20,000 air traffic controllers, is continually hiring new controllers. The FAA normally recruits controllers twice a year, in April and October.

There are three categories of air traffic control facilities:

- En route traffic control centers, which control aircraft operating under instrument flight rules between airport terminal areas
- Airport control towers, which handle flights in the terminal areas
- Flight service stations, which provide pilots with a range of weather and flight services

Much attention has been focused on the high stress of the air traffic controller's job. In fact, most of the time the work is very tedious and routine. The problem is that at any moment you could be looking down on tiny blinking lights on the screen and see a catastrophe about to happen.

> **INSIDE SECRET:** Applicants for air traffic controller jobs must pass a written exam and are ranked according to how they scored. Those chosen must attend a training course at the FAA academy.

Applicants who pass the written examination and meet other job qualifications are added to the list of persons eligible for controller jobs, according to individual rankings. Those chosen are sent to the FAA Academy at Oklahoma City for an initial training course of up to 15 weeks before moving on to a facility for additional on-the-job training. The starting salary is $21,000, but experienced controllers are well paid: In a large metropolitan facility such as New York, Chicago, or Los Angeles, experienced controllers can make as much as $90,000. Generally, candidates must not be over 30 years old.

Jobs with the FAA

Recently, the FAA was looking for a Deputy Director, Office of Airport Planning and Programming, at a base salary of $98,500–$141,300. The position shares the responsibility with the Director for developing and issuing the National Plan of Integrated Airport Systems, administering the airport Improvement and Passenger Facility Charge Programs, analyzing environmental and social factors affecting airport development, and overseeing the conveyance or lease of federal land and surplus property for airport purposes. Also, the Deputy Director oversees the management of $5 billion in federal programs and ensures the upgrading and efficient operation of the database systems to administer the programs. The position directs development for airport master and system planning, and oversees the processing of environmental actions for airport projects.

Other job openings at the FAA included an Engineering Research Psychologist, a Personnel Research Psychologist, a Customer Assurance Specialist, and a Quality Assurance Specialist (Electronics) in Oklahoma City; an Airway Transportation Systems Specialist, a Computer Specialist, and a Regional Operations Officer in Anchorage; a Manager of the Aircraft Certification Office in Wichita; and a combination Computer Specialist/Electronics Engineer/Computer Scientist/Mathematician in Atlantic City.

The FAA is also responsible for rule-making to ensure a safe system, and employs many attorneys on staff.

Contacts, Sources, and Leads

- **www.airportnet.org** has job postings but is accessible only to members.
- **The Federal Aviation Administration** Web site, www.faa.gov, posts jobs.
- Job openings at the FAA are advertised in the **Federal Register** and are listed by the Office of Personnel Management, which has offices in most large cities.

Port Management

The nation's leading maritime ports provide additional opportunities in transportation management.

Snapshot: Port Management

There are 28,000 people nationally who work in maritime port management, about one-third of whom work for the Port Authority of New York and New Jersey (which manages three airports and the World Trade Center in addition to the seaport).

There are 180 maritime ports in the United States. The largest, which handle millions of passengers a year (like the Port of Seattle), may have thousands of employees; the smallest might have only two or three (the director, the secretary, and an assistant). The busiest ports for passenger shipping are Miami, Port Everglades (Ft. Lauderdale), Port Canaveral, Los Angeles, Vancouver, New York, St. Petersburg, Palm Beach, San Juan, and San Diego. The average number of employees at these ports is 279.

Many ports are part of a Port Authority that may also manage the airport, and may be a public entity. Governmental port authorities are usually headed by political appointees, which help the authority negotiate the difficult political waters. The major passenger shipping ports likely have a marketing department that is responsible for attracting cruise lines to the port.

According to the American Association of Port Authorities, the average U.S. Port Director's salary was $79,518, with a range of $42,283 to $170,000.

Jobs in Port Management

The following recent classifieds for port management employees provide examples of titles, duties, and qualifications:

- **Port Director,** Port of Pasacagoula, Mississippi: Visionary, motivated, experienced maritime administrator, reporting to a nine-member Board of Commissioners (political appointees), responsible for the day-to-day operational and fiscal management of a growing port with capital budget of $12 million, 38-person staff, and more than 3,000 acres of port and industrial support facilities.

- **Director of Marketing,** South Carolina State Ports Authority: Responsible for management of both carrier and cargo domestic and international sales personnel and agents to include container and break-bulk clients, advertising and publications, marketing, and traffic and pricing function. Minimum of 10 years' experience with ocean carrier and/or ports with at least five years in middle or senior management. Needs leadership qualities, analytical skills, management abilities, and personal dynamics and energy level.

- **Director of Communications,** Port of Long Beach: Oversees a staff of eight and annual budget of $1.8 million; responsible for development, directing, overseeing, and implementing a comprehensive public relations program utilizing various media.

- **Transportation Planner,** Port of Long Beach (pays up to $5,600/month): Assists in traffic analyses and preparation of traffic duties for facilities, transportation projects, and environmental documents; manages and assists in review of traffic studies; conducts or assists in review/analysis of traffic issues, analysis of regulatory and legislative issues.

- **Senior Financial Economic Analyst,** Massachusetts Port Authority: Recommends and develops strategic and financial plans; recommends business plans and rates for maritime customers, long-term leases, and new ventures; prepares and manages economic impact studies.

- **Marine Marketing Director,** Port of Everett: Implements strategic marketing program, budget preparation and control, management, and securing new and maintaining existing marine cargo business.

Contacts, Sources, and Leads

- **American Association of Port Authorities,** 1010 Duke St., Alexandria, VA 22314; 703-684-5700; www.aapa-ports.org. Represents 150 port authorities in the U.S., Canada, the Caribbean, and Latin America. Professional opportunities are posted in its newsletter and on the Web site. The association helps field inquiries.

- The American Association of Port Authorities sponsors **Seaportsinfo.com**, the authoritative guide to the seaports, port authorities, and port industry of the Western Hemisphere.

Safety and Security

Every airline has a safety director, typically someone who has come up through engineering. A flight safety analyst reporting to the director of flight safety for one international carrier, for example, was responsible for identifying problems that could interfere with safe cockpit operations, analyzing flight accident-incident data, writing reports for management to use in preventing accidents/incidents, and investigating and reporting on serious incidents.

Safety-minded professionals might also consider contacting the National Transportation Safety Board, another federal agency. The NTSB has 315 employees, mostly accident investigators, computer professionals, and management people, who investigate accidents involving both airlines and ships.

Since the 1970s, when airliners became a popular target for hijackers and terrorists, the FAA and the aviation industry, particularly, have become concerned with security issues. Every airline now has a security department. They are involved with international terrorism, fraud (such as stolen tickets and credit card fraud), and drug trafficking.

Maritime security also presents a lot of opportunities with ship lines and ports. These professionals focus on detecting the smuggling of contraband and narcotics. (Multimillion-dollar fines levied by the government for drug discoveries have put some shipping companies out of business.) Increasingly, maritime security is also concerned with terrorism. Many cruise lines have small security departments and contract security companies at the ports of call. Every port has a security department, as well. The Port of Miami, for example, has 55 people.

Part of the responsibility of a port's security department is to work with the many federal, state, and local agencies also concerned with law enforcement, including Customs, Immigration, border patrol, Agriculture, Health, FBI, Secret Service (because dignitaries and presidents regularly pass through ports), the Coast Guard, and Marine patrol. They hold mock exercises to make sure all the appropriate agencies work together as a team—for example, to deflect a terrorist attack.

Contacts, Sources, and Leads

- **National Transportation Safety Board,** 800 Independence Ave. SW, Washington, DC 20594; www.ntsb.gov.
- **Office of Personnel Management,** 1900 E St. NW, Washington, DC 20415. Posts civil-service jobs.

WORKING BEHIND THE SCENES

CHAPTER 15

E-TRAVEL: THE TRAVEL INDUSTRY GOES WORLD WIDE WEB

Because travel suppliers essentially sell space-in-time, selling in cyberspace has proved a natural for the industry. Indeed, travel has become the largest category sold on the Internet, and sales are growing at phenomenal rates. The change is revolutionizing travel, transforming the industry on the same order of magnitude that the Industrial Revolution affected society. Deregulation, which had such a dramatic effect on the industry, was just a blip compared to the impact the ever-growing World Wide Web is having. This is by far the most significant factor affecting change in terms of travel professionals.

Virtually every supplier and every retailer is affected, with a vast proportion already having their own presence on the Web. There is a frenzy to establish links with new online travel companies, ranging from online retailers like Uniglobe.com, Vacation.com, and Virtuoso.com, to new online travel companies like Travelocity.com, Lowestfare.com, and Expedia.com, and new b2b2c entities like TravelGalileo.com and eGulliver.com.

Reshaping the Industry

At this writing, e-commerce is the most dynamic aspect of travel, with each day bringing new players, shifting strategies, new trends, new technologies, and new techniques. The Web is reshaping everything—and everyone—from marketing and sales to operations, to the travel services themselves, and even the travel products that are offered.

In many, many ways, the Web is also producing new travelers, by giving people access to real-time information that could dispel myths and misinformation about the effect of hurricanes, for example, or unrest.

This information could even overcome obstacles such as alleviating the concern about seasickness that might have kept someone from booking a cruise. By helping potential customers become better informed and easing access to the product, and even creating a new category of last-minute price-products, the Internet is also improving productivity, reducing the amount of time and effort to complete a booking. On the other hand, the industry is still wrestling with converting "lookers" to "bookers." But although the World Wide Web may ultimately be good for travel, it will prove devastating to some individual companies.

> **INSIDE SECRET:** While it is clear that e-commerce has a place to stay in travel, it is not clear which players will survive an inevitable shakeout and consolidation. This will be one of the riskiest segments for jobs.

A Natural Fit

Travel is a natural for e-commerce because it already had a well-established business-to-business technology link well in advance of other industries, in the form of Computer Reservations Systems and Global Distribution Systems that gave retailers real-time access to suppliers' inventory. But with travel agents selling only a proportion of any company's seats (albeit, up to 80 percent of airline seats sold and 98 percent of cruise cabins booked), that still left a significant volume of seats, cabins, and rooms unsold. Indeed, with airlines running load factors of 70 percent, some 500,000 seats go unsold and 1.5 million hotel rooms go unrented each day. It has been a fairly logical step for travel suppliers to seek a means of distribution directly to consumers, and the Internet has proved ideal.

The Internet is so ideal, in fact, that many suggest that it will cause the demise of retail travel agents altogether. Instead, travel agents are themselves embracing the Internet. (Vacation.com is a perfect example of a traditional travel agency consortium utilizing the Internet.) As an executive for Garber Travel, a Boston-based travel-management services company, said, "If the Internet were easy, why would America Online choose us to handle its corporate travel?"

As the Internet was taking hold, though, it seemed that instead of bypassing travel agents, the largest online entities were making efforts to embrace them. Galileo International, a global electronic distribution system created by 11 airlines, created TravelGalileo.com, a b2b2c travel Web portal, inviting agents to create a free, uniquely branded presence.

Phenomenal Growth

Total bookings of travel over the Web soared from $7 billion in 1999 to nearly $13 billion in 2000, according to the PhoCusWright 2000 Travel E-Commerce survey, and the number of people purchasing travel online in 2000 nearly doubled to 21 million from 11 million the prior year. Moreover, travel-related Web sites became the most preferred research tool among leisure travelers. Indeed, another study, by the Travel Industry Association, put the number of people using the Internet for planning at 52 million in 1999, a 1,500 percent increase from 1996.

The stunning increase in Internet business made headlines when in April 2000 consumers purchased more travel services online, $651 million worth, than any other consumer category. This was more than double the amount spent on computer hardware and software, which had been the leading e-commerce category.

Jupiter Communications, New York, a major research firm in the field, said that nearly half of all travelers who have access to the Net go online to research where to travel. The firm projected that the penetration of online travel bookings would climb steadily from 7.2 percent in 2000 to 14.2 percent in 2005. Meanwhile, another research firm, GartnerGroup, projected that online travel would generate $30 billion by the end of 2001.

Online bookings for air travel are expected to hit $18 billion by 2004. Southwest Airlines alone said it booked more than $1 billion worth in 2000.

The boom in online bookings is also expected to affect sales of packaged travel. A Forrester Research study projected that although online tour packages started relatively slow, at $175 million in 1998, they would generate approximately $4.8 billion by 2003. The Yankelovich Partners 2000 National Leisure Travel Monitor found that although tour packages make up a much smaller percentage of online travel bookings than single trip components such as hotel and airline reservations, the potential for growth is significant.

Affluent Customers

With online travelers' household incomes well above the 1999 U.S. median of $40,816, it is not surprising that they also prove to be frequent travelers, according to the TIA's study, *Travelers' Use of the Internet*. Of the 16.5 million who purchased travel online, 8.2 million were frequent travelers who made five or more trips during the preceding year.

"The wonderful part of the Internet is the ability to reach those 'hard-to-reach' affluent travelers," said Diane McDavitt, President of Luxury Link, a luxury e-travel site (www.luxurylink.com). "They really are everywhere, but hard to find. The medium allows us to really reach out to these affluent consumers. We are no longer limited to our backyards. The perfect client may be in California, Canada, or Australia."

However, though the affluent are also the most inclined to research and shop on the Internet, they also have the inclination to pay for expertise, once again suggesting that the World Wide Web will not mean the demise of travel counselors, but will be a significant force for change. "The Internet does not provide knowledge, wisdom, and experience, the ability to interpret the value of something, especially for us at the luxury end," said Bruce Good, the Director of Corporate Communications worldwide for Cunard Line. "The affluent can always make more money, but when you are talking about vacation, you are talking about time. That is their greatest luxury: time."

A New Battleground for Business

One trend that emerged in 2000 was the shift toward vertical integration, with airline-owned or dominated global distribution systems acquiring or linking with traditional retailers. For example, Amadeus, an airline-owned computer reservation system, acquired Vacation.com, a consortium of 8,500 travel agencies (24,000 agents) with a Web-site presence (www.amadeus.net has job listings).

Galileo, a global distribution company owned by 11 airlines, has a b2c presence with Trip.com, which has more than 200 employees who provide more than four million registered users with a host of tools and services. Services include around-the-clock reservation capabilities; city, restaurant, and hotel information; and 24-hour personalized customer service. It also maintains a b2b2c Web portal, TravelGalileo.com, an online travel booking solution that combines access through the Web to a preferred travel consultant.

Travelbyus.com, a Reno, Nevada–based travel industry "roll up," acquired two dozen companies in order to become a vertically integrated leisure-travel company. The e-travel company linked together 2,700 retail agencies, air consolidators, and a wholesale vacation operation, built around a branded Web site. The site was designed to enable consumers and travel agents to create their own vacation packages online. Users could bundle together their own air, hotel, car rental, tours, events, and cruises into a single package and get a price. The site also offered "virtual reality touring" and video streaming, and was integrated into global distribution systems (allowing for real-time reservations). Typifying the growing complexity of ownership in the New Economy, Travelbyus was owned by publicly traded Aviation Group, but Amadeus, the global distribution system that acquired the Vacation.com network of agencies, had a stake.

Leading online travel agencies include Travelocity.com (www.travelocity.com), Expedia (www.expedia.com), Priceline.com (www.priceline.com), Cheap Tickets (www.cheaptickets.com), Travelscape.com (www.travelscape.com), Lowestfare.com (www.lowestfare.com), Trip.com (www.trip.com), 1travel.com (www.1travel.com), and Biztravel.com (www.biztravel.com).

The Internet is producing an unprecedented pace of innovation. Rosenbluth International, a corporate travel-management services company, launched an entirely new business: Customer Interaction Management, its first venture outside of travel. CIM was aimed at providing nontravel clients with the same type of telephone and Web-based customer service Rosenbluth provided for travel clients.

The impact of the e-commerce technology also enabled a further trend of the mega-companies toward globalization, with data-tracking and reporting technology that did not exist before. However, the Internet has in some ways been a vast equalizer, giving smaller companies a worldwide presence and an ability to reach a targeted audience independently. But at the same time, it has made this a business of behemoths and Lilliputians.

New Job Titles, Career Paths

No matter how it all ultimately shakes out, the Internet is proving to be the biggest single generator of new jobs and job titles in the travel industry, affecting every element and aspect—marketing, sales, operations, administration, and finance. Any and all techies need apply.

The surge of new technology enterprises has fostered altogether new job titles in the industry. For example:

- American Express Corporate Services had a position for a **Senior Vice President and General Manager of Interactive Travel.**
- Sabre Travel Information Network had an opening for a **Managing Director of Global Agency Solutions.**
- Hilton Hotels Corp. had positions for a **Vice President of Marketing Distribution** and a **Director of E-Business Hotel Technology Marketing.**

- Choice Hotels had a **Senior Vice President of E-Commerce and Emerging Business.**

- Brendan Tours had a **Director of Information Services** and **Chief Information Officer.**

- United Airlines' new e-commerce division had a **Director of Strategic Planning, Marketing, and Sales.**

- Vacation.com was recently looking for an experienced **Online Community Manager,** who would work with the marketing, training, engineering, design, and content-production departments to communicate clearly to users and carry out Vacation.com's strategic plan for building community participation across its network of sites. The position required solid experience in online community programming, knowledge of the travel industry, and familiarity with HTML and chat and board software. The ideal candidate would have a minimum of a BS/BA degree, two to four years of applicable work experience, strong client relationship skills, and "be passionate about getting people involved in fun and meaningful interaction." Other employees sought included **Quality Assurance Engineers** and **Web Programmers.**

> **INSIDE SECRET:** The travel industry is being transformed by the World Wide Web, which is now the source of the greatest number of new jobs and job titles. Any and all techies need apply!

A **Director of Online Business** at a traditional travel company typically has 10 to 15 years of corporate experience and has come up through a company's marketing or information services department. A **Web Programmer** may have no corporate experience but will be fluent in several programming languages.

Best Bets

- Web Programmer
- Web Designer
- Director of Online Business Development
- Manager of Interactive Partnership Marketing
- Manager of Client Services

- NT Administrator
- Quality Assurance Engineer
- Customer Service Agents
- Producer

The pure e-travel companies do not have the same professional profile as "traditional" travel companies. And to a great degree, they are hiring their senior executives from outside the industry. Typically they have come from companies that have gone through an IPO (initial public offering) process or from publicly traded mega-million–dollar companies. Their senior management has the high-level profile, pedigree, and credentials of General Electric rather than General Tours.

Take, for example, James E. Barlett, the Chairman, President, and Chief Executive Officer of Galileo International, an electronic global distribution system founded initially by 11 airlines, including United Airlines. He came to Galileo from MasterCard International Corporation, where he oversaw the global program for innovative technology replacement, and previously had been at NBD Bancorp, where he directed the development of the Cirrus International automated teller switching system. He led Galileo through one of the 10 largest initial public offerings in the history of Wall Street in 1997. Or take Thomas Conland, the founder of ByeByeNOW, who has developed and acquired more than 15 companies in a variety of industries, predominantly in the office equipment industry.

> **INSIDE SECRET:** Although the travel industry is competing with other Internet and e-commerce companies and salaries are competitive, they still may be somewhat lower in the travel sector than other industries.

E-Travel professionals are coming from Information Technology (many are getting college training specifically in Internet and e-commerce) as well as Marketing (particularly brand marketing, database marketing, and frequency marketing) and Finance. But this is not a field for anyone looking for job security. The high-capital requirements, low profit margins, and intense competition are triggering waves of consolidation and failures. In this business, an old-timer is any company more than three years old.

LastMinuteTravel.com

The first Internet site to exploit the potential to turn over unsold space was LastMinuteTravel.com, founded in 1997 by David Miranda. Miranda was previously the Vice President of Brand Marketing for Holiday Inns Worldwide, responsible for corporate advertising, marketing programs, database marketing, and frequency marketing for the Holiday Inn Brand. He recognized the potential for technology to tap into the nearly 500,000 just-released travel offers available at any one time. The company enlisted more than 600 global travel and leisure providers—including major airlines like Delta, American, US Airways, Continental, and Lufthansa; hotels like Hyatt, Hilton, and Holiday Inn; cruise lines like Carnival and Norwegian; and rental-car companies including Avis—providing instant access to continually updated travel offers.

When the $110 million company needed to go for fourth-round financing, amounting to $40 million in venture capital, it tapped as Chief Financial Officer Kenneth C. Ray, formerly from BellSouth Telecommunications, where he was Vice President of Sales, Interconnection Services. Ray, who holds an MBA with Distinction from Harvard Graduate School, was part of a team that was responsible for generating $300 million in new revenues for 1999. Prior to joining BellSouth, Ray was with AFLAC; Booz, Allen & Hamilton, Inc.; and Procter & Gamble.

When the company set out to expand internationally, it tapped David J.C. Vis, considered an "international Internet intelligence pioneer," as Managing Director for Europe, Asia-Pacific, and the Middle East. Vis began his career as a travel journalist, then moved into the newly emerging field of travel technology and became the Director of Content for New Media for Reed Travel Group. In this position he developed, designed, and managed the Reed Travel Group's Traveler.Net Web sites. He was recruited by Amadeus Global Travel Distribution to manage the construction of its corporate site, www.amadeus.net, and subsequently launched a European Web company, Infocandy.com.

Next, the company tapped Elizabeth Ann Ward as Senior Vice President, Strategic Alliances, who joined LastMinuteTravel.com, her first foray into e-commerce, from her position as Vice President of Brand Development for KSL Recreation Corporation, a company whose investors include Kohlberg Kravis Roberts & Co. (KKR). Prior to joining KSL, Beth was Vice President of Marketing, Travel, and Entertainment for VISA USA. She also brought extensive hospitality and food service experience working with Hyatt Hotels and Resorts, Michael Jordan's Restaurant, and Rosebud Restaurant Group.

Other team members hail from iXL, *USA Today*, *Vogue*, *People* magazine, and Lockheed Martin.

Based in Atlanta, LastMinuteTravel.com offers candidates "competitive salaries, generous pre-IPO stock options, nice hats and shirts, bosses who listen to you." Among the positions it was hiring for: Java Architect, Internet Software Quality Assurance Engineer, Oracle Internet Developer, and Java Database Developer.

(For more information, see www.lastminutetravel.com.)

Why Go into Online Travel?

Online travel presents a new frontier for the travel industry, a chance to be part of the most creative and innovative facet, yet also share in the dynamics of the travel industry.

Expedia, one of the online travel companies, put it best:

> At Expedia, we see travel as a real trip. An intensely exciting experience. If you work at Expedia, you'll spread your wings and immerse yourself in all things travel. Career opportunities here offer lots of variety and the chance for you to transform our travel Web site into the richest, most useful, and engaging experience for the do-it-yourself business or leisure traveler. At the same time, you can help develop and support travel products from start to finish. It's interesting, fulfilling work. The kind you'll love telling your friends about.

Automation and Technology

The World Wide Web is almost an added layer to what had been known in the travel industry (and now seems quaint) as "automation." It is significant to remember that the airlines' computer reservations systems that predated the Internet were the most sophisticated computers used in civilian application, and cost billions of dollars to develop. These companies have been spun off into massive businesses in their own right, such as Sabre Inc., which started off as a division of American Airlines.

There is still all of the technology that existed before—automated back-office systems and reporting software now upgraded to sophisticated data warehousing and customer relationship marketing systems, and yield-management systems that accumulate data to forecast traffic and devise pricing that will stimulate, not dilute, demand.

Automation Products and Services

The 2000 edition of *Business Travel News' Automation Directory* includes 250 products or services designed specifically for the corporate travel market, from 74 vendors and 15 travel-management companies. (This is actually a decline from 300 products from 85 vendors and 15 travel-management companies in 1999, and 330 products from 100 vendors and 20 travel-management companies the year before that, due mainly to consolidation.) All of these vendors and companies provide significant job opportunities.

This is a multibillion-dollar business in its own right. Categories of products and services include the following:

- **Online booking systems:** Allow users direct and immediate access to a database of airfare, schedule, and availability displays for airlines and/or rate and availability data for hotels and cars. These also include agentless booking systems, electronic information exchanges, and dial-up systems.

Among the providers: Rosenbluth International, Commercial World.Net from Worldspan, Total Travel Management, Corporate TravelOnline from American Express, Corporate Travelpoint from Galileo International, E-Traveler from E-Travel Inc., GetThere Inc., PeopleSoft, Amadeus/SAP, and Sabre.

 INSIDE SECRET: Because online travel, automation, and technology vendors are so Web-oriented, their Web sites are excellent leads for job openings.

- **Trip-planning systems:** Allow users to search and book travel itineraries via fax, e-mail, voice response, computer, or other electronic means. These may have a delayed response time (perhaps two minutes) and require a person to act to complete the reservation. Some large travel-management services companies offer these systems, such as Worldspan, Trams, OAG Worldwide, SatoTravel, Travel and Transport, and Northwestern Travel.

- **Point of sale/pre-travel quality control software:** Addresses a corporate travel manager's need to make sure employees are following the company's travel policy. Companies offering these include American Express, McCord Travel Management, Travel and Transport, Rosenbluth, SatoTravel, Gelco, GetThere, Maritz, Omega, Total Travel Management, and Stevens Travel Management.

- **Web-based and client site reporting software:** Browser-based or reporting software located at the client site that allows corporate decision-makers to access corporate travel data and produce travel-management reports. Providers include Amadeus Global Travel Distribution, Northwestern Travel, Navigant International, E-Travel, GE Capital, Travel and Transport, American Express, Total Travel Management, and Rosenbluth.

 INSIDE SECRET: As e-travel is taking hold, two years of experience in e-travel is equivalent to 10 in other areas.

- **Frequent-flyer tracking software:** Software sold or licensed to track frequent-flyer points for corporations or their travelers. Providers include Northwestern Travel, GetThere, and Omega World Travel.

- **Global travel-management reporting software:** Consolidates global travel data from multiple locations around the world and produces travel-management reports that a corporate travel-management services company can provide to its clients.

- **T&E expense reporting:** Facilitates entry and processing of travel and entertainment expenses. The providers include Citicorp, Diners Club, and E-Travel.

- **End-to-end travel-management systems:** An integrated solution to travel-management issues such as automated booking, reporting, and travel and expense management, as well as policy compliance. Providers include Rosenbluth International, Northwestern Travel, and E-Travel.

- **Meeting-management software:** Facilitates planning, budgeting, execution, or financial analysis of meetings. Providers include Maritz and GetThere.

- **Hotel RFP:** Automates the hotel request for proposal systems, the transfer to the hotels, and the response back to corporate decision-makers.

Other Categories

Other categories include the following:

- **Profile management software or Web applications:** Designed to speed the creation and/or maintenance of passenger profiles.

- **Pre-travel reporting software:** Takes preticketed information and produces management reports.

- **E-ticket tracing software:** Used, licensed, or sold to track unused electronic tickets.

- **Travel-management reporting software:** Designed to generate management reports, so companies can provide their clients a means of viewing, forecasting, and analyzing travel bookings data, even globally.

Contacts, Sources, and Leads

- **Interactive Travel Services Association,** 1001 G St. NW, Ste. 900 E., Washington, DC 20001; 202-879-9305; www.interactivetravel.org.

- **WebTravelNews,** published by PhoCusWright, Inc., 1 Rte. 37 E., Ste. 200, Sherman, CT 06784-1430; 860-350-4084; www.webtravelnews.com.

- Business Travel News *Black Book.*

- Business Travel News *Automation Directory.*

CHAPTER 16

TRAVEL SUPPORT SERVICES: THE BEST OF BOTH WORLDS

An industry as large and as complex as travel and tourism gives rise to a whole host of support services and consultancies that indirectly make its activities possible. The list is virtually endless, but includes technology and computer services, research, marketing and advertising, insurance, credit card and financial services, law and accounting, and medical assistance.

Although many of these services may actually be outside the industry, those who work for support services have a specialized knowledge of that segment of the business and become integrated into the industry. They work with the same people, react to the same issues, develop the same product, and work toward the same goal of promoting travel and tourism. Many of these jobs also provide ample opportunity to travel. But there is an added advantage of working on the periphery of the industry: The pay levels reflect the industry you are actually in, rather than those of the travel industry. So the pay might be higher.

Frequently, too, working in a support service can be a way into the travel industry from a nontravel background, because you learn the industry as well as any insider, go to many of the same conferences and meetings, and make the same contacts. Similarly, travel people sometimes leave the industry to enter a consultancy or a service company that provides support to the industry.

For so many who come into the travel industry, working in travel fulfills a dream of traveling. But there are many other kinds of interests and activities that are equally compelling—such as journalism or photography. For many people who have been frustrated to find conventional career paths in those fields closed, these support companies provide a suitable alternative for realizing a professional dream. Working as a journalist for the travel trade press, for example, can enable you to practice your profession but also participate directly in the travel industry, travel extensively, and interact and form long-term associations with literally thousands of travel people.

INSIDE SECRET: Working in one of the many support services for the travel industry can be a "best of both worlds" situation: practicing a profession and earning a salary but being an active participant in the world of travel.

There are scores of activities that provide the same opportunity to practice a professional skill and yet enjoy the dynamism, vitality, and excitement of the travel industry and its people. We profile several of them in this chapter: research and marketing, advertising, public relations, travel writing, travel photography, education and training, association work, travel law, and nontravel services.

Research and Marketing

Seemingly picayune matters such as whether to change the number of seats in first class on an airplane, convert a floor in a hotel to make it women-only, or introduce a tiered price structure for ski-lift tickets can have vast financial consequences. Such decisions are not made without extensive market research.

Research guides decisions such as whether a business should open at all, whether there is a niche for a company, whether there is sufficient demand to move into another market, or whether a "package" for the product (the brochure, direct-mail piece, and hotel interior design) is effective.

As the travel industry has grown, become more sophisticated and professional, and the financial stakes have been raised, a whole industry of professional research companies has sprung up to service travel companies, destinations, governments, and developers. Generally, only larger companies can afford their own research staff person or department, or to commission a study. But, increasingly, even smaller entities are committing resources to research. Research professionals are employed by airlines and other transportation companies, hotel companies, tourist offices, trade associations, advertising agencies, and the consumer and trade press, in addition to specialized research companies.

The number of research companies specializing in travel and tourism has exploded in recent years. Many general companies, such as Gallup and Louis Harris, have also become active in the field. Most of the research firms dedicated to travel and tourism are small, but there are giants such as Pannell Kerr Foster, a company specializing in hotel research, which has offices worldwide and thousands of employees.

"We deal so much with the Vice Presidents of Marketing of airlines, cruise lines, and the like," stated Stanley Plog, President of Plog Research, a large research company in Reseda, California, which handles travel research projects and employs several hundred people. "You are at the heart of the dynamics of the industry. Markets are changing all the time."

Constant Change Necessitates Strategy

Even before deregulation, change was constant. But then, there was a certain predictability, even seasonality. Now, companies have to be able to respond sometimes the same day to a competitor's initiative.

"Clients have to figure out how to position themselves," said Plog. "That's what research does. We help

them develop a strategy. We help them think about the future in a different way. We help design new airplanes with the customer in mind. We work with cruise lines and destinations on how they should advertise themselves. We help developers design a resort, help transportation companies create an appropriate fare structure."

Companies also need to monitor themselves to make sure they are "delivering" what is promised. To measure how well companies are accomplishing this, a research company may survey travel agents. Research can also tell clients whether travel agents are "delivering" for them effectively.

INSIDE SECRET: Research and marketing are key growth areas in the travel industry, with positions opening at individual companies as well as in specialized research firms.

Getting In and Getting Ahead

Research companies usually look for people with a background in behavioral sciences and experimental methodology, statistics, or economics. Jobs include analysts, statisticians, interviewers, and computer specialists.

This is a field that demands creativity. "You better be creative to survive," said Thomas Lea Davidson, principal of Davidson-Peterson Associates, Inc. "Numbers are crunched by computer; people have to analyze them. We are not as concerned with statistics or research methods. We are concerned with personality—we look for a person who is brighter than average (this is a thinking business), willing to be involved in what we are doing, excited by the concept of research, inquisitive about why things work. They can have a tourism background."

Project managers travel to the places being researched, and in fact log lots of miles.

Growth depends on ability. At senior levels, salaries are on par with a senior account executive in an advertising agency. Research is just as much an art as a science and people who have a talent are well paid.

One of the exciting aspects of working in research is that you develop proprietary information and deal with the client's top management. Consequently, the research organization can also be a steppingstone to other areas of travel.

Like so many facets of the travel industry, there is a glut of people looking for entry-level jobs but a dearth of experienced people. Salary levels reflect supply and demand. There is no shortage of people to handle the "peripheral jobs"—mainly rote and manual work. But true researchers, those who are able to create a study and interpret the results, are in short supply.

Preparation for the work should involve academic courses in economics, statistics, and research methods, some of which are included in travel and tourism programs. It is much easier to get into travel research as a research professional than as a travel professional.

The Travel and Tourism Research Association is the key trade organization, with 800 members. TTRA does some job referrals, mostly in the academic arena. Its meetings and conferences bring together marketing and research people from all the companies and entities that employ them—airlines, hotel chains, car rental companies, universities and colleges, destinations, advertising agencies, consumer and trade publications—so it does provide a network for job-hopping. So far, only a few companies offer internships.

Contacts, Sources, and Leads

■ **Travel and Tourism Research Association,** P.O. Box 2133, Boise, ID 83701; 208-429-9511; www.ttra.com.

Advertising Agencies

Advertising agencies become intimately involved in the marketing and promotions strategy of a travel and tourism client—an airline, a hotel, a tour operator, a car rental company, a cruise line, or a destination. They are very much at the heart of the debate over whether travel can be marketed like a soap, a dream, or a service. They must be sensitive to changing lifestyles, values, and demographics, and whether "cheesecake" and sun-and-sand are the way to sell the Caribbean, or whether culture, sports, or some other theme would be more persuasive. They decide how the client should be positioned in the marketplace—to the upscale, sophisticated traveler, to the mass market, or somewhere in between.

For the account executive, there is considerable travel to the client destination, or considerable use of the client's product. On the other hand, an account executive's fortune rises and falls with the client's, so a bad season can put you out of a job.

The advertising executive can feel very much "in touch" with the travel industry. "I take the 'slings and arrows' more seriously even than my clients. I make myself as informed about the industry as I can," said Stuart Herman, Vice President of Herman Associates of New York, who started with a single travel account, found he adored the product, and slowly developed a specialty in the field.

INSIDE SECRET: Advertising executives become intimately involved in the success of their travel clients, and are at the epicenter of the maelstrom of change necessitating advertising response.

An agency like Herman Associates, which handles mainly international destinations and travel companies, may have the added role of explaining the American market to a foreign tourism director, who may be at the start of a three- or four-year stint here. The advertising agency has to identify the market, choose a theme, develop a concept, determine positioning for ads, and decide a strategy for running the ads—in short, it must "get the best bang for the buck." This is true for advertising any product, but travel is different. "So much of travel is illusion," said Herman.

Unpredictable but Rewarding

"Every type of business has its own eccentricities," Herman said, "it's good times and bad. But travel advertising has almost a total absence of long-range planning. You have to be extremely fast on your feet to respond to the changing situation—for example, the client who says his objective is to increase sales from individual travelers, and then four months later turns to groups or incentives. It is so volatile."

Unpredictable events such as earthquakes, hurricanes, airplane crashes, political unrest, currency fluctuations, and strikes can render an ad campaign useless. "Your biggest client may be a hotel in a country that becomes a hotbed overnight. There are tinderboxes all around the world. You don't know what to expect one day to the next," Herman said.

But there are definite rewards. There is a fair amount of travel, but not all of it subsidized. But the biggest benefit, to Herman, is that "I have clients all over the world; I have friends all over the world."

Smaller agencies afford some advantages. "There is a sense of involvement here that you might not have at a bigger agency. At a bigger agency, there may be so many layers, there is little exposure to the client, work is far removed, frequently comes back unrecognizable, and there is no control. Here, there is far less to cut through to make your ideas known and listened to."

Also, the staff is more likely to be working on several different campaigns at once rather than only one. The art director might be working with six to eight clients—largely because there isn't the volume from a single client.

Getting In and Salaries

"I hire people with advertising experience, but not necessarily travel advertising experience. I look for someone who is bright, who is also widely traveled. You can be the greatest art director in the world, but if you have never been to Europe, you haven't experienced travel," Herman said. The media planner also should have a "feeling" for matching up the product advertising with the correct media that will go to the right markets.

Salaries are modest at entry level but are excellent at senior levels.

Many ad agencies are also accommodating a trend toward clients who want other services as well, such as public relations. "Today, you are not just dealing with advertising, but communications," Herman said. "There used to be a war between public relations and advertising. But in the last decade, clients appreciate a coordinated marketing effort between public relations and advertising."

Advertising Space Sales

The other side of advertising is space sales—that is, working for print and broadcast media in the travel category to sell advertising space. Publications like the *New York Times, Texas Monthly, Food & Wine, Gourmet,* and *Connoisseur* (the list goes on and on) all employ advertising space salespeople to specialize in the travel category.

Contacts, Sources, and Leads

- Consult Standard Rate & Data's *Directory of Advertisers* and its *Directory of Advertising Agencies.*
- Also consult *Advertising Age* and *AdWeek,* the leading industry trade publications.

Public Relations

Some public relations firms specialize in travel accounts, particularly smaller, "boutique" agencies. Public relations also plays a vital role in the marketing process, but has a very different purpose from advertising. The object of public relations is to cultivate a positive image and awareness of a client, and generally to inform the public. The message generally has higher credibility than an advertisement because it is written by a third party—the journalist.

Public relations professionals handle press inquiries, write releases, use their contacts in the trade and consumer press to encourage reporters to follow up on stories, set up interviews and press conferences, and frequently arrange and conduct press trips.

Even large companies that already have a public relations staff will frequently go to outside agencies for additional support.

"It is possible to be a public relations practitioner who happens to have travel accounts," said Lynne Rutan, "but I personally feel I am part of the travel industry." Rutan got into "travel" as an Account Executive with a public relations firm handling the Greek National Tourist Office account. She then became the public relations officer for the American Society of Travel Agents, the leading trade association, which put her solidly in the middle of industry issues. She next went back to a public relations agency.

A Unique Spin on the PR Business

There are some unique aspects to representing a travel entity. For example, the public relations executive is more likely to be involved with press trips and will probably travel in conjunction with the trip. When Rutan worked on the Greek account, she spent about three to five days a month traveling for two years. When she worked at ASTA (by then she was a mother), she did not expect to travel, but had to travel to regional and national conferences, and also wound up producing a film where she had to travel around

the world for two months to handle the shooting.

Promoting travel is also different because the markets—the audience—and consequently the potential media you can place stories in are so much more varied than, for example, products such as computers, soap, or cereal. The same client can generate a story for trade, consumer travel, food and wine, lifestyle, news, or financial editors. Then there are the broadcast media, which provide even more opportunities for story placement. A key challenge for the public relations person is to think of the various story placements and how to "sell" the story to a skeptical editor who may not be in tune with travel.

Public relations agencies are set up different from one another and specialize in specific aspects of the field. Some are more promotions oriented, whereas others are more marketing oriented. In some agencies, "you are pigeonholed into doing just one thing for one client; in others, you do everything. It depends on the size and organization of the agency," said Rutan.

Public relations can be frustrating, as well. "You may have what you think is a terrific story, but the timing may be off, or the client may not be willing to present the product in such a way as to interest an editor. Also, it is frustrating to explain to the client that the presentation should be kept as objective as possible, that it is not a sales piece."

The publicist may have to tell the same story over 50 times to various editors, and then start over with the reporters. "But that can be fun, too, tailoring the pitch to the audience, picking out what is new and exciting," Rutan said.

Getting In and Salaries

Getting into public relations is not cut and dried. Many public relations people specializing in travel come from trade publications or travel companies such as hotels, and simply move over to an agency. Some get in by doing clerical support or interning. Many now are coming out of college Communications programs.

Generally, public relations agencies try to hire people who are already doing public relations for a travel entity. Sometimes, they try to hire from among the reporters for the trade press.

 INSIDE SECRET: Many get into travel-related public relations from the trade press.

Public relations requires writing and verbal communications skills, organization, the capability to take a campaign from conceptualization to implementation, and also salesmanship (to sell the concept to an editor). People skills, particularly in handling clients and editors and reporters, are also important.

Public relations can be lucrative as you move up—certainly better-paying than the trade publications. But not all areas pay the same. The account executive handling a bank's account is likely to be better paid than one handling a travel account because the travel accounts tend to be smaller.

Contacts, Sources, and Leads

- To find agencies that have a good chunk of travel clients, you can talk to reporters on trade publications such as *Travel Agent, Travel Weekly, Leisure Travel News,* and *Business Travel News.*
- Check *Jack O'Dwyer's Newsletter,* which announces which public relations agencies landed which accounts. This can give you an idea of which agencies might be needing to hire new people.
- Consult *P.R. Contacts* and *Media Notes.*
- Consult the **Public Relations Society of America,** 33 Irving Place, New York, NY 10003-2376; 212-995-2230; www.prsa.org. The Web site posts positions.

Travel Writing

Travel writing is an enormous field that encompasses the various media—newspapers, magazines, television, radio, guidebooks—and myriad audiences, including "consumers" (that is, the potential travelers) and "trade" (the industry). Within these categories are specialties; for example, you may be writing for a magazine catering to seniors, or to women, or to skiers.

The Trade Press

One of the best ways to enjoy the excitement, dynamics, and glamour of the travel industry is to join one of the many trade publications, such as *Travel Agent* magazine, *Travel Weekly, Leisure Travel News,* or *Business Travel News,* and literally dozens of others catering to the various industry segments (hospitality, airlines, meetings, incentives, and so on).

Trade publications are generally easier to get into than the consumer press (newspapers, guidebooks, and magazines for travelers), which have greater visibility and prestige. Trade publications also tend to be low paying. But the trade press affords an opportunity to take on more responsibility and to advance more rapidly. Reporting tends to have more depth than the consumer press; readers rely on the articles to keep them abreast of the latest developments, and the articles directly influence business decisions.

There is great satisfaction in being able to actually put "faces" on the readership—you meet your readers at industry meetings and conferences and wind up interviewing many. Trade reporters frequently become well known in their field and are often invited to speak at functions. Indeed, trade writing can frequently lead to positions in the industry, in public relations, marketing, consulting, or advertising.

Staffs tend to be smaller at trade publications, so there is greater opportunity to do many different kinds of reporting and have many different "beats."

Trade reporting is intrinsically different from consumer reporting. There is little in the way of on-the-spot flowery descriptions of sunsets, swaying palm trees, and powdery sand. Although there are many destination features (and tremendous opportunities to visit destinations), most of the articles are hard news accounts of developments in the industry—reports about companies, legal issues, and business issues. Most of the reporting is by telephone or face-to-face interviews.

There are frequent opportunities to travel, though. Because of the importance of travel and tourism to the economic vitality of nations and states, it is not uncommon to be in the company of presidents, prime ministers, and monarchs at major industry conferences.

It is best to start right out of college, preferably with an internship.

There are scores of travel trade publications for each specialty, including travel agents, aviation, hotels, incentive travel, corporate travel, meetings, and motorcoach.

Among some of the major travel industry publications: *Travel Agent* magazine, *Travel Weekly, Leisure Travel News, Travel Management Daily, Business Travel News, Jax Fax, Meeting News, Meetings & Conventions Magazine, Successful Meetings Magazine,* and *Aviation Weekly.*

Contacts, Sources, and Leads

- Check *The Writer's Market* and *Standard Rate & Data Service* for leads. Trade associations can also supply the names of leading publications.
- **American Business Media,** 675 Third Ave., New York, NY 10017; 212-661-6360; www.americanbusinessmedia.com.
- Publications regularly advertise for help in **local newspaper classified sections.**

The Consumer Press

Breaking into writing for consumer publications is much harder. Most of the major newspapers and journals already have some syndicated columnist or staff writer.

Most of the consumer-oriented travel magazines—*Travel & Leisure, Condé Nast Traveler*—rely on staff and freelance articles. *Vogue, Glamour, Seventeen,* and specialty publications such as *Gourmet, Town and Country, Tennis,* and *Ski* also have regular travel sections or features.

Travel writing is a hard club to get into. You may try to break in through a local newspaper. Once you establish credentials as a travel writer (you need to be published in order to get published), then it is possible to be included on press trips (although many publications have strict policies against writers accepting free travel).

One of the problems with the field is that everyone, including editors and amateur travel writers, assumes travel writing is a joy-ride, a lark, an endless spree of first-class air travel, of luxurious accommodations, and of being wined and dined. They fail to see the amount of work that goes into it, from the first hustle for assignments, to the pretrip research, to the sheer physical effort that a trip requires, to the arduous work of banging out the story by the deadline. As a result, fees for travel stories are well below those for any other kind of article, and sometimes do not cover the expense in time and effort that it took to write them.

The Life of a Freelancer

Eunice Juckett, a professional travel writer, had just turned 71 when her doctor diagnosed "fatigue syndrome" and advised her to cut down on her rigorous travel schedule.

(continues)

(continued)

"People don't think I work. They don't know how hard it is." She would rise at 4 a.m. to write for four or five hours before the phone started ringing. When traveling, she put in 16- to 18-hour days. "You try to do personal investigation, wander around the city, get a feel. You try to observe what's happening, the people, other tourists, where the popular places are. You ride the local transportation."

Even the writing is harder than it looks. "You have to go beyond the normal guidebook stuff—you must give insights about travel in relation to other destinations, not just the hours the museums are open and how much the hotels cost," she said.

As a freelancer, unattached to any single publication exclusively, Juckett maximized the value of her assignments by selling the story to as many publications or media as possible. She would do one story for about 15 different publications, changing the lead and the body to fit the audience. There are umpteen types of audiences: the trade press, local newspapers, special-interest magazines (such as food and wine, travel, in-flight magazines, sports, senior citizens, and religious publications).

Some assignments come from editors or are initiated by the public relations or promotional people for destinations and travel companies. But the good travel writer also comes up with ideas for stories, and simply by asking the questions, can influence the development of new products, programs, or policies. For example, Juckett did a story on what cruise lines do to make all the procedures that come on the last day of the cruise easier for passengers. "Many didn't even think about the issue until I asked about it," she said.

Breaking into travel writing is the hard part for several reasons. Just like everyone who can snap a picture and thinks they can be a photographer, everyone who can type and takes a trip thinks they can be a travel writer. Editors will generally never use an unpublished writer. "If your name isn't known, editors are skeptical about what you are saying," Juckett advised.

Another reason travel writing is difficult to get into is that there are only about 300 professional travel writers—those that make their living from travel writing and thousands more who write occasional travel pieces—and there is a closed clique among them. These writers, who typically are members of the Society of American Travel Writers (SATW), are invited to take trips by tourist offices, travel companies, and airlines, and have the credentials to get assignments from editors. There is usually a chicken-and-egg syndrome: A writer will be invited on a trip only when he or she already has an assignment.

The best way to break in, advised Juckett, is to "write about what you know well, and get two or three stories under your belt before you approach an editor."

Juckett, a fiction writer since her childhood, got into travel writing by doing articles about Long Island, where she lived. "I wrote a story about East Hampton celebrating its 300th anniversary and sent it to the *Herald Tribune*. It was printed in the Paris *Herald* before here. And I was off and running." The key is to cultivate an association with one publication and then expand.

A considerable amount of a travel writer's time is spent setting up assignments with editors, getting invitations for trips, reading background material and preparing for the trip, setting up interviews, handling correspondence, arranging an itinerary, and booking transportation and lodgings.

Publications have their own special audiences and their own policies. Some do not allow the travel writer to take any freebies; others insist that the articles support the advertisers, who are likely to be the expensive tours and resorts rather than cozy, inexpensive inns and do-it-yourself adventures.

Juckett has visited about 117 countries, including South Africa, Lebanon, and Northern Ireland. "As a travel journalist, my responsibility is to report what is there." She travels 75 to 80 percent of the year, typically.

Many travel writers around now have been in the field for decades, and have locked up syndicated columns and relationships with publications. But there is a new generation coming up.

"You have to study the market. You have to decide what facet of travel writing you want to be in. You can't be a specialist in everything. Some are better writers than others; others are mediocre but have good ideas; some are better at gathering facts but can't put them together in a publishable story; others are good writers but poor at research," Juckett said.

"Also, some are great writers, but you also have to be able to market the story and yourself—analyze the market, what will sell and when."

"You have to be able to sort out from all you see and experience, and write about what is important to the reader."

Traveling is physically strenuous. Juckett said, "You have to be able to keep up with 16- to 18-hour days, to keep going and do interviews even if you are suffering *turista* or some other ailment. You have to face hassles, like airline delays or cancellations or rerouted flights. You have to be an organized, detail-oriented person and keep tremendous files; read everything about the topic you intend to write about. You have to be flexible, adventurous, curious, interested in people, able to absorb, assess what you have seen.

"The travel writer has to be many things—that's why I got into photography, because the photographer was earning more than me. You have to sell yourself, and to know whether a trip will be profitable—if it is worth spending six days in Arkansas, for example.

"Travel writing can pay well, but only if you hustle. Many publications feel that travel is a perk and pay less—even one-third—for travel stories than other features."

Cash flow can be a problem. Travel writers have to lay out sums of money and wait for publications to reimburse them for their expenses and pay their fee, either after acceptance of the manuscript or after publication. Sometimes publications assign a story but then don't print it, and the travel writer has to collect a kill fee (a percentage of the full amount).

Travel writing, particularly freelancing, is an insecure field, one of feast and famine.

But travel writing is more than newspapers and magazines. It is also radio, television, cable television, Internet, cassettes, walking tours, lectures, and books. There are vast new markets for travel writing such as serving as a consultant to a large department store that may be tying a merchandise promotion to a foreign country. One must be creative to find new avenues and niches.

One of the difficulties in being a travel writer, Juckett reflected, is "you lose contact with your home town." On the other hand, a travel writer becomes part of a world community, forming friendships around the globe. "You are reminded of that when someone you met in India and haven't seen for years phones up out of the blue."

The Society of American Travel Writers does not offer much assistance to those trying to break into the field; indeed, membership is restricted to working professionals who meet criteria and are sponsored by members. However, SATW does offer members seminars and a base for networking.

(For more information, contact the Society of American Travel Writers, 4101 Lake Boone Trail, Ste. 201, Raleigh, NC 27607; 919-787-5181; www.satw.org.)

Contacts, Sources, and Leads

■ Check *The Writer's Market* for leads. Send a query and a self-addressed and stamped envelope for reply to the appropriate editor.

Guidebook Writing

Twenty years ago, there were few travel books and they vied for attention on cramped bookstore shelves. The popularity of guidebooks skyrocketed during the "go-go" 1980s. Today, there are massive travel sections and even entire bookstores devoted to travel, and a seemingly insatiable consumer appetite for guidebooks.

There are some 6,000 travel books in print today, with about 1,500 new titles published each year (about twice the number of cookbooks). Some of the biggest, best-selling brand-name series titles, such as Frommer's, Fodor's, Fielding, and Birnbaum, sell 50,000 to 100,000 copies a year, and industry-wide sales amount to more than $100 million a year.

Guidebooks have an enormous impact on travelers and the travel industry. They can literally put a destination, a hotel, or an attraction on the map. Many travelers regard their guidebooks as bibles, and follow the suggested itineraries religiously.

But the swelling demand for guidebooks is being met by an even greater outpouring of books, so competition is intense. Moreover, travel books are incredibly costly to research and produce, so publishers are hesitant to take on new authors.

Nonetheless, there are opportunities. Some of the brand-name publishing companies hire writers to produce whole books, write selected chapters, or research some special interest.

"Our writers are usually professionals with some association with the destination," related Arthur Frommer, whose *Europe on $5 A Day* spawned a revolution in mass travel when it was first published in the 1950s. "We get letters from people everywhere. We ask them to audition: Imagine you are writing a guide, give us 10 sample pages of a hotel chapter. Many times, people are hired that way. One of our writers had never written before, but she wanted to do Washington, D.C. For her audition, she compared the quality of government cafeterias. It was so colorful and fun to

read, we hired her to do Ireland, New Zealand, and Washington, D.C. She has made a career for herself."

It takes an author, or a battery of writers, an average of one to two years to research and write a guidebook. Frommer spent five years researching *Arthur Frommer's New World of Travel,* devoted to a new revolution in "intellectual, experiential" travel.

Margaret Zellers has authored Fielding's Caribbean guide since 1979, updating the book annually. Unlike most authors, she owns the book and holds the copyright. She is also scrupulous about paying her own way and not accepting any hospitality so that she can be free to set her own schedule and report her observations, even if it means warning readers against overcharging and surly immigration officials. Her book sells 50,000 to 100,000 copies a year. "Readers write to me," she said, pointing to the personal connection the guidebook writer sometimes forms with readers.

"When I first started in this business, it was wonderful," she related. "I wouldn't start today, though. The competition is vicious. Travel writers are running all over each other. It's a game of sharks. It's a lot of hard work—I travel three-fourths of the year [and pay my own way]. But it's been my life and I love it."

Contacts, Sources, and Leads

- Check *The Writer's Market* and *Publishers Weekly,* a trade magazine for book publishers.
- You can get a leg up by registering at **www.travelwriters.com**.
- An online source for markets for travel writers is the travel writing section of **Inkspot:** www.inkspot.com/genres/travel/markets.html.

Travel Photography

The professional travel photographer faces even greater frustrations than the travel writer: low pay, intense competition from everyone with a 35mm camera who thinks they can take a snapshot (including travel writers), and, as some have found out, a lack of creative outlets.

Lisle Dennis has been a professional travel photographer for more than 25 years. "You don't get into it for the money," she said with exasperation. Getting in 25 years ago was relatively easy—there were lots of press trips and invitations even without confirmed assignments from publications. "It's the end of the flying carpet era on the public relations side," she said. "Things have really tightened up." Now you need a letter confirming an assignment or an outlet for the photography before a sponsoring group will provide free travel. Then, as now, budding photographers would need to join the Society of American Travel Writers in order to network with magazine editors, but membership requires that a professional already be established in the field.

Even getting a plum assignment from a top publication like *National Geographic* or *Travel & Leisure* is no guarantee of future assignments.

Travel Photography Markets

To understand the problem, it is important to examine the markets for travel photography. There are scores of consumer magazines that feature travel articles. The trouble is, the articles may use only a single shot for illustration, and they rarely make assignments; many prefer to obtain photographs free from the tourist offices or buy from the stock houses.

Other markets for travel photography include airlines' own in-flight magazines, as well as newspapers, books, calendars, and even greeting cards. Advertising is a major market, but Dennis was very critical of the quality and creativity, which she attributed to the low budgets applied by travel companies. Other clients for travel photography include airlines, hotel companies, tour companies, and tourist offices.

Per diem rates are meager compared to other types of photography—on the order of $1,000, versus $2,500 for nontravel assignments.

About the only way a professional travel photographer can make a living is to shoot for stock houses—agencies that are libraries for millions of slides from hundreds of photographers. These agencies sell the rights to use the photographs to magazines, textbooks, calendar companies, advertising agencies, and so forth. Stock houses split the fee 50-50 with the photographer.

It is difficult to make a living as a full-time travel photographer; yet one cannot be a part-timer, either. Hustling assignments and shooting stock that is current and in demand takes a lot of time. "If you don't devote full time, you won't sell," said Dennis. "You may hit a local publication once or twice, or sell a few shots for postcards or calendars, but that's it."

A very different type of travel photography is shooting the "news" of the industry, working for the trade associations and trade publications, primarily at various industry functions and events.

Contacts, Sources, and Leads

- Consult *The Writer's Market* or *The Photographer's Market* for leads.
- An excellent online source for travel photography markets and stock houses is the **PhotoSecrets Travel Photography Home Page:** www.photosecrets.com/links.html.

Education and Training

Education and training has become a megabucks business within the travel industry. The intensifying pace of the industry, its growing sophistication, and the pervasiveness of computer systems have made on-the-job training virtually a thing of the past. Everyone wants to hire experienced people, and no one has time or money to hire trainees. It has become almost essential for anyone striving to enter the travel industry to get a foundation at a reputable travel school.

On the other hand, the lightning-fast changes in technology and the competitive landscape are creating a need for new training programs to keep employees up to speed. In addition to educating and training neophytes, companies are increasingly introducing their own programs to raise productivity or advance workers. Trade associations also mount training and education programs, employing a staffer to oversee programs.

Apart from the hundreds of colleges, universities, and community colleges that have introduced travel and tourism programs, scores of vocational schools have been opened by educators as well as travel agents. With tuition ranging up to several thousand dollars, travel training has become a significant profit center.

Although most of the teaching positions at the better vocational schools are reserved for industry people (such as working travel agents and executives from the airlines and hotels), there are certain kinds of courses that can be taught by professional educators.

Training and development is becoming a key area for many major travel companies. The hotel industry has always been particularly keen on training, but travel agency chains (such as Rosenbluth), car rental companies, and even Amtrak have programs, as well. This is an area where a professional educator can create his or her own position by targeting a company with a need.

There are travel and tourism programs at about 200 different two- and four-year colleges and graduate schools, and more than 600 vocational or proprietary schools.

Most educators come out of the industry first, sometimes winding up a career in travel in the education side. Many move into education in the middle of their careers, or even at the start. Some professors collect their master's degrees and Ph.D.s in recreation, hospitality, tourism, or some other related topic; teach; cultivate relationships in the industry; and then move into the industry. The demand for tourism professors has burgeoned with the explosion in enrollments and mass openings of programs at schools, and some instructors have been tapped from other disciplines.

Perhaps more so than in other disciplines taught in school, instructors do become directly involved in the industry. The dynamics of the industry demands it and there is pressure on the schools to offer more relevant presentations. Many professors become members of major trade associations. "That was one of the things that was wrong with some of the advanced degree programs of the past—they were disassociated from the industry," said one veteran.

Contacts, Sources, and Leads

- **International Society of Travel and Tourism Educators,** 19364 Woodcrest, Harper Woods, MI 48225; 313-526-0710; www.istte.org. An international organization of more than 300 educators in travel, tourism, and related fields, representing all levels of educational institutions, from professional schools and high schools to four-year colleges and graduate-degree–granting institutions. One of the aims of the society is to cultivate stronger ties with the industry in order to make programs more relevant. The Web site offers a section called "Finding a School."

- *A Guide to College Programs in Culinary Arts, Hospitality, and Tourism,* by The Council on Hotel, Restaurant, and Institutional Education, published by John Wiley & Sons (1999).

- The **American Society of Travel Agents' Scholarship Foundation** publishes a *Travel School Directory*.
- The **National Tour Foundation,** 546 E. Main St., Lexington, KY 40508; 800-682-8886; www.ntfonline.org. Publishes a listing of schools with tourism-related programs.

Travel Industry Associations

The travel industry is distinguished by its fragmentation and segmentation. Far from being a singular entity, it is composed of some 500,000 businesses in dozens of different categories. Consequently, there are dozens of associations to represent their separate interests and one massive umbrella organization, the Travel Industry Association of America (TIA), to represent them all.

Association work is a very specialized career, but working with travel-related associations presents yet another avenue for a career in travel.

Associations may be formed primarily as a lobbying group, such as the Airport Operators Council, or as a marketing organization, such as the Cruise Lines International Association.

Associations may have a staff of one or a few, but some employ hundreds of people, with much the same organization as a large corporation.

Pat Duricka Kelly was Director of Communications for the Travel Industry Association of America for 5½ years before moving on to become Public Relations Director for the International Association of Amusement Parks and Attractions. There she was responsible for media relations, developing industry promotional programs, and supervising the association's publications.

"In some ways, association work is analogous to corporate jobs," she commented. "The experience gained could be used as a jumping-off point to private enterprise, and vice-versa. But it is more common, at the higher level, to come from the private sector into the association, in the travel industry, especially."

Those who work in associations generally stay within the associations field, moving up through the ranks by moving from organization to organization, and rarely go from the associations into private enterprise, except perhaps as a consultant.

Kelly had been with a professional education society and then an association representing the construction industry before going to TIA. "I'm in the association business. I prefer the association slot in order to promote generically. We don't have to be concerned about carving out market share. One's livelihood is based on satisfying needs of members."

Associations have several key functions: professional development, holding annual meetings, information sharing, publications, government relations and lobbying, public relations, and membership development (which is similar to marketing in the private sector and may also include fundraising). Other functions include meetings planning, exhibit booth sales, and corporate travel; and, in the largest associations, legal counsel, research, administration, and trade show planning.

To fulfill these functions, associations employ educators and trainers, meetings planners, public relations specialists, writers, marketers, lawyers, research analysts, and administrators, as well as artists, designers, librarians, journalists, and filmmakers.

"For women and minorities, particularly, associations may provide a proving ground of what you can do, far beyond what is required in the paycheck." For example, working in associations provides an opportunity to head committees, speak at functions, and publish articles.

Working for a travel-related association has particular appeal. "The character of the industry is transcended into the character of the trade association," Kelly said. "The kind of members—people in travel tend to be creative, lively, gregarious, sociable. There is camaraderie. There is a travel industry 'type,' even more so a 'hotel type,' etc. It permeates the trade association."

There is also generally more opportunity to travel than at other trade organizations—primarily to annual conventions, trade shows, seminars, and board meetings, which may very well be held in exotic locations. However, "just wanting to travel is not a reason to work for an association. You must be interested in the association business, itself, and the industry it represents, in particular."

Deregulation has made for an especially exciting time, a period of challenge and flux, and has made the role of the trade associations even more vital. Organizations like the Air Transport Association and the National Tour Association had to change their focus (NTA even changed its name, from National Tour Brokers Association).

"As the industry's needs change, so does the association's," Kelly said. That was the case for IAAPA, where Kelly helped introduce marketing research.

Kelly noted that association management work has also changed with the times. "There was a time when you could say association work was institutional in terms of stability and growth. There were few cutbacks and jobs were dependable." There is less security today, but positions still tend to be longer term than in the private sector.

While the association field is becoming more professional, it is still relatively easy to get into, particularly through clerical positions, administration, or law. Advancement often comes by leaving one trade association for another.

Association work provides an opportunity to participate in an industry, but at a certain objective distance. It also provides a complete view of the entire industry. "It makes you a great generalist."

Salaries in Association Work

Salaries of association staff generally reflect those of the industry the association represents. A survey by the Foundation of the Greater Washington Society of Association Executives (GWSAE) reported median salaries of key positions (in 1996):

Title	Salary
Chief Staff Executive	$109,295
Conventions/Meetings/ Conferences Director	$50,025
Education/Training Director	$56,550
Conventions/Meetings/ Conferences Manager	$35,752
Exhibition/Trade Show Manager	$40,850
Education/Training Manager	$40,631

A 1999 salary survey of association meeting executives by The Professional Convention Management Association (PCMA) showed that the mean salary of meeting managers climbed to $49,073, while the mean for directors was $62,448. For the first time, in this survey, there was a nearly equal distribution of males and females among CEO and Vice President positions responding to the survey. The average salary of CEOs was $112,333, but 44 percent earned more than $125,000. The mean salary for Vice Presidents was $92,233.

The Associations

The travel industry is particularly rich in associations. Here is a sampling (unless noted otherwise, they are headquartered in Washington, D.C.):

- **Adventure Travel Society** (Salida, Colorado): www.adventuretravel.com
- **Air Transport Association:** www.air-transport.org
- **American Association of Airport Executives:** www.airportnet.org
- **American Association of Museums:** www.aam-us.org/index.htm
- **American Automobile Association:** www.aaa.com
- **American Hotel & Motel Association:** www.ahma.com/ahma/index.asp
- **American Bus Association:** www.buses.org
- **American Gaming Association:** www.americangaming.org

- **American Resort Development Association:** www.arda.org
- **American Society of Association Executives:** www.asaenet.org/main/
- **American Society of Travel Agents:** www.astanet.com
- **Americans for the Arts:** www.artsusa.org
- **Association of Corporate Travel Executives:** www.acte.org
- **Association of Retail Travel Agents:** www.artaonline.com
- **Cruise Lines International Association** (New York City): www.cruising.org
- **Hospitality Sales & Marketing Association International:** www.hsmai.org
- **Hotel Electronic Distribution Network Association:** www.hedna.org
- **International Association of Amusement Parks and Attractions:** www.iaapa.org
- **International Association of Convention & Visitor Bureaus:** www.iacvb.org
- **International Festivals & Events Association** (Port Angeles, Washington): www.ifea.com
- **Meeting Professionals International** (Dallas, Texas): www.mpiweb.org
- **National Air Transportation Association:** www.nata-online.org
- **National Business Travel Association:** www.nbta.org

- **National Association of RV Parks & Campgrounds:** www.gocamping.com
- **National Caves Association** (McMinnville, Tennessee): http://cavern.com
- **National Restaurant Association:** www.restaurant.org
- **National Tour Association** (Lexington, Kentucky): www.ntaonline.com
- **Professional Association of Innkeepers International** (Santa Barbara, California): www.paii.org/index.html
- **Professional Convention Management Association** (Chicago, Illinois): www.pcma.org
- **Recreation Vehicle Industry Association:** www.rvia.org
- **Regional Airline Association:** www.raa.org
- **Society for the Advancement of Travel for the Handicapped** (New York City): www.sath.org
- **Society of Incentive & Travel Executives** (New York City): www.site-intl.org
- **Society of Government Travel Professionals:** www.government-travel.org
- **The International Ecotourism Society** (Burlington, Vermont): www.ecotourism.org
- **Travel and Tourism Research Association:** www.ttra.com
- **United States Tour Operators Association** (New York City): www.ustoa.com

Contacts, Sources, and Leads

- **Greater Washington Society of Association Executives,** 1426 21st St. NW, Washington, DC 20036; 202-429-9370; www.gwsae.org. The Web site has a job-posting section.
- For additional leads, contact the **American Society of Association Executives,** 1575 I St. NW, Washington, DC 20005-1103; 202-626-2723; www.asaenet.org.
- Also, consult **TIA**'s Web site, www.tia.org, under "links."

Travel Industry Law

An elite but growing group of lawyers, skilled in the nuances and workings of the travel industry, are very much in the center of the activity of the industry.

Travel industry law entails labor relations, international law, contracts, property, liability—the standard fare of business law. But there are differences. The travel industry has rather unusual agent/client relationships, which are being established in precedent-setting consumer suits (such as one that found the travel agency liable for the murder by terrorists of an American passenger on the *Achille Lauro*). Deregulation and even e-commerce have raised new legal issues, particularly regarding antitrust. There are suits over rebates and competitive practices. Heightened merger and acquisitions activity has required the assistance of attorneys with an understanding of the relative values of the businesses.

Travel attorneys represent travel companies, travel agencies, and consumers in litigation against travel entities. They may also work for trade associations, lobbying government or pressing suits on behalf of the members.

The legal specialization has even produced its own trade group, the International Forum of Travel and Tourism Advocates, which includes professors who teach travel law. About 40 countries have members.

Alexander Anolik has made a career of offering "preventive legal care" to the travel industry and representing its interests. And, he says, he feels as much a part of the travel industry as he does the law.

"We speak differently," Anolik observed, while attending the American Society of Travel Agents World Congress in Rome. "We use different vocabulary. When you have litigation for the travel industry, we interpret and understand the travel industry issues and present them from a travel law standpoint."

Because of Anolik's expertise, he has been named by the court to appraise a travel agency. "You have to know the industry—the people, relationships. I can look at the same issue, such as banks in travel, and see what another lawyer cannot. I caught a bank giving

illegal rebates." He estimated that there are perhaps only 30 to 50 attorneys doing travel law more or less exclusively.

Anolik has served as general counsel to some airlines (with the proviso that he not be involved in anti–travel-agent litigation), and has represented a travel agency franchise, a consortium, some tour operators, and a hotel.

Anolik, who started out as a trial attorney working for other lawyers, reflected that the key difference in being a "travel attorney" is not the legal issues, but the people themselves. "Travel people are a more enjoyable group; good people, they know how to enjoy themselves. Not the greatest businesspeople, though. They need more preventive legal care."

The challenge comes from being in a new field, where precedents are being set. But the law is the law. "You still have to be a good paper man, good antitrust."

There is something different about the cases, too, as indicated by the fact that 20 percent of Anolik's clients come from referrals from other lawyers who do not feel qualified. Seemingly simple matters like the change in agency ownership makes a difference when the lawyer is an expert. The change in the regulatory environment is also key. A travel attorney needs to know the industry. "Read the trade press, get to know the people, spend time with them and learn what is bothering them," Anolik commented.

Travel law is a growing field. Besides the formation of an association, the International Bar Association has formed a committee on travel.

To prepare for the field, Anolik recommends studying contracts, antitrust, torts, and (given the present climate, especially) bankruptcy law. And if you're planning to work with travel agencies, you should study labor law. Then get into the industry, affiliate with the trade associations, and go to the functions.

Anolik, who is based in San Francisco, travels a lot, particularly as a speaker on "preventive legal care" for industry functions. He also writes articles for the trade press.

Others who specialize in travel law include Jeffrey Miller, Ward, Klein & Miller, Gaithersburg, Maryland; Pestronk & Associates, Fairfax, Virginia; and Arthur Schiff, New York.

Contacts, Sources, and Leads

■ Contact the **International Forum for Travel and Tourism Advocates,** www.iftta.org.

Nontravel Services

The travel industry is so pervasive, incorporating so many services, products, and needs, that it draws many other companies into the industry that you might not even consider.

AT&T and MCI are in the travel business because the industry, as well as travelers, utilizes communication. Most other major telecommunications companies are also in the business. AT&T employs travel industry specialists to market and sell its services.

Citicorp, Diners Club, American Express, and the other travel and entertainment card companies are very much in the travel business.

Insurance companies like Travel Guard (www.travelguard.com) specialize in products that travel agencies and tour operators offer their clients. Other insurance companies, like The Berkely Group, specialize in professional liability insurance for the travel industry.

There are visa agencies, such as Visa Advisors, Washington, D.C., that specialize in obtaining visas for individuals, companies, and travel agencies and tour operators.

There are currency-exchange companies that actively promote services for both the travelers and travel companies, like Deak Perera, New York, and Reusch International, Washington, D.C. These companies not only service travelers with foreign currency and traveler's checks, but also have various financial instruments that travel companies use for their international payments and receipts.

STRATEGIES FOR GETTING IN

John Crystal, an eminent career counselor, used to say that to get a job, you need the skills of a spy. It is more accurate to say that you need the skills of an investigative reporter. Finding a job is a matter of knowing where to find information, targeting specific potential employers, finding the appropriate person to contact, determining what questions to ask, and then assembling all the information into a convincing (and winning) presentation.

A Strategy for Success

The first questions to ask yourself are whether you want to pursue a career in travel and tourism at all, and whether you have what it takes to be successful in it. The industry is made up of about 500,000 separate businesses in some 15 different categories, each with different needs, issues, and approaches. Regardless of whether you have targeted an airline, a car rental company, a hotel, or a travel agency—and regardless of whether you believe travel is a dream or a commodity—what each of these companies sells is service.

The overriding quality employers look for is not "love people, love travel," but an ability to serve people selflessly. Travel and tourism goes on constantly. Most industry jobs of any responsibility are not weekdays 9 to 5; they require commitment and dedication.

Another common theme is the need to be very detail oriented; this is a business of minute detail and complicated logistics. Many jobs require someone who is organized, is patient, and can handle the constant changes and hassles that go with the job.

Many jobs, particularly at entry level, entail some sacrifice, particularly in terms of income, because the industry is relatively low paying in relation to other professions. Additionally, you may need to relocate to get a job or to advance later. Because the industry continues to expand, however, it affords excellent opportunities for rapid advancement into positions that do pay decently and have considerable responsibility and prestige.

Know Thyself

After you have decided that you have what it takes for a career in travel and tourism, the next task is to isolate where you want to focus your energies. The industry is so vast, so diversified; each segment manifests its own personality and style. Finding a job requires sorting through myriad choices so that you can focus your energies in one area.

Next, you have to establish priorities. What is important to you? Travel? Money, power, influence? The chance to work with people, to help people, to make a mark on society? To create; to grow personally or intellectually? To submerge yourself in art, culture, science, or business? To have free time for other interests or family? To work in a set routine, or in a dynamic situation where nothing is predictable? What is your ultimate goal? Where do you think you want to be in 5, 10, or 20 years?

Recognizing that your priorities will change, and that it is impossible to map out a career path precisely, make a list of your wants, desires, and needs on paper in order of their importance. Because few things in this world are perfect, any job you take will likely require some tradeoffs. Determine what is vitally important to you and what you can compromise. If you can be flexible about where you will live, for example, you will have a much easier time finding a job in travel and tourism. You will most likely have to weigh long-term benefits against short-term ones—higher pay for a learning experience; security for mobility; responsibility for free evenings and weekends to pursue outside interests.

Knowing who you are and what you really want can help expand your options. You may find that you can satisfy the same professional and personal objectives in a different industry segment than the one that first captured your imagination. For example, tour operations is a very limited field, but you can be a tour planner in many different contexts, such as hotels, incentive houses, travel agencies, airlines, motorcoach operators, and destination marketing organizations.

After you have established your priorities, you can begin focusing on potential employers. There are a few approaches, depending on your priorities. You can first decide what kind of professional you want to be (marketing, sales, public relations, administration, computer specialist—positions that are common to most businesses), then zero in on what segment of the industry appeals most to you. Or if getting into a particular segment of the industry—hotels, airlines, tour companies, or travel agencies, for example—is more important, start there. If you have targeted a particular company, you will probably have to be a little more open-minded about what position you take. You can be very clear on a resume about wanting a position in marketing, but many companies will fill those positions only from within and you may have to start in some entry-level position elsewhere in the company.

Finding Leads

After you have decided on an industry segment, consult the following sources (note that each chapter also lists specific leads, contacts, and sources for specific segments):

- **Trade journals** (both the articles and the ads). Trade journals include *Travel Weekly, Leisure Travel News, Business Travel News, Travel Agent, Corporate Travel, Aviation Weekly, Meetings and Conventions, Successful Meetings, Hotel & Resort Industry,* and *Lodgings.*

- **Trade associations.** Some have job banks on their Web sites as well as member listings, referral services, internship programs, and even scholarships. Some examples include the Travel Industry Association of America, www.tia.org; the American Society of Travel Agents (ASTA), www.astanet.com; and the International Association of Convention and Visitor Bureaus, www.iacvb.org.

- **Professional societies.** Examples include the Society of Incentive & Travel Executives (SITE), http://site-intl.org, and the Society of American Travel Writers, www.satw.org.

- **Newspapers.** Classifieds, display ads, as well as the news items, particularly the financial and travel sections; many newspapers now post their classifieds online.

- **Employment agencies.** Some specialize in travel.

- **Stock analyst reports about growth companies.**

Be particularly alert to the names of new companies, formations of new divisions, corporate expansions, reorganizations, new products, or projects and trends that may suggest new endeavors. One woman who landed a position as the Director of Administration and Personnel for the New York convention center had contacted the newly appointed chairman personally after reading about his appointment in the newspaper.

You might also try to attend vacation and travel expos, and trade shows. These are good venues to pick up business cards and directories of participants (which include titles, telephone numbers, and Web sites to follow up), and learn about different companies. It is also an excellent way to meet someone in a target company who can provide an introduction to a potential hiring manager in the company.

If you are restricted to finding a job within a geographical area, contact state travel offices, local convention and visitor bureaus, tourism information offices, or chambers of commerce to find out what travel companies might be potential employers in your area.

If you have targeted a specific company, try to do some research about that company to find out what positions they may be hiring for, and then personalize your approach. You might start with the human resources department, just to get an idea of what openings are available, before you make a formal introduction. After that, it is best, however, to try to contact people in specific departments. People in specific departments have a better idea about what the jobs entail, have the power to do the actual hiring, and will probably get you hired faster than if you went through formal channels.

The Internet has proved a veritable gold mine of contacts and information. Most major companies now have Web sites, and many of these offer job postings. The sites are an excellent place to get a sense of the company (check the press sections) as well as what kinds of openings it has. In addition, Web sites for trade associations may include job banks as well as links to members' sites.

Informational Interviews and Networking

Getting into the travel industry without prior experience requires creative approaches designed to personalize your application. Once you have isolated the names of the companies where you want to apply, one technique is to find out the name of someone who will allow you to come in and conduct an "informational interview." The purpose of the informational interview is to find out as much as possible about the organization—job titles, background, how people apply—and, with luck, to get a personal introduction to the person who would be doing the hiring. Just be sure that you don't impose on the informational interviewee by directly asking for a job during the interview. People don't mind helping by giving information, but they tend to feel used if the informational interview suddenly turns into a hiring pitch.

Another technique is networking, which can make the real difference for a person coming in from outside the industry with no prior experience. As many of the human resources professionals interviewed in this book noted, a lot depends on who you know. "We get thousands of unsolicited resumes from people with marketing degrees," said the Manager of Central Employment for TWA, "but there is a lot of networking going on."

How do you get into the network from outside? Start by asking every friend and relative, and friend of a friend or relative, if they know anyone in the target company or industry, even if that person is not in a hiring capacity. Being able to telephone someone and say, "So-and-so suggested that I give you a call," or, better, being introduced by an associate, makes a big difference. You have to realize that no matter how terrific your resume looks, it is only one of hundreds or even thousands that a personnel officer has to wade through, especially with the Internet now providing a flood of unsolicited resumes.

Using a Recruiter

Some recruiters specialize in one segment of the travel industry, such as hospitality, aviation, or travel agencies. There are several advantages to using a recruiter: A recruiter may know of openings that have not been advertised or publicized. A recruiter also knows in greater detail the job description and salary level the company is offering, and has a sense of what background and qualifications the company is looking for (which often changes after the company has conducted some interviews). In our practice at Travel Executive Search (TESINTL@aol.com), we also steer the candidate to background information about the company and the industry in order to prepare for the interview, to help the candidate evaluate the opportunity in comparison to others he or she may be considering, and to assist in negotiations and even relocation.

Choosing the Right Company

You should try to be selective about the company you work for. But if that is not possible, take anything just to get inside and have a travel company on your resume. If you can afford to be selective, the kinds of questions you should research include the following:

- How large, or how small?
- How new or old?
- What position does the company hold in its field?
- What is its reputation?
- How progressive, innovative, or conservative is the company?
- How many people are employed and in what kind of organization?
- What are the company's human resources policies and what kind of working environment does it offer?
- What has the company's record been during industry downturns?
- Is turnover particularly high or low?
- Is it affiliated with trade associations?
- What kinds of products and services does it offer and who are its customers?

You can get a sense of what your own advancement prospects will be by looking at the ages of your superiors and what turnover rates are like.

There are advantages and disadvantages of working at both large and small companies. The largest organizations generally have the most entry-level positions and better training and management programs (and usually, but not always, are better paying and offer better benefits). But they are also deluged by thousands of resumes and generally can afford the best-schooled, best-trained, or most-experienced people. Working in the largest organizations tends to be more specialized and advancement tends to be slower, although there are usually higher positions to advance into because there are more tiers. Smaller organizations can also be training grounds because these tend to pay less so they cannot afford the more skilled individuals; the working environment may be more cramped, but you are apt to get a more generalized education and greater responsibility more rapidly than in a larger organization. Frequently, smaller companies are used as steppingstones to larger ones, but they can also provide a more close-knit, comfortable atmosphere.

Getting In

To get a job, you have to see yourself as an entrepreneur—find a need and fill it. You have to demonstrate to an employer that you are not an expense, but a source of revenue. You have to see your resume as a sales presentation. Frequently, it means creating your own position; for example, if you are a corporate travel manager and you target a company that you know does not have that position, you are really making a business pitch rather than asking for a position.

Even if you do not have specific travel industry experience, try not to present yourself as a novice looking to break in. The travel and tourism industry draws on every professional background. From reading the chapters on the industry segments, you should have a sense of how you can present your own work or life experience as an asset in a position in a travel entity—even if you are just finishing school. If you are trying to change careers, it may be necessary to move into a parallel function in travel, even if you would really prefer to leave as far behind as possible what you were doing before—say accounting, teaching, or clerical work. Those who are returning to the workforce after raising a family should recognize their assets as managers and also realize that many organizations appreciate the maturity gained from that experience.

No matter where you are coming from or what your prior experience, your strategy should be to just get into the organization, because once you are inside the company and the industry, you can move within it or to another company much more easily. Getting in is the hard part; once you are over that hurdle, you can go as far as your abilities and ambition allow.

Education and Training Can Be a Ticket In

Given the fact that deregulation, information technology and the Internet, and growing professionalism are probably the most significant developments underway in the industry, the greatest opportunities for new hires are in marketing and research, sales, computer services, information management, telecommunications, training and development, quality control and customer service, and operations. Many of these positions require a college degree or some other training beyond high school.

The travel industry has had a tradition of on-the-job training, and sensational success stories of people rising through the ranks abound. But this has proved impractical in today's work environment. Reliance on specialized computer reservations systems and information technology, the incredibly fast pace, potential loss of valued customers to a competitor, and vulnerability to consumer liability suits have all forced agencies and other travel companies to rely more heavily on a growing body of academic institutions and vocational programs to provide them with entry-level people.

Although few believe the schools are capable of turning out graduates who can move right into a job, the industry is increasingly seeing the value to these programs: They weed out those who are looking for fun and glamour but have little comprehension of what the real world of work will be like in the travel business. They demonstrate the commitment of the job candidate, which is important because an employer makes a substantial investment in new hires. The programs provide a foundation that makes the required additional on-the-job training that much easier, particularly in geography, professional terms, and, even better, computer systems, and how the various industry segments function together. The best programs are now being designed with input from industry professionals, and include training on airline computer reservations systems, sales techniques, and industry ethics. Some of the programs are very specialized, such as those for ski resort management, hospitality, food and beverage, meetings, aviation, and travel agencies.

Many industry organizations also provide superb professional training and certification, such as the American Society of Travel Agents (ASTA even offers scholarships as well as home-study courses), Meeting

Professionals International, the Institute of Certified Travel Agents, and the American Hotels and Motels Association.

In terms of travel agency programs, there are no industry-set standards (states bestow accreditation), although the American Society of Travel Agents has been seeking to impose standards and has formed an associate membership category for travel schools (there are about 180 travel school members). Some programs are out-and-out rip-offs and offer little in the way of practical work experience. But a rapidly growing number offer a very solid program and, perhaps even more importantly, a more direct link to actual jobs through placement programs and industry alliances. Those enrolled in college programs can join ASTA's Future Travel Professionals Club, which provides access to a network of more than 26,000 ASTA members—leaders in the industry and potential employers (call 800-440-2782 for information).

There are hundreds of academic and vocational schools dedicated to travel agency training, some of which are affiliated with travel agencies and dozens more at two- and four-year colleges (particularly in areas heavily dependent on tourism, such as Hawaii, Colorado, and Florida). Colleges have made great improvement over the past decade in tailoring their programs to the needs of the industry. Many offering travel agency training, for example, have tailored their curriculum to the Institute of Certified Travel Agents program.

You should be discriminating when choosing a vocational school or college program. Make sure it is the appropriate program and training, and that it will lead to certification or licensing, if that is what is required (we have tried to indicate throughout this book which positions require certification or licensing). You should be wary if a school does not try to discover your own motivations or expectations about the travel business (for example, if you do not intend to be a travel agent, there is no reason to learn the airline computer reservation system). The best schools attempt to discourage people who have unrealistic expectations of salary, travel benefits, or work levels or who would simply be unsuited to a career in travel (such as people who are not people-oriented or detail-oriented).

When considering a school, check for the following:

- Faculty with industry experience.
- Curriculum that reflects the current needs and functions of the industry, particularly the quality and quantity of computer reservation training (using real computers, not generic dummies).
- The opportunity for hands-on experience, such as agency simulation and internships.
- The background of the school—how long it has been in business, its relationship and reputation with the industry, and citations by the local Better Business Bureau.
- Placement assistance and career guidance availability (some placement offices are very active in the process and have strong industry contacts).
- Licensing from the state's education department.
- Accreditation from appropriate agencies.
- Tuition that is neither too low nor too high.

Additionally, you should scrutinize the schools' recruitment, selection, grading procedures, attendance policies, and number of hours devoted to each area. You might interview recent graduates about the quality of education, the applicability of it to their work, and the effectiveness of the school's placement office.

Remember, you are taking the program in order to get a job. The degree is only as valuable as the school's reputation. A prospective employer will not consider your degree credible if the school does not have a reputation for turning out skilled graduates. The degree is helpful only in landing the first job; it becomes less significant with each successive job.

A degree in a reputable travel-tourism-transportation program is becoming more and more necessary in getting a first job. That is not to say that getting in is impossible without it; it's just a little easier. The background makes on-the-job training easier and faster, and makes advancement possible more quickly. Starting salaries also tend to be higher for new hires with a degree.

Sources to locate vocational travel schools and academic programs include the following:

- **International Society of Travel and Tourism Educators,** 19364 Woodcrest, Harper Woods, MI 48225; 313-526-0710; www.istte.org.
- **ASTA Foundation,** 1101 King St., Ste. 200, Alexandria, VA 22314; www.astanet.com. A "Travel Careers" packet is available (call 703-739-2782, ext. 4406) for a nominal fee. Scholarship information is available as well, by e-mailing scholarship@astanet.com.
- **International Council on Hotel, Restaurant, and Institutional Education,** 3205 Skipwith Rd., Richmond, VA 23294-4442; 804-747-4971; www.chrie.org; e-mail: info@chrie.org.
- **Educational Institute of the American Hotel and Motel Association,** 800 N. Magnolia Ave., Orlando, FL 32803; 800-349-0299; www.ei-ahma.org.
- **National Restaurant Association Educational Foundation,** 250 S. Wacker Dr., Ste. 1400, Chicago, IL 60606-5834; 800-765-2122; www.edfound.org.
- **National Tourism Foundation,** 546 E. Main St., Lexington, KY 40508; www.ntfonline.org. Publishes a listing of 600 schools offering tourism-related programs, available on their Web site.

Other facets of the industry also have specialized training, particularly aviation (see chapter 9) and even the ski and the theme park industries (see chapters 7 and 8).

Internships: A Foot in the Door

Internships can provide a first-class ticket into a company or industry. An internship not only gives real-world, on-the-job experience as well as knowledge of industry issues and contacts, but also gives you a chance to showcase your abilities and commitment. To a very high degree, internships (some are paid) lead to full-time positions.

Some entities—companies, trade associations, and public-sector agencies—have internships, including the Walt Disney Company, many airports, and many hotel companies. If you have targeted a particular company or industry association, contact them directly to ask about internship opportunities.

Opportunities for Career Changers

The increasing sophistication and evolution of the travel industry into "big business" has opened new opportunities for people from outside the travel industry. In the past, travel companies tended to insist on prior experience in travel (even within their own segment); now, there is much greater appreciation for professional experience outside. Indeed, when Club Med went searching for a new President/CEO-North America, it selected John Vanderslice, formerly the Senior Vice President, Concept Development, at Triarc Restaurant Group, whose subsidiaries include Arby's, T.J. Cinnamons, and Pasta Connection. Vanderslice, who also brought experience in brand management at Kraft General Foods, for Post Cereal, Kool-Aid, Country Time, and Crystal Light, was selected by Club Med for his expertise in brand management and repositioning. "It is important to hire from outside," said Philippe Bourguignon, Club Med's chairman. "Every industry becomes incestuous. There is no renewal of ideas."

Indeed, MBAs used to be shunned but now are coveted by travel companies, although the travel companies still have a way to go to be competitive with companies in other industries in terms of salaries and perks.

But many who come from outside the travel industry often are smug and condescending; they are lulled into thinking travel is simple, but it is actually deceptively complex. Those who fail to appreciate its unique dynamics tend to have a rude awakening.

Applying and Interviewing for Jobs in Travel

After researching and targeting a potential employer, you will make your initial introduction through a cover letter and a resume. People tend to focus mainly on the resume, but the cover letter is equally important because it allows you to customize and personalize your presentation, emphasize the strengths that are applicable to that employer or position, and inspire the potential employer to give attention to the resume. The resume is a necessary document, but it will not be what gets you a job (it will more likely cost you a job, if it is badly done or contains errors). The objective of the resume and the cover letter is to get you an interview.

Resumes

A resume should be neatly presented, with absolutely no spelling mistakes or typos, preferably word-processed or offset but definitely typed, on a quality white or off-white paper (not blue or gray, because these colors do not photocopy or fax well). These days, your resume should be scannable—that is, readable by a scanner, which converts it to a computer file. It should state your name, address, telephone number, and e-mail address if you have one. I discourage the use of a specific "job objective," on the resume because it will more likely eliminate you from consideration than cause you to be considered for an opening. Instead, you can state your "objective" in the cover letter. A better choice on the resume is to use a qualifications "summary" which will help the person reviewing it see you in context with an opening.

The summary can be a paragraph or sometimes a bulleted list; for example:

> Results-focused Sales and Marketing professional with a strong track record of success in travel-related services and telecommunications companies. Expertise in a variety of disciplines including Team Building, Sales Management, National Account Management, Negotiations, Marketing Promotions, Conference & Event Planning, Public Speaking, and Public Relations. Experience includes sales management responsibility for Divisions of two Fortune 500 companies.

Tailoring Your Resume to the Position

A resume is a living document that should be adapted as circumstances require. That absolutely does not mean that you should include false information. It does mean that a resume necessarily is selective in what information is presented, and you can reorder and reprioritize the items to make the clearest statement to the reviewer as to why you are a strong candidate for the position.

Resumes are extremely subjective—the same resume that is effective in one situation will work against you in another. It is almost impossible to know what the person is looking for (except if you are working with a recruiter who has already received clues). I strongly advise my candidates to tailor the resume as much as possible to each job opportunity, based on what is known from the job description, about the company, and even about the people who are likely to be reviewing it. There is nothing underhanded about this—the resume is exactly like a sales presentation. You would not send the same sales presentation to every potential client, and you would not send the same resume to every potential employer. My rule is that the resume should have impact and be designed to get your message across with the greatest effectiveness.

I have observed that there is a different style and tone in the resume of someone seeking an upper-management position versus a low-level position. That stands to reason because the upper-management person would have a greater grasp of dollar figures and results. But it carries over that if you are an executive-level person or are looking to make a step up the ladder, the resume should have that commanding tone and upscale look.

Tailoring your resume for different situations is not so difficult if you have a word processor. But if that is not practical, you can get around that by writing a convincing, tailored "sales" presentation in each cover letter.

Resume Formats

There are two broad resume formats: the chronological (a classic style that lists jobs and titles in reverse chronological order and lists responsibilities and results under each); and the functional (which lists responsibilities and achievements, followed by a listing of job titles and employers). My rule of thumb is that the closer your prior experience matches the industry, the more you should use the chronological style. The further away you are (such as a career-changer), the more you should use a functional style, because it will enable you to highlight experience and accomplishments that are applicable.

An example of a chronological resume. The job titles are the best advantage of this resume; the time spent at each job is the disadvantage. The titles are capitalized and prominent (extending out to the left margin); the years follow after the employer name; we also made them years instead of months-years. Does an excellent job of showing achievements (preferably bulleted), not just job descriptions.

SALLY SMITH
17 S. Fairlawn, Aurora, IL 60606
(213) 555-1212
ssmith@email.com

SUMMARY

Fifteen years of experience in hospitality marketing, and planning and managing high-level corporate and association meetings, conferences, and special events. Track record of success in utilizing marketing and communications skills and business expertise.

CAREER HIGHLIGHTS

DIRECTOR OF CONFERENCES AND SPECIAL EVENTS
Nonprofit Association, New York, 2000–Present

Direct conferences and development of sales/marketing strategies for conference promotions, sponsorships, and trade show exhibits sales. Manage conference programs, board of directors meetings, annual conventions, and trade show expositions. Advise on Web site content development, brochures, and print advertisements. Negotiate and review venue and vendor contracts. Direct all on-site management, merchandising, exhibit sales, and audiovisual staging. Manage team of two full-time staff, contractors/vendors, and on-site staff.

Sales and Marketing Accomplishments:

- Identified and developed revenue-generating sponsorship and exhibit programs and cross-selling advertising opportunities (first time for this organization). Researched and targeted potential sales leads.

- Within first four months of employment, sold corporate sponsorships totaling $100K in revenues not budgeted for fiscal year. Developed pricing strategies and customized sponsorship programs.

- Collaborated with editorial and design consultants for print and online promotions of conferences.

- Wrote promotional copy that was used in print materials, ads, and online. Directed marketing campaigns to drive conference exposure, including use of Web site, print brochures, magazine advertisements, targeted e-mails, and press releases.

- Established press policy for press/media attendance at conferences.

The Nonprofit Association is the preeminent professional organization in the field of advertising, marketing, and media research. Its combined membership represents more than 400 advertisers, advertising agencies, research firms, media companies, educational institutions, and international organizations.

INDEPENDENT CONSULTING ASSIGNMENTS—1998–2000
Consulting for corporate meetings, special events, and board meetings. Advisor for corporate gifts and promotional merchandise. Temporary legal administrative assistant assignments for senior partner, legal. Assignments included Ad Agency, New York; Major Bank, New York; Famous Department Store, New York.

DIRECTOR OF INTERNATIONAL CONFERENCES AND SPECIAL EVENTS
Financial Association, New York, 1994–1998

Responsible for financial trade association program development, marketing strategies, and management of more than 30 high-level conferences, special events, meetings, and incentive programs throughout Europe, the Americas, and Asia. Traveled extensively—approximately 70%—to 30 global cities to provide site selection and on-site management. Event attendance from 20 to 700+ delegates, press, and trade show exhibitors. Controlled $2 million annual budget, contracts, and vendor negotiation. Provided creative direction of marketing brochures, invitations, print advertisements, signage, and logo interpretation. Established cost-cutting brochure production, and distribution methods. Managed two assistants plus contractors/vendors.

Sales and Marketing Accomplishments:

- Developed and expanded revenue source from 9 to 30 annual conference programs.

- Researched and targeted potential sales leads from member and nonmember corporations.

- Sold $300,000 in corporate sponsorship/exhibits in 1997.

- Increased revenues in 1998 and sold additional $450,000 in corporate and press sponsorships and exhibits.

- Spearheaded merchandising program and enhanced association's name recognition worldwide.

- Achieved the first fully sponsored annual general meeting program in the association's history.

- Increased registration revenues through telemarketing and direct-mail strategies.

SPECIAL EVENTS PLANNER
Financial Institutions Consulting Group, New York, 1993–1994

Planned top-level client forums and incentive events attended by chief executives of banking institutions. Event attendance of 25. Coordinated logistics at deluxe resorts (golf outings, social programs, hotel contract negotiation, reconciliation, menus, accommodations, and transportation arrangements).

ADMINISTRATIVE ASSISTANT TO VICE PRESIDENT
Film Corporation, New York, 1992–1993

Provided office management and administrative support to senior-level corporate executive with offices in Hong Kong and New York. Managed business and personal schedule, travel arrangements, and business events. Traveled to Los Angeles to participate in the office start-up and launch of the channel.

ACCOUNT REPRESENTATIVE
Marketing/PR Inc., New York, 1988–1992

Serviced Eastern accounts and new business development for Los Angeles–based menu design and hospitality marketing agency. Followed up with leads, provided customer support, and expedited orders.

SALES AND MARKETING, DELUXE HOTEL
Deluxe Hotel, New York, 1985–1988

Supported group sales and marketing efforts. Conducted conference services duties for corporations, conventions, and VIPs. Represented hotel at sales presentations and promotional events.

COMPUTER/OFFICE SKILLS
Microsoft Office, including Word, Excel, and Outlook. Use the Internet for research.

EDUCATION
Attended State University

PROFESSIONAL AFFILIATIONS
Meeting Professionals International (MPI); Council of Protocol Executives (COPE)

There are also hybrid styles, such as a resume that offers a summary, then a list of key accomplishments, followed by the chronological listing of jobs (sometimes called a "combination" resume). The choice of style depends on which would have the greatest impact and would get your message across most effectively.

An example of a combination resume, which starts with a functional presentation. This is a model of a career in call-centers, customer service management, and operations utilized by airlines, transportation, hospitality companies, travel agencies and e-travel companies. Persuasive presentation of achievements and qualifications. Detailed but not overwhelming. Shows a record of rapid promotions at a company during a 14-year tenure.

GERALD FRANK

OBJECTIVE

A leadership position in Program Management or Customer Service Management with an airline that values proven skills and experience in

- Managing large-scale projects to improve service levels and productivity
- Creating and implementing effective sales, service, and support programs
- Developing and facilitating training programs to achieve maximum results
- Clearly communicating new sales/service processes to improve overall efficiencies
- Establishing, building, and managing large corporate accounts to maximize revenues

QUALIFICATIONS

A strategy-oriented, productive, and thorough professional with 15+ years of experience including

- Program strategy
- Customer service
- Project management
- Process improvement
- Quality assurance
- Program management
- Written communications
- Sales/service training
- Curriculum development
- Service management
- Marketing strategy
- Product implementation
- Account management
- Sales
- Group leadership

SELECTED ACHIEVEMENTS

- Managed key project to migrate customer-service functions from a centralized center to three regional service centers within a 3-month period, including project plan development, headcount needs, training, systems and tools, process flows, and management reporting.
- Managed the successful migration of order-entry functions for two national service centers over a 3-month period by developing a comprehensive project plan and coordinating execution with senior management through weekly conference calls and meetings.
- Collaborated with a marketing team to develop a successful communications and training program for 64 field sales offices that allowed them to better leverage the service they provide in the telecommunications industry.
- Coordinated the communications and marketing of a new billing support program to 300 field service representatives without interruption to the billing resolution process; this program allowed service representatives to spend more quality time with their customers.
- Developed a sales and service training program and communications for over 35 field sales offices that allowed them to differentiate the service they provide and increase revenues.
- Coordinated development of new Credit Review process for Global Account sales teams that enabled them to order and implement services in 50% less time.
- Orchestrated a new 3-year, $100 million contract for a large corporate customer by building customer relationships, resolving billing problems, and reconfiguring their network.
- Signed new 2-year, $40 million contract with major account within first 9 months in position, by improving customer relationships and fixing longstanding customer billing problems.
- Contributed to the successful implementation of the first Vnet (CSI) network in the state of Virginia by managing customer expectations, creating detailed project plans, and coordinating smooth order entry and circuit implementation across the state.

PROFESSIONAL EXPERIENCE

❑ **GLOBAL COMMUNICATIONS CO.**   **1986-Present**

$37 billion global communications company providing fully integrated local, long distance, international, and Internet services.

Project Manager, Service Center Operations—City (11/99–Present)

Manage projects to support Service Centers nationwide, including development of project plans, leading executive management conference calls and meetings, and developing strategies for process improvements.

Program Manager, Global Service Solutions—City (2/98–11/99)

Managed *Service Plan* programs for field sales and service teams; developed program strategies to differentiate global sales and service; hosted strategy sessions with sales-management teams; developed training curriculum; delivered sales training; conducted sales presentations and monitored *Service Plan* quality.

Regional Manager, Regional Revenue Services Support—City (5/97–2/98)

Managed resolution of customer billing and contract disputes for Global East Region and developed/implemented process improvements in billing and contract areas.

Program Manager, Brand Marketing—City (8/94–5/97)

Managed *Proof Positive Account Review* sales/service program, which included developing and implementing marketing strategies, writing field communications, developing and delivering sales training programs, and assisting with field sales calls.

Major Account Support Consultant/Group Leader—City (5/93–8/94)

Identified, analyzed, and resolved customer-service issues for major accounts; recommended new products and services; developed sales proposals; implemented new services; trained new Major Account Support Consultants.

National Account Support Consultant—City (1/92–5/93)

Managed voice services for largest national account in the state, including implementation, maintenance, and trouble-handling of voice services; developed and presented proposals; analyzed account activity and maintained reports on order status.

National Account Support Consultant—City (8/88–1/92)

Managed multiple national accounts in the area, generating $7 million in annual revenues; conducted quarterly service reviews, implemented new services, and managed customer-service issues.

Customer Sales Representative, Major Account Manager—City (5/86–8/88)

Developed inbound and outbound sales of telecommunication services for small to medium-sized businesses and managed the resolution of customer network issues.

❑ **MAJOR AIRLINE—City**   **1985-1986**

An innovative, low-fare U.S. airline that generated annual revenues of nearly $1 billion by 1985.

Customer Service Manager, Flight Attendant—City (2/85–3/86)

EDUCATION

B.S., AERONAUTICAL SCIENCE, 19--

Embry-Riddle Aeronautical University—Daytona Beach, FL

Resume Presentation, Content, and Organization

My rule is that a resume should be designed to get your message across to someone scanning down from top to bottom, beginning to end, in about 13 seconds. I suggest bulleted points, rather than run-on paragraphs. Depending on whether you need to fit the resume into one or two pages, you might use more or less white space. You may also use boldface headings, where appropriate. Try to use a typeface no smaller than 11 points and no bigger than 12 points unless it is unavoidable to fit the space. (If you are e-mailing your resume, you can preserve the formatting by sending the resume as a Word attachment, rather than pasting it into the message; if you are sending out the resume "cold," you may be better off pasting it into the message.)

The organization of the resume varies depending on what arrangement best presents your case. It should always contain your work experience, with dates, name of employer, city and state, and title (if you had several promotions at one company, put the years you were at the company on the first line, and the dates you had each job on the same line as each title) for each job. You may choose to use an italic description of the company, such as "*$1 billion global transportation company.*"

Follow this with a bulleted list that describes your duties, responsibilities, and any major accomplishments. This is a vital point: You do not just list "responsibilities" generically, but instead show achievements and accomplishments that show you did the job well. The kinds of details you should mention (in bulleted statements) include the number of staff managed, how sales grew during your tenure, and any new program or innovation you created or implemented and with what result: "During my tenure, sales increased 50 percent"; "opened new territory"; "devised and implemented new campaign that achieved a five percent increase in market share"; "won company's top sales award"; "introduced new product"; and so on. Use active words (managed, directed, oversaw, initiated, created, conceived, designed, implemented, managed) and do not keep repeating the same ones.

Always specify whether you managed people (how many), called on clients (corporations, travel agencies, or groups), made presentations, wrote proposals, or had responsibility for a budget (how much?). You should be more specific, naming names and being more detailed, if your background matches the job description. You should be a bit more generic if the position you are seeking is out of your direct experience.

Use clipped sentences; for example, never use "I." You can eliminate words like "and" and "a" or "the" unless they are necessary for meaning.

You should list your educational background, including dates of graduation, degree, name of school, and any special awards or honors. Some people leave off the year of graduation; this is risky because leaving out such an item could be perceived as an attempt to disguise something unfavorable about you or something untrue on your resume. You might include a list of extracurricular activities (but only if you are a recent graduate or if it was something really significant, like captain of the NCAA championship team). Include any military experience. You should list any memberships in professional or community organizations, awards, honors, distinctions, any published works, job-related activities, certificates or licenses (such as a pilot's license), and special skills (such as computers, foreign languages, or photography) or assets (extensive travel; lived abroad).

Recent graduates need to emphasize their educational backgrounds and stress any internships, summer employment, or work-study experience, especially anything that relates directly to the travel industry, such as membership in an industry-oriented club.

Your resume should not be longer than two pages; it should be only one page if you are a recent graduate or have had only a few jobs in your career. But do not leave out important detail about your accomplishments just to keep your resume to one page.

Instead of ignoring or downplaying something that might be perceived as a negative, hoping that the employer will not notice, turn the negative into a positive. For example, some employers are skittish when they see someone has changed jobs every two years.

You need to note that you had a rapid advance with a steady increase in responsibility. Or you can explain in terms such as these: that you were contracted for a one-year project; you were recruited by the CEO for a one-year project; recruited by a client; the position was moved to Minneapolis and you chose not to move with it; the company was merged, acquired, or went out of business. Potential employers will generally ask why you left your last job, so have a good answer planned. (You don't have to say you were "fired"; you could instead say that there was a wave of layoffs or re-structuring, and the company was forced to cut costs.) Never lie; just choose your wording strategically.

This is an example of one-page executive resume. Very detailed in showing dollar figures, results, and percentages. Shows a command of the business process. Active words. Excellent use of accomplishments at the beginning, which positions the candidate to apply skills outside his immediate industry. Shows progression from a food-and-beverage company to hospitality management. When you have had several positions within one company, show the full number of years on a line with the employer, and dates for each position as they are listed.

MARK JONES

5030 Park Avenue, Trenton, NJ 06234. (212) 654-1212. mjones@aol.com

Senior executive with experience in P&L management, business development, operations, and strategic planning.
- Played pivotal role in company's growth from $30 million to $200+ million.
- Grew EBITDA tenfold (from $6 million to $60 million).
- Turned $100 million investment into $200+ million asset value within 3 years.

Results-driven leader adept at maximizing profit by leveraging organizational strengths to meet market demands.
- Increased profit 25% and revenue 15% by repositioning key departments after acquisitions.
- Turned around struggling $2 million company with $100K debt into $4 million business with $500K profit.
- Doubled value of company in 3 years by identifying and seizing business line expansion opportunities.
- Built $35 million, 12-site operation generating 30%+ profit margin within 4 years.

Effective manager with track record of surpassing objectives for growth and profitability.
- Attained 200%+ of competitive growth rates as reported by leading industry organization.
- 30% reduction in management turnover realized through better selection process and staff-development initiatives.
- 15% decrease in labor costs achieved by improving forecasting and control procedures.
- 14.8% saved annually by revamping purchasing through e-commerce and national contract negotiations.

Business strategist with exceptional ability to turn problems into sources of increased revenue and profit.

Undergraduate studies, College, IL
Certified Hotel Administrator (CHA) · Certified Food and Beverage Executive (CFBE)
Company Value Creation Award (two-time winner)
Achievements featured in the *Wall Street Journal, USA Today,* the *Washington Post,* ABC News-Washington, and others.

PROFESSIONAL EXPERIENCE

INTERNATIONAL HOSPITALITY CO., D.C.   1992–Present
Vice President, Operations (1994–Present)
Vice President, Food and Beverage (1993–1994)
General Manager (1992–1993)
Instrumental in growth from $30 million to $200+ million in revenue (and from 12 to 90 hotels).
- Key in site evaluation/acquisition, establishment of managerial structure/financial goals and repositioning operations to capitalize on local market situations. Improved customer service, cut costs, and reduced management turnover.
- Spearheaded new concepts including extended stay, nationally branded food court, and theme restaurant.

HOTEL MANAGEMENT, TX   1987–1992
Regional Food and Beverage Director (1987–1992)
Food and Beverage Director (1987)
Increased revenue 15% and profit 25% through strategic leadership of F&B operations across 20 hotels.
- Repositioned departments to penetrate new markets and strengthen profitability.
- Developed strategies for resort properties to enhance customer satisfaction while controlling costs.

FOREIGN FOOD CO., FL   1984–1987
Managing Partner
Turned around $2 million company with $100K debt into $4 million business generating $500K profit.
- Negotiated contracts with British firms to become leading U.S. importer.
- Added manufacturing/distribution operations. Clients included Famous Attractions Co. and International Airlines.

NATIONAL RESTAURANT CO., Chicago, IL   1980–1984
Director of Operations
Introduced company to Chicago market. Within 4 years, grew to $35 million, 12-site operation generating 30%+ profit. #1 company-wide in both revenue and profit margins.

This is a resume for a travel industry financial executive with experience in the dot-com milieu. It's a good example of a one-page executive resume. Good use of "buzz words" and results-oriented data.

ROGER SMITH, CPA, CMA

1501 Bass Drive
Chico, CA 95624
(901) 777-7777
rsmith@email.com

OBJECTIVE: CFO / CONTROLLER

EXPERIENCE:

VICE PRESIDENT, FINANCE AND ADMINISTRATION
Travel dot.com   **2000–Present**
Created Finance Department for "near-start-up" Internet travel company. Designed all financial systems including domestic and foreign credit card procedures. Negotiated Customer Reservations System (CRS) automation contract that will earn $1.5 million in third year of contract. Developed all budget, financial, and cash-flow projections. Negotiated the purchase of a travel agency. Negotiated airline ticket fulfillment services contract with host agency and coordinated implementation procedures.

CONTROLLER
InternetTravelAgency.com   **1995–1999**
Created Finance Department for a start-up, entrepreneurial Internet travel agency that grew to $300 million in annual revenue in four years. Key member of senior management team that achieved profitability in second year of operation. Established all accounting, financial reporting, budgeting, and internal control procedures. Created financial models to maximize profitability and determine product pricing. Performed financial analysis to evaluate Internet product line. Hired and trained 40 professional and clerical staff. Prepared pro-forma financial statements for IPO.

DIRECTOR, SALES / REFUND ACCOUNTING
International Airlines, Inc.   **1994–1995**
Directed 200 clerical and 10 professional staff in processing airline ticket sales and refund transactions. Conducted quality circles to identify process improvements and improve employee productivity and morale. Identified and recommended efficiencies in ticket-processing procedures.

CHIEF FINANCIAL OFFICER
Travel Company   **1992–1993**
Provided financial leadership to $170 million corporate travel-management company. Directed all aspects of Accounting, Finance, and Information Systems. Created financial models and budgets that established target performance. Identified cost reductions of $1.7 million. Implemented accounts receivable collection program that reduced accounts receivable by $700,000 (35%). Strengthened profitability by eliminating unprofitable accounts, saving $100,000 annually. Developed Information Systems (IS) development plan by identifying and evaluating potential system enhancements and related cost / benefits. Designed Total Quality Management (TQM) program.

ASSISTANT CONTROLLER, REVENUE ACCOUNTING
DIRECTOR, REVENUE ACCOUNTING
MANAGER, INTERNAL AUDIT
Travel Management Co.   **1986–1992**
Managed branch accounting function for $3 billion travel-management company with 500 branches nationwide. Directed 20 managers and 100 clerical employees in performing airline ticket reconciliation, accounts receivable, accounts payable, and accounting procedures functions. Directed a regional Information Systems function and created the internal audit department. Consolidated four regional accounting centers, saving $500,000 annually. Developed customer service program for accounting department. Directed audits of 100 branch offices, comparing individual branch performance to corporate benchmarks and saving $300,000.

EDUCATION:
University of XXX (B.S., Accounting)
Passed Certified Public Accountant (CPA) and Certified Management Accountant (CMA) exams.

An example of a tour operations professional who has worked in only one company so far. Uses one page in the classic chronological style. Good detail. Would be enhanced by adding numbers (number of staff managed, number of passengers carried on programs, dollar volumes and results in terms of market share, profitability).

ANNA JEFFRIES

PROFESSIONAL EXPERIENCE

TOUR OPERATOR, INC.,   *1980–Present*

Product Manager/Escorted Tours Division   **1998–Present**
- Responsible for negotiating and contracting, planning and developing, budgeting and pricing, and handling all aspects of South Pacific, Orient and China, France, Turkey, Greece, and Egypt, plus holiday tours in New York
- Manage, train, and develop department staff.
- Work closely with worldwide representatives of hotel chains in the U.S. and abroad; develop and maintain cooperative relationships with suppliers.

Product Manager/Escorted Tours Division/Special Groups/Barging   **1988–1998**
- Responsible for planning and developing new tours and day-to-day operation of the current product.
- Negotiated and finalized all contracts for hotels, ground operators, excursions, restaurants, etc.
- Developed operating instructions and tipping schedules to prepare tour managers, prepared budgets, and determined margins, packaging, and pricing of actual tours, including air (net + margins).
- Wrote and edited brochure copy.
- Headed new department handling Special Groups and Barging in Europe, including hiring and supervising staff, training, and scheduling; assisted with preparation of marketing plan and development of department budget and operating costs; developed needed materials; set company policies.
- Worked closely with other department managers to train, develop, and coordinate the smooth transition of a new department and to integrate different computer systems and methods to achieve department goals.
- Provided oversight for France, the Orient (including SE Asia, Vietnam, etc.), and China for Escorted Tours; responsible for the entire world for Special Groups/Extensions; and customized Barging in France/Holland/England programs with clients.
- Responsible for South Pacific (Australia, New Zealand, Fiji, Papua New Guinea), Turkey, Italy, Greece, Hawaii, Canada, and the United States (Texas, New York, eastern seaboard, South Carolina, California, Montana, and Washington).
- Served as company translator for all French and German communications.
- Traveled to sites to evaluate accommodations, restaurants, sightseeing excursions; aid in the development of new destinations and tours; and to ensure quality control of product.

Manager, Reservations and Sales Department   **1984–1988**
- Responsible for hiring and developing staff, delegating job duties, charting productivity, and developing reservations system.
- Made sales calls to travel agencies
- Gave presentations at sales seminars.

Supervisor Reservations and Sales Department   **1983–1984**
Assistant Supervisor Reservations and Sales Department   **1980–1983**
Reservationist   **Mar.–Nov. 1980**

COMPUTER SKILLS: IBM System 400. Protour System. Familiar with Excel. PARS.

OTHER SKILLS: Negotiations, sales and training presentations, fluent in French and German.

EDUCATION
B.A., Education (French and German), University, 19--
Additional courses in Japanese, University, 19--

Here is an excellent example of a resume from a new graduate. Because he does not have a lot of work experience, the emphasis is on his educational background as well as internships, summer employment, and so on. Although the experience may not be applicable, the resume shows a high level of responsibility and strengths that would be applicable.

JAMES GREEN

9999 Lemon Lane
San Diego, CA 95024
(904) 555-1212
jgreen@internet.com

EDUCATION

B.A., Finance, University: 1999
G.P.A. in major: 3.7

HONORS AND ACTIVITIES

Honors Program
Scholarship Recipient
Finance Club Member
Dean's List
National Merit Commended Student

COMPUTER SKILLS

Microsoft Windows, Word, Excel, PowerPoint, Access, and Exchange; Lotus Notes; Netscape Communicator; mainframes

WORK EXPERIENCE

Bank & Trust Company, June 1999–Present
Accountant

- Accounting services for short-term bond and international equity mutual funds
- Researched and tracked global complex corporate actions

Mortgage Company
Loss Analysis Department Intern, June 1998–April 1999

- Utilized Access database to research and resolve default loans
- Reconciled discrepancies as part of post-merger clean-up process
- Performed loss analysis on post-foreclosure loans to identify recoverable funds and report control weaknesses to senior management

What Travel Companies Want

Remember the key qualities that travel companies want and try to weave them into your resume and cover letter. Provide example accomplishments that show that you possess these qualities. Travel companies look for people who are

- Service-oriented
- People-oriented
- Detail-oriented
- Good communicators

If you have broad experience, say so; if you are a specialist, say so.

Do not assume that the person reading your resume is going to understand how your experience applies to his or her organization. Explain (in the cover letter) how your experience is relevant. If you are coming from outside the travel industry, you can use a summary of job expertise—sales and marketing, operations, public relations, calling on corporations, making presentations—all of which are directly applicable to travel. Use to your advantage the fact that you bring experience from outside the industry: for example, you can speak the language of another industry and have wide contacts to better sell corporate clients on your travel services.

It is helpful to show an understanding of the employer's industry, and even their particular company. You can gather such an understanding from the material in this book and from doing your own additional research.

Some people think that if they happen to leave something relevant out of the resume, they can mention it in an interview. That is not going to happen. A resume that does not address the employer's needs will not get the candidate an interview.

Cover Letters

If you are approaching a company cold, the cover letter ideally should start off with "so and so suggested I contact you directly about a position as…, given my interest and experience." Try to be as specific and to-the-point as possible. You might want to mention any outstanding qualifications for the job or attention-getting achievements in the cover letter, rather than depend on the resume. The cover letter should be designed to get you an appointment for an interview. Instead of merely asking for an interview at some time, suggest a time that you would like to visit for an interview and state that you will call to confirm the date. Be assertive but not pushy. Be respectful and polite.

If you know of a specific position you want to go after, try to learn as much as possible about the company—its corporate philosophy, its human-resource philosophy, its plans to expand into new products or markets—and weave these concepts into your letter: "Knowing that your company is diversifying into…[expanding into]…[opening]…I wanted to contact you directly concerning how I might contribute directly to your company's success."

The following are a few example cover letters:

Written to accompany resume sample 4. An example of a cold solicitation letter, which gets attention with important phrases and buzz words.

ROGER SMITH, CPA, CMA
1501 Bass Drive
Chico, CA 95624
(901) 777-7777
rsmith@email.com

July 10, 2001

Ms. Karen Rubin, President
Travel Executive Search
5 Rose Avenue
Great Neck, NY 11021

Dear Ms. Rubin

Are you currently recruiting for a dynamic CFO with start-up and Internet experience? If so, I would appreciate your consideration of my enclosed resume.

I am currently the Controller of Travel dot.com, where I established the Accounting/Finance department for this $300 million start-up, entrepreneurial travel company. I created and implemented all start-up accounting procedures relating to every aspect of accounting.

Prior to this position, I was Chief Financial Officer of Travel Company, where I directed all aspects of the Accounting, Finance, and Information Systems functions.

If you are looking for an energetic financial leader with strong start-up and Internet experience, I would appreciate the opportunity to speak to you about my career objectives.

Sincerely,

Roger Smith

JOE LEAHY
220 First Ave.
Buffalo, NY 10065
(516) 555-1212
leahy@email.com

February 22, 2001

Karen Rubin, President
Travel Executive Search
5 Rose Avenue
Great Neck, NY 11021

Dear Ms. Rubin:

In the course of your work with present and future clients, you may have the need for an experienced problem solver with a track record of impacting company profits. Over the past 10 years, I have enjoyed a progressive career with the XYZ Attraction. My background includes

- Promotions through sales-management positions
- Demonstrated strengths in leadership, training, and organizational improvement
- Well-rounded experience within a company focused on customer satisfaction
- Proven ability to define problems and develop change strategies

I am seeking to relocate to the southeastern United States. To achieve this goal, I am considering positions outside my current industry, sports and entertainment. You should know that in recent years, my compensation has been in the range of $xx,xxx to $xx,xxx

Please consider my qualifications for search assignments.

Very truly yours,

JOE LEAHY

Written to accompany resume sample 6. This letter comes from a new graduate hoping to land his first position in the industry.

JAMES GREEN
9999 Lemon Lane
San Diego, CA 95024
(904) 555-1212
jgreen@internet.com

December 12, 2001

Ms. Karen Rubin
Travel Executive Search
5 Rose Avenue
Great Neck, NY 11021

Dear Ms. Rubin

I recently graduated from college and have been working for the past year as a mutual fund accountant. I have, however, come to find the work unfulfilling and wish to utilize my skills elsewhere.

My interest lies in travel, most particularly in tour operations and product development. I am looking for a job in the Chicago area that would allow me to combine my business training with my passion and creativity.

Your name was given to me by Susan at XYZ as a resource who might be able to assist me in my search. I have enclosed my resume and would greatly appreciate any assistance you could provide.

Thank you very much.

Sincerely,

JAMES GREEN

Interviews

Prepare yourself for the interview by learning as much as possible about the company and the industry (such as competitors and key issues), and even the people you are likely to meet (including the department head you would be working for). Prepare questions you might have about the company and the position for which you are interviewing. This will go far to set you apart from other candidates. It will impress the interviewer that you are serious and committed, as well as demonstrate the skills that you can bring to the job.

There is a great difference between whether the interviewer is a professional personnel officer, the owner or manager of the firm, or the department head for whom you would be working. Each person comes to the interview with different perspectives and agendas, and you must understand these in order to respond appropriately.

You may think the function of the Human Resources department is to recruit talent into the company; on the contrary, human resource professionals are like guardians to the castle: Their task is to keep out undesirables, and they are trained to detect any sign that suggests undesirability. They will pose questions to determine whether you are who you say you are and whether your credentials fit the bill. Frequently, they do not have actual knowledge of the position, but only a listing of criteria to match you against. They may use open-ended questions, where you have to go into lengthy detail, or directed questions that require a straightforward answer. There are no right or wrong answers; in fact, it may not be the answer that is important at all, but what you don't say or the manner in which you answer. They are looking for "chemistry," "the right personality," and long-term suitability for the organization, and are trained to look for any hint of misinformation or evasiveness.

In contrast, the department head is more likely to direct questions to gauge your knowledge, experience, and assets you bring, but is also trying to gauge whether you have the right personality to fit into the "team." Although some managers are looking for a "clone" of the person who had the job before (or a person who is doing this successfully for the competition), or someone who can bring a "book" of business (their clients), others prefer to train people in their own methods and are more interested in your intelligence, willingness to learn, and energy. (Unfortunately, you probably won't have a clue which type the hiring executive is looking for.)

What employers are looking for is highly subjective. But what we have found to be most common are a "people-orientation" (that is, the ability to work with people and serve others), good communication skills (the ability to organize thoughts and express them clearly when speaking or in writing), a willingness to accept responsibility, energy, motivation, commitment, flexibility, and experience. A knowledge of geography and keyboarding are very desirable for front-line travel positions. You will probably also be rated on personal appearance, manners, social grace, leadership potential, and maturity. At more senior levels, recruiters are increasingly being asked for candidates who have analytical skills and computer skills (such as experience with spreadsheets or PowerPoint presentations).

Follow-Up

Follow-up is critical. After an interview, you should follow up with a note thanking the interviewer for spending the time with you and summarizing your key selling points (your assets) for the job. For example: "Based on our discussion and how you described the position, I know I have the qualifications you seek. I am skilled at meeting planning, I have a sales background, I have excellent communications skills, and I can represent the company in a professional manner. I am a go-getter who can spot new business opportunities. I very much want to be a part of a people-oriented, growth-oriented leader in the travel industry, such as your company."

Such a letter gives you the opportunity to make your last sales pitch; in fact, it is the same as a follow-up letter to a sales presentation. An interview follow-up letter also shows that you care about getting the job, helps you stand out from the crowd, and refreshes the interviewer's memory (the interviewer might have also seen dozens of other people that week for the same job). Moreover, it demonstrates the communications skills (listening and writing) and professionalism that you would present to a potential client or customer. Also, the letter gives you the opportunity to correct any misunderstandings or false impressions the interviewer might have had. Do not assume the interviewer heard, understood correctly, or remembered everything you said in the interview.

A follow-up letter will not land you the job; its function is to get you a second interview, when an offer might be extended.

Don't Give Up!

You should not feel discouraged or rejected if you do not get a job. Frustration is an inevitable part of the process. Timing may have a lot to do with it. Be persistent (but not obnoxious). Dick Sundby of Tauck Tours had to try four times before landing a job at Tauck as a Tour Manager—that was 20 years ago, and he has since risen to Manager of Tour Directors. Be creative; be enterprising. Be persistent but not obnoxious.

Getting Ahead

You are likely to stay in your first job in the travel industry only two or three years. How far and how fast you progress depends largely on the company or entity you are working for, as well as your own ability and aggressiveness. "Make yourself indispensable," advised Trudy Baron, who started her career in travel as a secretary and rose to be a vice president of a major international hotel company.

Don't just settle for the job description; go beyond it. Be entrepreneurial. Grow your own job, or grow yourself into one (see a need and fill it). The Public Relations Manager of one prominent New York City hotel began to create packages for the hotel with the aim of working into a position that reflected her expanded role. Don't be locked into preconceived roles or plans. Be flexible. Join trade organizations. Network. Read the trade press for your own field as well as other travel segments; read beyond the headlines and between the lines. If necessary, take additional training or schooling toward certifications (the Institute of Certified Travel Agents' CTC is one of the most coveted designations in the industry).

It is very difficult to plot out a career path in travel because there are so many avenues you could take. Still, you should have a plan for yourself—plotting your next move, where you want to be in 5 years and 10 years—but be ready to change it. There are countless examples of people who have had successful careers that weren't exactly what they planned: Robert Coffey, Vice President–Market Planning for Alamo Rent-A-Car, who started in the airlines; Richard Valerio, President of American Sightseeing International, who also started with the airlines; Colin Marshall, Chief Executive of British Airways, who was with Avis before; Gideon Spitz, President of Golden-Tulip Hotels, who started in public relations; and Pat Foley, Chairman of Hyatt Hotels, who started out as a front-office supervisor nearly 30 years ago.

The industry lore is full of sensational success stories of people attaining the heights of their profession coming from humble beginnings. Such amazing successes will continue to happen because the industry is still growing and innovating. It is likely that in the future, however, the top positions will require more education and professionalism than in the past.

Indeed, the whole concept of "career" in the travel industry has changed. Not too long ago, people tended to spend their entire careers in a single segment, such as airlines or hotels, and even a single company, and their career paths were vertical. Now there is much greater integration of the elements, and career paths tend to be more horizontal and diagonal, from segment to segment.

People frequently attribute their success to "being in the right place at the right time." But on closer inspection, in most instances it is a matter of perceiving an opportunity or making an opportunity happen.

However, you should not be so focused on the next rung on the ladder that you miss the enjoyment of the view from where you are. I often have people come to me asking for help in finding a new position merely because they feel they have been too long in one place and are itchy to move. Yet they may have what others might consider a "dream job" in an ideal company, earning an excellent salary that would be hard to match, let alone improve. That too could be the nature of the people who find their way into this business—anxious to move on and experience new things.

Where Dreams Come True

You spend most of your waking life in a job, so it should be something that is satisfying and fulfilling. So many people fall into a career or fit themselves into some slot, where they feel stifled and frustrated because their natural abilities are not given expression.

The travel industry utilizes so many different professional skills and personal talents, it offers a dream come true not only for those seeking to travel, but also for those who seek other forms of creative or professional expression.

It used to be said that travel was a dream of a lifetime, and those who worked in the industry, when I would ask what they enjoyed most about their jobs, would frequently reply that they "fulfilled dreams." For so many who seek to work at something that is personally satisfying, and for those who started at the lowest rung of a career ladder and rose to top management, being a part of the travel industry has been the means to fulfilling a personal dream. It can be for you, too.

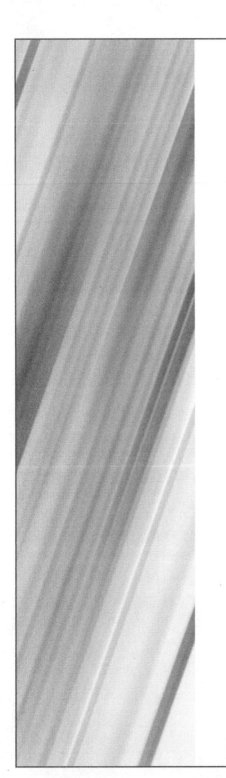

APPENDIXES

BEST BETS IN TRAVEL

Choosing an Industry

The travel industry is full of great opportunities; however, some are better than others. The following pages show you which sectors of the travel industry are the best to get into depending on your particular priorities and skills.

Best Opportunity to Combine Work and Lifestyle

- Ski industry
- Spa resorts

Best Opportunity to Earn a High Income

- Incentives
- E-travel

Best Opportunity to Live/ Work Abroad

- Hospitality
- Tour management

Best Opportunity to Travel

- Travel agents
- Airlines
- Tour operations
- Cruise lines

Best Entry-Level Opportunity

- Hospitality

Best Opportunity to Climb the Corporate Ladder

- Hospitality

Least Appreciated Opportunity

- Car rental
- Motorcoach industry
- Receptive travel/destination management companies
- Convention and visitor bureaus

Jobs That Afford the Greatest Creativity

- Travel agents
- Tour operators
- Incentives

Jobs in Highest Demand

- Web
- Internet
- E-commerce
- Hospitality

Newest Titles

- Global sales
- Internet partnership marketing
- Convention Services Manager
- Process Manager

Most Eclectic Industries

- Theme parks
- Attractions
- Hospitality
- Aviation/port management

Best Places for "Techies"

- Airlines
- Car rentals
- Aviation/port management
- E-travel

Best Places for Those with a Grasp of the "Nuts and Bolts"

- Ski industry
- Car rentals
- Airlines
- Hospitality
- Motorcoach
- Aviation/port management

Best Places to Escape "Burnout" Jobs

- Travel agents
- Tour operations
- Ski areas
- Spa resorts

Highest Stress

- Incentives
- Airlines
- Aviation/port management
- Corporate travel management
- Convention planning

Most Fun

- Ski industry
- Theme parks

Best for the Politically Savvy

- Aviation/port management
- Convention and visitor bureaus/state travel offices
- Ski industry
- Association management

Best for Entrepreneurs

- Travel agents
- Tour operators
- Convention/meetings planning
- Destination management companies
- E-travel

Best for Working at Home

- Travel agents
- Tour operators
- Bed-and-breakfast

Best Emerging Fields in Which to Write Your Own Ticket

- Cultural tourism
- Sports marketing commissions
- Corporate travel management
- E-travel
- Global sales

Best Opportunity to Bring Peace and Prosperity to the World

- Tour operations

Most "Employee-Oriented" Companies

- Southwest Airlines
- Club Med (hospitality)
- Globus & Cosmos (tour operator)

Hottest Jobs

The travel and hospitality industry is being transformed by the Internet; every company now has a Web presence, and many entrepreneurs are adapting traditional "bricks-and-mortar" businesses as e-commerce "clicks-and-mortar" businesses.

Best Leads

Most major companies have Web sites, and these sites often have career listings. Trade associations' Web sites also provide links to other sites and industry statistics. Many also host job banks (see the "Contacts, Sources, and Leads" sections in individual chapters, or Appendix B).

Best Bets for International Jobs

People assume that because travel is an international endeavor, there must be travel jobs abroad. There are actually limited opportunities to be posted abroad (the best for these would be hospitality, tour operations, airlines, and destination promotion). Although travel is a global business, this is accomplished mainly through alliances with foreign entities, relationships that are negotiated and maintained by an executive from headquarters. Essentially, though, travel is an international export business. Most of the jobs that entail foreign travel are in the form of sales missions, with a growing number of global alliances.

New International Positions

New positions are opening up:

- **Global Sales** (such as at corporate travel management companies): A high-level corporate sales position, this involves securing foreign-based divisions or subsidiaries of U.S.-based multinational corporate clients as well as international clients. This is a relatively new position that has arisen mainly as more U.S. companies have established foreign bases and U.S. corporate agencies have joined with foreign affiliates. It can often take years to secure the account, first by selling the headquarters and then by systematically selling foreign offices, which typically function autonomously. Involves building relationships abroad; a knowledge, understanding, and sensitivity to cultural differences, regulations for doing business in that country, as well as the client's business travel needs, and a strong understanding of competitive business issues. Requires strong follow-up, particularly to avoid any miscommunication; although English may be the language of international business, some points of the deal may not be fully understood. Usually this is a senior sales position; however, because the position is still emerging, you can make your own opportunity, particularly if you have experience selling other services in an international setting. The position involves a great deal of travel—even 80 percent of the time.

- **International Group Sales** (cruise line, attraction): Serves as sales liaison to foreign wholesalers, tour operators, and the lines' appointed general sales agent. Responsible for enhancing customer service and satisfaction and increasing sales of key markets such as leisure groups and corporate incentive groups. Conducts foreign and domestic sales calls. Represents the company at international trade shows and promotional events. Plans affinity groups with foreign incentive houses and coordinates specialized requirements.

- **International Sales Manager** (hotel, transportation company, destination marketing organization): Cultivates travel from a particular foreign market, such as Japan, Germany, or England, which requires an understanding of that country's travel industry, language, and culture. Requires market research, untangling different or complex distribution channels, and cultivating solid business relationships with industry leaders. Can go so far as to develop and implement new services to cater to the market, such as an "International Floor" at a hotel or guide programs and itineraries at a destination. Streamlines operations for incoming tours from the country and works to keep a high level of customer satisfaction. Knowledge of foreign language, business customs, strong selling skills, and marketing savvy are key. There are not too many steps up to this position, and typically a hotel sales manager creates the position for himself/herself.

- **Manager, International Sales and Marketing** (transportation): Sells and negotiates large contracts with international clients. Develops and expands representation networks in foreign countries. Develops innovative pricing schemes. Creates advertising, brochures, and sales promotion literature. Coordinates a worldwide distribution system.

- **Director of International Sales** (tour operator): Directs, produces, and distributes a product line for Visit USA international travelers. May be responsible for researching and appointing a General Sales Agent Network in foreign countries. Oversees costs, legal specifications, currency conversions, customs requirements, and consumer protection laws associated with marketing in foreign countries. Travels often to market countries.

Best Sources for International Jobs

- Working Abroad, a collection of articles on the Gonyea Online Career Center (www.iccweb.com).

- *Transitions Abroad* magazine (800-293-0373; www.TransitionsAbroad.com).

Best Bets by Industry

If you know which sector of the travel industry you would like to be in, here are the fastest growing and most promising jobs within each sector.

Travel Agencies

- Webmaster
- Frontline Agent
- Quality control
- Training
- Information Technology
- Groups Specialist

Corporate Travel Management

- Information Technology

Tour Operations

- Web Designer
- Web Programmer
- Quality Control
- Marketing

Incentive Travel

- Client Services Manager
- Account Executive
- Quality Control

Conventions and Meetings

- Convention Services Manager
- Event Manager
- Direct Marketing
- Information Technology

Hospitality

- Guest Services Manager
- Group Sales Manager
- Convention Services Coordinator
- Executive Housekeeper
- Front Office Manager

Ski and Spa

- International Sales Manager
- Marketing Director

- Corporate Sponsorships Manager
- Group Sales Coordinator
- Environmental Manager
- Resort Services
- Resort Planning and Development Manager
- Risk-Management Director
- Mountain Manager
- Grooming Operations Manager
- Lift Maintenance Manager
- Ski Patrol
- Ski School Director
- Day Care Supervisor
- Webmaster
- Government Relations Manager

Theme Parks and Attractions

- Global Sales Manager
- Manager of Corporate Sponsorships and Partnership Marketing
- Incentive Sales and Corporate Sales
- Product and Sales Development Manager
- Productivity and Process Improvement Manager
- Financial Planner
- Games and Attractions Manager
- Information Technology Manager
- Technical Designer
- Training and Recruitment Manager
- Director of Employee Experience

Airlines

- Customer Service Agent
- Partnership Marketing Manager
- Manager of Internet Distribution
- Global Sales Manager
- Manager of Yield Management

- Manager of Quality Assurance
- Training Manager

Car Rental

- Customer Service Agent
- Director of Partnership Marketing
- Manager of Internet Distribution
- Director of Global Sales
- Manager of Yield Management
- Manager of Quality Assurance
- Training Manager
- Manager of Fleet Utilization

Motorcoach and Rail

- Customer Service Agent

Cruises

- Counselor
- Sales Representative
- Incentive Sales Specialist
- Conventions and Meeting Services
- Manager of Partnership Marketing
- Revenue Management Analyst
- Webmaster
- Reservations Agent

Destination Marketing Organizations

- Convention Sales Manager
- Convention Services Manager
- Leisure Travel Specialist
- Tourism Marketing Manager
- Market Research Analyst
- Director of Public Relations
- Advertising Manager
- Manager of Information Technology

Port Management

- Air Traffic Controller
- Facilities Manager
- Marketing Manager

E-Travel

- Web Programmer
- Web Designer

- Director of Online Business Development
- Manager of Interactive Partnership Marketing
- Manager of Client Services
- NT Administrator
- Quality Assurance Engineer
- Customer Service Agents
- Producer

DIRECTORY OF INTERNET TRAVEL RESOURCES

Chapter 1—Travel Agents

Organization	Web Address
Airlines Reporting Corporation	www.arccorp.com
American Society of Travel Agents (ASTA)	www.astanet.com
Association of Retail Travel Agents (ARTA)	www.artaonline.com
Education Systems/The Center for Travel Education	www.educationsystems.com
Institute of Certified Travel Agents	www.icta.com
International Airlines Travel Agent Network (IATAN)	www.iatan.org
National Association of Commissioned Travel Agents (NACTA)	www.nacta.com
Rosenbluth International	www.rosenbluth.com
The Boyd School	www.boydschool.com
Uniglobe Travel	www.uniglobe.com
Vacation.com	www.vacation.com

Chapter 2—Corporate Travel Management

Organization	Web Address
Association of Corporate Travel Executives	www.acte.org
National Business Travel Association	www.nbta.org

Chapter 3—Tour Operators

Organization	Web Address
American Sightseeing International	www.americansightseeing.org
American Society of Travel Agents (ASTA)	www.astanet.com
Backroads Bicycle Touring	www.backroads.com
Flying Wheels Travel Service	www.flyingwheelstravel.com
Globus & Cosmos	www.globusandcosmos.com
National Tour Association	www.ntaonline.com
SATH (Society for Accessible Travel & Hospitality	
Specialty Travel Index	www.specialtytravel.com
TKTS-N-TOURS TRAVEL, Inc.	www.ticketsntours.com
Travel Aides International	http://members.tripod.com/ ~Travel_us/index.html
Travel Industry Association of America (TIA)	www.tia.org
U.S. Tour Operators Association (USTOA)	www.ustoa.com
Wilderness Inquiry	www.wildernessinquiry.org

Chapter 4—Incentive Travel

Organization	Web Address
Maritz	www.maritz.com
TravelAwardsOnline	www.travelawardsonline.com
The Journeymasters	www.journeymasters.com
The Society of Incentive & Travel Executives (SITE)	www.site-intl.org
Incentive magazine	www.incentivemag.com
Meetings & Conventions magazine	www.meetings-conventions.com
Successful Meetings magazine	www.successmtgs.com

Chapter 5—Conventions and Meetings

Organization	Web Address
Association of Destination Management Executives	www.adme.org
b-there.com	www.b-there.com
Convene magazine	www.pcma.org/convene/default.htm
Corporate Meetings & Incentives	www.meetingsnet.com
International Association of Conference Centers	www.iacconline.com
International Association of Exposition Managers (IAEM)	www.iaem.org
Meeting Guide Directory	www.mmaweb.com/meetings/Directory/
Meeting News	www.meetingnews.com
Meeting Professionals International	www.mpiweb.org
Meetings & Conventions magazine	www.meetings-conventions.com
Passkey.com	www.paskey.com
PlanSoft	www.plansoft.com
Professional Convention Management Association	www.pcma.org
Society of Corporate Meeting Professionals	www.scmp.org
Successful Meetings magazine	www.successmtgs.com
Tradeshow Week	www.TradeshowWeek.com

Chapter 6—Hospitality

Organization	Web Address
AH&MA	www.ahma.com
American Hotel Foundation	www.ei-ahma.org/ahf.scholarships
American Resort Development Association	www.arda.org
Club Med	www.clubmed.com
Educational Institute of AH&MA	www.ei-ahma.org

(continues)

(continued)

Chapter 6—Hospitality

Organization	Web Address
Executive Recruiters, Inc.	www.hotelrecruiters.com
Hospitality Business Alliance	www.h-b-a.org
Hospitality Recruiters	www.hospitalityrecruiters.com
Hotel & Motel Management	www.hmm.online.com
Hotel Business	www.hotelbusiness.com
Hotels; Innkeeping World; Lodging Hospitality	www.Llhonline.com
Interval International	www.intervalworld.com
Lodging	www.lodgingmagazine.com
Marriott International—Jobs	http://careers.marriott.com/ http://jobsearch.marriott.newjobs.com/
National Restaurant Association Educational Foundation	www.edfound.org
Nation's Restaurant News	www.nrn.com
Resort Condominiums International	www.rci.com
Restaurant Business	www.restaurant.biz.com
Restaurants & Institutions	www.rimag.com
Restaurants USA	www.restaurant.org
The Council on Hotel, Restaurant and Institutional Education (CHRIE)	www.chrie.org
Trades Publishing Company	www.resorttrades.com

Chapter 7—Ski and Spa

Organization	Web Address
American Skiing Company	www.peaks.com
Aspen Skiing Company	www.skiaspen.com
Booth Creek Ski Holdings	www.boothcreek.com
Colorado Mountain College	www.coloradomtn.edu
Colorado Ski Country, USA	www.coloradoski.com
Cool Works	www.coolworks.com

Organization	Web Address
Intrawest Corporation	www.intrawest.com
K&M Rocky Mountain Tours	www.skithewest.com
Lyndon State College	www.lsc.vsc.edu
National Ski Areas Association	www.nsaa.org
National Sports Center for the Disabled	www.nscd.org
Sierra Nevada College	www.sierranevada.edu
SkiTops	www.skitops.com
SnowSports Industries America	www.snowsports.org www.snowlink.com
SpaFinders	www.spafinders.com
Spa-Therapy.com	www.spa-therapy.com
University of Colorado	http://bus.colorado.edu
Vail Resorts, Inc.	www.snow.com
Vermont Ski Areas Association, Ski Vermont	www.skivermont.com www.ridevermont.com

Chapter 8—Theme Parks and Attractions

Organization	Web Address
Amusement Business magazine	www.amusementbusiness.com
Association for Living History, Farm and Agricultural Museums	www.alhfam.org/alhfam.jobs.html
Disney Casting	www.Disneycareers.com
International Association of Amusement Parks and Attractions	www.iaapa.org
International Theme Park Services	www.internationalthemepark.com

Chapter 9—Airlines

Organization	Web Address
Air Line Pilots Association	www.alpa.org
Air Transport Association	www.air-transport.org
Aviation Career magazine	www.aviationcareer.net

(continues)

(continued)

Chapter 9—Airlines

Organization	Web Address
Aviation Employee Placement Service	www.aeps.com
Aviation Information Resources	www.jet-jobs.com
BidJetCharter.com	www.bidjetcharter.com
College of Aeronautics, La Guardia Airport	www.aero.edu
Ejets	www.ejets.com
Embry-Riddle Aeronautical University	www.embryriddle.edu
FlightSafety International	www.flightsafety.com
International Air Transport Association	www.iata.org
JetBlue Airlines	www.jetblue.com
Regional Airline Association	www.raa.org
Southwest Airlines	www.southwest.com

Chapter 10—Car Rental

Organization	Web Address
DollarTravel.com	www.dollartravel.com
Enterprise Rent-A-Car	www.erac.com/recruit/
Hertz Corporation	www.hertz.com/company/hr/index.cfm
Avis Group	www.avis.com/company/employment/
Budget Rent a Car	www.drivebudget.com
National Car Rental System	www.nationalcar.com
Alamo Rent-A-Car	www.alamo.com
Dollar Rent A Car	www.dollar.com/company_information/employment_opportunities.asp
Thrifty Car Rental	www.thrifty.com/careers.asp
Advantage Rent-A-Car	www.advantagerentacar.com/cgi-bin/employ.cgi
Payless Car Rental	www.800-payless.com/CareFrameSet1.html

Chapter 11—Motorcoach and Rail

Organization	Web Address
Greyhound Lines, Inc.	www.greyhound.com
National Motorcoach Marketing Network	www.motorcoach.com
American Bus Association	www.buses.org
National Tour Association	www.ntaonline.com
Amtrak National Railroad Passenger Corporation	www.amtrak.com
Rail Europe	www.raileurope.com
Copper Canyon Tours	www.ss-tours.com
Premier Selections Inc.	www.premierselections.com
Rail Travel Center	www.railtravelcenter.com
Specialty Travel Index	www.specialtytravel.com
Yahoo (Railroad information)	http://dir.yahoo.com/Economy/ Transportation/Trains_and_Railroads/
Orient Express	www.orient-express.com

Chapter 12—Cruises

Organization	Web Address
American Classic Voyages Company	www.amcv.com
Carnival Cruise Lines	www.carnival.com
Cruise Lines International Association (CLIA)	www.cruising.org
Crystal Cruises	www.crystalcruises.com
Disney Cruise Line	http://disney.go.com/DisneyCruise/
Freighter World Cruises	www.freighterworld.com
International Council of Cruise Lines	www.iccl.org
ResidenSea	www.residensea.com
Seabourn Cruise Line	www.seabourn.com
Windstar Cruises	www.windstarcruises.com

Chapter 13—Destination Marketing Organizations

Organization	Web Address
International Association of Convention & Visitor Bureaus	www.iacvb.org
NYC & Co.	www.nycvisit.com
Tourism Offices Worldwide Directory	www.towd.com
Travel Industry Association of America (TIA)	www.tia.org

Chapter 14—Airport, Aviation, and Port Management

Organization	Web Address
American Association of Airport Executives	www.airportnet.org
American Association of Port Authorities	www.aapa-ports.org
College of Aeronautics, La Guardia Airport	www.aero.edu
Denver International Airport	www.flydenver.com
Embry-Riddle Aeronautical University	www.embryriddle.edu
Federal Aviation Administration (FAA)	www.faa.gov
Hartsfield Atlanta Airport	www.atlanta-airport.com
National Air Transportation Association	www.nata-online.org
National Transportation Safety Board (NTSB)	www.ntsb.gov

Chapter 15—E-Travel

Organization	Web Address
1travel.com	www.1travel.com
Amadeus	www.amadeus.net
Biztravel	www.biztravel.com
Cheap Tickets	www.cheaptickets.com
Expedia	www.expedia.com
Interactive Travel Services Association	www.interactivetravel.org
LastMinuteTravel.com	www.lastminutetravel.com
Lowestfare.com	www.lowestfare.com

Chapter 15—E-Travel

Organization	Web Address
Luxury Link	www.luxurylink.com
Priceline.com	www.priceline.com
Travelocity	www.travelocity.com
Travelscape.com	www.travelscape.com
Trip.com	www.trip.com
WebTravelNews	www.webtravelnews.com

Chapter 16—Travel Support Services

Organization	Web Address
Adventure Travel Society	www.adventuretravel.com
Air Transport Association	www.air-transport.org
American Association of Airport Executives	www.airportnet.org
American Association of Museums	www.aam-us.org/index.htm
American Automobile Association	www.aaa.com
American Bus Association	www.buses.org
American Business Media	www.americanbusinessmedia.com
American Gaming Association	www.americangaming.org
American Hotel & Motel Association	www.ahma.com/ahma/index.asp
American Resort Development Association	www.arda.org
American Society of Association Executives	www.asaenet.org
American Society of Travel Agents	www.astanet.com
Americans for the Arts	www.artsusa.org
Association of Corporate Travel Executives	www.acte.org
Association of Retail Travel Agents	www.artaonline.com
Cruise Lines International Association	www.cruising.org
Greater Washington Society of Association Executives	www.gwsae.org
Hospitality Sales & Marketing Association International	www.hsmai.org

(continues)

(continued)

Chapter 16—Travel Support Services

Organization	Web Address
Hotel Electronic Distribution Network Association	www.hedna.org
Inkspot (Travel Writer's Spot)	www.inkspot.com/genres/travel/markets.html
International Association of Amusement Parks and Attractions	www.iaapa.org
International Association of Convention & Visitor Bureaus	www.iacvb.org
International Ecotourism Society	www.ecotourism.org
International Festivals & Events Association	www.ifea.com
International Forum for Travel and Tourism Advocates	www.iftta.org
International Society of Travel and Tourism Educators	www.istte.org
Meeting Professionals International	www.mpiweb.org
National Air Transportation Association	www.nata-online.org
National Association of RV Parks & Campgrounds	www.gocamping.com
National Business Travel Association	www.nbta.org
National Caves Association	http://cavern.com
National Restaurant Association	www.restaurant.org
National Tour Association	www.ntaonline.com
National Tour Foundation	www.ntfonline.org
PhotoSecrets Travel Photography	www.photosecrets.com/links.html
Professional Association of Innkeepers International	www.paii.org/index.html
Professional Convention Management Association	www.pcma.org
Public Relations Society of America (PRSA)	www.prsa.org
Recreation Vehicle Industry Association	www.rvia.org
Regional Airline Association	www.raa.org

Organization	Web Address
Society for Accessible Travel & Hospitality	
Society of American Travel Writers	www.satw.org
Society of Government Travel Professionals	www.government-travel.org
Society of Incentive & Travel Executives	www.site-intl.org
Travel and Tourism Research Association	www.ttra.com
Travel Guard	www.travelguard.com
Travelwriters.com	www.travelwriters.com
United States Tour Operators Association	www.ustoa.com

INDEX

F

National Railroad Passenger Corporation. *See* rail travel
National Restaurant Association, 74, 222
National Tour Foundation, 20, 174, 211, 222
Navigant International, 12
neighborhoods, car rental, 135
networking
   job search, 218–219
   travel agencies, 20
newspapers, job search, 218
noise abatement officer, airport/aviation
  management, 182
NT administrator, 194, 250
NYC & Co., 167–168

O

on-the-job training, 221
1travel.com, 193
online business development. *See* e-commerce;
  e-travel; Internet
online reservations. *See* Internet; reservations
operations, 6
   airlines, 124
   airport/aviation management, 181
   see also *tour operations*
Orbitz, 122
Orient Express, 146
Outside Sales Agents, 21

P

package tours, 34–35
partnership marketing
   airlines, 123, 249
   car rental, 137, 249
   cruise lines, 155, 249
   ski and spa resorts, 98, 249
   theme parks/attractions, 111
passenger service, airlines, 126
Payless Car Rental, 134, 140
personality of travel agents, 2, 217
photography, 209
pilots, airlines, 124
point of sale/pre-travel quality control software, 196
politics, state travel offices, 172–173
port management, 178, 180
   air traffic control, 250
   contacts, sources, and leads, 188
   employment outlook, 187
   facilities, 250

   information technology, 246
   marketing, 187, 250
   port management, 187
   safety, 188
   stress, 246
   transportation, 187
   Web sites, 258
presentation, resumes, 229–230
Priceline.com, 193
pricing. *See* cost
print buyers, incentive travel, 61
priorities, job search, 217–218
Producer, 194
product and sales development, 6
   amusement and recreation services, 111, 249
   tour operations, 38–39
productivity and process improvement, amusement
  and recreation services, 111, 249
professional certification, 20
professional societies, 218
programming. *See* information technology
promotional tours
   convention and visitor bureaus, 166
   incentive travel, 59
   tour operations, 52
promotions, job, 1, 15, 30, 84–85, 240–241, 245
property management, airport/aviation
  management, 182
Protix Agent Support Network, 26
public relations, 6, 166, 203–204
   contacts, sources, and leads, 204
   convention and visitor bureaus, 168–169
   destination marketing, 168, 249
   salaries, 203
   theme parks/attractions, 111
purchasing, 61, 111

Q

quality assurance, 194
   airlines, 123
   car rental, 137
   e-travel, 250
   tour operations, 40
quality control, 17
   incentive travel, 60, 248
   tour operations, 39, 248
   travel agents, 248

Y